THE THEOLOGY OF THE
RESURRECTION

THE THEOLOGY
OF THE
RESURRECTION

WALTER KÜNNETH

CONCORDIA PUBLISHING HOUSE
ST LOUIS, MISSOURI

Translated by James W. Leitch on the basis of a
draft prepared by E. H. Robertson and Brian Battershaw
from the German
Theologie der Auferstehung (new edition)
Claudius Verlag, Munich, 1951

Library of Congress Catalog Card No. 65-25571

FIRST ENGLISH EDITION 1965
© SCM PRESS LTD 1965
PRINTED IN GREAT BRITAIN BY
ROBERT CUNNINGHAM AND SONS LTD
ALVA, SCOTLAND

IN REMEMBRANCE OF MY FATHER
LORENZ KÜNNETH
AND MY FATHER-IN-LAW
MAX VON AMMON

CONTENTS

Part Two

THE DOGMATIC SIGNIFICANCE OF THE RESURRECTION

Part Three

THE RESURRECTION AND ITS CONSUMMATION

PREFACE TO THE GERMAN EDITION OF
1951

M ORE than a decade and a half has passed since the third edition of *The Theology of the Resurrection* was sent upon its way. Since its first appearance in 1933, the face of the world has radically changed. But the burning questions of humanity have remained the same, and so has the decisive answer of the truth of the Bible. The course of history, as it has so terribly disclosed itself to us, can only be a confirmation of the Christian insight that all mankind is trembling on the brink of destruction and groaning under the tyranny of death. In this dark night of the world there is only one single source of light: the joyful news, 'Christ is risen!' Thus precisely for our day a 'Theology of the Resurrection' becomes an urgent necessity and its message the redeeming answer.

The book has met with delighted assent among those to whom the proclamation of the word is entrusted, and received understanding appreciation in technical theological circles. Above all I have to be grateful for the assessment of Folke Holmström, who welcomed the book as an 'energetic new attempt' 'to make a fundamental idea of the Bible fruitful for dogmatics today' and a 'radical effort towards a methodical re-orientation', and thereby acknowledged the work to be 'a sign of a late renaissance of the biblical way of thinking' in the world of dogmatics (*Das eschatologische Denken der Gegenwart*, 1936, pp. 382, 387).

The cause which this 'Theology of the Resurrection' sought to uphold has meantime, considering the general new evaluation of the resurrection message, widely prevailed. Yet now as always the questions of method implied in this fundamental theological insight, as well as the individual dogmatic problems, are still the subject of scholarly discussion. There was therefore no material reason for making any essential change in the lay-out and content of the book, except for the necessary additions. Consideration has been given to the theological discussion that has meanwhile arisen, and especially to the significant debate which P. Althaus has conducted with *The Theology of the Resurrection* in his various publications. The reply which is given in this edition would wish to be understood as an expression of my esteem, and at the same time of my thanks for this conversation.

Meanwhile the theses advanced by R. Bultmann have deeply stirred theology and the Church. It has therefore proved necessary in the revision to make special and detailed reference to Bultmann's approach. A biblical approach to these problems on the basis of a 'Theology of the Resurrection' brings out their topical significance with renewed clarity.

The last section of the book, which deals with Christian eschatology, has undergone a thorough recasting and supplementing. The introduction of the biblical 'doctrine of aeons', and above all the exposition of the 'Aeon of Christ's Lordship', as well as the new consideration of the problems of the 'Intermediate State' and the *'apokatastasis'*, involved an expansion so great that it proved advisable to gather these different thought complexes together into a new third part. In doing so I have indeed ventured to allow the operation in eschatology of points of view which have so far received little attention in theology. The biblical view which culminates in the 'Theology of the Resurrection' can be the only valid norm for doing so.

Finally, the new edition offers additional scripture references, an enlarged index of subjects and a new index of names. For this help, too, I now express again my thanks to my father, who until the end of his earthly pilgrimage assisted me as a loyal friend with expert advice on the problems here involved.

WALTER KÜNNETH

Erlangen, Summer 1951

PREFACE TO THE FIRST EDITION

At a time when a thousand subjective opinions and speculative world-views, religions and substitute religions are competing for recognition, and when we can also hardly speak of a unified dogmatic line in the Protestant Church and its theology, there is more need than ever for radical reflection on the primary and proper content of the proclamation of the Gospel, for referring back to the substance of the Church. The future of the Reformation Church will depend on the purity of its doctrine, which has been threatened for generations and has been lost even in the widest circles within the Church, but the absence of which provides a welcome opening for a kind of spirituality foreign to the Gospel. The proclamation of the Gospel in the sense of the Reformation, however, can mean nothing else but taking our proper bearings from the biblical witness to revelation, for it is with the validity of that witness that the claims of the Church's message stand or fall.

In the context of this theological task, the present book finds itself committed to take its stand at a decisive point: to strive for a clear understanding of the primitive Christian message of the resurrection and to make a contribution to the struggle for a deeper understanding of Christ. The study thus sets out from a problem which has so far received strikingly little attention in theological discussion, but is certainly convinced that it is precisely the witness to the resurrection of Jesus that sums up the essential problem of Christology, if not of theology altogether. It seeks to sketch a *Theology of the Resurrection*. Its aim is therefore to expound systematically the whole content of the resurrection message and to trace the dogmatic lines from this point to the major questions of a Christian theology.

To be sure, a sense of appreciation for this inquiry will be possible only to those for whom the world of Pauline thought is a real world, and who are able to see in the chapter on the resurrection in I Corinthians the decisive intellectual turning point between biblical thought and extra-Christian speculation. It is from this standpoint, therefore, that we would wish an assessment to be made of our attempt to find precisely in the resurrection of Jesus the basis of what theology has to say.

Thus this study is at bottom concerned for the attainment of a *new theological outlook*, which is unequivocally determined by the reality of the resurrection of the Kyrios.

I express my heartfelt thanks to my father, Pastor L. Künneth of Hersbruck near Nürnberg, for the reading of the proofs and the preparation of the subject index, but also for much understanding advice during the preparing and executing of the work.

WALTER KÜNNETH

Berlin, February 1933

INTRODUCTION

W HEN we speak of the resurrection of Jesus, we are not discussing a possible result of religious speculation, nor do we mean an idealistic postulate or a philosophical construction, but we are basing ourselves on the given 'word of the resurrection'. This is always already given as a fundamental theological presupposition before theological reflection begins; it is presupposed both in the New Testament kerygma and in the confession of the Church.

Our theological concern with this word of the resurrection is an expression of our being inevitably committed to the actual content of the primitive Christian message, which certainly does not merely contain the word of the resurrection as one declaration among others, but finds its essential focus and determination in the testimony, 'Christ is risen'.[1] This Good News puts the specific stamp on the faith and confession of the primitive Church,[2] as also on its missionary preaching.[3]

Moreover, we are driven to theological reflection on the Church's witness to the resurrection. Are the words, 'on the third day he rose from the dead' only a tradition which has no significance for today, or do they have imperishable validity and the intimacy of a living faith? Modern scepticism and criticism of church dogma summon us with special urgency to deeper reflection on this article of the creed. A thorough-going explanation of it is thus an essential part of the Church's task in seeking to understand its own faith.

If theology sought to evade a discussion of the witness to the resurrection, then on the one hand it would be moving dangerously far from

---

[1] The Easter cry, 'The Lord is risen indeed' (Luke 24.34) certainly belongs to the earliest witness of the primitive Church.

[2] I Cor. 15.3-7; Rom. 8.34; I Cor. 12.3; Phil. 2.11; the confession in Rom. 10.9; II Tim. 2.8. Cf. R. Bultmann in *Deutsche Theologie* III, *Vom Worte Gottes*, 1931, p. 16: the theme of the preaching is 'life and death'. Further, *Die Offenbarung im Neuen Testament*, 1929.

[3] Acts 2.32; 4.2; 4.33; 13.32-41, where the resurrection is related to several Old Testament passages, including Isa. 55.3; Ps. 16.10; Acts 24.21; 25.19; 26.6-8; 23.6; 17.31. That the event of the resurrection stands at the very centre especially of Pauline theology will become clearer as this work proceeds.

its basis in the New Testament, while on the other hand it would all too easily become the victim of an arbitrary, undoctrinal subjectivism. There is no doubt about the importance of the theme. But the significance of the task is equalled by its peculiar difficulty.

The word of the resurrection of Jesus provides a focal point for the intersection of very various and heterogeneous lines. At this point there cross each other, as it were, the judgments of historical research, the views of the historian of religions, the ideologies of general metaphysics, the findings of New Testament scholarship and of dogmatic theology. Which authority is competent to apprehend the 'matter' to which this word bears witness; which is the appropriate epistemological method? The answer to the question as to the real character and the authentic meaning of the resurrection is beset by a multiplicity of problems. For this reason it is with the special question of the resurrection that the divergence of theological views and positions becomes most evident. And so the resurrection witness becomes a 'sore point' in the theological field, indeed an absolute stone of stumbling. It is the sort of thing we would prefer to leave alone—or it will kindle a thorough-going discussion which involves the ultimate depths of our world-view. *To ask about the resurrection of Jesus is thus to take the risk of entering the least secure and most sharply contested sector of the theological front. But it might be precisely at this point that the decision must fall.*

This raises acutely the question of what contribution the history of theology can make to the problem of the resurrection. Modern theology[4] shows many signs of uncertainty in its handling of the problem, a tendency to illegitimate interpretation and manifest distortion of the facts. This bankruptcy of a secularized theology in face of the problem of the resurrection is of course largely due to Schleiermacher, who declared that 'The facts of the resurrection and the ascension of Christ ... cannot be taken as an authentic part of the doctrine of his person.'[5] Nor is this typical indifference of Schleiermacher to the resurrection really remedied by the statements of Ritschl, who regards all assertions that can be made about the exalted Christ as already 'attributes of his

---

[4] Within the scope of this work we must dispense with an analysis of the history of dogma, however important and interesting that would be in itself. For this, cf. K. Holl, *Der Osten*, Tübingen 1928.

[5] *Der christliche Glaube* III, p. 96, § 99 (ET, *The Christian Faith*, 1928), where he points out that 'the spiritual presence which he (Jesus) promised, and all that he said of his continuing influence upon those left behind, is not mediated by either of these two facts', accordingly 'the real influence of Christ can, and also did, make its impact without any news of these facts', pp. 97, 88. Further, 'faith in these facts is thus not an independent element in the original content of faith in Christ', p. 99.

existence in time'.[6] Accordingly most of the theologians influenced by these leaders adopt a similar reserve towards the question of the resurrection. The result is, that the resurrection of Jesus is no longer regarded by them as a necessary element of the Christian faith; at least it does not have the force of a ground of faith as it had in the primitive Church.[7] In rejecting views so disastrous to the resurrection witness and aligning itself with the Reformers and Orthodoxy, the so-called 'positive theology' has preserved the content and substance of the teaching of the New Testament and the Church, yet without providing a new theological basis for a more fruitful approach to the problem of the resurrection. The sharp criticism of Schleiermacher by R. Frank is worth noting: 'One cannot imagine anything more contrary to the witness of scripture than these assertions . . . that the fact of the resurrection of Christ is not to be taken as an essential part of the doctrine of the Person of Christ. . . . So the attempt to formulate a Christian dogmatic . . . without emphasizing this fact must be described as senseless'—a criticism which at least drew the attention of dogmatic theology once more to the New Testament message of the resurrection.[8] But a more profound understanding of the theological importance of the resurrection of Jesus came only with the special inquiries of L. Ihmels[9] and C. Stange.[10] According to Ihmels, 'Nothing less than the whole understanding of Christianity' depends on the resurrection. 'We may say without exaggeration: at the

[6] *Rechtfertigung und Versöhnung* III, pp. 383 f., 415 f., 423 f., 441. According to Ritschl 'the statement that Christ is exalted to the right hand of God is either meaningless to us, since Christ as the Exalted Lord is directly hidden from us, or else it will open for us the door to fanatical views of every conceivable kind', for the activity of Christ *in statu exaltationis* 'must be described as an expression of the permanent effect of his historical appearance' (pp. 407 f.).

[7] Typical of this outlook is the point of view of H. Stephan in his *Glaubenslehre* II, pp. 197 f. To be sure, he is clearly aware that 'the resurrection of Jesus is inextricably interwoven with the apostolic witness to Christ and occupies an important place in the faith of the disciples'. But at the same time he avers that 'the experience of the disciples does not have the same significance for us', indeed, 'we do not require it to the same extent'. For the knowledge of faith the resurrection is not something 'independent or of totally new content'. 'Even without the experience of meeting the Risen Lord, the disciples would inevitably have acquired the right understanding of his life and death.' 'In the light of all this, when we talk of the resurrection of Jesus today, we are not discussing an insight which provides a specific basis for faith.' The most it can do for the believer is to 'confirm his own guesses', 'enrich and deepen his own thoughts'—an evaluation which at all events stands in complete contradiction to the primitive Christian message.

[8] *Die christliche Wahrheit* II, pp. 208-209.

[9] *Die Auferstehung Jesu Christi*, Leipzig 1917.

[10] 'Die Auferstehung Jesu', in the *Zeitschrift für systematische Theologie*, vol. 24, part 4, pp. 724, 735: 'In view of its historical effect, faith in the resurrection claims absolute primacy of place'; 'in the destiny of Jesus the destiny of the world is fulfilled.'

tomb in Jerusalem the ultimate choice will be made between two totally different world-views.'[11] These fundamental insights, together with ideas taken over from M. Kähler,[12] are affirmed also by P. Althaus, whose theological expositions always presuppose the event of Easter,[13] and they are reaffirmed in the theology of Karl Heim, whose thought both in dogmatics and in the philosophy of religion would be impossible without the fact of the resurrection.[14] Finally, the question of the resurrection has been raised urgently once more by the dialectical theologians. Karl Barth, who was strongly influenced by the living resurrection faith of Christoph Blumhardt, refers in impressive terms to the 'central importance' of the resurrection of Jesus. For him the resurrection is the point 'from which light falls on the whole'; it is the 'assault upon Christendom'.[15] 'The content of the proclamation of Christ is, that he has been raised from the dead.[16] The pivot of primitive Christian thought has at all events not been neglected by Karl Barth,[17] and has been taken seriously by E. Brunner and F. Gogarten.[18]

This brief glance at the history of theological discussion on the subject of the resurrection makes clear that in itself there is no lack of valuable approaches towards a theological formulation of the problem,[19]

[11] *Op. cit.*, p. 27.
[12] *Christliche Wissenschaft*, § 365, p. 327.
[13] P. Althaus, *Die letzten Dinge*, 1927, p. 56; *Theologische Aufsätze*, 1929, pp. 2, 123 f., 219; *Grundriss der Dogmatik* II, 1932, p. 92.
[14] *Dogmatik* I, pp. 43 ff.; *Dogmatik* II, p. 86; *Glaube und Leben*, 1926, pp. 419 f.; *Die neue Welt Gottes*, 1929, pp. 62 ff., 69 f., 77.
[15] *Die Auferstehung der Toten*, 1924, pp. 1 f., 86ff., 125 (ET, *The Resurrection of the Dead*, 1933, pp. 11f., 156 ff., 217).
[16] *Dogmatik* I, p. 275.
[17] Cf. *Römerbrief*, pp. 62, 68, 71, 82, 87, 126 f., 348 f., 413 f., 464 (ET, *The Epistle to the Romans*, 1933, pp. 88, 94, 97, 108, 113, 150 ff., 427 f., 462, 513).
[18] E. Brunner, *Der Mittler*, 1937, pp. 511, 522, 528 (ET, *The Mediator*, 1949, pp. 563, 574, 581); 'All faith in Christ is vain, if Christ is not risen, really risen. . . . Everything else is a sham: both materially and historically—the coincidence is a necessary one—Easter is the foundation of the Christian faith and of the Christian community.' 'Easter is the epistemological ground of the apostles' knowledge of Christ.' 'Easter is the focal point in relation to which everything else that the Gospel says first acquires its "rightness". Take away this one thing, and there remains nothing at all.' Cf. also F. Gogarten, *Ich glaube an den dreieinigen Gott*, 1926, pp. 164 ff.: the Christian message is 'word of the resurrection and as such Word of God'. The resurrection is 'the first and the last word' of the message. Gogarten perceives that for the apostles the decisive accent lies on the resurrection, 'for it is only in the light of the resurrection that what the apostles have experienced in Jesus acquires such a significance that they must speak of it. It is now no longer something which concerns only them, but something which concerns all men.'
[19] Mention should be made of the 'Easter Theology' of Kähler's pupil Adolf Schneider-Posen, cf. *Ges. Aufsätze*, 1929, pp. ix ff., 40 ff., 82 ff. It is worth noting also that the 'Union of Evangelical Christians for all Russia' attaches a special importance to faith in the resurrection. The programmatic essay published by the president, J. S. Prochanov, bears the title 'The Resurrection Cry'

and in particular that contemporary theological reflection shows the time is ripe for a new start in this field. But on the whole, the insight concerning the resurrection has so far not yet been given comprehensive theological expression in one systematic work. The event of the resurrection is spoken of in customary terms as one event among others, without ever raising the question of the adequacy of these means of expression. The method of equating and co-ordinating the resurrection with other articles of faith necessarily hinders the proper development of the basic theological insight and ill accords with the primitive Christian interest in the resurrection message.[20]

The task of theology, which the present work finds to be urgent, is clear from this brief survey. On the negative side, we have to overcome first the failure to recognize the importance of the resurrection witness, and second the refusal to make a determined attempt at theological construction. On the positive side we have to show the fundamental basis of the resurrection knowledge in the New Testament and the Church and develop it in its systematic aspects and in the context of dogmatics and particularly of Christology. The immediate result of that is to develop the basic lines which in the course of modern theology's debates on the question of the resurrection have proved to be essential.

The whole problem can be summed up in three main thought complexes. First we have to examine from every angle the radical problem of the resurrection of Jesus, and to ask what kind of reality is actually meant when the primitive Christian witness speaks of the 'resurrection of Jesus'. We have thus to discuss the 'essence' and 'nature' of this event, rigorously excluding inappropriate interpretations and forming adequate concepts. Then the dogmatic meaning of the declaration that

---

(first written Easter 1928, prepared for publication Easter 1930). The hymns of this Union are called 'Resurrection Songs', 'because that is the best way of reflecting the inward attitude of the Russian believers, whose enthusiasm flows from a quite specially profound grasp of the Easter Act of Jesus Christ.'

[20] Typical of this attitude is the method used by Schlatter when in his otherwise most valuable dogmatics he fits the resurrection of Jesus into the general pattern of his thought. Without any attempt to work out systematically the universal importance of the resurrection of Jesus, it is not until paragraph 79 that he comes to deal with it too (*Das christliche Dogma*, 1923, pp. 307 ff.). Also typical are the Christologies of R. Frank and R. Seeberg. Thus R. Frank in the second part of his work, under the head of 'Regeneration', observes that from the standpoint of the exaltation of Jesus 'the necessity and the significance of the resurrection at once' emerges (*Die christliche Wahrheit* II, p. 207). According to R. Seeberg, various motives were at work in the emergence of faith in Christ, and therefore faith must not restrict itself to the life and sufferings of Jesus but 'includes within itself also' the resurrection of Jesus. The presenting of the resurrection thus forms the necessary conclusion of a Christology. (*Christliche Glaubenslehre* II, pp. 204, 212, 223.)

Christ is risen has to be systematically investigated and developed. Independent Christological examination of this kind, however, does not by any means imply that it is merely declared to be a specialized internal concern of theology, but consciously seeks, on the basis of the resurrection aspect here perceived, to make a contribution towards the understanding of reality as a whole and so to relate the message of the resurrection to the spiritual life and questions of our time. Thirdly, we have to develop these fundamental insights in relation to the problems of specific eschatology, and to reject inadequate eschatological theses and postulates.

There remains the final task of theologically recapturing the primitive Christian situation and advancing to a deeper understanding of the true significance of its resurrection message. That is, we have to aim at nothing less than the writing of a *Theology of the Resurrection*. In this case the key to primitive Christian theology is recognized from the outset to lie in the witness to the resurrection, and this is taken as the fundamental principle, the presupposition and point of departure for theological thinking. In contrast to all theological misunderstandings and confusions, such an effort to construct a theology of the resurrection knows something of the *infinite importance of the word of the resurrection of Jesus not only for theological knowledge in general, but also for the living problems of contemporary man*. How far a theology of the resurrection can prove itself legitimate and meaningful is for the present inquiry to establish.[21]

[21] Cf. Ewald Burger, *Der lebendige Christus*, Stuttgart 1933, which has recognized the importance of such an undertaking. Also H. Schreiner, *Die Verkündigung des Wortes Gottes*, 1936 (new edition, Friedrich-Wittig-Verlag, Hamburg, 1949), who from the point of view of the demands of practical theology has been able to give his full support to the new approach here proposed (pp. 185, 227).

Part One

THE REALITY OF THE RESURRECTION

A THEOLOGICAL work which concerns itself with the understanding of the resurrection of Jesus has the task of *grasping the resurrection of Jesus as a reality*. By '*reality*' is not meant simply 'substantial fact', which can apply equally well to a thing.* By 'reality' is meant the creative, reconstitutive truth of an event that lays claim to validity. Does the resurrection of Jesus qualify as a reality at all, and what characteristics has this reality? The necessity of stating the question thus, creates a series of problems, raises critical objections which threaten partly to destroy the resurrection's character of reality and partly to obscure it or prevent an appropriate understanding of it. The problematical character of the resurrection becomes manifest.

* The connection is perhaps not quite so clear in English as in German, where *Realität* (here translated 'substantial fact') still has the force of the Latin root *res* (thing), while *Wirklichkeit* ('reality') retains the notion of the root *wirken* (to work, effect)—*Translator*.

I

THE PROBLEMATICAL CHARACTER OF
THE RESURRECTION OF JESUS

THE hindrances to understanding the resurrection as a reality are best dealt with under five heads. There are then five problem complexes: resurrection and history, resurrection and the idea of life, resurrection and existentialism, resurrection and myth, and resurrection and world-picture. This means that the problem of the resurrection involves in the first instance questions of historical research, of the philosophy of religion, of existentialism, and of the history of religion, as well as the question of modern knowledge of the world. Now the task is to discover what kind of conclusions are reached by relating the resurrection to these concepts, and whether by means of this approach to the problem we can find an answer to the question of the reality of the resurrection.

I. RESURRECTION AND HISTORY

(a) The Question of the Historicality of the Resurrection of Jesus

Since the days of Orthodoxy, it has been widely accepted that the resurrection of Jesus was a 'historical fact', and this opinion is deeply rooted in the Church. The *historicality of the resurrection* appears to be the strongest bulwark against any denial of the resurrection and any attack upon the Christian faith which has been built upon it. This view holds that only the historic is real, without raising the question as to whether the concept of reality might not include more than what is merely historical. The understanding of the resurrection as a fact in history involves three factors: that the resurrection is a historical fact implies that it is concrete, completed, and unique. The resurrection is accordingly an event which took place in a quite definite way, at a quite definite time, to quite definite people, in the context of quite definite external phenomena. It is concrete, and therefore has a character which is personal, historic, and within space and time. It concerns an event which took place on the morning of the third day and hence in time, outside the gates of Jerusalem and hence in space, before the eyes of individual men and hence in the midst of human history. As a concrete fact, however, the resurrection is also a completed one. That marks it as a happening in the past, as an accomplished act in history. The perfect tense excludes the timeless and the supra-historic; it denotes an accomplished event, and one that has no longer to be completed and supplemented. The resurrection as a historic fact, however, is also a unique event. This statement seeks to define the resurrection as a unique act in contradistinction to all undifferentiated eternal ideas. The uniqueness of the event gives expression to the glory of history. Unique means unrepeatable.

If the resurrection of Jesus is to be asserted as a historic fact, then it can be compared with other events in the life of Jesus. If, however, the life and death of Jesus is to be judged from the point of view of its historical reality, then to apply these same principles to the resurrection is only a question of the degree of clarity of the historic tradition. There arises the need to establish the historicality of the resurrection of Jesus, i.e. to provide a historical proof of the historic fact of the resurrection of Jesus. It is thought possible to 'establish' this by valid historical means, either on the basis of the evidence given by witnesses according to the New Testament tradition or by pointing to the historic after-affects of the resurrection event. The result of the labours of this supra-naturalistic historism is the verdict: the 'evidence' for the historicity of the resurrection appears to be 'good', and indeed 'of the best'; the resurrection is a historically verifiable fact, which differs from other historic events only in virtue of the peculiar metaphysical causality and extraordinary quality of its effects.[1]

Yet the very description of the resurrection as a historical fact raises a complex of difficult *problems*. The historicality of the resurrection has been fundamentally and radically called in question both by historical research and by the possibility of rationalization. If the resurrection is an event on the plane of history, then it also participates in all that determines the nature of history. The resurrection event is then a relative fact in the context of the phenomena and life of history, stands in continuity with a multitude of other known and unknown factors belonging to this world, is an element in historical existence and as such possesses no absolute validity but is subject to conditions and thus to the uncertainties and probabilities of all history. To insist upon the

[1] Cf. Kahnis, *Die Auferstehung Christi als geschichtliche Tatsache*, Leipzig 1873; Greiner, *Die Auferstehung Jesu Christi von den Toten nach ihrer Tatsächlichkeit und ihrer Bedeutung für den christlichen Glauben*, Karlsruhe 1869; Uhlhorn, *Die Auferstehung Christi als heilsgeschichtliche Tatsache*, Gotha 1869.

historic character of the resurrection has the result of objectifying it. The historic fact of the resurrection becomes a possible object of historical criticism and an object of rational analysis. That means, however, that the assertion of its historicality leads to an irresistible process of dissolution, which ominously threatens the reality of the resurrection itself.

First of all the historic fact of the resurrection becomes an object for the impartial examinations of historical science. Different methods have been tried. There is the method of arguing back from the existence of belief in the resurrection in the primitive Church to the fact which must originally have given rise to this belief. There is the method of applying the historical and psychological principles of analogy and relation. Or there is the method of understandingly feeling one's way into the atmosphere of the primitive Church and then reconstructing the situation and using one's sense of congeniality to grasp the meaning of the reports. At all events the resurrection message becomes a problem of historical research. Even when we pay due regard to all the methods of historical criticism, still we are under the influence of different philosophical and speculative assumptions and according to these we reach different interpretations of the resurrection traditions which lie before us. The milder historical criticism is inclined to recognize at least the subjective convictions of the faith of the primitive Church with regard to the resurrection of Jesus, but reckons at the same time with the possibility of a later legendary embellishment of the original experiences. Yet it also sees itself compelled to give up the attempt to throw light on the origins of belief in the resurrection. After all the research into history, there is 'an inexplicable remainder', a 'historical riddle', which 'can never be completely analysed' by historical methods.[2] Thorough-going historical relativism, on the other hand, is not satisfied with the concession of an ultimate inexplicability, but is convinced that all the statements on the resurrection are historically untenable. The radical application of the principles of historical criticism results in the complete breakdown of the resurrection witness.[3] The sharpest attempts of supranaturalism to repulse this attack by the science of history are understandable, but hopeless. For indeed it is precisely the historical thesis of the resurrection of

[2] A. Deissmann, *Paulus*, 1911, pp. 97 f., 100; E. Brunner, *Der Mittler*, pp. 526 ff. (ET, pp. 578 ff.); F. Loofs, *Die Auferstehungsberichte und ihr Wert*, 1908, p. 39.
[3] R. Bultmann, *Jesus*, 1926, pp. 12, 15 (ET, *Jesus and the Word*, 1934, pp. 8 f., 12); *Geschichte der synoptischen Tradition*, 1930 (ET, *History of the Synoptic Tradition*, 1963); *Die Erforschung der synoptischen Evangelien*, Giessen 1930, pp. 14, 35 f.

Jesus that the supranaturalist feels compelled to maintain and that now provokes the criticism. All his historical arguments go to pieces under the fire of the criticisms of the science of history. *At the end of the road of historical research into the resurrection of Jesus stands a question mark with the whole burden of historical uncertainty and scepticism.*

Secondly, however, the problems of the historicality of the resurrection are sharpened by attempts to rationalize it. A historical process is open to the possibility of rational explanation. Such attempts have been made repeatedly with the most diverse variations, from Celsus, who saw the resurrection as a piece of self-deception on the part of the disciples or an intentional fraud,[4] through the Wolfenbüttel fragments and D. F. Strauss, to the rationalizing efforts of contemporary theology. Above all D. F. Strauss is of course the classic representative of the famous subjective-vision hypothesis, according to which the resurrection appearances are explained as inward, subjective experiences of the beholder. The emotions of the soul crystallize into visible pictorial shape; the imagination intensifies into a vision that has subjective value without absolute validity. The resurrection experience has its origin in the soul of the disciples, in an emotional climax for which their previous experiences had prepared them, and which, as they remembered the imperishable dignity of Jesus, assumed a visionary character that put an end to their doubts. The 'historical fact' of the resurrection of Jesus is thus seen to be a phenomenon that is humanly and historically understandable and psychologically explicable.[5] Special mention is due also

---

[4] Cf. Origen, *Contra Celsum*, 2.55.

[5] D. F. Strauss, *Leben Jesu* II, pp. 631 f., 634 ff. Cf. the following line of thought: Accordingly 'the powerful impression of the magnificent personality of Jesus will doubtless have been capable of inspiring his immediate disciples . . . to visions'. There arose in the disciples 'automatically the psychological need to resolve the contradiction between the final fate of Jesus and their assured opinion of him'. 'Thus the Jesus who had been executed in shame was not lost to them, but remained: he had only entered through death into his Messianic glory.' 'How easy it is, finally, to imagine that these feelings were occasionally intensified in a purely subjective fashion in individuals, especially women, to become real visions; whereas on others . . . the sight of an unknown person occasionally perhaps made the impression of a revelation or appearance of Jesus; an intensity of pious visionariness.' It was of course a very simple matter for the disciples to take their earlier Jewish view of the eternity of the Messiah and 're-establish it by means of the idea of an actual return to life of the dead Christ'. Quite near to D. F. Strauss are R. Bultmann's observations on the 'appearances' of the Risen Lord. They are reduced to 'visionary experiences' of the disciples, the factual character of which appears to be disputed. At all events Bultmann does not consider these 'appearances' to be of any special material importance for theology: on the contrary, they are to be regarded as 'concessions to the weakness' of the disciples and consequently 'non-essential' and 'unnecessary' to the Easter event. We have not to demand the outward 'sign' of 'appearances', but the word alone, quite apart from any visionary circumstances,

to Harnack's grandiosely conceived attempt at psychological explanation. Here we have to do with a combination of the transfiguration story and certain subjective experiences on the part of Peter after Jesus' death—which is supposed to explain the 'vision of Peter'. For Harnack, the question how Peter's vision came about is 'a religious-historical problem of the first order', for the explanation of the first act of Easter faith implies the explanation of the 'visions' of the rest of the apostles which we must consider to depend, as it were, on the suggestiveness of Peter's vision and to have been due to a kind of visionary infection.[6] Even E. Hirsch's thought on the resurrection of Jesus, which is of course also conditioned by his basic historical approach, is not free of rationalizing

---

must have the power to convince and to awake faith. Bultmann therefore thinks that this Easter tradition is based upon 'a false interpretation of reality by the disciples': *Das Evangelium des Johannes*, 1941, p. 539; see *Kerygma und Mythos*, 1951, p. 47 (ET in *Kerygma and Myth*, 1953, p. 42).

[6] Cf. *Sitzungsbericht der Akademie der Wissenschaften*, 1922, pp. 73, 75 ff. In support of this construction he brings in also the story of the transfiguration and thereby adopts again the line of E. Meyer and Wellhausen (E. Meyer, *Ursprung und Anfang des Christentums* II, p. 156: 'The resurrection and the appearances of the Risen One grew out of the transfiguration. The latter is the ultimate root of Christianity.' An exposition of the transfiguration story as a story of the resurrection, with special reference to II Peter, is found also in Wellhausen, who speaks of Jesus being 'transported into heaven immediately after his death'. Cf. Bertram in *Die Himmelfahrt Jesu vom Kreuze aus*). Accordingly Harnack avers: 'If ever a vision appeared well and sufficiently motivated and explained by what had taken place in the visionary, and if such a vision has ever been credibly explained, then it is certainly so if Peter since the day of Caesarea Philippi had lived and moved in the overwhelming conviction that the Rabbi Jesus was the Messiah. . . . If he was disposed to visions at all, then all the conditions for one would be given now, particularly as Jesus . . . had withdrawn to a high mountain with him in solitude.' Thus Peter is psychologically prepared by hunger, thirst and sunburn to experience the first vision of Christ, the Messiahship of Jesus. This first event, however, acquires an 'extraordinary significance'. 'For now we have to notice that Peter, when the catastrophe of the crucifixion broke and everything in him must have bristled at the idea of allowing it the last word, did not need to cling only to the words of Jesus and the deep impression of his earthly life—all of which now seemed to be proved false—but that he had to his hand also a reminiscence that triumphed over the death of the cross already in advance: he had once on the mountainside seen Jesus as the Messiah in heavenly glory. For him that was a fact, and precisely on the basis of that fact his faith sprang up anew, overcoming every doubt, and made him experience a second vision of the Lord in his glory.' Thus the first vision of Christ 'came to the help of his wounded and dying faith, lifted it high again from his subconscious mind and worked so powerfully that it repeated itself'. Accordingly Peter 'experienced two visions, one during the earthly life of Jesus and the other after the crucifixion; the second stood in the closest connection with the first and was brought about, or made possible, by it. . . . Later the two certainly blended, as it were, in Peter's soul, and from them there then arose the others' experiences of the Risen Christ . . .' (p. 80). More recently, it is true, Harnack himself seems to have recognized the uncertainty of this hypothesis, cf. *Die Entstehung der christlichen Theologie und des kirchlichen Dogmas*, Gotha 1927, p. 46: 'Thus so far as the visions permit of an explanation at all, they are to be traced to the continuing effect of the impression of the person of Jesus himself; but even this explanation is not entirely satisfying.'

explanations. Easter becomes the 'story of the heart' of Peter and then 'the story of the first church'. He would identify Peter's subjective experience of the forgiveness of sin with 'the true secret of the Easter story'.[7] Every rationalizing attempt to make the historical process of the resurrection understandable, however, not only fails at bottom to provide any safeguard against explaining it away as subjective, but also leaves the door open to pathological or spiritist methods of explanation. In the sphere of history, one is perfectly entitled in face of an unusual phenomenon to adopt also an approach which in itself belongs to the field of medicine.[8] Thus alongside of historical criticism we must regard

[7] *Jesus der Herr*, 1927, pp. 38 ff. Since then, in *Die Auferstehungsgeschichten und der christliche Glaube*, Tübingen 1940, E. Hirsch has dropped his theological mask and—if in modern form, yet substantially in the sense of the older liberalism—has used the allegedly established methods of critical historical examination to bring about the radical dissolution of the Christian Church's faith in the resurrection as 'Easter legend' and 'Easter myth'. It is the merit of P. Althaus that he has made a clear critical reply in determined opposition to the methods of demolition employed by this kind of pseudo-theology (*Die Wahrheit des kirchlichen Osterglaubens: Einspruch gegen E. Hirsch*, Gütersloh 1940). In doing so he refers with a wide measure of agreement to *The Theology of the Resurrection*. It is only to be regretted that Althaus himself is still, as I think, under the spell of historism and considers it necessary to accept with Hirsch 'the fundamental demand' 'that the Easter stories must be submitted to historical criticism in order to ascertain the actuality of their content, or their possible legendary character as the case may be' (p. 13). On this plane Althaus arrives at the conviction—a highly disputable one even from the standpoint of historical study of the New Testament and a fatal one for the Church and its doctrine—that the accounts in John 20 are of a 'legendary nature', though to be sure 'while making full allowance for their poetic character' we may read and understand them as a 'true witness to the nature and lordship of Jesus' (p. 14). In contrast to Althaus we consider this whole approach to be erroneous from the start and must reject his seemingly ambiguous verdict as an unnecessary concession to a critical attitude that is out of date. The critical views asserted by Althaus against Hirsch turn, if I am not mistaken, against his own admissions. Christians who listen to historical criticism, so Althaus tells us, pass 'from dependence on the New Testament scriptures to dependence on the historians'. . . . They 'are furthermore then in the difficult position . . . of having to choose between the historians, for the results of their analyses are in many points contradictory' (*op. cit.*, pp. 64-65).

[8] On this point see J. Leipoldt, *Vom Jesusbilde der Gegenwart*, 1925, pp. 168 ff. A special kind of rationalizing of the 'historical fact' of the resurrection of Jesus is found in the attempts at a spiritist or anthroposophical interpretation. Cf. R. A. Hoffmann, *Das Geheimnis der Auferstehung Jesu*, Vienna 1921.

One result of the rationalistic approach is the attempt to provide a pathological explanation of the reports of the resurrection of Jesus as a psychological abnormality, a morbid disturbance of the soul, intensified to the point of hallucination. This, it is true, has a long history, but is without any ground in the facts themselves. The psychological examination of the disciples' characters does not provide the slightest reason for accepting the possibility of such an assertion: on the contrary, to suggest a hallucination which even medicine could not account for in such intensity, temporal duration and persistence as this, is to raise new problems more insoluble than ever. It is true that the fact of historical immanence does imply the possibility of examining the historical data also from the medical standpoint. Such an investigation, however, is totally void of scien-

also the psychological-vision hypotheses and the various rationalizing explanations of a cruder or more refined, more primitive or more ingenious kind, as consequences of equating the resurrection of Jesus with a fact of history—consequences which, for all their recognition of the historic character of the resurrection, destroy the authentic nature of the resurrection message.[9]

(b) The Untenability of the Thesis of the 'Historicality' of the Resurrection of Jesus

It is important to understand the justification of this concern with the 'historical'. Undoubtedly the primitive Christian witness to the resurrection has something to do with history. On the surface, it would appear that this witness to the resurrection is a declaration by historic people, information about certain experiences in the past which have affected the course of history. For this reason, it is difficult to agree with K. Barth in his view that for the resurrection message, 'place and time is quite unimportant', and the fact of the disciples' 'seeing' is immaterial.[10] Sharpest contradiction, however, must be the reaction to R. Bultmann's verdict that the eye-witness accounts of the resurrection of Jesus cited by Paul, and his arguments in I Cor. 15.3-8, are 'fatal' because that is to turn the message of the New Testament upside down and remove the basis of the disciples' faith in the resurrection.[11] There is no doubt that the New Testament has an interest in the connection between resurrection and historicality. The concept of the historic not only aims at the exclusion of the subjective, but also includes indispensable elements of value in its definitions of the concrete, the completed and the unique. It is a question of the unique and unrepeatable character of the resurrection event, which took place independently of man's consciousness and his powers of discernment. The cardinal point of the resurrection story is thus necessarily the testimony of the eye-witnesses. 'We have seen the Lord', is a message which marks the uniqueness of par-

---

tific seriousness if it refrains from taking the given facts as the basis of the examination and is compelled on the contrary to twist the facts to suit medical hypotheses.

[9] Cf. also Holsten, *Zum Evangelium des Paulus und Petrus*, 1868, pp. 65 ff.; J. Weiss, *Das Urchristentum*, 1917, pp. 20 ff. (ET, *The History of Primitive Christianity*, 1937, pp. 28 ff.); F. Barth, *Hauptproblem des Lebens Jesu*, 1893; W. Baldensperger, *Urchristliche Apologie: die älteste Auferstehungskontoverse*, Strassburg 1909; K. Kautzsch, *Ist die Ostertatsache die bestverbürgte Tatsache der Weltgeschichte?*, Leipzig 1910; E. Riggenbach, *Die Auferstehung Jesu* (Bibl. Z. u. Str. Fr.) 1908.

[10] *Die Auferstehung der Toten*, p. 78 (ET, p. 143).

[11] Cf. *Kerygma und Mythos*, p. 45 (ET, p. 39: 'dangerous').

ticular events that became the cause and the primary ground of the Easter faith. The truth which is enshrined in the description of the resurrection as a 'historical fact', and the earnest intention thereby expressed to preserve the statements about the resurrection from meaninglessness, must not be overlooked.[12]

Nevertheless the thesis must be recognized as the expression of an inadequate theological understanding of the matter. The formulation is false, because it is simply not capable of doing justice to the claims of the primitive Christian witness. No matter how important the historical relationships may be in detail, when the resurrection message is looked at in its essential character it does not exhaust itself in history but points decisively beyond the sphere of history. The whole weight and extra-ordinary character of the witness to the resurrection of Jesus simply does not depend at all on its historicality. What makes the witness to the resurrection different from other statements lies beyond the historic plane. Therefore the definition of it as a historical fact involves an un-tenable shift of emphasis, in which the deepest meaning of the message is the very thing which cannot be validly expressed. If the resurrection of Jesus were to be understood as a merely historical happening, then it would stand among other historic events and other miracles which were played out on the stage of history. Such a comparison, however, fundamentally destroys the uniqueness of the resurrection and thus fails to grasp the basic newness of the witness to the resurrection. The real goal of historical supranaturalism, which is to ward off the danger of a reduction to the subjective level by emphasizing the historic char-acter of the resurrection of Jesus, is not attained. Rather, the attempt falls a prey to the historical levelling process.

In rejection of the 'historical' thesis we have first of all in a general sense to stress the resurrection's transcendence of history, i.e. its superiority to history. Here the dialectical attack on making the resur-rection into mere history is justified. It is asserted against all the histor-ian's efforts that the tradition has no desire for a 'historical proof of the resurrection', that in the end of the day 'the historical approach as such,

---

[12] In this connection it is worth noting the verdict of E. Lohmeyer in *Die Grundlagen paulinischer Theologie*, 1929. According to Paul the resurrection is 'vérité de fait'. 'For one thing the resurrection must be spoken of, precisely because of its purely metaphysical validity, as a historical fact; and secondly, because of this its factuality, it sets itself up in its own right and its own actuality alongside the fact of death' (pp. 95 f., 101). Cf. also F. Kattenbusch in the *Festschrift für R. Müller*, 1922, pp. 322 ff.; W. Mundle in the *Zeitschrift für N. T. Wissenschaft*, 1922, pp. 22 ff. Similarly H. Wobbermin, *Wesen und Wahr-heit des Christentums*, Leipzig 1925, p. 286.

if not eliminated, is certainly relativized'.[13] The resurrection of Jesus is 'the boundary of history', it is 'primal history', it is 'the denial of all this-worldly assertions and denials', which can no longer be spoken of in historical categories at all.[14] Here we are also able to understand Bultmann's aim in his repeated attack on all attempts to ensure 'the historical controllability of revelation'. It is quite true that historical arguments of that kind are impossible and pointless. Whatever way we may have to interpret the resurrection of Jesus in detail, the decisive thing is, that in contrast to the concepts that are formed on the basis of historical presuppositions, it must be understood as essentially also a reality that is beyond history. Speaking in an entirely general sense, the word of the resurrection of Jesus signifies at all events not a historical, if also metaphysically exceptional fact, but a reality of God's revelation—and one which as such falls outside the realm of history and by its very essence leaps the bounds of the merely historical.

If the defining of the resurrection as a purely historic fact on the basis of the witness to the resurrection is to be rejected, then the historic problems involved in the resurrection appear in a totally new light. The questions of the science of history, as also of the attempts at rationalization, will have to be raised in an intrinsically different form.

In the first place there can be no more talk of the science of history threatening the truth of the resurrection event, if the latter is a revelational reality of an absolute character. The assumption from which the historical approach sets out, that the resurrection is an objectively ascertainable object of knowledge and accessible to impartial observation, is then seen to be fundamentally incorrect. The resurrection of Jesus is actually not a point on the historical plane to which we could conceivably have an objective relation. The historian's way of looking at it 'from outside' enables him at best to observe certain points at which it has entered the course of history and left its mark upon it, yet the proper interpretation of these things is denied him because he sets out from a false presupposition. The significance of the real content of the resurrection witness, however, does not lie within the range of the historian's vision. Accordingly, *historical research is not a competent authority at all when it comes to the question of knowledge of the resurrec-*

---

[13] K. Barth, *Die Auferstehung der Toten*, pp. 74 ff. (ET, pp. 137 ff.).
[14] K. Barth, *Dogmatik* I, 1927, pp. 80 f., 232 ff., 247 f., 254, 262 f., 273 f., 340 ff. Also F. Gogarten, *Der dreieinige Gott*, p. 172: 'To the extent that this is the story of a past event, which as such is finished, it has absolutely nothing to do with us.' Cf. also E. Brunner, *Der Mittler*, pp. 138, 140 ff. (ET, pp. 163, 165 ff.).

tion, which essentially cannot be grasped by historical formulae and is beyond the reach of an impartial examination. Between the reality of the resurrection, which transcends history, and the historical method of investigation, there is an incongruity which cannot be bridged. The resurrection witness is not given to us as a problem of the science of history, but has a specifically 'theological' character. To realize that an identification of the resurrection of Jesus with history has to be rejected is to liberate theological reflection from the paralysing bane of the methods of the science of history, and to face the task of comprehending the reality of the resurrection as a thing that transcends all two-dimensional objectivity.

Secondly, all rationalizing explanations of the resurrection are likewise seen to be fundamentally groundless when we assert the resurrection's transcendence of history. So long as the resurrection as a fact of history is made the object of every conceivable exercise of our perceptive faculties, then it is justly open to rational and pyschological analysis. If, however, the resurrection is understood as an 'absolute' which transcends all rational possibilities, then any kind of rationalizing is ruled out as inappropriate. In the case of something that belongs to history, we require an explanation which is as complete as possible and fits in with the laws that govern other phenomena; where, however, the reality is one that transcends history, it remains impossible to make it intelligible by rational means and any attempt to do so is pointless. There is therefore no need at all for a penetrating criticism of the hypothesis of subjective vision and similar rationalizing tendencies, such as has often been presented and in itself is thoroughly commendable. But instead of detailed criticisms, which will then repeatedly have to face new counter-arguments, we must question the whole possibility of rationalizing at all. The rationalist approach in terms of immanence cannot even begin to understand the resurrection witness and its pointers to something 'more than history', nor can it reach the real heart of the 'matter'.[15]

[15] Characteristic of rationalistic explanations is the lack of clarity on the relation of the 'appearances' of Jesus to the resurrection of Jesus itself. The two are frequently identified without more ado. Stange's criticism is noteworthy: 'The question must not be put in the form: how were the disciples able to come to belief in the resuscitation of their dead master? The question must rather have the much more precise form: how were the disciples able to come to the belief that the end of Jesus' life has significance for the history of the world?' For according to Jesus' view it is in itself certain 'that the return of someone from the dead would not widen the range of religious ideas in any way' (Luke 16.29 ff.). According to the rationalistic explanations 'it would have to be assumed that belief in the resurrection must also often have arisen elsewhere in history. . . . If the motive behind the belief in the resurrection is supposed to have been the love of the disciples, then that motive is at work everywhere in

From this point of view what remains open is no longer the possibility of a rational explanation, but only the possibility of a clear choice between two alternatives: either we accept the resurrection witness—a witness which in principle rules out any attempt at rationalization—or we reject it entirely.

This examination of the problem of the resurrection and history has led to the conclusion that *there are certainly notable relations between the resurrection of Jesus and history, but that the concept of 'historicality' cannot grasp the essence of the resurrection witness, which points rather to something that transcends history.*

2. RESURRECTION AND THE IDEA OF LIFE

(a) The Idea of Life and the Notion of Immortality

Another way to attempt an understanding of the resurrection of Jesus is through the philosophy of religion. Primitive ideas of the life value, of the soul and its immortality, refined by the thought of Plato and Aristotle, are held to form a broad basis for the comprehending of the resurrection witness. In such discussions the question of the historicality of the resurrection and of the possibilities of historical criticism is a matter of indifference. Here it is rather a case of including the resurrection of Jesus in the general history of ideas and relating it to the true idea of life, which is independent of all concrete history.

The *idea of life* is the fundamental idea of human existence as such, born of experience of the psycho-physical facts of the origin, growth and organic self-development of living things according to teleological patterns. It asserts the contrast with everything that is dead, everything that is detached from the framework of reality. Life is 'unity, movement, continuity, coherence, articulation', and therefore 'the prevailing of the life-values happiness and pleasure in the peculiar sense'.[16] The idea of life therefore originally appears already in the primitive consciousness of being, is intensified eudaimonistically in the struggle for existence as a battle for the preservation and advancement of life, and is finally sublimated in every experience of value which contributes to the fulfilment of personal, individual life. The life-value concentrates itself decisively, however, in the concept of 'soul', which is seen as the self-creating origin and driving-force of all living things as distinct from the inani-

---

history—and yet belief in the resurrection does not arise on the death of any and every man' (*Zeitschrift für Syst. Theologie*, 1923-24, pp. 733, 734 f.).

[16] Cf. F. Brunstäd, *Die Idee der Religion*, 1922, pp. 140, 15 f., 20, 302.

mate. From the early animistic representations, originating particularly in the phenomena of sleep and dreams, mental abnormalities and death, right on to the philosophical theories of most diverse motives and types, the soul is seen as an incorporeal, independent entity which bears our life within it. The soul element is identical with the life element, and the idea of the soul is therefore of necessity combined with that of the immortality of the soul.

The idea of life comes to its fulfilment in the *notion of immortality*. The notion of the continuing life of the soul after death—no doubt originally postulated on the ground of the soul's re-awakening from sleep and the rising of dead vegetation to new life on the one hand, and of man's urge for self-preservation and his striving for happiness on the other hand—is given a fourfold basis and explanation in detail. First, the soul means an immaterial factor. Assuming the metaphysical anti-thesis of spirit or soul and matter or corporeality, the soul possesses a higher 'infinite value'. Whereas material things are subject to transience, the immortal soul is not affected by the decay of the body. Secondly, the soul is to be thought of as indestructible. Its immortality rests upon the unified form and indissolubility of its substance. It is indestructible like an atom. Thirdly, the idea of immortality derives from the element of continuity in the soul, which extends beyond our bodily existence and has its own existence even apart from the latter. From this there comes the idea of a Beyond as an extension of the soul-life of this world —i.e. the Beyond is the equivalent of a bodiless, spiritual form of this world. Death therefore causes no break in the continuity of the soul, but rather brings its liberation from the material world, since the soul as such already spans the grave. Finally, the idea of the soul and immor-tality is evaluated essentially in anthropocentric terms. The notion of immortality is the highest expression of the imperishable worth of human personality. Personality itself by its own nature already com-mands immortality, without raising the question of God at all. The idea of the soul is ultimately indifferent towards faith in God, because it becomes itself a substitute for faith.

The detailed development of this idea takes as many different forms as there are different philosophies among men. We may classify them into four basic types, though in fact these types are intermingled in manifold ways. The idea of immortality expresses itself, firstly, in the picture of a continuing life of the soul, free from the body and all material things—whereby the purely spiritual state is generally reckoned to be higher. The second type is closely bound up with this: the idea of the continued life of the soul after death, only with the help of a sensual substratum. The in itself bodiless soul strives after death to attain to a real existence, a new incarnation. Here lies the starting point for the notion of the transmigration of souls. The idea of life comes to expression, thirdly, also in the picture of a material resurrection from the grave in the sense of a reconstituting of corporeality at the end of time —ideas which are to be found in the popular traditions of Egyptian cults and among the ancient Prussians, as well as in Zoroastrianism and in Judaism.[17] Finally, the idea of development is transferred also to the notion of the soul, so that immortality of the soul means a higher development towards perfection in other spheres even to the point of merging into the Godhead.

It appears a simple matter to pass from this world of ideas to an understanding of the resurrection of Jesus. The resurrection of Jesus supports a declaration about the life after death, stands as it were on the frontier between life and death. Accordingly, the ideas contained in the concepts of life, soul and immortality are applied to the 'phenomenon' of the resurrection of Jesus and the concept of resurrection is deduced from the general idea of life. On this basis an attempt is made to understand the resurrection in a twofold way: the resurrection of Jesus is *a symbol of life*, and it is *a revelation of the immortality of the soul*.

The idea of life occurs to the human spirit of itself. It is found as a general human idea quite apart from the witness of the resurrection. The word of the resurrection of Jesus therefore cannot impart something fundamentally new, but is rather a special expression and confirmation of something already known. The real significance of the resurrection is that it gives individual and concrete expression to the abstract idea of life. The resurrection of Jesus becomes a symbol of life, an open expression in concrete and personal terms of the character and ideal resources already latent in, and in actual fact given with, the life of nature and of man. The eternal, timeless, non-historic truth of the imperishable quality of life appears in the resurrection of Jesus clothed in the form of history and time—with the result that the idea of the resurrection 'is neither proved nor disproved by historical knowledge' but on the contrary 'its foreignness and offensiveness' can 'be tranquilly noted'. Such is R. Otto's verdict on the symbolic character of the resurrection witness: 'sacred legends, in which the irrational relation of the eternal to the temporal is reflected in ways appropriate to the views

---

[17] Cf. R. Bultmann's article in *RGG*² IV, cols. 390 ff.: 'Mythus und Mythologie im Neuen Testament'.

of those days. They retain for us the value of incomparable, powerful symbols and ideograms of the mystery itself.'[18] Thus the message of the resurrection of Jesus is not grasped in its concrete peculiarity, but expanded into the general idea of the triumph of life over death, into the 'idea of the moral consummation of the world'. Hence the fact of the resurrection is turned into a resurrection idea, which does not need to be bound to the resurrection fact.[19]

The interpretation of the resurrection of Jesus in terms of the notion of immortality is also governed by the general idea of life. In this case, either the philosophical concepts of 'soul' and 'immortality' are foisted on the primitive Christian witness to the resurrection, or at least it is held that in this world of ideas we have the necessary first step towards an understanding of the resurrection, however much these ideas may individually be broadened in a certain sense by the resurrection of Jesus. Holsten, for example, is of the opinion that in the resurrection of Jesus the 'philosophic concept of the immortality of the soul comes to its own'.[20] Jesus possesses an 'immortal core', the immortal substance of the soul which cannot be destroyed by death. From the point of view of the idea of immortality the message of the resurrection of Jesus, if it is understood only in terms of the history of ideas, loses all its offensiveness and incomprehensibility. Rather, the resurrection of Jesus, i.e. the continuing life of the immortal soul of Jesus after death, appears as an obvious consequence of these premises. 'Those who believe in immortality will have no objection to accepting that Jesus came alive again after his death', asserts R. Seeberg, who for the rest has vital things to say about the resurrection of Jesus, but nevertheless thinks he cannot

[18] *Aufsätze, das Numinose betreffend,*[2] 1925, p. 170.
[19] Cf. A. Schweitzer, *Geschichte der Leben-Jesu-Forschung,* 1913, pp. 632 ff. R. Paulus, *Das Christusproblem der Gegenwart,* 1922, does not get beyond this circle of ideas either. If for him dogmatics is 'an application and working out of the premises of the philosophy of religion to something historically given and personally experienced' (p. 123), then the lack of understanding in face of the fact of the resurrection is easy to comprehend. 'Jesus arose in the realm of the divine spirit' (p. 170), 'by the expression "Christ", we mean God in this his nearness'; 'suffering, death and resurrection' are primarily 'abiding forms of the Christ life', the realization of a 'supra-historically grounded law of life' (p. 177). The content of the Bible is here manifestly evaporated in philosophical specu-lation. The 'Christ symbol' designates the new relation between God and men. If the resurrection of Jesus is cut out of the Christian message, then its absolute-ness also goes by the board, then we have 'the decisive thing for us: the historic embodiment of the Christian life . . . in Jesus and in the primitive Christian workings of the Spirit, but also further in Christendom and beyond' (p. 178). The parallel with the history of religion is thereby fundamentally complete, 'even if the figure of Jesus' remains 'the mightiest and purest bearer of the Christ life' (pp. 178, 172).
[20] *Zum Evangelium des Paulus und Petrus,* 1868, pp. 65 f.

avoid thus linking up with the idea of life.[21] The resurrection of Jesus thus represents a direct continuation of the already existing postulate of immortality. The starting point in the Platonic doctrine of the soul makes it possible to reflect on the question of a manifestation of Jesus after his death, as also on the question of a new incarnation of his soul. Undoubtedly, the uncritical equating of the resurrection with the idea of a mere continuing life of the soul in some form of existence after death is an essential over-simplification of our problem.

Whether such a synthesis with Platonic thought in conjunction with symbolism is valid, must be critically examined. This very approach reveals a significant part of the problematical character of the resurrection.

(b) The Resurrection as Antithesis to the Idea of Life and Immortality

The attempt to explain the nature of the resurrection of Jesus on the basis of the idea of life and immortality has unmistakable elements of truth about it. To inquire into the reality of true life that is not subject to transience, is in itself already to ask a proper question. The resurrection message takes up this question again, in order to give an answer to it. The resurrection of Jesus does in fact, as a fulfilment of the universal longings for life and inklings of immortal life, have a bearing on the idea of life. Further, in the notion of immortality there lurks the knowledge of the fragmentary character of the existence of earthly objects. It points as such beyond this existence and asks about the possibility of another reality. In so far as the resurrection witness knows about this other reality, it can understand the postulate of immortality. The idea of personality, too—generally reduced to the concept of soul and thereby foreshortened—is an experience of man's being unconditionally addressed by a Thou, and an expression of the state of responsibility that stretches beyond the context of the merely relative and conditional; and as such it provides a significant setting for the word of the resurrection. For the resurrection witness, too, is a declaration about individual, personal life. The idea of life and immortality is the philosophic expression of man's being made for unbroken living. But what kind of reality is it that presents or guarantees this perfect life? That is the decisive problem.

Despite such positive relations and notable points of contact, the

[21] *Christl. Dogmatik* II, p. 210, cf. also I, pp. 49 f., 141, 503; II, pp. 580 f. It is significant that in E. Troeltsch's *Glaubenslehre*, 1925, there is no room for the resurrection of Jesus, but that all the more importance is attached to the 'infinite worth of the soul'—that is to say, philosophy's concept of the soul supplants the New Testament's message of the resurrection. Cf. pp. 285 f., 288, 347, 296, 362.

resurrection of Jesus, unless we would hopelessly bar the way to the deepest understanding of its reality, must be regarded as the antithesis to the idea of life and immortality. In contrast to these ideal constructions, its fundamentally paradoxical character and its heterogeneity must be brought out in detail.

The *resurrection witness* appears to be a contradiction to the tenets of man: it is a *paradox*. And indeed this contradiction is a fundamental one, directed not simply against individual statements, but against the basic structure of the philosophic attitude to life. Ideas are factors that are given with humanity, presented in the course of intellectual development, waiting to be used in the process of philosophic thought. The resurrection of Jesus, however, is not an idea, and is not to be confused with ideas of reanimation or reincarnation such as are found here and there in metaphysics. It cannot, therefore, be classified within the scheme of general ideas, nor can we drive the witness to it from a superior, antecedently given idea and constructively develop the nature and meaning of it from that. The word of the resurrection of Jesus is not a product of the history of ideas, but rather the interruption of the regularity and continuity of the ideas of life and immortality. The resurrection of Jesus is absolutely foreign to all existing theories of life and is, therefore, unable to serve as a symbol of the abstract idea of life. Symbolism demands some adequacy between the symbol and the things to be expressed by it; between the resurrection of Jesus, however, and the ideologies produced by philosophic reflection on life there is an essentially inadequate relationship. Not timeless symbolism but concreteness, not a floating dialectical relation between the temporal and the eternal but once-for-all completeness, is the characteristic mark of the resurrection. The resurrection confronts the existing range of ideas as something unique and original—but precisely in its difference and its refusal to bow to the prevailing ideas, a *skandalon* for the ideas of life and immortality. The rejection of the resurrection witness in the surrounding Jewish and Hellenistic world can only be understood on the basis of the anti-ideal character of the message.[22]

The second element in the resurrection paradox finds expression in the calling in question of all ideas of life by the resurrection of Jesus. The validity of the postulates of everlasting life and of the ideas of immortality becomes questionable in principle when seen in the light of the reality of the resurrection of Jesus. On what ground do we have the right to speak at all of the extension of life and the continuing of the

[22] Cf. Acts 17.32.

soul as an immortal quality? The fact of the law of death allows us at all events to contest these theories, but the resurrection witness itself produces a crisis for every philosophical optimism which imagines it can command life and immortality. The resurrection of Jesus testifies in the first instance to the unbroken reality of the lordship of death over all earthly life, including that of the soul. From this standpoint the idea of the immortality of the soul appears to be an attempt to escape the fatal destiny of the world, a piece of philosophical self-deception regarding the situation of mortal man. It is only in unreserved acceptance of the necessity of dying that the message of the re-awakening from the dead becomes the message of a life that is not given as such, but established for the first time in the resurrection of Jesus. The idea of life and immortality then means a life which does not lie at all within the power of man, but which is first grounded in the resurrection of Jesus.

The third paradoxical feature of the resurrection witness in relation to the realm of ideas can be seen from the difference in the presuppositions that determine what is said in either case. The forming of the idea of life, as of that of immortality, is dependent upon immanent facts and the speculation based upon them; the resurrection message on the other hand claims to have its ground in an unconditional revelation of God. The resurrection witness reckons with the reality of God which in the resurrection of Jesus showed itself in a way that is paradoxical for all immanent thinking. That is why the 'substance' of the resurrection of Jesus is in itself totally incomprehensible to man. Every attempt to understand it philosophically, i.e. to employ the idea of life as our epistemological principle, must lead to an essential transformation, and indeed destruction, of the resurrection message. A philosophical removal of the 'scandal' of the resurrection of Jesus, however, discards also its content. The resurrection, therefore, is not a matter of philosophical knowledge, but stands in a relationship of fundamental antithesis to it.

The *heterogeneous character* of the resurrection in relation to the concepts of soul and of immortality becomes particularly clear in detail in the following points: The word of the resurrection does not speak of the continued existence of an immaterial, immortal soul-substance, but its presupposition is precisely the destruction of the whole psychophysical existence of man in death. Jesus dies in the totality of his manhood, without possessing in his soul the guarantee of resurrection. The very resurrection itself demonstrates that there is no bridge, anchored somehow in the soul, to be built from this transitory life to the reality of everlasting life. Resurrection is therefore the overcoming of death through a new awakening of life out of death by God; it is a new creation of new bodily life. Thus the resurrection stands in contrast to any spiritualizing which abstracts from corporeality and concentrates only on the soul. This rejection of the Greek concept of the soul and emphasizing of the totality of death does not, however, by any means imply the denial of a continued existence of man in an 'intermediate state'. The concern of the primitive Christian preaching was not with the continued existence of Jesus after death in a bodiless abstraction of soul, but with witnessing to the resurrection as a new reality embracing also bodily existence. Just as little, of course, does this general description imply the restoration of the mere material features of bodily earthly existence, as it has often been misinterpreted by a supranatural historism, but it resists the drawing of any kind of parallels with the Platonic world of ideas. An identification of the idea of immortality with the resurrection message, or indeed even any direct relating of the content of the two, fails to understand the heterogeneous character of the resurrection message and of the specifically anti-anthropological, or rather theocentric, view of the world that is rooted in it.

The discussion of the problem of the philosophy of religion leads to the realization that although in the *idea of life and of immortality* there are insights of value, yet these concepts *do not do justice to the uniqueness of the resurrection of Jesus, and indeed even obscure it and level it down.* In contrast to these ways of thinking we have to deal with the concrete, personal and corporeal reality of the resurrection of Jesus.

3. RESURRECTION AND EXISTENTIALISM

(a) *The Existentialist Interpretation of the Resurrection of Jesus*

The concern for a new understanding of the resurrection of Jesus finds its peculiar expression in the relating of the resurrection to the fundamental principles of existentialism in R. Bultmann. His attempt at an 'existentialist' interpretation of the revelation of Christ is necessarily of decisive significance for the question of the resurrection of Jesus.

The starting point for the theological explanation of the resurrection event lies for Bultmann in existentialist philosophy. The premises for his thinking are the basic ideas of Martin Heidegger and Karl Jaspers. He is concerned with the 'being' and the 'self-understanding' of man. Accordingly, the general theme of Bultmann's theologico-philosophical inquiry is the question, How does man attain to his true self-understanding, to his 'authenticity'? In reply to Schniewind, Bultmann therefore formulates his position thus: 'I present theology as anthropology', because all 'genuine theological statements are statements about existence'.[23]

From these philosophical and anthropological presuppositions there results the method of the 'existentialist interpretation', the effort to make the message of revelation understandable in its existential reference. Bultmann believes that in this way he can determine 'the real intention' of the New Testament, the real meaning of the resurrection of Jesus, quite apart from the question of historical factuality—i.e. that he can answer the question, 'What is the self-understanding implied by the Christian Easter message?[24]

For the existentialist understanding of the New Testament revelation it is first of all essential, according to Bultmann, to distinguish between 'historical fact' and 'historic encounter', between the historical Jesus of Nazareth who once lived in the years AD 1-30 and the 'Christ of the kerygma'. Bultmann radically turns his back on all historical circumstances and determines to apply himself solely to the one all-important encounter with the Christ proclaimed in the 'kerygma', to the message of the Risen One. 'Just as my book on Jesus is not kerygma, so in the kerygma we do not encounter the historical Christ. Rather, in it we encounter Jesus as the Christ, as an eschatological phenomenon. . . .' 'The significance of his history lies in what God wishes to say to me through it.'[25] Specially pregnant is the verdict: 'Jesus' teaching and Jesus' ideas are understood as what they are in the concrete situation of a man living in time: as the exposition of his own existence in its movement, in its insecurity, in its decisions.'[26] The risen Christ thus encounters us as a 'question how we ourselves seek to grasp our existence'.

From this philosophical starting point comes Bultmann's 'concept of revelation', which he wrongly identifies with the New Testament's understanding of revelation. 'Revelation is an event which places me in a new state of my selfhood', so that man attains 'to salvation, to his authenticity', which he cannot attain on his own.[27] Revelation is thus concerned 'not with simple imparting of information', but it can be 'understood only as address'. In revelation, 'man is seen in his limited-

---

[23] *Kerygma und Mythos*, p. 126 (ET, p. 107, a paraphrase).
[24] *Op. cit.*, p. 22 (ET, p. 10).
[25] *Op. cit.*, p. 41 (ET, p. 35).
[26] *Jesus*, pp. 14 f. (ET, p. 11).
[27] *Der Begriff der Offenbarung im Neuen Testament*, pp. 6 f.

42 THE REALITY OF THE RESURRECTION

ness', for man is limited by death. 'But revelation gives life.'[28] The message of revelation is therefore essentially a message of life and resurrection. For revelation consists 'in nothing else than in the fact of Jesus Christ', which can only be grasped through faith in Jesus Christ, 'who died and rose again for us'.[29] But the essential point is, that this event of salvation is given 'manifestly only as proclamation, in the word'. The word of revelation concerning the risen Christ is therefore 'an event which affects us immediately and happens to us ourselves'. It has nothing to do with the past, but takes place 'in the present, in my present'. The revelation is not a thing that once happened 'somewhere and sometime', but the decisive point is, how I have to interpret the revelation event for myself today.[30] 'What, then, has been revealed? Nothing at all, if the question is one . . . about doctrines . . . which no one could ever have discovered, secrets which, once imparted, are known once and for all. But everything, if we mean the opening of man's eyes to himself and his being able to understand himself.'[31]

On this basis in existentialist philosophy rests the corresponding interpretation of the resurrection event. It is not as a fact of the past that the resurrection of Jesus becomes the saving event, but only in its existential reference. 'The cross and resurrection of Jesus' are therefore not to be understood as past acts of salvation; but they become present phenomena, 'inherent parts of my self-understanding',[32] to which I stand in a contemporary relationship. To the question, 'How do we come to believe in the resurrection as an event of salvation?', Bultmann has only one answer: 'because it is proclaimed to us as such'. 'The crucified and risen Christ encounters us in the word of proclamation, nowhere else. It is precisely faith in this word that is the true Easter faith.'[33]

Under the spell of this finding of existentialist philosophy, Bultmann comes to the following negative conclusions about the resurrection of Jesus as a reality revealed in the past: 'The Christian Easter faith is not interested in the historical question. . . . The Easter faith of the first disciples is not a fact on which we can base our faith.'[34] The resurrection of Jesus is 'myth' when considered as 'a nature miracle like the resuscitating of one who is dead'. 'If anyone knows that he will rise after three

---

[28] *Op. cit.*, pp. 12, 20.   [29] *Op. cit.*, pp. 24 f.
[30] *Op. cit.*, pp. 26, 29.   [31] *Op. cit.*, p. 38.
[32] Cf. H. Thielicke, 'Die Frage der Entmythologisierung des Neuen Testamentes', in *Theologie der Anfechtung*, Tübingen 1949, p. 151.
[33] Bultmann, *op. cit.*, p. 50.
[34] *Op. cit.*, p. 51.

days, then clearly death will not mean very much to him.'[35] The message of the resurrection does not mean 'a certifying miracle in view of which ... we can believe assuredly in Christ', neither does it mean 'the return of one who is dead back to the life of this world', for such a message would be 'incredible'.[36] Hence Bultmann delivers the summary verdict: 'That puts an end to the stories of the ascension and of the descent into hell.'[37] A final consequence of this is the statement that the 'intercession of the exalted Lord in the New Testament, and his position of lordship, as well as prayer to him as an expression of a personal relation to the risen Lord, must be described as "mythological" '.[38]

All the same, Bultmann believes that he can maintain the proper and positive sense of the resurrection message and of the Christian Easter faith by means of the existentialist interpretation. 'The cross and the resurrection of Jesus' represent no 'mythical event', no exceptional, miraculous happening in the past, but a 'historic event' affecting me also here and now, which summons me 'to die with Christ and with him to rise from the dead'.[39] If we are to 'believe in the cross of Christ', to 'take up the cross as our own', without thereby having to believe in an event in the past, then believing in the 'resurrection of Jesus' means knowing the point of voluntary acceptance of suffering, for the 'resurrection of Christ' is 'an expression of the significance of the cross'. The resurrection faith means an 'eschatological event', which takes place again and again in the present; the content of that faith is 'rising together with him as an event in the present'. The Easter faith, the 'taking part in the resurrection of Jesus', 'shows itself in the concrete act of living'.[40] Through this 'rising with Christ' there comes about the transformation of man's self-understanding. By means of the kerygma of the cross and resurrection, the authentic life of man is first made possible, and he attains to surrender, to faith, to love, and thus to a 'Christian understanding of being'. This is realized in the 'confidence that precisely the invisible ... encounters man as love, brings him his future, and means for him not death, but life'.[41]

The existentialist interpretation of the resurrection, according to Bultmann, is able to give the decisive answer to the anthropological problem posed by contemporary existentialist philosophy.[42]

[35] *Op. cit.*, p. 21.　　[36] *Op. cit.*, pp. 48 f., 50, 51.
[37] *Op. cit.*, p. 18.　　[38] *Kerygma und Mythos*, p. 127 (ET, p. 109).
[39] *Op. cit.*, pp. 43 ff. (ET, pp. 37 ff). 　[40] *Op. cit.*, pp. 45 ff. (ET, pp. 40 ff).
[41] *Op. cit.*, pp. 29, 40 (ET, pp. 19, 33).
[42] Cf. to sum up the publications of R. Bultmann which are vitally relevant in this context: 'Neues Testament und Mythologie' in *Offenbarung und Heilsgeschehen*, 1941 and in H. W. Bartsch (ed.), *Kerygma und Mythos* I, 1948, 2nd

(b) The History-bound Perfect Tense of the Resurrection

In face of these theses of Bultmann's, which appear to surmount all the difficulties of historical criticism and thus to offer a most enticing solution to the complex problems of the resurrection of Jesus, we have to ask whether this answer is valid in the sense of the New Testament accounts, and whether it proves to be theologically tenable in principle and also to hold water from the existentialist standpoint.

Undoubtedly there can be no denying to Bultmann's view a certain partial recognition of the truth. He rightly stresses the existential reality of the resurrection message, which rules out the impartial attitude of a mere observer and puts the hearer in the position of immediate decision. He also rightly brings out, in agreement with the primitive Christian witnesses,[43] the common destiny of the believing community in fellowship with the living Christ. If Bultmann's concern were simply to move the emphasis from the objective side of the resurrection to the necessity of a subjective decision in faith, then a discussion with him would be both possible and meaningful. Here, however, an ominous question arises. Does the existentialist interpretation not constitute altogether a serious threat to the objective reality of the resurrection of Jesus, or indeed even destroy it? Is it properly speaking still concerned at all with the unique event of the resurrection of Jesus in the past, or is the whole Easter witness not transformed into the momentary subjective consciousness of the interpreter's faith?

The following critical questions and objections have to be raised in face of Bultmann's interpretation of the resurrection in terms of existentialist philosophy:

First, we must examine how far Bultmann's interpretation calls in question the actual fact of the resurrection itself. Admittedly, the discussion with Bultmann is made a lot more difficult by the imprecise means of expression he uses. The events of revelation, history and faith are enshrined so to speak in a twilight so dim that all the contours

---

ed. 1951 (ET, pp. 1 ff.); *Die Theologie des Neuen Testaments*, 1948 (ET, 1952, 1955); *Das Evangelium des Johannes*, 1941; *Glauben und Verstehen* I, Tübingen 1933, esp. 'Zur Frage der Christologie' (p. 85) and 'Die Christologie des Neuen Testaments' (p. 245); *Der Begriff der Offenbarung im Neuen Testament*, 1929; *Jesus*, Berlin 1926 (ET, *Jesus and the Word*, 1935); *Das Urchristentum im Rahmen der antiken Religionen*, 1949 (ET, *Primitive Christianity in its Contemporary Setting*, 1956). Further, W. H. Kümmel, *Mythologische Rede und Heilsgeschehen im Neuen Testament*, Coniectanea Neutest. XI, Lund 1947; W. Klaas, *Der moderne Mensch in der Theologie R. Bultmanns*, 1947; K. Barth, *Kirchliche Dogmatik* III/2, 1948, pp. 531 ff (ET, pp. 442 ff.); E. Brunner, *Dogmatik* II, 1950, pp. 221 f., 311 f. (ET, 1952, pp. 186 f., 263 f.).
[43] Cf. Gal. 2.20, 21; Rom. 7.6; Col. 2.13; Eph. 2.5; Phil. 3.20.

disappear. On the one hand, in the presentation of the event of revelation its historical author Jesus of Nazareth is not dispensed with entirely, so that we have obviously after all to do with more than a mere 'event of consciousness'[44] in man. On the other hand the outstanding thing is only the present act of self-understanding and there is a complete lack of interest in any kind of historic factuality, which can also be done without, of which we know nothing, and do not need to know anything either. Here we must certainly ask: Is this Easter faith of which Bultmann talks still necessarily bound to the quite definite revelational fact of the resurrection of Jesus—and that, too, as the sole ground of faith and as the content of faith? Does he hold to the event of the resurrection, quite apart from its result in the succeeding resurrection faith? From Bultmann's standpoint, the answer to that question can only be, 'No'. Accordingly, there is justification for asserting that in Bultmann's interpretation we have at bottom a repetition of the process that already took place in classical German idealism. As with Kant, Fichte, Hegel and others, we find full-sounding Christian statements, but the concepts mean something totally different from what they say: they have a different content. Thus despite all the will to truth that attends the existentialist philosopher's efforts, the result is a masked alteration of the very substance of the Christian resurrection message—masked by the use of biblical terms. Despite all the outward marks of a legitimate Christian theology, we have here in actual fact a philosophical reinterpretation of the Christian faith, a metamorphosis of the theological content of the resurrection reality. Bultmann's kerygma is then at all events no longer identical with the kerygma of the evangelists and apostles.[45]

Secondly, Bultmann's concept of revelation is distorted by excessive one-sidedness. Revelation is not in fact simply 'address' *in actu*, not simply the proclaimed word of promised resurrection life, but also, and indeed fundamentally, information about a fact, the message of a completed act of salvation, of the past perfect of the resurrection of Jesus.

[44] Cf. the criticism by H. Thielicke in *Theologie der Anfechtung*, p. 113. Because Bultmann concentrates everything on the situation of the 'moment', he loses the firm ground of history under his feet, history not being exhausted in the *hic et nunc*. The impression given by Bultmann's interpretation of the New Testament is described by H. Thielicke as follows: 'The New Testament narratives become ghostly forms that haunt the twilight between "being" and "validity", between "reality" and "mere contents of the consciousness" ' (*Theologie der Anfechtung*, p. 152).

[45] This philosophical dilution of the Christian truth leads to the conclusion that theology has to dissolve itself into an atheistic philosophy, as has happened in Bultmann's disciple W. Kamlah—to be sure in contrast to the intentions of his master. Cf. Wilhelm Kamlah, *Christentum und Selbstbehauptung*, Frankfurt on Main 1940.

That, at any rate, is the view which alone accords with the New Testament concept of revelation. Wherever revelation is cut from its moorings in history, we find a tendency to reduce it to general 'truths of reason'. What Bultmann, precisely in view of the results of liberalism, seeks to avoid is directly provoked in the course of his own 'interpretation'; rejecting the category of the 'historically past, unique, completed' in favour of the 'presently actual, summoning to decision' leads necessarily into the sphere of that conception of religion and of revelation which belongs to idealism and mysticism. Bultmann is not able to rescue the decisive 'once for all' by means of his principles and methods,[46] but ends, against his will, in a philosophical metaphysic of timelessness. Thus the 'resurrection of Jesus' is reduced to a timeless symbol, to the ideogram of a general truth. The existentialist interpretation of the resurrection is thus ultimately unable to take us beyond the solution which the 'idea of life' believed it could offer us.

Thirdly, it becomes clear that in Bultmann the Christian view of faith is also not protected against a process of increasing inward dissolution which leads ultimately to total destruction. The concept of the 'contemporaneity' of the believer with the Christ who is present in the proclamation must not deceive us as to the true state of affairs. Genuine 'contemporaneity' as understood by Kierkegaard is only possible in paradoxically holding fast to the past perfect of revelation *extra hominem*. Precisely this, however, is called in question by Bultmann. But how is the believer to become 'contemporary', if the risen Lord as the historically crucified Jesus of Nazareth has not appeared on the scene at all as a reality in the past upon which salvation is based? The active event of 'dying with Christ' and 'rising with Christ' falls to pieces as a reality and is reduced to the mere idea of a life-process unless the fact of the resurrection of Jesus is firmly established as something that 'has been' and is thereby given 'once for all'. If the saving Easter faith of the disciples is grounded only on their own interpretation and their subjective understanding of existence, then that very faith as such becomes meaningless and loses all declaratory power. It is not for nothing that Paul, in contrast to Bultmann's theses, defined Christian faith as faith in the past perfect saving act of the resurrection of Jesus. 'But if Christ is not risen, then our preaching is vain, and your faith is also vain.' 'If thou believe . . . that God hath raised him from the dead, thou shalt be saved.'[47] Thus precisely the existentialist interpretation tragically fails

---

[46] Cf. Schniewind in *Kerygma und Mythos*, p. 105 (ET, pp. 80 f.).
[47] I Cor. 15.14 ff.; Rom. 10.9.

to bring out the existential significance of the resurrection of Jesus.

In irreconcilable antithesis to Bultmann's attempt at interpretation stands the whole witness of the primitive Christians to the resurrection of Jesus. It is not that the experience created in the consciousness by the kerygma is the origin of faith, which can then argue back to some unknown and indistinct historical 'X' standing behind the message; but on the contrary the past perfect resurrection of Jesus is the unique reality which produces faith. The increasing separation of revelation from its moorings in history—here it must not be overlooked that while revelation is more than history, yet it does not become existent without history—leads to the triumph of a new form of *gnosis* divorced from history. Thus Bultmann's theology bears the stamp of a 'gnostic myth',[48] which is contradicted by the reality of the history-bound perfect tense of the resurrection of Jesus.

4. RESURRECTION AND MYTH

(a) The Mythifying of the Resurrection of Jesus

The fourth problem complex is defined by bringing together *resurrection and myth*. Taking the message of the resurrection as witness of a myth, or as a product of various mythical ideas, seems to the modern mind to offer the best possible solution, which both avoids the difficulties of the historical approach and also allows for the difference between the content of the statements and the general concepts of the life-idea which are found in the philosophy of religion. But what are we to understand by the much-used word 'myth'? The concept is today very much in the centre of academic thought. From the various analyses comes a multitude of definitions. We must first of all, then, determine what we mean by the concept of myth, before it can be applied to the resurrection.

(i) The Basic Features of the Mythical Way of Thinking

The meaning of the concept 'myth' is distinguished on the one hand from historic reality and on the other from the mere play of fantasy or poetic invention. Myth suggests non-historicality, but certainly not for that reason something unreal. The mythical points beyond the sphere of history to the realm of pre-history and of what stands behind all history. According to J. J. Bachofen, 'the beginning of all development lies in myth. It is myth that enshrines the origins . . . the origins condition all future advance.'[49] Thus myth is a pointer to what lies beyond

---

[48] Cf. E. Stauffer, *Entmythologisierung oder Realtheologie*, 1949, p. 11.
[49] Cf. C. A. Bernoulli, *Joh. Jak. Bachofen und das Natursymbol*, 1924; Manfred Schröter, *Der Mythus von Orient und Okzident*, 1926, quoting Bachofen.

space and time, to something pre-historic, supra-historic, supra-natural, to the complex of what can be described as 'proto-history', as a happening which is the 'original' basis of historic earthly life. Myth does, as Cassirer says, mean the 'world in itself',[50] yet not by any means a reality of inferior objectivity or of primitive thinking. 'Reality is the mark of myth as opposed to fiction.'[51]

If myth's claim to reality is not to be denied, as the rationalistic age of the Enlightenment believed, but means that it takes its bearings from a more immanent reality which bears the stamp of the irrational when seen from the standpoint of everyday history, then the connection of the mythical with the religious becomes clear. At all events a 'part of the realm of religion is in truth . . . wholly identical in nature with myth',[52] and religious cults have always some kind of bearing on the content of myths, which for their part have in turn a qualifying effect on the piety. Myth and religion meet in the concept of 'symbol', in the expression of the unconditionally Beyond. Thus for religion the mythical idea is a symbolic image of the transcendent. The symbols are borrowed according to definite laws from the perceptual world of space and time, and the mythical material is submitted to transformation according to the particular state of consciousness, yet the symbolic pointer in the language of myth to a transcendent Being remains in all religions. Myth is therefore according to P. Tillich 'a religious category'. His 'symbolico-realistic' understanding of the mythical leads to a mature and notable definition: 'Myth is constructed out of elements of reality to form a symbol of what the religious act means by the Unconditional and the Beyond-of-being.'[53]

The understanding of myth as a symbolic expression for that which, while not historical and natural, is yet real transcendent being, leaves open in the first instance the question of the origin of the mythical way of thinking. To put it in schematic form, myth springs from a threefold root:

First, the mythical motif can have its ground in the inherited memory

---

[50] E. Cassirer, *Die Begriffsform im mythischen Denken*, 1922; *Sprache und Mythos*, 1925 (ET, *Language and Myth*, 1946).

[51] Erich Unger, *Wirklichkeit, Mythos, Erkenntnis*, Munich and Berlin 1930, p. 42.   [52] E. Unger, *op. cit.*, p. 45.

[53] P. Tillich in *RGG²* on 'Mythos', col. 364; *Die religiöse Verwirklichung*, 1929, pp. 88, 142. Cf. also Arthur Titius, *Ist systematische Theologie als Wissenschaft möglich?*, Berlin 1931, pp. 16 f. According to Titius, 'Myth stands for a way of representation which transcends the means of philosophical analysis and synthesis and seeks to express the ineffable in plastic images.' Georg Koepken, *Die Gnosis des Christentums*, Leipzig 1940. Cf. also E. Spranger, 'Weltfrömmigkeit', in *Magie der Seele*, Berlin 1947.

of pre-history, living on in the subconscious in manifold dress and imaginative form. The unconscious insights that have not yet attained conceptual clarity, such as we find in part of the world of folk-tale, saga and myth, have their deepest ground in the memory of realities of pre-history, in primordial experiences which have become elements of the human spirit. From such primordial grounds in the realm of the human soul the rise of the myth of creation and fall, as it is found in some form or other in the most varied cultures, is conceivable. The cause of the formation of myth is accordingly a prehistoric reality whose influence continues to work in the sub-conscious mind of man.

As a second factor in the formation of myth, the impression caused by the experience of the 'numinous' has to be taken into account. Man finds himself exposed to the powerful impulses of certain natural phenomena and historic experiences, which essentially determine his existence and give rise to mythical themes. Thus aetiological myths are attempts to explain particular events in nature or in the life of man, whether in the form of nature myths and astral myths, or in the form of cosmogonies. Likewise, unusual impressions given by history light up its mythical background and lead to surmounting and comprehensively interpreting the life of history in mythical terms. The strongest numinous experience, however, always bears a peculiarly metaphysical stamp and creates the need to give expression to the fulness of religious ideas in the plastic form of myth. That, according to P. Tillich, is why myth has essentially to do with stories of the gods which are acted and experienced in space and time.[54] The experience of the divine in moments of deep emotion and longing leads through intensification of the earthly in idealistic and poetic contemplation to theogonies which deal with the genesis, struggles and character of the gods,[55] as also to the soteriological myths concerning saviour gods and the coming of redeemers and mediators.[56]

Finally, the third factor in the forming of myths is the creative power

---

[54] P. Tillich distinguishes a pre-mythical stage where the idea of gods is as yet unknown, and a post-mythical stage in which divine action and suffering in space and time is spoken of in ways that no longer accord with the consciousness of the unconditional transcendence of God. In the latter case we have to speak of a 'broken myth', such as is presented by Christian dogma on the basis of a post-mythical attitude of mind.

[55] Cf. the mythical motif of the supernatural birth of the god.

[56] Cf. Friedrich Creuzer, *Symbolik und Mythologie der alten Völker*, 1829; F. G. Lipps, *Mythenbildung und Erkenntnis*, 1907; Leesmann, *Aufgaben und Ziele der vergleichenden Mythenforschung*, 1908; P. Ehrenreich, *Die allgemeine Mythologie und ihre ethnologischen Grundlagen*, 1910; O. Rühle, *Sonne und Mond im primitiven Mythus*, 1925; E. Howald, *Der Kampf um Creuzers Symbolik*, 1926.

of the human spirit. Accordingly myths arise not only from the unfolding of a primitive consciousness going back to pre-history, not only as
reactions to experiences, but also as the act and product of the spirit.
Thus the attempt is made to explain myth either on the basis of psychic
tendencies and the laws that govern the life of the mind, as the objectifying of emotion or the symbolic expression of subconscious desires,
particularly of an erotic character. Or else on the other hand the
mythical creations of the spirit can be ascribed a significance of their
own, if mythical thinking is understood as an element in intellectual
life alongside aesthetics and 'science', as the 'working of an area of the
mind that is meaningful in itself'.[57] The supremely important thing is,
that here the human spirit is particularly clearly recognized as the power
that creates myth, without it being necessary for that reason to designate
the object of myth as unreal.

In most cases there is an intermingling and varied interconnection
of the several origins and themes that go to make up myth, so that none
of the various theories need be without some truth and yet the multifarious depths of the reality of myth can be grasped only by one of the
comprehensive views of systematic mythology.

(ii) *The 'Resurrection Myths'*

Once we accept this world of mythical ideas, it is a simple step to
classify the primitive Christian witness to the resurrection as part of it,
and to explain it in that light. The turning of the resurrection of Jesus
into a myth is carried out in detail on the basis of two sets of ideas—
first, in terms of the myths of deities returning to life again, and secondly
under the influence of the myth of the primordial man.

The oriental myths which are brought into association with the
resurrection of Jesus originally derive on the one hand from the harvest
and fertility cults based on the ever-recurring natural phenomena of
growth and decay, of winter and spring, while on the other hand it is a
case of astral myths based upon the interchange of sun and moon and
the experience of a macrocosmic and microcosmic coherence in nature.
Even if the myths are later separated from the immediate happening in
nature, yet their fundamental basis in nature remains, so that the centre
of the picture is occupied exclusively by the gods of vegetation and
fertility, alike in the Phoenician Adonis cult and astral divinities and in
the Babylonian Marduk cult. The idea of the dying and re-awakening
of vegetation, which originally found its solemn expression in the nature

[57] Cf. P. Tillich, *RGG*[2], cols. 360 ff.

cults, is brought into connection with the fates of gods. In the Babylonian material there is the notion of suffering and re-exalted kings, in parallel to the setting and rising again of the light deities and stars, yet without a relation to any idea of redemption. In the Phrygian Attis cult there was the great new year orgy of lamentation over the dead god, which changed into a festival of rejoicing on assuming his resurrection from the dead.[58] At an early stage, the Greek thought of immortality is connected with these rites. They develop finally into mystery cults with washings and initiation rites, with a novitiate, with blood baptisms, meals and dramatic ceremonies, as symbolic expressions for the death and resurrection of the deities and their devotees with the aim of rebirth and mystical union.

Beside these general mythical ideas much attention has recently been given above all to the Persian gnostic redemption myth of the primordial man. Precisely these mythical themes are supposed to have determined the Christian Easter story. Thus E. Lohmeyer assumes that behind the classical formulation of primitive Christology (Phil. 2.5-11) there stands the ideas of Persian cosmology, 'a cosmogonous myth of creation and temptation'. We find traces of the idea 'of a divine being coming down from heaven', although 'on Jewish soil this myth never existed as a coherent whole'. 'We naturally think of the myth of the primordial man as the divine redeemer.'[59] E. Seeberg, too, despite his clear statement of the difference between myth and Christianity, is convinced that the ancient myths 'came half way to meet it [Christianity]', that 'the ideal of the new humanity, humiliated, overcoming and overcome, here played the decisive role'. 'There is also no doubt that in Christ the original myth of man very soon crossed and combined with the related, but differently constructed myth of the saving lord who ushers in the new age.'[60] In agreement with this, M. Dibelius likewise sees in the myth-abounding world of that time the basis for the rise of the Christ myth. Although the source of the formation of this myth

[58] The same sort of thing happened also in Egyptian Isis worship. After the dismembered corpse of Osiris has been sought by Isis in great pain, there follows the jubilantly proclaimed raising of him from the dead by Thot and Horus. The assurance of immortality was connected with this cult too. The bull has special significance as a symbol of the life-conveying power of nature, and so also in the Marduk resurrection rite has the morning sun. Cf. M. Brückner, *Der sterbende und auferstehende Gottheiland*, 1908.

[59] E. Lohmeyer, *Kyrios Jesus*, Heidelberg 1928, pp. 23, 26, 68 ff.; cf. also R. Reitzenstein, *Die hellenistischen Mysterienreligionen*, Leipzig 1920, and especially *Das iranische Erlösungsmysterium*, 1921.

[60] *Ideen zur Theologie der Geschichte des Christentums*, Leipzig 1929, pp. 22 f.

cannot be clearly established, yet it is possible that 'foreign stories of
the gods' were 'transferred to native figures'.[61]

These investigations were carried to a sort of crowning extreme by
R. Bultmann. Taking up especially the ideas of Wrede, Johannes Weiss,
M. Dibelius and Reitzenstein and thinking them radically to the end,
Bultmann places the whole New Testament tradition under the judgment of 'mythology' and sees precisely this as proof of the need to
'demythologize' the New Testament. He is convinced that primitive
Christianity can be understood only from the history of the religions of
its environment, and that motifs of two kinds provide an explanation
of it. According to Bultmann, it is 'easy to trace the individual themes
of primitive Christianity back to the contemporary mythology of Jewish
apocalyptic and of the gnostic redemption-myth'. The New Testament
tradition is inserted into this mythological setting, and hence a great
many elements and ideas in the New Testament, such as belief in angels
and demons, eschatological ideas, the thought of pre-existence, the
doctrine of 'vicarious satisfaction through the death of Christ', and
above all the witness to the resurrection of Jesus, bear the stamp of
'myth'.[62]

Bultmann has thus set the problem of 'resurrection and myth' in the
centre of theological and philosophical discussion. It is precisely the
solution of this problem that decides the place of the message of Christ
in the history of religion and answers the question of absoluteness
thereby implied.

On the question of the dependence of the resurrection statements on
these various mythological themes, the following points of analogy must
be regarded as important. In the centre of the cult of the oriental and
hellenistic religions in question, there stands the death and resurrection
of a redeemer-god. Secondly, the Easter celebration of the resurrection
is paralleled in the mystery religions with a celebration likewise about
the beginning of spring. Further, the concept 'on the third day' or
'after three days', as well as the alternating use of these two statements,
plays an important role.[63] Fourthly, the event of the dying and returning
to life of the deity is bound up with thoughts of rebirth, of continuing

[61] *Evangelium und Welt*, 1929, pp. 81 f.

[62] *Kerygma und Mythos*, pp. 15 f., 20 f. (ET, pp. 2, 7 f.); R. Bultmann, 'Zur
Geschichte der Paulus-Forschung', *Theol. Rundschau* 1929, vol. I, pp. 45 f.;
Primitive Christianity in its Contemporary Setting.

[63] According to Pfleiderer and Brückner the resurrection of Osiris took place
on the third day after his death, that of Attis on the fourth. Another interpretation is, that the three-day period is connected with the three days in which
the moon is invisible at the time of the new moon in spring.

life after death, and of mystical union with the deity through the magical working of sacred rites.[64] Further, it seems worth noting that 'those pagan cults also flourished precisely in the places which came to be the first centres of the rise and spread of Christian congregations'.[65]

Turning the message of the resurrection into a myth calls in question its specifically Christian character as such. If the resurrection of Jesus is 'the primary datum of New Testament Christology as such',[66] then the recognition of its dependence on mythology means its utter dissolution.[67] The question of the tenability of a relation between myth and the resurrection of Jesus and of the right to attempt to make it into a myth, therefore certainly becomes a decisive one. For that reason we must entirely agree with Harnack in his judgment that if the present 'widespread and supposedly scientific opinion' that the Christian affirmation of the resurrection arose from myths is correct, 'then that is the end of historic Christianity'.[68]

(b) The Anti-mythical Character of the Resurrection of Jesus

(i) The Question of the Appropriateness of the Concept Myth

We have first to consider in principle whether the concept of 'myth' can express in an appropriate way what primitive Christianity is concerned with in the resurrection witness. Because it transcends the objective world, this witness, too, finds itself dependent on the use of picture and simile and moves, at least in part, in a symbolic language. The possibility of mythological ideas breaking into the world of Christian thought does exist at this point—that is rightly recognized by those whose approach is from the history of religion. The orientation of the resurrection message towards a 'transcendent Beyond' appears to require the form of myth to give it shape, but at the same time that seems to render more difficult the exclusion of mythical elements essentially foreign to it. A relation between the resurrection of Jesus and myth

[64] Cf. H. Gressmann, *RGG*[2] I, col. 623. The resurrection is then often interpreted as a marriage.
[65] M. Brückner, *op. cit.*, pp. 36 f.; H. Gunkel, *Zum rel.-gesch. Verständnis des N.T.*, 1903; Hermann Wirth, *Der Aufgang der Menschheit*, 1930.
[66] M. Brückner, *op. cit.*, p. 35.
[67] Cf. A. Drews, *Die Christusmythe* (ET, *The Christ Myth*, 1910). According to this Paul, who was a 'man of taurian and pharisaic education', heard 'of the god of a Jewish sect, Jesus by name' and 'connected this idea with the death and resurrection of Adonis and the notion of the suffering Servant of God in Isa. 53', with the result that 'there arose the idea of redemption by a God-man effected through death and resurrection'.
[68] *Die Entstehung der christlichen Theologie und des kirchlichen Dogmas*, Gotha 1927, p. 45.

would accordingly already be given in principle by the fact that the resurrection witness, as a religious statement, not only moves on the same plane as myth, but also necessarily shares in its laws and its forms of expression. In that case it would be a question of using the formal concept 'myth' in order to make the resurrection intelligible, however much its content may differ from the world of the mythical.

We find this view in K. Barth, who describes the resurrection of Jesus by the mythical concept of 'proto-history' as opposed to history, and declares unequivocally: 'Jesus as the Christ can be understood within the framework of the historical outlook *only* as . . . myth'.[69] According to this, the concept of myth would be the only appropriate way of expressing the 'more than historic character' of the resurrection of Jesus, while at the same time in its ambiguity also a sign of the veiled and offence-giving character of revelation, and the question of dependence on other myths would no longer have to be raised with the same sharpness, because the mythical determination has already been conceded from the start. How far the primitive Christian 'resurrection myth' nevertheless differs from non-Christian myths, i.e. how far it is 'true', remains solely for faith to decide. E. Brunner also speaks of a Christian 'mythology', since in fact all Christian statements of faith are 'mythological, that is, in a quite definite way inappropriate'. This mythological form is 'the only form' in which 'to express and maintain' the Christian faith. Brunner's postulate of a 'Christian myth' is the more striking since he clearly distinguishes it both from the abstract statements of the philosophy of religion and also from pagan mythology, and is concerned to assert precisely 'a difference expressible in strictly categorical terms'.[70]

This tendency to understand the resurrection of Jesus from the point of view of the mythical must nevertheless be judged to be inappropriate when seen in the light of ultimate principles. Even if the form of every theological statement about the resurrection of Jesus must be recognized to be intrinsically inappropriate and certain basic features of myth seem to come a long way towards what Christianity, too, is after; even if it is true that the world of primitive Christian thought is also not free of mythical elements and cannot dispense with a specific mythological symbolism, yet such considerations still do not imply any justification for taking over the concept of myth uncritically into our theology, and

---

[69] *Römerbrief*², p. 6 (ET, p. 30); *Dogmatik* I, pp. 43 f., 230 f. In his *Kirchliche Dogmatik* III/2, Barth has abandoned his previous supra-historic theories. His earlier position, however, retains the historical significance of a characteristic theological type.

[70] E. Brunner, *Der Mittler*, pp. 337 ff. (ET, pp. 377 ff.).

do not release us from the theological obligation to think through anew and fundamentally the question of the appropriateness of our choice of concepts. The problem of the appropriateness of theology's conceptual language to express the content of biblical revelation has been set in motion again by Bultmann's motto of 'demythologizing'. In opposition to this slogan Schniewind says, 'As men, we can never escape myth'[71]; and H. Thielicke declares, 'The mythical is the form of our thinking . . . the valid form for the perception and description of religious objects.'[72] Accordingly, a 'demythologizing' of our thinking is not possible at all and the demand for a 'demythologizing of the New Testament' is meaningless, if the mythical represents a human form of thinking.

On this matter the following fundamental observations have to be made. The need for interpreters, for a translation of the message of Christ, is self-evident. The reason lies in the otherness of the divine revelation event, which utterly shatters the bounds of our earthly think-ing and representation. The 'revelation of God' is given in the form of human speech, and that sets our proclamation the task of making clear what is 'really' meant by these earthly 'words, pictures, similes, repre-sentations, concepts', what the 'substance' of revelation in these 'earthen vessels' in actual fact is. The task is, to transpose the biblical message into our way of thinking and our framework of ideas without its content being lost. This work of translation, however, has nothing to do with demythologizing in Bultmann's sense, since the Christian revelation is of course anything but a myth. It is simply a question of the fundamental fact that God's revelation in itself is beyond contemplating and thinking out, and is accessible to us at all only in pictorial language. 'Now we see in a glass darkly.'[73] Without pictorial language and conceptual material which must be taken from the realm of the experience of our earthly world if it is to be intelligible, there is no message at all, but only an abandoning of communication, only a mystical silence.

The question can only be: Which pictures, which concepts, are ade-quate to express the revelation of God? Adequacy in the proper sense is fundamentally impossible in this present age, but the decision on the choice of appropriate concepts and means of expression has already been made by the apostles and evangelists. Their choice has made specific words and concepts into 'primary words' and 'basic concepts', which are irreplaceable, inexchangeable. Every modern translation of

[71] *Kerygma und Mythos*, p. 79 (ET, p. 48).
[72] *Ibid.*, p. 175 (ET, p. 158).
[73] I Cor. 13.12.

biblical expressions must ultimately lead to translating them back into the biblical 'primary concept'.

From the standpoint of epistemological theory there is no possibility at all of escaping picture language. Even Bultmann cannot do so. He, too, speaks of 'God', 'God's action', of 'Christ', 'grace', 'faith', 'sin', 'love', and so on. Either these are empty terms behind which there stands no reality, and thus mere symbols for products of the consciousness, or they are 'remainders' which cannot be further demythologized because they are indissolubly bound up with a reality and consequently have primal significance.

In practice this means that Bultmann's efforts are an attempt to do the impossible: to strip off the pictorial and representational material which is given with human nature as such. Hence from the standpoint of epistemological theory, too, 'demythologizing' is condemned to failure. The greater the measure of 'demythologizing', the greater becomes the distance from true reality. In the abstract, airless atmosphere attainable by this means, we can no longer breathe, and Christian theology can no longer live. The concepts and pictorial representations of the New Testament are inseparably bound up with the 'matter' they express. If the concept of the mythical is in itself already burdened by not inconsiderable unclarities and varying possibilities of interpretation' and therefore hardly to be utilized for the theological task, then for two reasons its application to the resurrection of Jesus is to be rejected in principle.

On the basis of Tillich's definition, which speaks of an 'unconditional, and a 'beyond-of-being' to which myth gives symbolic expression, the word of the resurrection of Jesus would in the first instance be a symbol for something transcendent and unconditional. For this reality, however, a whole multitude of mythological symbols can serve, since the unconditional is of course the universal, ever-existent, the ground underlying all visible phenomena. To myth belongs the timelessness of pre-history or proto-history; it is the symbolic expression, in the religious-historical field, of the *revelatio generalis*. In the mythical is expressed the general religious orientation towards a Beyond—whereby it is characteristic that this Beyond is abstractly and neutrally conceived, while the definition of its content is of secondary importance. In contrast to this, however, the message of the resurrection has to do precisely with a *revelatio specialis*: its content is not something of a general mythical kind, but the particular and concrete amid the varied mythical forms. The purport of the resurrection of Jesus is not a powerful symbolic expression of a general condition, of a timeless background of being, but the strict once-for-allness and uniqueness of a concrete event which interrupts as it were the course of time and therefore, as a completed act, cannot be fitted into the general scheme of mythological ideas. The resurrection of Jesus is what it is only in the peculiar concreteness of the risen Jesus, and thus in direct opposition to every mythological tendency. In agreement with H. Bornkamm, we must point out here that 'the event of salvation *extra nos*' is at stake at this point, that 'Jesus Christ' is indeed 'not simply a fact of salvation', but also must not cease 'to be a person'. The *quod* of revelation is given only along with the *quid* of revelation, with its concrete content. The 'force of the *est*' must not be abandoned in favour of a mere '*significat*'.[74] This concrete '*est*' of the Risen One, however, stands unequivocally opposed to every general concept of myth. Any mythical elements which there may be in the resurrection witness, and which it has in common with every human form of presentation, are precisely the non-essential part of it. *The application of the concept of myth to the resurrection of Jesus means a levelling down of the particular to the universal, the changing of the* 'revelatio specialis' *into a general revelation*, the confusing of the accidental with the essential. The idea of myth must be designated absolutely inadequate to the resurrection of Jesus, if the unique quality of the primitive Christian proclamation is not to be lost in the wastes of the general history of religion.

To this there also comes a second and no less fundamental point, which shows the inappropriateness of the concept of myth for the resurrection of Jesus. The very consideration of the sources which give rise to the formation of myth shows at once that, however many influences from 'without' there may have been, the decisive part in the birth of the myths was played by the creative mind of man. Myth is the expression of anthropocentric religion. To combine myth and the resurrection of Jesus therefore manifestly represents a fundamental misunderstanding of the totally other nature of the claim of the resurrection message. Its claim stands essentially in contradiction to the existing religion of man as such. The word of the resurrection of Jesus does not seek to be a symbolic expression of the religious movement of the soul, but rather the proclamation of a reality which is not at the disposal of man in himself, of which he cannot be even mythologically aware, and which must first be told him. The resurrection witness speaks precisely

[74] Cf. H. Bornkamm and W. Klaas, *Mythus und Evangelium: Zum Programm Bultmann*, Munich 1951.

of what 'no eye hath seen, nor ear heard, neither hath entered into the heart of man',[75] of the absolutely transcendent. What happens in the resurrection is the revealing of the *mysterium* of the hidden, unknown, silent God; what happens is the *actio Dei*, not the realizing of a potentiality of the human spirit, the attesting of the *Deus revelatus*. The resurrection of Jesus has therefore a theocentric character, i.e. it is not a reflection of the general idea of the divine in mythical symbols, but a special revealing of the word of God as distinct from all human potentialities. Thus the message of the resurrection demands the abandoning of the original starting point in anthropocentric religion, the abandoning of man's basic mythical outlook, and the radical reversing of the whole approach to take its bearings from the new 'theological' centre. Whereas in myth 'eternal' religious truths so to speak are presented, experienced and contemplated, the content of the resurrection statements cannot be grasped at all by any attitude of that kind. The message of the resurrection is addressed to man in terms demanding a decision, and is indeed a judgment on all anthropocentric mythological attempts to master the truths of another, unconditional world.[76] The secondary question of whether, and how far, elements from the world of mythological thought were recast in the primitive Christian proclamation, must not obscure the decisive insight that the resurrection of Jesus is anti-mythological in character. Certainly, to the non-Christian religious world the Christian message of the resurrection must appear to be mythology, because unbelief cannot of itself recognize or understand the 'revelation of God'. From this standpoint, religion and revelation, myth and revelation, are inevitably confused with each other. But it is not the task of Christian theology to encourage this error by holding on to an inadequate interpretation of concepts and applying concepts like 'myth' and 'legend' to the realities of salvation.

(ii) *Specific Criticisms of the Myth Analogies*

It is superficial and unfounded to say that the study of the history of religion has shown the dependence of the resurrection of Jesus on mythology. On the contrary, it is precisely the comparison with the history of religion that gives rise to the strongest objections to any kind of mythifying of the resurrection of Jesus. Not least the sharp-sighted critique of K. Holl and the extensive researches of A. Schweitzer have shown the sheer gulf between primitive Christianity and the mythology

---

[75] Cf. I Cor. 2.9.
[76] Cf. E. Brunner, *Der Mittler*, p. 344 (ET, pp. 383 f.), where he rightly refers in substance precisely to this discrepancy between myth and Christian doctrine.

and mystery cults of the hellenistic and oriental world.[77] The following critical arguments against the fact of myth being blended with the Christian witness to the resurrection may be listed:

First: The fact that the theme of the dying and returning deity is a general one in the history of religion, and that a transference of this theme is possible, must not be made the occasion for speaking at once of dependence, of influence, or indeed of identity of content. Rather, the scientific task is not to overlook the essential differences in form, content and ultimate tendency, and even in cases of apparent formal analogy to work out the decisive difference of content.

To this methodological point we add the fact emphasized especially by Harnack: 'There is ... no tradition that leads to the assumption that in the circles from which Peter and the first disciples came, or among the pious Jews of that time in Palestine, such a myth was known at all, far less had any place in their religion.' The foreignness of the resurrection of Jesus is indicated also by 'the complete surprise with which the Easter experience comes upon the Twelve'.[78] The special character of the spiritual atmosphere of Israel as distinct from the syncretistic world around calls for primary consideration. Its whole outlook stands in contrast to mythological assumptions.

A decisive argument which establishes that the resurrection of Jesus stands diametrically opposed to the customary formation of myths and processes analogous to it, is the relatedness of the resurrection of Jesus

[77] K. Holl, *Urchristentum und Religionsgeschichte*, 1918, pp. 10 ff., 34 (ET, *The Distinctive Elements in Christianity*, 1937, pp. 6 ff, 33); A. Schweitzer, *Geschichte der Leben-Jesu Forschung*, 1921, pp. 536 ff.; *Geschichte der paulinischen Forschung*, 1911, pp. 141 ff., 184 (ET, *Paul and his Interpreters*, 1912, pp. 179 ff., 235 f.) and in the same work a list of further literature on this problem; *Die Mystik des Apostels Paulus*, 1930, pp. 27 ff. (ET, *The Mysticism of Paul the Apostle*, 1931, pp. 26 ff.). A radical historical criticism of Bultmann's attempt to derive the primitive church's Christology from gnostic myth is found in E. Stauffer, *Entmythologisierung oder Realtheologie*, 1949, pp. 10 f. According to Stauffer's analysis of the sources, Bultmann's myth theory is impossible already on chronological grounds. Bultmann's chief source is the Mandaean literature. This, however, represents 'a medley of post-Christian syncretism with an admixture of Christian elements'. Accordingly, a mythological interpretation of the New Testament is without object, since the men of the New Testament did not know these sources at all.

[78] A. Harnack, *Die Entstehung der christlichen Theologie und des kirchlichen Dogmas*, Gotha 1927, p. 46. Cf. also Gunkel's verdict in *RGG*[2] IV, col. 381: 'Israel did not look upon myth with favour. Myth is polytheistic by nature. . . . To that we must add the infinite respect which was felt in Israel for Yahweh, and not least the close relation between religion and morals. . . . It is no small wonder among the civilized peoples of the Orient' that Israel, 'although its imagination, too, was richly developed . . . nevertheless adopted a stolid attitude towards the myths and finally rejected them as far as was possible. . . . Israel, as far as we can see, did not create myths at all, or only very few.'

to history. The ultimate aim of supranatural historism is here correct. The resurrection of Jesus has as its content an event which happened to a quite definite historical person, an event which in its once-for-allness and non-repeatability bears concrete marks of historic reality. A myth has to do with a series of relatively important events which could have happened one way or also another, but the resurrection of Jesus exists only in the peculiar concreteness of this relatedness to history or it does not exist at all. On this point every analogy which relates it to nature cults or vegetation rites breaks down, adapted as these are to the constantly recurring rythm of nature. That the resurrection of Jesus is clearly rooted in history, although it is not in itself a historical fact, shatters the basic pattern of all mythological symbolism,[79] which is always nature-bound and timeless in contrast to the history-bound character and temporal fixation of the resurrection of Jesus.

Connected with this is the further insight that the resurrection witness was not interested in proclaiming a general religious truth in the symbolic language of myth, but in 'actual experienced facts'. The very concern of the Christian witnesses to confirm as far as possible the factuality of the resurrection of Jesus 'disproves the assumption' that this confession 'is to be explained by their acceptance of the myth about the dead and resurrected god'.[80] Paul emphasizes in regard to the 'Easter history', according to G. Kittel, 'that the fact of it is assuredly certified and that one can go and ask the eye-witnesses'. He 'refers the Church neither to his own visions and inner experiences . . . nor to what is true because we tell ourselves so or because it is so widely accepted in the Church, but he gives a list of critically sifted and accredited witnesses.' The message of the resurrection of Jesus is accordingly passionately interested in the concrete and completed reality of the event—an attitude totally foreign to the mythical frame of mind.[81] The witness tells of the resurrection of Jesus not as something pre-historic and supra-temporal, but as an event which has had its effect in the realm of con-

---

[79] Cf. Harnack, *op. cit.*, p. 47; M. Brückner, *op. cit.*, p. 48.
[80] Harnack, *op. cit.*, p. 46.
[81] Cf. Gerhard Kittel, 'Der "historische" Jesus', in *Mysterium Christi*, 1931, pp. 51 f., 54. Specially to the point, p. 52: 'The myths and speculations and philosophies of the time know of redeemers and redemption. But with none of them, neither with one of the gods like Osiris, nor with one of the demigods like Heracles, nor with the heavenly figures of the gnostics either, does the believer have the slightest interest in any historical realism. The redeemer stands out-with the categories of time; whether and when the things of which the myth speaks were once real, actual history in some dim and distant past, is a question which cannot seriously be discussed at all, because it is a matter of supreme indifference. The timeless encounter with the symbolism of the myth, given in ritual and liturgical contemplation, is the perfect gift, is redemption.'

temporary history and was experienced by men living in history and still alive.

Further, it is to be noted that the word of the resurrection of Jesus, in contrast to the most multifarious myths, is not concerned at all with a 'deity' who dies and comes to life again, but with the man Jesus of Nazareth. The extraordinary thing is, that a resurrection is proclaimed which, after the historically ascertainable death of Jesus, took place precisely in this historic person. Thus the decisive point for a comparison with the mythical analogies—the theme of the dying and rising 'deity' —is missing from the start. The unique thing about the resurrection message is the raising of a man from the dead, of which nothing whatever is said in the myths.

Moreover, it is significant that while the myths do speak of a dying, they never testify concretely to a death by crucifixion. Transitoriness exists also in nature and the cosmos, and transitoriness is the stuff of myth; but the death of Jesus on the cross is an act in history. Because myth is concerned with the symbolic presentation of a natural process, which ultimately develops autonomously according to laws of its own, and which accordingly even while the dying goes on has already within it the vital forces of resuscitation, the question as to the means by which the resurrection comes about simply cannot arise.[82] In a myth it is of no consequence whether the deity awakes to life again himself or whether magical powers come to him through the influence and help of the devotees. For the Christian understanding of the resurrection, on the other hand, it is of supreme importance that death and resurrection do not have a natural connection as a matter of course but—though the usual practice is to overlook this—that it is God's intervention alone which overcomes death and raises Jesus from the dead. The resurrection is here no autonomous natural process, but a sovereign act of God, which has no parallel in mythology.

The same ineradicable difference can be seen in regard to the significance which the resurrection has for the believer. Greek thought, living as it does in the realm of mythology, sets in the centre the mystical union with the divine, the magical sacramental experience of immortality. The primitive Christian confession of the resurrection, however, knows nothing of any such mystical deification and enjoyment of immortality, but proclaims on the contrary that Christ died and rose for the sins of

---

[82] Typical of this is the formula τῇ τρίτῃ ἡμέρᾳ, which in actual fact goes back originally to the periodicity of the laws of nature. Applied to history it denotes in general a short period of time, and concretely an ascertainable point of time for historic experience in its uniqueness.

the world. At this fundamental point, too, the anti-mythical character
of the resurrection of Jesus and the lack of any analogy is evident. The
resurrection message, on the contrary, says the opposite of what the
mysteries and their mythologies promise their followers.

Finally, something has also to be said of the unique character of the
primitive Church's missionary consciousness with its basis in the resurrection. Although it was proclaimed in the centres of heathen religions,
the message of the resurrection was not by any means felt to be a new,
but fundamentally similar, myth: on the contrary, it was recognized and
rejected in its offensive otherness. If the resurrection of Jesus had been
nothing more than a myth, the witness to it would have been just as
palatable as a hundred other myths. The message of the resurrection
did *not* appear to the contemporary world to be one of the customary
cult legends, so that Jesus Christ would be a new cult hero standing
harmoniously side by side with other cult heroes. But the message was
in terms of strict exclusiveness: One alone is the Kyrios. Here every
analogy fails. This witness, in contrast to the tolerance of the whole
mythical world, comes with an intolerant claim to absoluteness which
calls in question the validity and truth of all mythology.[83]

We come to the conclusion that the study of the history of religion
cannot by any means be regarded as authority for the mythifying of the
resurrection of Jesus and that any such claim does not stand serious
testing. *The complete otherness of the reality of the resurrection forbids in
principle any application of the concept of myth and brings out in detail the
impossibility of any analogical relationship with the myths of religious
history.* In its unequivocal relatedness to history the resurrection of
Jesus is secure against every mythological misunderstanding, yet at the
same time it is also at bottom *the fulfilment of myth.* In regard to the
questions of inter-testamental apocalyptic, the resurrection of Jesus
gives the answer of the dawning of the new world of God and brings
the promise of eschatological fulfilment. In regard to the gnostic myth
with its longing for light and life and its questions about the right way
to heaven, the message of the resurrection gives the answer that 'light
and life', 'way and truth', are grounded solely in the Risen One. The
extent to which the resurrection of Jesus can fulfil what all myth ultimately means, can be shown only in the further course of our study.[84]

---

[83] Cf. Tor Andrae, *Die letzten Dinge*, 1940 (German translation by Hans
Heinrich Schäder).

[84] Harnack too, *op. cit.*, p. 16, avers: 'The Gospel in its ultimate essence, i.e.
in its historic reality, was not a new myth alongside the others, but the fulfilment
of myth.' Similarly also E. Seeberg, *op. cit.*, p. 21: 'It was as the fulfilment of

5. RESURRECTION AND WORLD-PICTURE

(a) The Resurrection Statements as bound to their Age

The validity of the primitive Christian resurrection message is, finally, also radically called in question by the criticisms of modern science-conditioned thinking and its secular view of the world. The profoundly problematical character of the resurrection of Jesus is due to its close connection with a quite definite picture of the world and its dependence on ideas rooted in this world-picture. This type of critical attitude, taken seriously in theology so far chiefly by R. Bultmann, has long been widely adopted and has impressed itself on public opinion in general.

The significance of the resurrection of Jesus for contemporary man is not to be contested because historical research is unable to attain to unequivocal knowledge of it, but because the idea of resurrection from the dead is rooted in a different picture of the world which has become untenable for modern man. All primitive Christian statements about the resurrection of Jesus are conditioned by their time. While there is no need to dispute the subjective conviction of the primitive Church, yet the value of that conviction is bound up with the contemporary picture of the world. The *world-picture of primitive Christianity* is pre-Copernican. It is the naive cosmology of geocentricity. The earth is seen in the centre as a flat disc over which arches the heavenly sphere of the stars and beneath which extends the underworld of the dead. Heaven and the underworld are conceived, like the earth, in terms of spatial objectivity. This massive static picture of the world provides the framework within which the great cosmic drama of redemption can be played out. Bultmann speaks especially of the three storeys—earth, heaven, and hell—by which he says the New Testament's picture of the world is marked as 'mythical'. 'The earth is not only the scene of natural everyday happenings, but also the stage for the working of supernatural powers.'[85] Hence Paul's Christology is also built on this three-fold division of the universe.[86] 'The Son of Man belonged to three realms, as a divine figure, as a servant, and in death. Thus there are also three realms which after his ascension are put under his feet: the heavenly, the earthly, and the underworldly.'[87] On the hypothesis of a three-storey universe, it is possible to understand the idea that a

myth that it (Christianity) prevailed, and thus, in fulfilling it, at the same time transforming myth and abolishing it.'
[85] *Kerygma und Mythos*, pp. 15 f. (ET, p. 1).
[86] Phil. 2.5 ff.
[87] E. Lohmeyer, *Kyrios Jesus*, 1928, p. 43; R. Bultmann, *ibid.*

heavenly being comes down from heaven to earth, lives upon it, enters after death into the realm of the dead under the earth, is resurrected, i.e. rises up again from the grave and the realm of death under the earths and by an 'ascension into heaven' returns to the 'upper' world and sit, on the throne of the Lord of the universe 'at the right hand of God'. R. Bultmann avers: 'The saving event which forms the real content of the New Testament proclamation is presented in accordance with the mythical picture of the world. . . . The Risen One has been exalted up to heaven to the right hand of God; he has been made "Lord" and "King". . . .' The word of the resurrection of Jesus is therefore to be understood as a thoroughly naive idea bound to a primitive picture of the world. Only when we take our stand on that world-picture can we hope to reach an understanding of the message of the resurrection.

A change in world-picture, however, brings at once a crisis for the idea of the resurrection, because it dissolves the preliminary conditions on which the thought of a resurrection of the dead appears possible and meaningful. The fundamental revolution in the ancient picture of the world since Copernicus and Giordano Bruno seems to have created a totally new situation also for religious statements, not merely by abandoning geocentrism, but also by abolishing the boundaries of space and the old ideas of space. The whole idea of an earthly sphere separated from a spatially conceived heavenly world and underworld has become impossible. The universe extends without boundary and without earthly centre into infinity, to the utter insignificance of the planet earth. The ideas of a divine dwelling-place in 'heaven' and of a realm of the dead have, astronomically speaking, no place in the modern world-picture. Consequently the thought of a resurrection of Jesus from the sphere of the dead and an ascension into the divine realm is also regarded as inconceivable. Thus M. Dibelius, too, comes to the conclusion that belief in the resurrection arises from a situation which is 'for us unrepeatable'; it is immediately related to an 'apocalyptic, geocentric picture of the world, for which miracles are credible'.[88]

Pursuing these thoughts further, R. Bultmann actually bases his new theological position on the constraint which the situation of modern man places upon any theology that is to be taken seriously. The 'mythical world-picture' of the Bible is 'past' for modern man, and therefore the 'mythological talk' in which that past world-picture indulges has 'become incredible'. Modern man accordingly cannot be expected to subscribe to the myth of the resurrection with its moorings in the old

[88] *Evangelium und Welt*, 1929, pp. 81 ff.

world-picture, since modern man lives with a completely different world-picture which is 'determined by modern science'. 'And this other world-picture dominates men through the influence of the school, the press, the cinema, and technology in general.'

Theology must reckon with the situation created by the new world-picture. 'The theologian and preacher owes it to the Church to be absolutely plain and clearcut.' It is a case of considering where within the framework of the 'no longer contemporary world-picture' the proclamation has to find its starting point. 'The preacher must not leave the hearers in any doubt as to what they really hold to be true and what not.' Since according to Bultmann a refurbishing of the mythological ideas and pictures of the New Testament will not do for the man of today and he is no longer able to repeat in his own mind the mythological thinking of the Bible, the thing is 'to uncover the truth of the kerygma as kerygma for the non-mythologically thinking man'. This means, however, that according to Bultmann, 'the word of the resurrection of Jesus' has lost its validity because of the change in the world-picture.[89]

There is no doubt that modern thinking stands under the overwhelming influence of the new situation created by the changed world-picture, and that to the same extent the Christian witness to the resurrection of Jesus confronts it as strange and unintelligible. On the one hand the concept 'resurrection' seems to belong to the language of an archaic and outmoded world, which has an anachronistic flavour and can claim no interest now. The word 'resurrection' thus points to a situation which is no longer valid today, to the naive world-picture of antiquity. On the other hand it is believed that natural science, whose insights made possible the building of the new world-picture, can be cited as an authority against the possibility of the resurrection of Jesus. Thus a new attitude born of the contemporary situation bars the way to an understanding of the resurrection and makes it more problematical than ever.

(b) The Independence of the Resurrection of Jesus from the World-picture

The discussion with this radical attack on the resurrection faith has to begin with the concept of world-picture. What are we to understand by this much used and much interpreted term? *The concept 'world-picture' does not mean a metaphysical statement, nor a religious interpretation of a situation, but a conclusion about the universe based upon immanent knowledge.* The world-picture means the gathering together

[89] Cf. *Kerygma und Mythos*, pp. 21 f., 26 also 123 f. (ET, pp. 9, 15, 104 f.).

at a given moment of experiences, impressions of the surrounding world, results of investigation, into a unified order determined by definite laws. Thus there arises a coherent picture of the universe, whose extent, form and content are dependent upon the amount of knowledge of the world, the width of the horizon, and the accuracy of research. The variety of world-pictures is accordingly due to the manifold gradations of knowledge of the surrounding world and its laws, so that according to the perceptive powers involved we can speak respectively of a primitive world-picture or a scientific world-picture. A world-picture, however, is always only a relative quantity, which stands in relation to the developing and changing knowledge of the world. The changeableness of the world-picture belongs essentially to its very character. It is always engaged in a process of change as ever new insights into the ordering of world elements are gained.[90]

Considering the change that has come over the classical, mechanical world-picture of nineteenth-century science as a result of modern researches on energy and the atom, Bultmann's standpoint appears thoroughly antiquated. This fundamental change in the scientific situation opens up unexpectedly new possibilities for the relating of faith and science. The world-picture of a mechanistic and materialistic science and the speculative world-view based upon it, to which Bultmann still appeals, is today at all events obsolete. The concepts of a universally calculable causal system and determinism which labels every extraordinary occurrence, such as miracle, as 'breaking' the laws of nature, are in process of dissolution. Far more typical of the principles of scientific thinking today are the ideas of the 'freedom' of natural phenomena and the 'indeterminacy' of final patterns. According to the theories of this contemporary world-picture, we must reckon in principle with the breaking into the cosmos at any moment of new, perhaps hitherto unknown energies, and consequently with the alteration of present researches, judgments and laws.

That is certainly not to say that the new world-picture could give us any proof of the truth of the Christian faith, or that we may talk of a dependence of faith on the results of modern research. The new scientific position displays only a recognition of the 'possibility' of miraculous

[90] Cf. W. Künneth, *Naturwissenschaft und Glaube*, Stuttgart 1930, pp. 14 f.; cf. Ernst, *Die Weltanschauung und ihre Problematik*, Gütersloh 1930. More recently the comprehensive examination by K. Heim: *Christian Faith and Natural Science*, ET 1953, as also *The Transformation of the Scientific World View*, ET 1953. Otto A. Dilschneider, *Das christliche Weltbild*, Gütersloh 1951.

events, for the earlier verdict of 'impossible' can no longer be legitimately passed in the name of science today.[91]

Strictly to be distinguished from the concept of world-picture (*Weltbild*) is the speculative world-view (*Weltanschauung*)—the metaphysical interpretation of the universe, the attempt to master intellectually the recognized facts of the surrounding world and to make sense of them. No matter whether our knowledge of nature be primitive or refined, it can be bound up with 'ultimate' questions which are no longer to be solved intellectually and lie beyond the explorable realm of the immanent. The questions of the ultimate basis of the cosmos, of its goal and the sense of its laws, of the significance of man and of his relation to the universe, of God and divine revelation, are totally independent of the nature and transformations of the world-picture, but are inevitably posed by every attempt to comprehend the world. Religious statements are in no way threatened by the progress of natural science, since the latter has to do neither with interpreting the meaning of existence nor with the reality of God. On the contrary, both the primitive geocentric world-picture, and the Copernican world-picture, and also the world-picture of modern atomic physics, can all be speculatively interpreted in the same way, whether in terms of atheistic materialism or in terms of pagan religious myth, or, as it may also be, in the sense of biblical faith in the Creator. The momentary interpretation of natural events, and of the results of research as determined by their day, is in principle independent of the nature and shape of the world-picture. Accordingly, a new world-picture does not abolish the metaphysical questions that already arise at once even with a primitive world-picture, nor invalidate the religious answers given to them.

This general recognition of the necessity for a *distinction between world-picture and world-view*, i.e. religious interpretation and explanation, is of importance for the relation between the resurrection of Jesus and the world-picture. The message of the resurrection of Jesus is in essence not a declaration made with an eye to the world-picture or the study of world structure, but it belongs to the sphere of man's relation with God, which natural science can neither affirm nor deny. The word of the resurrection of Jesus is a declaration which is concerned with God, with his revelation and its importance for men, and thus has no more interest in the pre-Copernican primitive world-picture than it has in a modern world-picture. A scientific objection to the resurrection of Jesus does not lie within the bounds of possibility at all. Scientific

[91] Cf. Oepke, *Geschichte und übergeschtichliche Schriftauslegung*, 1946, p. 58.

knowledge is concerned with the immanent and leaves religious judgments open, and outside the realm of its investigation. The dissolution
of the world-picture of primitive Christianity therefore cannot upset
the witness to the resurrection in any way, since the latter is independent
of changes in the understanding of the world, and of the questions
raised by a changing knowledge of nature. The assumption that the
resurrection of Jesus is endangered by changes in the world-picture is
based upon a serious misunderstanding both of the character of the
resurrection and also of the possibilities of scientific knowledge. Bultmann's fundamental error is thus to be seen in his confusing of 'world-
picture' with 'world-view'.

With this fundamental insight, however, the problem is not yet
solved. We come to the root of the matter only with the question of the
means of expression of a religious statement and its relation to the
world-picture. Every religious experience, every revelation and every
witness of God is inevitably committed to take the content of something
that has laid hold of man and convinced him, and communicate it to
others who know nothing of it. No matter what form such a communication may take, whether the form of action or of speech, it is always a
proclamation whose means of expression are drawn from the world of
man, from his world-picture. To make the transcendent revelation and
the reality of God immediately understandable, without any use of
immanent ideas and concepts, is impossible. Everything which is not
part of the objective world can be spoken of only by means of pictures
and likenesses, signs and symbols. But all these come to man out of
the material provided by his world-picture. For that reason all speech
is ultimately pictorial and all talk of God anthropomorphic. It is accordingly necessary to distinguish between the religious 'substance', which
remains untouched by the world-picture, and the means of expressing
this 'substance', which must be drawn from the material of the world-
picture. Thus the witness to the resurrection stands on the one hand
beyond all questions of world-picture, while on the other hand its
linguistic form bears the stamp of ideas that were originally connected
with a world-picture. The concepts 'resurrection', 'ascension', 'session
at the right hand of God'—figures of speech rooted in the immanent—
accordingly must not be confused with the 'substance' itself. An identification of this kind would presuppose the spatial character of heaven
and of God's 'throne', and thereby alter the real 'substance' itself.

At this point it must be seriously asked whether biblical thought was
in actual fact so bound up in the space-time pattern of the word-picture

of antiquity that it could think and speak even of the reality of God only in these limited categories. There can, however, be no question of that. The Bible itself already maintains that faith and its judgments are independent of the world. Even the Old Testament, to say nothing of the New Testament, on countless occasions broke through the three-storey theories of the mythological world-picture with their 'localizing' of God. Of the infinite majesty of God it is said, 'Behold, heaven and the heaven of heavens cannot contain thee.'[92] Of the all-pervading presence of God it says, 'Can any hide himself in secret places that I shall not see him? saith the Lord. Do not I fill heaven and earth? saith the Lord.'[93] For the biblical witness to revelation the space-time pattern of the world-picture is accordingly not authoritative at all, and at this point Bultmann is doing battle on a front which in essence does not exist.[94]

The early Christian witness, however, although derived from a primitive world-picture, is itself convinced of the inadequacy of its terms and therefore seeks to describe the reality of the resurrection in ever new variations. This provides an important safeguard against a literal interpretation of the witness, which would inevitably lead to objectifying and secularizing the resurrection of Jesus. The literal interpretation does not do justice to the aim of the resurrection witness and must be fundamentally rejected as inappropriate. This knowledge of the improperness of the terms can exist independently of the world-picture and its transformations. The classical example of that is Luther, who still adopted the pre-Copernican world-picture, but was convinced that heaven 'as the place of God' is 'not a place in the spatial sense', that Jesus' 'ascension into heaven' is not a spatial event, and that Jesus' 'exaltation' certainly cannot mean a localizing of his body in heaven, but on the contrary the formula *'dextra Dei ubique est'* ('the right hand of God is everywhere') is the decisive answer of faith to all questions raised by the world-picture. That proves that the 'mythological' world-picture of antiquity remains without any influence on the real and intrinsic knowledge of faith. But precisely when this is recognized, the distinction between God's revelation and the form man gives to it can be made theologically fruitful.[95] If we maintain this fundamental viewpoint, then

---

[92] I Kings 8.27. [93] Jer. 23.24, cf. also Ps. 139; Acts 17.27 ff.
[94] Hence E. Schlink rightly says: 'To seek to demythologize the Bible would be to overlook the fact that its witness is without exception already demythologized, since God's word, by entering in revelation into the language of man, broke through the myths of man' (*Studium Generale*, 1948, p. 203).
[95] Cf. the excellent expositions by W. Elert in *Morphologie des Luthertums*, 1932, I, pp. 364, 355 ff.

an alteration of the world-picture can never lead to criticism of the resurrection of Jesus itself, though it can certainly provoke new reflection on the significance of the form of expression. The very impossibility of spatial ideas of 'heaven' or 'the realm of the dead' in the new world-picture becomes a valuable corrective to an inadequate concept of the resurrection. What is critically called in question here is neither the 'substance' nor the in itself necessary means of expression, but the literal, intrinsically inappropriate interpretation of the word 'resurrection' as an inner-worldly, objective, spatial event. The change of world-picture bids us recall the difference between 'substance' and linguistic form, and at the same time consider what is 'really' meant by the concept 'resurrection', what it means in the proper sense.

The problem is thus summed up in the *question of the appropriateness of the concept of the 'resurrection'*. If it is a matter of representational inadequacy, then it might look as if the concept could be replaced by a different term corresponding to the new world-picture and its material possibilities. If the word 'resurrection' is merely a pictorial image, merely an explanatory symbol for something totally different, then its place could be taken equally well by another image derived from the new state of the world-picture. Then the change in world-picture would not indeed alter the actual 'substance', but it would demand a change in the pictorial form of expression.[96] Now there is no disputing the fact that a new and profounder picture of nature brings new possibilities of expounding the unchanged content of revelation in new terms. The decisive theological question, however, is whether the recognition of this can be made the ground for renouncing in principle the old religious terms like resurrection, redemption, ascension, in so far as the new substitutes we have chosen appear more appropriate to the 'substance'.[97] Against this, however, the following points have to be made clear:

To admit the inadequacy which the space-time structure of all earthly, human existence imposes on our means of expressing the divine revelation, is still not the same as to say the concepts are unsuitable. The words resurrection, rising, ascension, exaltation admittedly do not give direct and non-pictorial expression to the event of revelation; but for all that, they do represent essentially suitable concepts. These are *root words in the forming of religious language, which are more than pictorial similes and signs exchangeable at will*, and consequently they lay claim to appro-

[96] Cf. Heinrich Frick's profound study, 'Ideogramm, Mythologie und das Wort', in *Marburger Theologische Studien*, Gotha 1931.

[97] P. Tillich rightly points to the importance of the 'choice of models' for religious and theological language. Cf. *Die religiöse Verwirklichung*, 1930, p. 88.

priateness. Concepts like God, heaven, the spatial designation 'above' for the eternal and divine, the spatial designation 'below' for the earthly, transitory and the dead, and likewise 'resurrection' as denoting the transition from 'below' to 'above', from death to the life of God, are technical terms of biblical religion; and while they do share in the fragmentary character of all earthly representations of an unconditional reality, which means they can comprehend it only in a pictorial space-time pattern, yet at the same time they are valid and appropriate for every world-picture, since even an advance in our knowledge of the world does not free us from the need to use spatial and temporal forms of expression. Even modern man is compelled to think and to express himself in these forms of speech. The primitive Christian root word 'resurrection' therefore cannot, even in the modern world-picture, be appropriately replaced by any other concept. It is a substantial, technical term, so bound up with the technical 'object' of which it speaks, that in surrendering the term we should perforce lose the 'substance' also. The message of the resurrection is therefore not merely picture, likeness, symbol, but a 'technical term' by which alone, despite all its basic inadequacy, the reality of the resurrection is unequivocally and suitably expressed. Hand in hand with the appropriateness of the concept of resurrection goes its irreplaceability. This provides the safeguard against the sort of subjective arbitrariness in the choice of figure and model that would seem to lie at hand with every change of the world-picture.

To sum up, the witness of the resurrection is in principle independent of the world-picture and its changes. *However much the linguistic terms of the message belong to the world-picture, the concept of resurrection constitutes a root word of religious language and one that has ineradicable significance at every stage of our knowledge of the world.*

This discussion of all the aspects of the problematical character of the resurrection of Jesus has led to the recognition that its reality cannot be understood by means of the concepts of history and the life-idea[98] or of existentialism, nor yet by the approach from mythology[99] and the world-picture. With that we have described as it were in a negative sense the 'theological place' of the resurrection of Jesus.

[98] Mattiesen's study, *Der jenseitige Mensch*, 1925, moves in the same direction as Hoffmann's metapsychology.

[99] For further reference see especially Alfred Jeremias, *Die ausserbiblische Erlösererwartung*, Leipzig 1928, and above all the same author's important study, *Die Bedeutung des Mythos für die Dogmatik*.

II

THE THEOLOGICAL CONCEPT OF THE RESURRECTION

THE starting point of a scientific discussion of the resurrection problem seems as a matter of course to lie in an established position already given as such. The reality of spatio-temporal existence is equated with absolute reality, and in that light the resurrection of Jesus is subjected to a detached and critical examination. In face of this immanent state of affairs an attempt is made to confront the resurrection with the given criterion of reality, to understand and test it according to the conditions of immanent existence, to classify it under these scientific laws and to prove it by their means. This way of looking at things, however, though natural enough in itself, must be radically challenged. If the resurrection message's claim to bear witness to a reality is valid, then that kind of attempt to understand it must be radically unsound. It might be that the resurrection of Jesus is a reality compared to which the given facts of our immanent world cannot make the same claim to reality, and that indeed our spatio-temporal existence is radically called in question by the reality of the resurrection. In that case the criterion of reality which is accepted uncritically as known and given would have to be subjected to revision. On the erroneous assumption that rightly speaking there exists only an immanent reality, it is quite clear that the resurrection of Jesus is placed in a false perspective and can be seen only in distortion. On the contrary, *the reality of the resurrection does not allege the existence of a criterion of reality outside of, and in abstraction from itself, but rather demands the adoption of a criterion and standpoint based on the reality of the resurrection.* This insight requires an about-turn, so to speak, in our thinking: it demands *a thinking based on the resurrection, a specifically 'theological' conception of its reality.* The theological concept of the resurrection means the acknowledgment of the presupposition that the 'substance' of the resurrection is absolute reality, which cannot be measured according to the norms of other realities beside itself or subordinated to them.

A proper understanding of the resurrection of Jesus is conceivable only if it comes of a radical change in the whole approach. The theological task is to *expound the basic characteristics of the reality of the resurrection*, as it is mediated to us by the primitive Christian message of the resurrection. *Three distinct themes* have to be dealt with: first, *the event of the resurrection of Jesus, the primal miracle (Urwunder)*—then as distinct from this, *the revelation of the Risen One in the realm of space and time*—and thirdly, the question *how a knowledge of the resurrection is made possible.*

I. THE PRIMAL MIRACLE OF THE RESURRECTION OF JESUS

In general, theologians do not usually speak of the 'substance' of the resurrection of Jesus itself, i.e. the event of Jesus' being raised from the dead by an act of God. Any reflections on this event, which we designate the primal miracle (*Urwunder*) of God, and which must be clearly distinguished in the first instance from the appearances of the Risen One, appear to be exposed to the danger of speculation. And yet, the primitive Christian kerygma deals primarily with nothing else but this primal event of resurrection which takes place beyond all the happenings of history; and it is only secondarily that it goes on to add, so to speak in confirmation, the account of specific facts and circumstances. The content of the resurrection message is the primal miracle of God's act in raising Jesus from the dead. Our task, then, in the first instance is to conceive this event 'theologically', i.e. to define it sharply in our mind as against misinterpretations and let it stand out in its own peculiarity. To dispense with such reflections would cause us to overlook something of decisive importance and concentrate the whole discussion on the problem of the appearances. But that would be precisely the way to shift the emphasis and foreshorten the central content of the resurrection witness.

(a) The Establishing of the Reality of Life

In the resurrection of Jesus God brings about the establishing of a new reality of life. This activity of God in the raising of Jesus bears the stamp of a primal miracle. The concept *primal miracle* means two things. First, it expresses the activity of God. The reality of the new life of the resurrection is not something self-existent and self-contained, but is grounded only in the act of God. Resurrection life is no static being. Only in the primal miracle of the resurrection does God found new life out of himself; it is a dynamic event proceeding from God. If God is the fountain of all life, then he alone controls the reality of life which he causes to break forth in the primal act of the resurrection. *The primal miracle of the resurrection is God's creative act, which in essence must be set parallel to the primal miracle of creating the world.* As the sovereign act of God in creating the world is a *creatio ex nihilo*, so the intervention of God in the resurrection produces something new, the creative power of God creates life from the dead. The resurrection miracle is after the creation of the world the second and decisive attestation of the fulness of life and power of life that is in God.

But the concept primal miracle at the same time also describes the reality of the resurrection as a special kind of life. The life of the resurrection is therefore to be understood as a 'primal life' (*Urleben*). Karl Heim has pointed out the significance of the prefix '*Ur-*' (primal) as a mark of peculiar theological content.[1] The life which is established in the primal miracle of the resurrection stands in contrast to immanent reality. It is not a transitory life, and is therefore not to be conceived on the basis of the reality that is limited by death. As original life from God it is a primal datum, which is not derivable from any other given fact and does not allow of any immanent grounding. The primal life of the resurrection of Jesus means the genuine life to which all other life bears a secondary relation. The reality of the resurrection is the genuine and true reality, and by claiming to be such it challenges the genuineness and validity of every other living reality: it unmasks the life of immanent existence as a non-genuine and untrue life, as a pseudo-life.[2] What Heinrich Frick has maintained to be the fundamental task of a theological doctrine of reality, is one that must be specially pursued here.[3] The reality of the new life founded by God in the resurrection cannot now by any means be interpreted as a merely pictorial or symbolic expression, but the situation of man and his understanding of reality have been radically altered. *The primal life of the resurrection of Jesus is the reality upon which all life depends.* And indeed *vice versa* the pseudo-life[4] of the immanent world can only be a likeness and symbol

---

[1] *Glaube und Denken*[1,2], 1931, pp. 386 ff. (ET, *God Transcendent*, 1935, is of 3rd, revised and much smaller edition, 1934).

[2] The concepts 'pseudo-reality', 'pseudo-life' stand in radical antithesis to the true reality of the resurrection life. The reality of the immanent world as such is not affected thereby. I am surely hardly likely to be misunderstood as teaching docetism.

[3] H. Frick, *Ideogramm, Mythologie und das Wort*, 1931, pp. 17 ff. In connection with Eph. 3.15 he rightly avers: 'The fatherhood of God is not "merely a metaphor" but reality, whereas the merely metaphorical character belongs precisely to the earthly "fatherhood" which commentators call "the real thing".... For whatever "reality" this reality of ours has, it has only from God.'

[4] 'Pseudo-life' means the unauthentic existence which does not express the true essence, as distinct from the authentic, true and essential life.

of the genuine life of the resurrection. The fragmentary life of space and time, which is dependent on the true life that comes from God, can become a pointer towards the perfect resurrection life. All positions based upon the usual view of reality are in the last resort illusory, inasmuch as they deceive themselves in regard to the non-genuineness of our own existence and seek to conceive the reality of the resurrection only as an improper and postulated reality. The reality of life, however, is not discovered by making a choice among the various possibilities of life, but is established in the resurrection of Jesus, which alone makes possible the vantage-point from which it can be determined what is genuine and non-genuine, transitory and eternal reality. What real life is, is known for the first time on the ground of the resurrection of Jesus, in which is established the underivable primal reality of life.

This revaluation of the concepts of life and reality sheds a new light on the idea of life and immortality as well as on the thought-world of myth. The life of the resurrection helps us to recognize these ideas and mythologies which concentrate on the overcoming of death as presentiments of perfect life and postulates of genuine reality; but at the same time it denies their claim to validity by revealing the questionableness of all transitory existence apart from the word of the resurrection. The relation of the reality of the resurrection to the life-idea and the life-myth is that of fulfilment and cancellation. It overcomes the inadequacy of their claims and perfects the life which they seek, but do not know. This recognition of the *fulfilment of all life in the resurrection* likewise means a promise, in accordance with the character of the resurrection life. The primal miracle of the resurrection has an eschatological determination. It is a primal miracle like the creation of the world, but in contrast to the provisional and transitory character of the latter, there breaks through for the first time in the former the conclusiveness and intransience of a new and final creation. The resurrection of Jesus marks the start of the reality of eternal life. It is the beginning of the final reality, which claims to be a universal consummation in contrast to all penultimate and broken realities. The primal eschatological miracle of the resurrection of Jesus contains an inner dynamic, a tension between the dawning of life in this primal act of God and its ultimate consummation. That is why in the word of the resurrection of Jesus the reality of life counters the world of pseudo-life, that is why it becomes the denial of all pseudo-solutions of the problem of life in philosophical ideas and mythologies, and that is why it also becomes a promise of ultimate consummation of life for all transitory existence. *The reality of the resurrection is the assault of life upon the spatio-temporal reality of death.*

But this general description of the primal miracle of the resurrection must not give occasion for empty abstractions. The establishment of the reality of life by God is not an abstract event, nor an event which, as the parallel with the creation of the world might suggest, could be appropriately described only in general terms: it is a very work of God, which is accomplished unequivocally in the raising of the man Jesus of Nazareth. *The resurrection life is given a concrete and personal determination in Christ*, guaranteeing the singularity of the past perfect act as resurrection *of Jesus.* The noticeable theological formalism in regard to the conceptual grasp of the resurrection in K. Barth, who is content with a vacillating terminology, consequently hardly does justice to the concreteness of the primal miracle of the resurrection of Jesus. If the resurrection according to Barth is a concept synonymous with 'righteousness', 'kingdom', 'exercise of kingly power', 'redemption', 'the turning-point in time', 'the cancelling of everything that we mean here and now by man and world', 'eternity', 'mercy of God', 'the revolution, the impossibly possible',[5] then however apposite these descriptions individually may be, the resurrection becomes an epitome of general Christian statements and 'values'. To be sure, Barth is correct in understanding the resurrection as a summing up of the whole Christian message. But this insight must not lead to a diffuse and ambiguous description which is in danger of failing to see the essential feature of the resurrection witness. The decisive thing for the understanding of the reality of the resurrection is its concrete and personalistic character. That is to say that God has not everywhere or in many places revealed the reality of his life, but has bound it to one, single point. *God realizes in the resurrection the 'novum' of life, in Christ.* Therefore, there is not a life and a reality which exists somewhere and reveals itself sometime, not a neutral, impersonal, abstract life-reality, but only a Christ-reality. *The risen Christ is the life, the primal life, the true everlasting life*; he is the authentic reality beyond death, the existence which alone can be meaningfully described as real. This exclusiveness in the binding of all the reality of life to the Risen One is extraordinarily important. In it the absolute claim of the resurrection message has its ground, and with that ground the message stands

---

[5] Cf. *Römerbrief*, pp. 175, 446, 62 ff., 126 f., 187 (ET, pp. 193 f., 462, 87 ff., 150, 206 f., *Wort Gottes*, 1925, pp. 95 ff. (ET, *The Word of God and the Word of Man*, 1928, pp. 90 ff); *Auferstehung der Toten*, pp. 60, 82 (ET, pp. 111, 148). Cf. also Schmidt-Japping, 'Die christologischen Anschauungen der dialektischen Theologie' in *Apol. Jahrbücher* 1925, pp. 98 f., 106 ff., and especially Werner Weisner's study, *Das Offenbarungsproblem in der dialektischen Theologie*, Munich 1930. Further, the critique by H. W. Schmidt in *Zeit und Ewigkeit*, 1927, pp. 37 f., 276 f.

or falls. This is the exclusiveness of life as opposed to death, but it appears awkward and difficult precisely because it is related to the concrete life of the Christ raised from concrete death. The abstract philosophical way of thinking, which has often come to dominate also in theology, is prepared, it is true, to speak of a victory of life over death; yet it views with hostility the assertion of a concrete resurrection bound to Christ. The primal miracle of the resurrection, however, is concretely Christocentric, or it is nothing at all—but in that case there is also no establishing of a life-reality superior to death. The personalistic, concrete character of the resurrection of Jesus is in fact an inconceivability, a *skandalon*, for the thinking which sets out from the presuppositions of immanence—all the more so when on the basis of this Christ-reality a critical judgment is passed on the improperness of all 'reality' apart from Christ.

One final characteristic is important for the understanding of the reality of the resurrection. As personalistic life it is safe against any views of a neuter and organic kind, and cannot be identified with natural phenomena. Rather, the real life of the Christ bears the stamp of the spiritual—whereby 'spirit' does not by any means imply non-corporeal and non-natural spiritualizing. Our relation to a spiritual and personalistic reality is not magical, immediate, or mythical, but has the form of personal address, in which the word of the resurrection also shares.

(b) The Uniqueness of the Resurrection

From the recognition of the primal miracle of the resurrection of Jesus as a new creation of life by God there arises the further question: What relation does this resurrection reality have to the world of space and time? This is *the question of the uniqueness of the resurrection life*, and of the comprehending of its structure in the category appropriate to it. The discussion so far has shown that this primal miracle of God cannot be understood as an element in the ordered continuity of the complex of being, and therefore rules out a historifying treatment. The decisive thing, however, is to discover which set of concepts lies at our disposal to give uncurtailed expression to the uniqueness of the resurrection.

On the lines of K. Heim's inquiries into the spheres of existence or the dimensions, the concept *'dimension'* appears suitable for application to what the resurrection message means to say.[6] The concept of dimension is to be considered appropriate to the subject if it can express the uniqueness of the reality of the resurrection and its difference from the

[6] Cf. *Glaube und Denken*, pp. 54 ff., 76 f., 307 ff., 363 ff.

immanent world. The conceptual definition of the resurrection of Jesus as 'dimension' involves three further statements.

The dimension of the resurrection reality stands in a paradoxical relation to the dimensions of the spatio-temporal world. As the primal miracle of God it has the character of the unconditional, and is therefore not conditioned by any factor within the world nor classifiable under the schema of the inanimate world and its relationships. An unconditional reality is not objectifiable: it is non-objective and cannot become an object of observation and external ascertainment. The unconditional and non-objective character of the reality of the resurrection is accordingly contradictory to the multiplicities of all immanent being: it shatters their bounds and cannot express itself in their sphere in unified statements. Because the resurrection of Jesus embodies a new dimension that is not existent in the world, it is absolutely impossible of contemplation. There are no earthly spectators of the primal miracle of the resurrection of Jesus any more than of the creation of the world. It is therefore of the highest significance, and in keeping with the dimensional understanding of the resurrection, that in the New Testament there is no description of the resurrection event itself. The reality of the resurrection of Jesus lies beyond our earthly categories; hence it is necessarily impossible to represent it, and the absence of reports about the primal miracle itself is a sign of the pertinence of the primitive Christian witness. Every attempt to remove the impossibility of contemplating the resurrection of Jesus, and thus to depart from the basis of the resurrection message, means a failure to understand the dimensional determination of the resurrection, and a destruction of its uniqueness.

The dimension of the resurrection is consequently also not a possible object of knowledge in the immanent world, that could be perceived by sense or thought or could be grasped by way of feeling. It is not susceptible of any proof and is not, as supranatural historism still thought, demonstrable by a multitude of arguments. It finds itself in its relation to the world dependent solely on the word of the message which by its very essence is exposed to contradiction and denial from the side of the immanent world. The fundamental lack of any means of proof makes its message appear within the framework of the categories of world reality to be empty fantasy, subjective fancy, at best myth. The dimensional character of the reality of the resurrection means its radical insecurity. This is the unprotectedness of true life in the midst of the world of illusory life. The resurrection dimension can certainly be pointed to in terms of witness; it becomes a reality, however, only to those upon whom its truth has dawned, to whom it has attested itself.

According to these two statements, the reality of the resurrection could be understood in exclusive antithesis to immanent existence. But the resurrection of Jesus as a dimension of life is not merely the 'wholly other' in contrast to the world of objects, nor is it a transcendent kind of being that remains in unrelated isolation from everything conditional, but on the contrary it is constitutive of all being as such. Dimensions can be left out of account, and therefore the resurrection dimension, too, is subject to the possibility of abstraction. Nonetheless, this dimension is of fundamental importance for the whole of the world's reality in so far as that reality is in fact real and is oriented towards a true life beyond the transient. There is no life in the world which is not essentially determined by the dimension of the perfect life of the resurrection of Jesus. Reality in the proper sense attaches to the being of the world only so far as light falls upon it from the resurrection dimension, only so far as it is oriented towards the reality of Christ.[7]

An understanding of existence that takes no account of the resurrection dimension which gives direction to all existence, is ultimately fragmentary, and the very thing it misses is real being. The dimension of the resurrection has existential significance for the world as a whole. From this point of view it becomes clear that the moment the knowledge of this dimension dawns upon us, there must come about a radical change in our whole understanding of existence.[8] Knowledge of the reality of life in the resurrection of Jesus necessarily alters our knowledge of the existential situation of man and his world. The comprehending of the resurrection as a new dimension implies the indication of a world-change of colossal proportions. Thus the uniqueness of the reality of the resurrection comes to appropriate expression in the concept of dimension.

The dimension of the resurrection of Jesus has a structure of its own, which is incommensurable with the forms in which other dimensions are expressed. A consequence of this is the often overlooked *difference of the resurrection from the miracles in history*. An identification of the resurrection with the preceding and succeeding miracles in the history of salvation, especially with the raising of the dead by Jesus himself, is accordingly no longer possible—however true it may be, as will have to be shown elsewhere, that there is an inner connection between them.

[7] Cf. K. Heim, *op. cit.*, p. 61: 'A dimension is a respect in which each thing must be defined if the question what it is is to be fully answered.'
[8] Cf. K. Heim, *op. cit.*, p. 66.

Certainly the resurrection of Jesus, too, is to be understood as a miracle; but the understanding of the resurrection as a miracle calls for special modification in order to bring out the uniqueness of this miracle.[9] Every miracle presents within the immanent sphere a special emergence of a reality formed by divine activity; the resurrection of Jesus on the other hand is a primal miracle and as such lies as it were behind and beyond the spatio-temporal plane, though of course not without having important repercussions on it. This outcome within the sphere of history, however, is not the thing itself, as with other miracles, but only a pointer to the primal miracle beyond the bounds of the immanent world. *The reality of the resurrection of Jesus is accordingly to be understood as an event of a qualitatively different kind from all other prophetic, messianic or apostolic miracles.* Even the miracle of Jesus' raising someone from the dead does not lead us beyond the created reality of space and time. The man snatched from death by Jesus stands afterwards, as he did before, under the laws of the earthly limitations of existence, and his life is still menaced as before by the final necessity of dying. Resurrecting in history does not give final liberation from the law of death that dominates history, and there can therefore be repetitions of it in the epoch of saving history. None of these happenings can kindle any kerygma of a new 'eternal' life, nor even be the basis for such a thing. The primal miracle of the resurrection of Jesus, on the other hand, in its stringent exclusiveness and non-repeatability does not mean the restitution of a life bound to history, but the unique and incomparable reality of ever-lasting life. *The resurrection message proclaims an event* 'sui generis'. Every weakening of its uniqueness obscures precisely the central thing to which that primitive Christian message testifies.

2. THE REVEALING OF THE RISEN ONE

The basic definition of a theological concept of the resurrection of Jesus as primal miracle appears to justify dispensing with any further reflection on the resurrection event. The concept of 'primal miracle' alters fundamentally the theological outlook, which has often concentrated only on the problem of the appearances of the Risen One. Thus the statements of dialectical theology on the resurrection find it possible to relinquish any relation to the sphere of history and to disregard any special concreteness of content. However great may be the importance of this fundamental insight—that the resurrection of Jesus is not to be

[9] Cf. W. Künneth, *Das Wunder als apologetisch-theologisches Problem*, Gütersloh 1931.

identified with the appearances of Jesus—yet it must not become a reason for setting aside the detailed problems of the resurrection as partly insoluble and partly of no consequence. Such evasion of the special questions posed by the resurrection of Jesus is supported neither by the 'substance' of the resurrection itself nor by the witness to the resurrection.

The recognition of the resurrection as primal miracle implies at the same time also the statement of the *revealing of this new reality of life*. Revelation, however, means the disclosure within the concrete realm of history of that which was not previously present and knowable. If there is a revealing of the Risen One, an emerging of the new resurrection reality from its state of hiddenness, then the primal miracle of the resurrection has also a face towards history. This reflection in history of the resurrection reality is not the 'substance' of the resurrection of Jesus itself, but the latter does not exist without the revealing outcome in history. This does not result in a return to the historical approach, but in a clear recognition that the theological understanding of the resurrection of Jesus is dependent on the resurrection witness.

The whole New Testament witness is in full agreement that the reality of the resurrection proves to have a real effect also in the realm of space and time, that the revealing of the Risen One takes place in the 'appearances' and, secondarily, has some connection with the 'empty tomb'. This leads to the abundance of concrete, detailed statements in the earliest Christian tradition,[10] which, although their individual features are certainly not all to be uncritically accepted, nevertheless set an inescapable theological task. The thing is, to understand the ultimate concern of the resurrection witness, expressed as it was precisely also in plastic, concrete form, and to expound it theologically in the light of the concept of the primal miracle of the resurrection. The strict relation to the substantial content provides the safeguard against any shifting of the emphasis from the central fact of the resurrection reality itself to the peripheral and secondary statements about the revealing of it.

(a) The Reality of the 'Appearances'

Dogmatic study cannot avoid the task of making a contribution towards the explanation of the *appearances of the Risen One*. The question is essentially not one of historical criticism and of exegesis, but of dogmatics. Hence it is not a case either of examining how many appearances

[10] Cf. especially Matt. 28.6 and Mark 16.6: 'Come, see the place where he lay', 'Behold the place where they laid him'; John 20.27: 'Behold my hands.'

took place, where, when, and to whom, and what differences there may have been between them. Rather, the important thing is to inquire into the special character of the revealing of the Risen One which is customarily expressed by the word 'appearance'.

(i) *The Problem of the Biblical Analogies*

The decisive question is whether the appearances of the Risen One can be classified among the phenomena of the history of revelation, or whether a proper understanding of them is only obscured by so doing.

The biblical parallels that correspond to the Easter experiences of the disciples would seem to be the prophetic visions in the Spirit, the 'experience of calling, ordination, installation'.[11] The *prophetic vision* of a divine revelation is not to be rated as the product of emotional excitement, but as the emerging of a reality which lays hold of man, and is accompanied at the same time by auditions which communicate new knowledge. Such a theophany is conditioned by the belief that God and heavenly beings can 'show themselves and take a form recognizable to man'.[12] The constitutive concept to describe this is *ōphthē*, i.e. God 'appears', 'shows himself', 'lets himself be seen'. Though to be sure a theophany is only 'possible by God's appearing on earth in disguise, in human form', as 'man' or 'angel', or by his hiding himself in natural phenomena, thunder, storm, earthquake, fire cloud.[13] The human witness to such theophanies moves in the form of pictures, as they were seen in the ecstatic vision, and in relative ritual ideas and tradition-bound language[14]—whereby there is the accompanying note of the indefiniteness and terribleness of what was seen.

When this is recognized, the explanation of the resurrection appearances seems to be that they are analogous to the well known prophetic visions. According to R. Otto, the appearances of the Risen One are an 'experience of the mysterious', a 'mystical experience', an 'experience of the Spirit'.[15] It is possible 'to fit the resurrection experiences clearly into a general class of experiences which we call mystical and spiritual, and of which there are typical repetitions among the other great figures called by God'. Like the prophets before them, especially Ezekiel, the apostles possess a special spiritual faculty which can rise to the *horasis* of the 'secret vision', to the ecstasy of being carried away in mystical

[11] Cf. Isa. 6; Amos 1; Hos. 1; Jer. 1; R. Otto, *Aufsätze, das Numinose betreffend*, p. 162.

[12] Cf. the excellent study by E. Fascher, *Deus invisibilis*, Gotha 1931, p. 69.

[13] E. Fascher, *op. cit.*, pp. 47, 55, 46; and on the LXX version of Gen. 12.7 ('and someone appeared to Abraham'): pp. 45 f.

[14] Cf. *op. cit.*, p. 44.   [15] R. Otto, *op. cit.*, pp. 161 f.

experience. The experience of the appearances represents a 'first break-through of the Spirit', it is 'only a link in the chain of spiritual occurrences'.[16] The vision of the appearances of the Risen One stands side by side with the visionary experiences at the baptism and transfiguration of Jesus and provides a typical special case of the prophetic experiences of God.

This view is strengthened by the themes in the 'resurrection stories', which appear analogous in essential points to the prophetic theophanies. We find with the appearances the themes of fear, doubt, astonishment, the report of the sudden appearing and disappearing of the Risen One,[17] which 'points back to primeval epiphanies where the deity makes itself invisible as quickly as it became visible'.[18] Likewise the 'brilliant light' plays 'an important role, as already in the Old Testament'.[19] Further, as E. Fascher likewise points out, a difference can be seen in the narrative form—on the one hand a naive realism with possibilities of legendary embellishment even so 'intense as to be crudely sensual', on the other hand theological reflection like that of Paul, in which the appearance is 'not described in outward and visible form'.[20] Above all we find in the appearances also the idea of veiling, like that of the Old Testament stories, as the form of revelation suited to men. The Risen One, since he takes the place of God, is not for all to see, nor visible everywhere, and often even for the chosen disciples not to be seen immediately and directly. In place of 'Yahweh walking and eating' appears the Risen Lord. He also bears, precisely in his veiled garb, the marks of the 'pilgrim God'.[21]

Our observations so far have without doubt shown that a formal similarity exists between the events of revelation in the prophets and the appearances of Jesus, and that in regard to thematic form and means of expression the traditions agree at a number of points. To be sure, the recognition of an analogy of this kind does not in itself as yet have an immediate effect on the reality of the resurrection, but we do have to reckon with the possibility of a repercussion on the actual understanding of the resurrection. If the appearances are to be regarded only as a phenomenon belonging to the vast array of revelation events in the spiritual realm, then the unique character of the resurrection of Jesus itself is endangered. If, however, the peculiar character of the resurrection as the primal miracle of God has become plain, then we have rather

---

[16] *Ibid.*, p. 165. [17] Luke 24.31. [18] E. Fascher, *op. cit.*, pp. 67 f.
[19] *Op. cit.*, pp. 69 f., footnote; Acts 9.3; 22.11; 26.13.
[20] *Op. cit.*, pp. 68-9.
[21] Cf. Gen. 18; Luke 24.15 ff.; John 20; E. Fascher, p. 48.

to ask on the contrary whether the same peculiarity must not belong also
to the revealing of the Risen One in the appearances. The seeming parallel between the appearances and spiritual experiences must not deceive
us as to the profound differences, which we have now to examine in detail.

(ii) *The Peculiar Character of the Appearances*

In the first place, an examination of the real state of the New Testament shows that according to the judgment of the earliest Christian
witnesses, the appearances of the Risen One are in no way to be identified with general theophanies, or with visions of angels and experiences
of spiritual ecstasy in Old Testament prophecy. Although the disciples
and the primitive Church knew of spiritual experiences in their circle
and possessed charismatic gifts, they nevertheless distinguished such
happenings sharply from the appearances. Paul experienced ecstatic
raptures[22] and knew himself to be under spiritual guidance[23]; nevertheless he recognizes the qualitative difference between these experiences
and the wholly other, incomparable event of Christ's appearance on the
Damascus road. Here he experiences not ecstasies, not a prophetic
dream with vision and audition, not a mystical spiritual experience, but
a unique encounter with the neither previously nor subsequently experienced reality of the Risen One, which was fundamental for his life.
Accordingly, in the appearance on the Damascus road we have an event
which, while from the empirical standpoint it can certainly be interpreted
as vision and audition, is nevertheless not exhausted by these concepts,
and in its peculiarity cannot be compared with known spiritual states
but on the contrary defies all attempts to classify it.[24] Thus no spiritual
and charismatic experiences of the Church had independent significance
alongside the resurrection event, but all were subordinated to it as to
their foundation.[25]

[22] II Cor. 12.2 f.; Acts 22.17 ff.

[23] I Cor. 14.15; II Cor. 12.9; Acts 16.6 f.; 20.23.

[24] Cf. also Acts 9.10 with the account of the appearance on the Damascus
road and at the same time in contrast to it the vision of Ananias '*en horamati*'.
Cf. also Acts 7.54 ff. Further, Ottfried Kietzig, *Die Bekehrung des Paulus,
religionsgeschichtlich und religionspsychologisch neu untersucht*, Leipzig 1932.

[25] K. Holl, too, states that the primitive Church makes a sharp distinction
between the appearances and other visions: 'That is why the visions of the
martyrs were never recognized as on a par with the appearances to the apostles'
(*Sitzungs-Bericht der Akad. der Wissenschaften* 1921, p. 927). Schlatter, too,
aptly remarks: 'If the disciples had considered their faith in Jesus to be the
product of movements within their own souls, then instead of the Church there
would have been a body of mystics busy creating in themselves the ecstatic state
by means of which the Christ becomes visible also to them' (*Geschichte des
Christus*, pp. 523, 520). It is significant that the definition of the content of the
ōphthē is totally different in the case of the appearances and in the case of the

The peculiar character of the appearances is to be noted in the following detailed points. The uniqueness of the resurrection appearances is most clearly expressed in the identity of the Risen One with the historical and crucified Jesus of Nazareth. The specific and at the same time extraordinary characteristic of the event is, that the disciples recognize in the appearance the Jesus of history in all his concreteness. The Risen One is neither a phantasy, nor a theophany, but the appearance of a new, living mode of existence. The appearance expresses the connection between life beyond death and life within history. That is why the Risen One stands before the disciples as the one who bears the marks of his wounds[26] and whose words and actions remind them of their earlier fellowship with him[27]—and why in the short span of his revealing appearances[28] he grants them a peculiar relation to himself, that they may know the reality of his new life. The Risen One is in fact precisely *not* God himself in some kind of disguise, but Jesus of Nazareth, raised and exalted by God. With that, all the decisive presuppositions for any identifying of the appearances with prophetic revelations or spiritual visions fall to the ground. The concreteness of the appearances in their relatedness to history made any confusion with Old Testament theophanies impossible.[29]

Secondly, in the appearances we have to do not with a typical prophetic experience of the divine, but with a once-for-all experience which has no analogy either before or after. The spiritual visions of the prophets could be repeated any number of times before and during their ministries. The resurrection appearances have the character of strict once-for-allness, so that the apostles never afterwards expected nor experienced a similar event, even though visions occurred also in their later life.

Further, it is to be noted that for the apostles not only the fact, but also the character and content of the resurrection appearances was of decisive importance. For the prophetic task, it was in itself a matter of indifference in what way God attested himself to the bearers of this calling. For that reason the prophets also received the divine commission in varied forms. The vision by which they are called is certainly the first cause of their prophesying, yet their spiritual experience is not

---

other biblical narratives in which this term is found. Hence E. Fascher also says emphatically, 'The appearances of the Risen One are certainly of a different kind and have a totally different purpose' (*op. cit.*, p. 48).

[26] Cf. E. Fascher, *op. cit.*, p. 55: God appears 'on the scene as if he were a well known "historically human" person'.

[27] Luke 24.39 ff.; John 20.27.

[28] Luke 24.30 f.; John 21.6 f., 12 ff.   [29] Acts 1.2.

by any means the central content of their preaching. However important
the spiritual experiences may have been for them personally, they could
be silent about them, so long as they carried out God's command. In
contrast, the one thing that is characteristic of the resurrection message
is, that the revealing of the Risen One in the appearances not only
became the outward cause of their mission, but was at the same time
the foundation on which the substance of the Easter witness was based.
The witnesses of the resurrection appearances all undergo the same
explicit experience that the crucified and dead Jesus encounters them
as the living Lord. This absolutely new fact was not a matter of subjective experiences of accidental importance, but rather had perforce
to become the centre of their proclamation.

(iii) *The Significance of the Appearances*

Connected with the peculiarity of the appearances is the question
what special meaning attaches to this event. The investigation so far
has shown that to understand it in terms of spiritual prophetic vision is
out of place, denies its uniqueness, and at the same time is a projection
onto the plane of religious history. The reality of the appearances of the
Risen One is therefore to be understood as in a category by itself. Like
the primal miracle of the resurrection, the revealing of this new reality
of life in the appearances can also only be understood as an event *sui
generis*, without analogy and without parallel. The concept 'appearance'
stands on its own and can be applied in this special sense only to the
revealing of the Risen One.

The essential significance of the appearances is to be seen as twofold.
Firstly, in the appearances the reality of the resurrection of Jesus reveals
itself. In them Jesus shows himself as the Christ and the Exalted Lord
—which, however, means in a new mode of existence. The appearances
are, as has already been said, not the primal miracle of the resurrection
itself but the revealing of it. What the Risen One reveals in the appearances is his new life, which can always only be revealed in veiled form
to the disciples who still stand this side of death and within the dimension of history. The appearances of the Risen One therefore do not mean
for the disciples an emerging of the reality of the new existence direct,
but a revealing of it in a form appropriate to the history-bound situation
of the disciples. We must therefore *differentiate between the reality of the
resurrection as such and its 'appearance', as also on the other hand between
an unmediated, full revelation, for which the disciples still wait, and a
fragmentary revealing in veiled form which they received in the appearances.*

The concept *ōphthē* means: the Risen One lets himself be seen, so that this statement implies that the 'showing of himself' takes place only on the scale which the revealing makes necessary. Consequently, the question 'how' the appearances took place is unanswerable, just as a detailed portrayal of the events remains out of the question. The whole primitive Christian witness to the appearances has therefore in the nature of the case a fluctuating character. It witnesses to the fact of the new Christ life, but is not in a position to comprehend adequately the detailed characteristics of this reality which transcends its powers of representation. The concept 'appearance of the Risen One' thus means a boundary statement, which on the one hand expresses the revealing of the resurrection life of Jesus, and on the other hand merely points to the newness of this life as a mean between the mutually exclusive dimensions of death and life.[30]

This recognition that the appearances present a reality which stands on the boundary between the immanent world and the resurrection world of God and therefore allows no unbroken description of the reality here appearing, does not, however, require us to renounce making any statement about the appearances at all. The thing is rather, to pay due regard to the peculiar character of the witnesses' reports and to develop their boundary statements in the direction of the primal miracle of the resurrection which they reveal. The appearances mark as it were the point at which the reality of the resurrection opens itself towards history. Hence in their own reality we can recognize the same basic characteristics as in the primal miracle of the resurrection itself.

The decisive statement is: '*The Risen One reveals in the appearances his glorified existence.*' Constitutive for the *concept of existence*, however, is the idea of *corporeality*. Thus the appearance of the Risen One becomes a revealing of the corporeal reality of the new life. The old dispute as to whether we are to speak of a resurrection simply as such, or of a bodily resurrection, is to be dismissed as a false antithesis. The reality of the resurrection means indeed in particular also the refashioning of concrete corporeal being, so that a consequence of this must also be found in the appearances. That is why in the appearances we have always a recognition of the new corporeality of the Risen One, which as such

---

[30] Cf. the dispute between Ihmels and T. Häring, *ZTK* 1923, p. 46; *ZTK* 1889, pp. 331 ff., 468; 1898, pp. 129 ff.; further, Häring together with M. Reischle, *Festschrift für Bonwetsch*, 1917, pp. 120 ff.; L. Ihmels, *Festschrift für Häring*, 1918, 'Zur Frage der Auferstehung Jesu'. In addition, J. Wellhausen, *Kritische Analyse der Apostelgeschichte*, Berlin 1914, p. 17; E. Fascher, 'Die Auferstehung Jesu und ihr Verhältnis zur urchristlichen Verkündigung', *ZNW* 1927, pp. 1-26.

points precisely to the realness of his new being. The 'glorified character' of the risen Christ marks the complete otherness and newness of
his bodily mode of existence. This constitutes at the same time also a
clear repudiation both of all false spiritualizing views and also of any
kind of materializing.[31]

The statements of the witnesses are obviously vitally concerned to
confirm the undoubted reality of the appearances as it expresses itself
most unequivocally in corporeal existence. Pointing out the corporeality
of the Risen One makes it impossible to spiritualize the event till it
evaporates into a psychical phenomenon or a spiritual experience.
Emphasis is laid on the fact that the one who appears has a real body,
which can be handled, which is apprehensible in space,[32] that he bears
the marks of the wounds, that he can be said to eat and drink and walk
about. This way of speaking of the appearances with downright four-
square realism springs not from poetic fantasy nor the tendency to
legendary embellishment, but from the most intrinsic and necessary
interest in the bodily realness of the Risen One. Though theological
reflection may alter the form in which the appearances are presented, it
must stick to the 'substance' itself and also pay serious attention to the
purpose that underlies the crudely sensual statements of the witnesses.

At the same time, however, the concept of glorified corporeality also
safeguards the event against a physiological and naturalist approach.
The bodily appearance is no proof of the supranatural theory of the
physical, material identity of the resurrection body of Jesus with the
body laid in the tomb. Though the appearances do present a reflection
of the resurrection life in the realm of history, yet they are not spatio-
temporal phenomena in the sense that the appearances could be mater-
ialistically regarded in terms of things and objects.[33] That the glorified
body of Christ who appeared is not to be identified with any resuscitation of a corpse can be learned from the witnesses' depositions as plainly
as that they repudiate any idea of incorporeality. The appearance is not
bound by the limitations of space as an earthly body is, but has a strange
and unapproachable air, and reveals the shining glory of the Risen One.[34]

[31] T. Häring rightly avers that the task is 'to preserve' the resurrection of
Jesus 'on the one hand from being emptied and on the other from being
coarsened' (*ZTK* 1923, p. 46).   [32] John 20; Luke 24.36 ff.
[33] The transience of the *koilia*, I Cor. 6.12-20. R. Frank likewise rejects the
idea of a material identity, *System der christl. Wahrheit* II, pp. 478 f. On the
other hand we find in Quenstedt and Hollaz the typical expression of naturalistic
error: the resurrection of Jesus is '*reproductio sive reparatio* of precisely the
same body as was destroyed by death, *ex atomis seu particulis illius corporis hinc
inde disiectis atque dissipatis*' (Schmidt, *Bekenntnisschriften*[5], pp. 383 f.).
[34] Luke 24.16, 31, 36; John 20.14, 17, 19; Acts 9.3; John 20.28. According to

The Risen One appears in the glorified form of an inconceivable corporeality, in which a new and wholly other reality is proleptically revealed.[35]

Every statement about the glorified mode of existence of the Risen One as it emerges in the appearances finds itself determined by this double-edged verdict which cannot be resolved. Hence, too, the twin verdicts do not supply any explanation of the appearances, but an appropriate description of their significance.

The second factor which illuminates the meaning of the appearances lies in the restoration of relations of fellowship between the Risen One and the disciples, and, bound up with that, in the *founding of the apostolate*. Not only did the death of Jesus bring a break in the earlier words and commissions of Jesus to his disciples, but also the behaviour of the disciples themselves at the time of his passion had called in question their fellowship with Jesus. Betrayal, denial, and weakness formed a searing burden of guilt upon the whole circle of disciples. Only the appearances of the Risen One precisely to these guilty disciples bridged the gap, and were already in themselves an expression to the disciples of their being forgiven.[36] Therefore it was necessarily of central importance to the disciples to take part in these appearances. For them, they meant not only the revelation of his life, but also the making possible and establishing of new fellowship with him. For the primitive Christian consciousness the witnesses' report that they had 'seen' the appearance of the Risen One and 'heard' his words, was in fact decisive. According to the New Testament tradition it is a case of the reality of repeated appearances to individual disciples and to a larger circle of disciples during a definite period which comes to a close with a specially impressive appearance, the ascension, while the Damascus road appearance is a special case.[37]

---

this, the appearances are already a pointer to a *sōma tēs doxēs* (Phil. 3.21) and *sōma pneumatikon* (I Cor. 15.42 ff.). On the problem of the glorified body cf. the detailed examination by Traugott Schmidt in *Der Leib Christi*, 1919, pp. 8 ff.

[35] E. Hirsch avers: 'This miracle does not consist, however, in the fact that now a different life was seen from the one our Lord had on his earthly way, a different life from that of the despised son of man and suffering servant of God' (*Jesus der Herr*, p. 40)—which, although it does rightly emphasize the Risen One's link with concrete history, nevertheless overlooks precisely the fact of his glorification.

[36] Significant and understandable in this context is the general testimony to a first appearance of Jesus precisely to Peter: Luke 24.34; I Cor. 15.5.

[37] It is a fact whose full significance must not be overlooked that the apostles, and especially Paul, in order to confirm the truth of their proclamation, sometimes in dispute with opponents and critics, speak of their having been witnesses of the appearances, e.g., Acts 1.2 f.; 10.41; 13.31; (9.3 f.); 22.6 f.; 26.13 f.;

This general significance of the appearances for the disciples is deepened, however, by the fact that these events form the basis for the rise of the missionary consciousness of the apostles. *The primitive Christian apostolate does not stand in dependence on the historical sending out of the disciples by the Rabbi of Nazareth but is founded by the appearance of the Risen One.* The characteristic mark of the apostle was recognized to be that he had been witness of an appearance (Acts 1.22).[38] Paul, too, proves the validity of his apostleship, which is neither historically determined nor self-chosen, by pointing out that he had seen an appearance of the Lord (I Cor. 9.1).[39] The appointment to the office of messenger and the sending out of the messengers have their foundation in the resurrection appearances, in that on the one hand the Risen One renews and confirms the apostolic status of his disciples and on the other hand gives it a completely new ground. With that, the Risen One's own statements during the appearances acquire special importance.[40] Insep-

Gal. 1.16. The conscientious listing of the valid groups of witnesses is therefore a matter of course.

Cf. I Cor. 15.3 f. This primitive apostolic confession is also in Harnack's view 'the oldest tradition that we have concerning the conclusion of Jesus' life'. He also says 'the text is sound'. Harnack distinguishes different groups of tradition: 1. the main witness of Peter and the apostles, 2. the witness of the appearance to 'more than five hundred brethren in Jerusalem', 3. the double witness of James and his people, which would mean that the twelve apostles are identical with 'all the apostles', 4. the witness of Paul himself (*Sitzungsbericht der Pr. Akademie der Wissenschaften*, 1922, pp. 62 ff.).

In the same way K. Holl emphasizes 'the documentary significance' of I Cor. 15.3 ff. He notes that this passage brings only *the* appearances 'which the Christian Church regards as basic or as essential'. For Paul, however, according to the view of the Jews and of antiquity, the appearances to women are not regarded as conclusive testimony. (*Sitzungsbericht Pr. A. d. W.*, 1921, pp. 922 ff.)

On the question of the 'Ascension' of Jesus it has to be added that it does not by any means mark the end of Jesus' renewed sojourn upon earth for a period of forty days after the resurrection—which would be a complete misunderstanding not merely of the character of the appearances, but also of the resurrection event itself. The 'ascension' is to be understood only when it is given a place within the revelation of the appearances as a whole and in subordination to it, and is not to be assessed as a saving event parallel to the resurrection. It is the last, specially significant appearance of the Risen One.

[38] To be an apostle, it was necessary to belong to the circle of which Peter says, 'we, who did eat and drink with him after he rose from the dead', Acts 10.41.

[39] Paul sees the *diakonia* (Acts 20.24) and the *apostolē* to world mission (Rom. 1.5; Gal. 1.1) as received directly from the Christ who has risen and appeared to him. Accordingly he knows himself to be an ambassador, a *leitourgos*, a *doulos* of the Lord (Rom. 15.16; Gal. 1.10 f.).

[40] Matt. 28.18 ff.; Luke 24.46 ff. Cf. R. Seeberg, *Dogmatik* II, pp. 207 ff.; 'Evangelium quadraginta dierum', *NKZ* 1905; *Der Ursprung des Christenglaubens*, 1914. Schlatter also strongly emphasizes this: 'In the intercourse of the Risen One with his disciples his *own statement* seems to be the great and important thing which the whole incident serves'; 'incidentally the suggestion that the words of the Easter story could or must only have come from a later age is worthless. Certain is, that there was never an Easter story without Easter

arably bound up with the revealing of the risen corporeality of Jesus in the appearances is a special verbal revelation in which Jesus himself announces his resurrection and exaltation, addresses words of comfort and exhortation to his disciples, calls them anew and gives them new instructions, has conversations with them which on the one hand link up with earlier events and discoveries and on the other hand convey new insights into God's plan of salvation, and promises to impart the power of the Spirit.[41] *The appearances place the apostles in a unique situation in the story of salvation, because of their nearness to these events— a situation that was unattainable to other men of their own day or of later ages.* Thus in the end the criterion of what is 'apostolic', and thereby of what is 'evangelical', becomes identical with the fact of being directly determined by the reality of the appearances.[42]

(b) The Question of the 'Empty Tomb'

The concept of the resurrection of Jesus as a reality of life newly founded by God in Christ does not include *the question of the empty tomb*. Rather, the recognition of it as a non-immanent factor appears to stand in direct opposition to the ideas usually associated with the empty tomb. In itself it could be that the whole problem of the empty tomb with its most varied critical historical controversies is a false trail, in that here the accent is laid on a point in history which does not have theological interest at all. On theological principles it would be conceivable to dispense with the discussion of this question, if it could be done without prejudice to the reality of the resurrection and the witness to it. But the thing that causes systematic reflection to deal with the question of the empty tomb has its basis, despite all considerations of principle, in the statements of the primitive Christian witness. The facts of the case— that all the gospel reports attest the empty tomb, and that this report is inseparably bound up with the message of the resurrection and as specific 'Easter Gospel' is rooted in the faith of the primitive Church—

---

words—a story that described Jesus as a dumb shadow like a ghost that cannot speak' (*Die Geschichte des Christus*, p. 534). Also the examination by C. Stange, 'Das letzte Wort des Auferstandenen', *Zeitschr. f. syst. Theol.* 1931-2, part 4, p. 637.

[41] Cf. E. Schlink, *Der Erhöhte spricht*, 1948, pp. 49 ff.

[42] K. Holl, too, points out that what is 'apostolic' is characterized by the fact that the disciples were sent by the Risen One to bring to the world 'the resurrection as the crowning of his Gospel'. 'Something similar to what is recounted in Matt. 28.19 and Acts 1.8 must in actual fact once have taken place, an appearance with a formal command by Jesus' (*Sitzungsbericht d. A. d. W.*, 1921, p. 931). Likewise the special apostolic authority of Peter and James in the primitive Church is grounded in the appearance of the Lord granted specially to them (I Cor. 15.5, 7). Cf. their 'position as pillars', Gal. 2.9.

require serious theological consideration.[43] A message of the resurrection of Jesus without news of the empty tomb does not exist at all events in the tradition of the primitive Church, and is a theological abstraction.

Although there are thus objections to eliminating the question of the empty tomb, the attempt has been made, and is not yet abandoned even today, to avoid the material problem by opposing the Pauline accounts to the Gospel tradition. Thus E. Brunner declares that Paul makes no mention of the empty tomb: 'None of the Epistles mentions it. . . . Does Paul, do the earliest apostles, whose witness has come down to us only in fragments, mean the same as what is told in the Gospel records we have today?. . . Can we so easily pass over the plain fact that Paul reckons his encounter with the Risen One, which is quite different from those depicted in the Gospels, to be identical with those of the original apostles, and that it is accepted by them as such?. . . Was the resurrection witness of the original apostles and of the "five hundred brethren" perhaps more like that of Paul than like what is now reported in the Gospels?'[44] This raises the much discussed question of the contradiction between the view of Paul and the first apostles on the one hand and the Gospel records on the other.[45] Even if we feel that the critical historical approach, radically in need of revision though it is, must be due some concessions, if we reckon with the possibility that 'imaginative embellishment' took control of the resurrection story already at an early stage,[46] and if we believe we can detect the 'intrusion of legendary and apologetic motives'[47]—even then it is extremely difficult to see how the Gospel accounts of the resurrection could arise in opposition to the original apostolic preaching and that of Paul. Critical historical analysis and construction offer no satisfying solution to the question of the differences, but only deepen the problem. The authority of the apostolic eye-witnesses was extraordinarily strong. It would be inconceivable how

[43] It may be that the other evangelists have taken over the original Markan account of the empty tomb and that 'alongside the Jerusalem tradition, which in itself can be very ancient and dependable, there existed also another tradition' which took its rise 'far from the tomb of Jesus' in Galilee; certain is, that in the primitive Christian Easter tradition the empty tomb does play a role. Even if like H. Sasse we feel it must be conceded that the Gospels show 'an unmistakable tendency to connect the appearances more and more with the tomb of Jesus', the decisive question still remains open, how far an essential concern of the primitive Christian Church is expressed precisely in this tendency. Cf. H. Sasse, 'Jesus Christus der Herr', in *Mysterium Christi*, 1931, pp. 121 f.

[44] *Der Mittler*, pp. 524 f. (ET, pp. 576 f.).

[45] According to the church tradition about the resurrection event handed down by Paul in I Cor. 15.1 ff., a difference between the experience of Paul and of the original apostles seems impossible.

[46] Thus E. Brunner, *op. cit.*, p. 524 (ET, p. 576).

[47] Cf. H. Sasse, *op. cit.*, p. 121.

there should have arisen in opposition to the authoritative witness of the original apostles a harmonious tradition telling of an event that has no basis in the message of the eye-witnesses. The interest of the primitive Church surely centred solely on handing on the witness of the apostles as unspoiled as possible, and most especially the witness to the resurrection of Jesus which was of such decisive importance. Here the very details of the account were of priceless worth and invention by the Church contrary to the apostolic witness had no place among the Church's interests, nor could it have failed to be sharply contradicted by the apostles or their pupils. Must we not rather in face of these critical objections reckon precisely on the contrary with the possibility that the various pieces of witness are essentially the same in kind? Could it not be that Paul and the original apostles mean the same as the Gospel accounts, even when they do not tell the story so colourfully as the latter? The 'fact' of the difference is still unproven, or at least cannot be proved from the silence of the apostles.

It appears indeed to be as good as certain that the account of the empty tomb was definitely included in the apostolic tradition, and that it is therefore completely impossible to speak of any silence of the apostles on the matter. Paul asserts both that 'he died' and that 'he was buried', and expressly affirms his agreement with these statements.[48] Hence according to the apostolic tradition the resurrection of Jesus can hardly have been thought of otherwise than as being raised from the tomb, and the statement of the empty tomb must have been indirectly included already in that tradition. This conclusion is strengthened by the symbolic interpretation of baptism as being buried and rising again, whereby significance attaches precisely to the burial as a precondition of the latter[49]; and it is likewise strengthened by the parallel between the raising of men and the resurrection of Jesus, which again suggests the thought of a resurrection from the tomb.

Attention must also be paid to the examination of the Jewish and biblical ideas about death and resurrection, which cannot have been without influence on the composition of the apostolic tradition. In contrast to the spiritualizing character of hellenistic thinking, for which the notion of the empty tomb must have been inconceivable, the Judaic thought-world appears to be chiefly materialistic and concretely historic.[50]

---

[48] I Cor. 15.4. Cf. also the exposition of I Cor. 15 by H. D. Wendland in *Die Briefe an die Korinther*, Göttingen 1932, pp. 78 ff.   [49] Rom. 6.3 ff.

[50] Noteworthy is the verdict of H. S. Chamberlain, *Die Grundlagen des 19. Jahrhunderts* I, pp. 436 ff.; E. Brunner, *op. cit.*, pp. 514, 518, 520, 527 (ET, pp. 566 f., 570 f., 572, 580).

According to it, the future resurrection of the dead was not conceivable at all except as a bringing to life of the dead bones laid in the tomb, and thus in crassly realistic terms.[51] From this point of view, no matter whether it be theologically acceptable or not, Paul's statements on the resurrection necessarily move into the neighbourhood of the Gospel presentations.[52] The postulation of a Greek influence on the

[51] Cf. Ezek. 37. K. Barth, *Die Auferstehung der Toten*, pp. 65 ff., 56 f., 114: 'A soul living on after death—that is a thing it is at least wonderfully easy to assert without disturbing a unified world-picture. . . . Resurrection of the body, however . . . is obviously a merciless destroying of that unity, is offensive and irrational and religious materialism' (ET, pp. 120 ff., 105 f., 201, esp. 123 f.).

[52] Cf. for this point the observations of K. Bornhäuser in his study, to which theology has paid too little attention, *Die Gebeine der Toten*, Gütersloh 1921. Bornhäuser thoroughly examines the views on the resurrection of the dead at the time of the New Testament, and comes to conclusions which are of the highest significance for the understanding of the resurrection accounts and the resurrection faith of the primitive Church, including Paul. Starting from the view that the grave is 'the place of the wasting of the body and the storing and preserving of the bones', which are not consumed in the grave but 'continue', he says that accordingly in the resurrection we have to do with 'a resurrecting of the bones'. Resurrecting of the bones then means 'restoring of the whole man'. 'Under the continuing influence of the rationalism of the Enlightenment we repeatedly forget, or at least do not pay sufficient attention to, the fact that for the Jews the perfected man lives on the *new* earth.' 'The view of the continuing of the bones in the grave is not, however, the necessary presupposition of any possible perfecting. The Jew, too, knows that the hope of resurrection is not tied to that, but affirms the power of God to raise man even without the bones being present', as is suggested above all by the story of the martyrs. Jesus' view corresponds to that of the Pharisees. He does not dispute 'that the bones continue in the grave and that that gives a starting point for the resurrection', but he specially emphasizes that our being raised is totally independent of the fate of the dead bones. 'Without disputing their significance for the resurrection where they still exist, the sole ground and possibility of being raised is found to be in "the power of God".' The same is true of Paul's teaching on resurrection. Bornhäuser aptly observes: 'It should never have come to the point that in spite of the *etaphē*, "he was buried", of I Cor. 15.3 f. the phrase "he was raised again the third day" was understood in any other way than as raising from the tomb.' Accordingly the saying, 'Flesh and blood cannot inherit the kingdom of God' (v. 50) must also be ascribed a different meaning from the accepted one. 'There are not many verses on which more false comments have been written than this one.' Paul is thinking 'as a Pharisee entirely realistically of the fact that flesh and blood in actual fact decay in the grave'. Thus here, too, it is a case 'of a resurrecting of the bones', 'which by a creative act of God are clothed again with flesh and blood'. We can speak of a resurrection of the body, 'only we must not connect this with the idea that the body of the man who is raised is formed precisely from *the* dust which it turned into when it decayed' (cf. pp. 9, 20, 26 ff., 31, 33, 36-7). Cf. also K. Bornhäuser, *Das Wirken des Christus*, pp. 251 ff. However critical we may be of these statements in detail, as for example Althaus is (*Wahrheit des kirchl. Osterglaubens*, 1940, note 27), at all events they give proof of a unified attitude on the part of the primitive Church.

In the light of Bornhäuser's examination the conclusions in regard to the resurrection of Jesus appear to be as follows: 1. The raising of Jesus can have been thought of by Paul and by the whole primitive Church only as a bodily one. 2. Consequently the conviction of the empty tomb of Jesus becomes as a matter of course an element in faith in the resurrection of Jesus. 3. The fact of the empty tomb as such, however, does not have any power to prove the resurrec-

Pauline world of ideas also breaks down on the fact of Paul's complete agreement with the original apostles on the question of the resurrection, and cannot prove a difference between him and the Gospels. In view of all this, it appears hazardous to maintain the thesis of a contradiction between the apostolic and the Gospel tradition; at all events, an unequivocal proof that the report about the empty tomb is foreign to the apostles is absolutely impossible. On the contrary, a number of notable features create the impression that the views of the apostles and the Gospels on the question of the empty tomb are homogeneous in content. 'Only an uncritical critic can today still describe the news of the empty tomb as legendary. All the historical evidence and critical consideration of the sources favours the conclusion that the tomb of Jesus was empty on Easter morning.'[53] The apostles do not speak expressly of the empty tomb, not because they know nothing of it or because they deny the fact of it, but because in the context of the reality of the resurrection the empty tomb was for them as for the whole Jewish and Christian world a matter of course, without this fact being the ground of their faith.[54]

If the content of the whole Easter witness is to be seen along these lines, then it will no longer do to speak 'vaguely and obscurely' about it, as Albert Schweitzer rightly accuses theology of doing.[55] *The dogmatic theologian of all people must not give the appearance of wanting to pass*

---

tion, since the latter in itself is wholly independent of any substratum of a material kind, so that Paul, too, like the rest of the New Testament, does not adduce the fact of the empty tomb as a specific argument.

[53] Cf. E. Stauffer, *Entmythologisierung oder Realtheologie*, p. 20.

[54] Cf. H. J. Holtzmann, 'Das leere Grab und die gegenwärtigen Verhandlungen über die Auferstehung Jesu', *Theol. Rundschau* 1906 (9), pp. 79-86, 119-132. Also R. Seeberg, *Dogmatik* II, p. 205.

In this context we must refer to E. Bickermann's study on 'the empty tomb' in the light of the Markan account: *ZNW* 1924, pp. 281-292. Bickermann sets out from a fundamental distinction between the structure of a story of translation and that of a story of resurrection. The proof of the translation is given by establishing the disappearance of the corpse, or by the empty tomb, without any sort of reflection on the reality of the death, whereas the proof of a resurrection is possible only through the appearing of the resuscitated one, of his being there again, whereby the empty tomb remains of no significance for the resurrection. The result of applying this religious-historical theory to the Markan account is the assertion that in Mark we have the combination of two series of motifs. First the older translation legend, the story of the tomb, and second the hellenistic idea of resurrection. This mystery faith, it is alleged, gradually transformed the old view of the primitive Church. It is hardly possible to agree with this questionable theory.

[55] *Geschichte der Leben-Jesu-Forschung*, p. 630. The double judgment of E. Brunner is also unsatisfactory and not in accordance with the existing facts: 'We shall have to content ourselves with the fact that there is no unequivocal answer for us to the question what happened then. . . . Just as little can we take the responsibility of asserting that the first apostles, when they witnessed to the Risen One, certainly did not mean what the gospel accounts have transmitted to us': *Der Mittler*, p. 525 (ET, p. 578).

over what is perhaps a painful question without making clear where he stands. The thing is, to examine what theological character belongs to the statement on the empty tomb, and what is its relation to the primal miracle of the resurrection.

The theological understanding of the empty tomb is often made more difficult by the false approach to the question, which sets out from the possibility of proving the resurrection of Jesus from this fact. Thus on the one hand supranaturalism has claimed the empty tomb as the surest support for belief in the resurrection, while in reaction to this view the newer theology has not only denied that it has the character of proof but has at the same time rejected any consideration of its possible significance. The report of the empty tomb no more proves the resurrection than do the appearances of the Risen One.[56] We are not here concerned at all with the question whether the empty tomb in itself would already have provided sufficient ground for the assurance of the resurrection of Jesus, but with the problem whether this primitive Christian report has theological significance, and if so, what significance.[57] The primitive Christian declaration, 'the tomb of Jesus is empty', must also be seen from the standpoint of the revealing of the Risen One. This, it is true, takes place decisively in the appearances, yet also in the outwardly visible and ascertainable result of the empty tomb. The bare fact of this spatially ascertainable result does not permit us to argue back from it to the character, content and significance of the event that stands behind it; it is not a proof, but a pointer to something which is yet to encounter the disciples. The empty tomb becomes a sign set up by God, which waits for its interpretation; as such it is an open question which only receives its valid answer in the appearances of the Risen One. This explains why the empty tomb cannot by any means be the basis and point of the resurrection witness, and why it recedes into the background in the apostolic preaching whereas the appearances stand in the foreground. These, however, lead back illuminatingly to the empty tomb, in that it is from them that this fact receives its interpretation. The empty tomb's character as sign and pointer is significant as a means of creating an openness for the resurrection message and

---

[56] See the following section, 3*a*.

[57] Cf. E. Brunner, *op. cit.*, pp. 523 f. (ET, p. 576); W. Michaelis, *Täufer, Jesus, Urgemeinde*, 1928, pp. 116 f. Thus Michaelis' view too—that 'the empty tomb is only a secondary proof compared with the appearances', that it is 'hardly a fully valid cause for the rise of the assurance of the resurrection', that 'the tradition of the empty tomb as a proof' is 'wholly secondary'—misses precisely the essential point. A gradation into primary and secondary degrees of proof is impossible, since the question of proof is not to be raised at all.

preparing the way for understanding the revelation of the resurrection.

In itself there is no identity between the empty tomb and the primal miracle of the resurrection of Jesus. The idea of *creatio ex nihilo* is valid in principle here also. But the theological reflection required of us has not to speculate on the possibility of what in itself may be: it has to attempt to grasp the proper meaning of the primitive Christian message, which is aware of a connection between the resurrection of Jesus and the empty tomb. As little as God's work of creation is bound to any immanent substratum, as little can we speak of the impossibility of including these elements in the reshaping of being. Precisely the absolute freedom of the creative power of God is able to include in the primal miracle of the resurrection of Jesus also the material elements of the transitory world. The acceptance of the empty tomb is to be theologically understood ultimately on the principle of *infinitum capax finiti*, which rules out any dualistic metaphysical separation of time and eternity and recognizes precisely in the resurrection of Jesus the ending of the temporal, which has been penetrated anew, fulfilled and consummated by God. Accordingly, the empty tomb as a spatio-temporal datum is a symptom of the power exercised in the immanent world by the reality of the resurrection.

Finally, the meaning of the empty tomb is given as an expression of the concrete, bodily reality of the resurrection of Jesus. It is true that the resurrection of Jesus implies a wholly new corporeality, yet at the same time also a corporeal existence which is inwardly and essentially connected with the historic concreteness of life. This, the resurrection's face towards history, is expressed by the empty tomb. It establishes on the one hand the genuineness of the death in the domination of man by the tomb, and on the other hand correspondingly, the genuineness of the life in the freeing of the body from the tomb. The empty tomb thus becomes the strongest expression of the Easter message's concern with the concrete, bodily resurrection, and at the same time the clear safeguard against every spiritualizing tendency to evaporate the central declarations of the resurrection. To that extent it is by no means a matter of indifference whether theology takes the empty tomb seriously. There is hardly another point at which the Platonizing of theology shows itself more clearly than precisely on this question. For a theologian to take offence at the report of the empty tomb is therefore a mark of the ultimate motives and principles of his basic theological outlook.[58]

[58] Cf. C. Stange, *Die Wahrheit des Christusglaubens*, p. 39: 'For Christian faith

3. THE KNOWLEDGE OF THE RESURRECTION OF JESUS

All that has been said so far about the reality of the resurrection and the revealing of it in history is valid only on the presupposition that it is grounded in the act of faith. This raises *the problem of the relation between the revelation of the resurrection and faith*, i.e. in particular the question of the knowledge of the resurrection of Jesus.

(a) The Believing Situation

If the primal miracle of the resurrection of Jesus is to be understood as non-objective transcendence, which must not by any means be identified with the appearances of the Risen One, then the medium for the revealing of this reality can only be the kerygma. This proclamation which reveals the resurrection can take place in two forms: first, in the form of communicative proclamation of the word, and second, in the form of visible testimony. The relation between these different revelatory forms of the proclamation of the resurrection and faith requires closer examination.

It appears significant, although often too little attention is paid to the point, that the revealing of the resurrection reality takes place decisively through the *proclamation of the word*. Awareness of a resurrection life beyond the world of objectivity exists only when something is said about it. *The word of the resurrection of Jesus is primarily the message which gives information about this reality.*[59] Through the word a non-objective relation is established between the resurrection miracle and the hearer, and the latter is thereby placed in the situation of belief, or unbelief as the case may be. Only through this proclamation is it possible to adopt the attitude of belief as assent to the primal miracle of God and of unbelief as the denial of this event. Although the Risen One reveals himself in the word, it becomes a means of revelation only for the believer, while for the unbeliever it must have the character of an offence. The revelatory word of the resurrection thus rules out any merely neutral attitude and constitutes as its necessary correlate either the believing situation or the contradiction of unbelief. A knowledge of the

---

in the resurrection precisely this is a vital element, that the Lord did not remain in the tomb, but that his body was raised.' We must refer also to E. Meyer, *Ursprung und Anfänge des Christentums*, vol. III, 1923, who describes the corporeal resurrection of the body that was laid in the tomb as a 'fundamental dogma of Christianity'—a verdict which is doubtless untenable in the sense in which E. Meyer applies it, but which nevertheless acutely perceives the essential otherness of the Christian world-view as distinct from Greek thought.

[59] Cf. the first proclamation of the resurrection of Jesus at the tomb and the subsequent spreading of this message in the circle of the disciples.

resurrection of Jesus is accordingly grounded exclusively in the faith which assents to the word as the bearer of revelation, whereas it is absolutely denied to unbelief.

The relation between the proclamation of the word and faith has to be defined still more closely. On the one hand the word awakens faith, because in the word the Risen One, and therewith the reality of the resurrection itself, encounters the hearer. The communicative proclamation thereby becomes personal address by the Risen One, and the word of the resurrection becomes a claim upon man which cannot be overheard. Faith arises on the ground of this verbally mediated encounter between the 'Thou' of the Risen One and the 'I' of the hearer, through the experience of being overwhelmed in conscience. The uttering and hearing of the word of the resurrection is therefore an essentially existential event, which both calls in question the existence of man and also founds it anew in his awakening to faith. Faith is thus to be understood as an act of the Risen One in man, which will be experienced by the believer as being absolutely convinced in conscience and unable to do otherwise. On the other hand, however, the revealing character of the word that informs and claims can be understood in turn only on the basis of faith. The attitude of faith becomes an act of man, because it is on him that the assurance of the new dimension of the resurrection dawns. Man is not able to bring about this assurance himself, but it is given to him, without his doing anything, by the presence of the Risen One in the encounter with the word. Faith has essentially the stamp of a reacting element of the resurrection reality itself, so that the man who knows in faith and on the ground of faith is one who stands 'in the resurrection' and can know only as one who at the same time is 'known' by the Risen One. To the miracle of the resurrection there inevitably corresponds the miracle of faith.

The word of the resurrection bears within itself a creative power to be the ground of faith. The actualizing of faith comes only through our being inwardly laid hold of by the Spirit of the Risen One bound up with the word. In a logically insoluble antithesis to this assertion, however, stands the previous statement about the decisive character of the proclamation. The word calls man out from his totally unrelated separation or 'cision' from God's primal miracle and places him in a state of 'de-cision'. In this decision, either the claim of Christ becomes effectual as the gift of life, or man denies that claim and thereby rejects the gift. Man on the point of decision has the possibility of closing his heart to the preaching of the resurrection, i.e. the possibility of unbelief, but at the same time also the possibility of making room for the working of the word. This possibility of opening oneself to the proclamation, however, is not yet to be identified with the possibility of believing. Faith in the resurrection is not man's to command, but is grounded in the freedom of the Christ who proves his effectual working in the word of the resurrection. The knowledge of the resurrection of Jesus which is given in this faith is always in fundamental tension with the verdict of unbelief, which shuts itself off from any understanding of the resurrection. The only source of true knowledge, the existential surrender in the decision of faith, must become an offence from the standpoint of unbelief. Believing knowledge is therefore a knowledge constantly threatened by unbelief, even as all statements about the resurrection of Jesus are determined either by faith or by unbelief.

This shifting of the emphasis to the knowledge of the resurrection as a believing knowledge raises *the question of the relation between this faith-awakening proclamation of the word and the kerygma of the visible attestation in the appearances, and of the relation between the event of the appearances and faith.*

First it has to be noted that theoretically a distinction can be made between the word of the resurrection and the appearances as such, but that in content the two constitute inseparably the inner unity of the same period of revelation of the reality of the resurrection. The word is proclaimed, quite apart from the appearances, to men who have had no experience of an appearance; but in content the proclamation of the word is always at the same time essentially connected with the appearances. There is no proclamation of the resurrection which does not at the same time either point to the appearances or presuppose them. There can therefore be no talk of any abandoning of the reality of the appearances in favour of a general proclamation of the word of the resurrection. The decisive thing however is, that the appearance itself is not a dumb event, but precisely as a revealing of the Risen One it is an encounter that speaks. Thus there is no resurrection appearance which does not have proclamation bound up with it. It is only through the accompanying word, as the factor appropriately interpreting the event, that the appearance becomes completely the kerygma in which the Risen One reveals himself. Unless the appearance is interpreted by the revealing word, it would become a silent phenomenon subject to arbitrary subjective interpretation and indistinguishable from the vague realm of mystical experience. The appearance becomes true revelation through the clear-minded words of address by the Risen One. Thus the appearance bears the character of a *verbum visibile* and is so to speak the incarnating of the kerygma of the resurrection.

If, however, the appearance is the word of the resurrection become visible, then that also determines the relation between appearance and faith and answers the question of the knowledge of the Risen One. Two misunderstandings have to be guarded against. For the one view, the important thing is to emphasize that the reality of the resurrection involves a real seeing of the Risen One. Knowledge of the Appearer depends on being an eye-witness and not on faith. 'If it is affirmed that here (in the appearances) we have incidents which can be known only by faith, then that is to ascribe to faith a property which it does not possess.'[60] On the other hand, it is maintained conversely that the 'mystery' of the resurrection of Jesus would be completely abolished if the conviction of the resurrection were '*not* faith, but a piece of empirical knowledge'. The resurrection witness of the disciples 'is not that of eye-witnesses, but of faith-witnesses'.[61] Here an empirical seeing of the appearances is contrasted with a believing knowledge independent of the appearances. This antithesis, however, does not do justice to the facts. Both opinions contain a partial truth, but the one ignores the fact that the appearances are bound to the word, while the other fails to see that the word of the resurrection takes corporeal form in the appearances. If the appearances are to be understood as a corporeal word of the Risen One, then the knowledge of them as revelation is given only to the 'seeing' of 'faith'. It is precisely this paradoxical combination that appropriately describes the character of the knowledge of the resurrection where the appearances are concerned. *There is no discrepancy between being an eye-witness and giving the judgment of faith, for the former is made possible by faith, and the latter finds its confirmation or its awakening in the Risen One's becoming visible.*

The appearances are not events which inwardly disinterested, 'objective' observation apart from faith could discern to be a revealing of the Risen One. It is quite true that the 'empty tomb' and the actual appearances as such may be undeniable facts for the unbeliever. Then no doubt they bear for him the mark of the extraordinary, the unusual, the miraculous; but they are not in any way the vehicle of a divine revelation. The unbeliever, to be sure, is ultimately in a position to ascertain that extraordinary events could have happened; but that does

---

[60] Cf. C. Stange, *Zeitschr. für syst. Theol.* 1923-4, part 4, p. 721.
[61] Cf. R. Otto, *Aufsätze, das Numinose betreffend*, pp. 160, 161 f.; E. Brunner, *Der Mittler*, p. 523 (ET, p. 575).

not yet lead him to a knowledge of the resurrection. Those happenings are immanent conditionalities, and as such are open at any time to attempts at empirical explanation, so that even an appearance of Jesus to unbelievers would have given them no proof of the resurrection.[62] Unbelief does not have the knowledge of the appearances at its command; and thus on this basis, too, the question of the bare facts having the power of proof is decided in the negative. Knowledge of the resurrection comes only with the passage from unbelief to faith. Faith does not produce the miracle, but the miracle discloses itself only to faith, which alone can recognize in these events the signs of the primal miracle of the resurrection.

The kerygma of the resurrection of Jesus, both in the form of verbal proclamation and also as expressed in the appearances, is discernible only in the situation of faith. Thus faith becomes the universal and decisive basis for the knowledge of the resurrection. Nevertheless, we must not diminish the *difference between the primary testimony to the resurrection in the* 'verbum visibile' *of the appearances, as the foundation of the original believing knowledge, and the subsequent secondary proclamation of the resurrection* which presupposes that fundamental testimony. It is always only to faith that knowledge is given; but the chosen believers' special nearness to revelation as eye-witnesses is the precondition of all later resurrection faith. This distinction, however, is only a special case of the essential distinction between the bearers of revelation and those who in dependence on them receive the message of revelation. The bracket which holds together both the bearers of revelation (the apostles) and those who come by means of their proclamation to a knowledge of the resurrection of Jesus is faith.

(b) The Theological Significance of Believing Knowledge

To show that the situation of faith alone accords with the reality of

[62] Both the empty tomb and the appearances can be given a purely immanent explanation quite apart from faith in the most varied ways without it being compellingly necessary to accept a miracle. Even an appearance of Jesus to the high priest or Pilate would not have spared them the decision of faith. Their unbelief had perforce to reject also the 'seeing' of the appearances as an illusion. From this standpoint it also becomes understandable why we are told of appearances of the Risen One only to the disciples' circle. A confirmation of the fact that the revelational character of these events manifests itself only to the attitude of faith is supplied also by the appearance on the Damascus road. The appearance as such is for the unbelieving Paul certainly an unheard-of event, but in the first instance not yet a revelation of Christ. His unbelief does not know how to interpret the event properly, and questions arise in his mind. Only when the word of the Risen One reaches him is he faced by the decision of faith. Is this really an appearance of Christ, or a demonic deceit? Only when Paul becomes believing does the appearance reveal itself to him as an encounter with the Risen One.

the resurrection, and that in it alone the possibility of a knowledge of the resurrection of Jesus is given, has far-reaching consequences for epistemological methodology, for the evaluating of the resurrection tradition in the New Testament, and for the task of theology.

If *the knowledge of the resurrection of Jesus* is to be described as *specifically believing knowledge*, then that first of all excludes all attempts to arrive at an understanding of the resurrection that are foreign to faith. Different in kind from the outlook of faith is the effort of metaphysical and philosophical speculation to expound the ideal content of the resurrection witness on the basis of some *a priori* assumption. Inner subjective processes, reflections on mysticism, and consideration of the religious *a priori* within the psychic sphere, do not pass beyond the bounds of the facts and possibilities existing in the immanent world. Philosophical reflection which disregards faith is therefore not able to reach the transcendence of the resurrection, but that is the very thing it is in danger of denying. The same epistemological inadequacy is found in the critical historical approach. On the one hand it is governed by the erroneous assumption that by eliminating the standpoint of faith it can exercise its cognitive functions free of presuppositions, while on the other hand it is concerned to give an impartial account of the historic situation as it was apart from faith. In accordance with these presuppositions, the assertions of the resurrection witness are examined like the statements of a historical document to test their genuineness and validity—and that, too, according to the criteria of historical research and the rules of the historic development of religious ideas. This inevitably leads to the usually convulsive attempts to explain the resurrection of Jesus somehow or other—which, however, means to project it into the objective plane, and to find a place for it within the previously given concepts and ideas and subject to them. Yet if the knowledge of the resurrection is open only to faith, then every method that is detached from faith must in principle lead to failure.[63] Likewise the thesis that the resurrection message is relative, because bound to an outworn cosmology, is also possible only when we ignore the standpoint of faith from which the witness is made. Since faith has precisely *no* eye to the description of the momentary world-picture, and its knowledge is not conditioned by changes in the immanent knowledge of the world-picture, any exclusion of faith as the foundation means the start of a process of

---

[63] Cf. the specifically form-critical examination of the resurrection story, Albertz, *ZNW* 1922, pp. 259-268; L. Brun, *Die Auferstehung des Christus*, 1925; W. Michaelis, 'Himmelfahrtsgeschichte', *Theol. Blätter* 1925, cols. 101-109.

relativizing in accordance with the advance in our knowledge of the world.

To sum up: every discussion of the resurrection of Jesus must become problematical when it begins in abstraction from the knowledge of faith. We have therefore to point out a twofold ground of the problematical character of the resurrection. It is not only properly grounded in the uniqueness of the reality of the resurrection, which cannot be unequivocally expressed in the categories of the objective and constitutes a problem which is theologically warranted, but it likewise has its ground also in the inappropriateness of a basic approach which brackets out the knowledge of faith. The method of abstracting from faith causes an improper, theologically mistaken problematicalness and shuts itself off from the possibility of knowledge.

Believing knowledge marks the structure and content of the whole *New Testament witness to the resurrection*. The fundamental presupposition for an understanding of this tradition is therefore the recognition of its *confessional character*. The tradition speaks of the resurrection of Jesus only in the form of confession, as the expression of a believing decision whose truth must remain totally inaccessible to those who stand outside the range of this confession. The resurrection witness has only one concern: to present its believing knowledge as appropriately as possible. The 'resurrection narratives' are of all things not documents or legal articles, but confessing statements which consciously spring from the faith of the primitive Church and therefore mediate the knowledge of the resurrection as a knowledge conditioned by faith.[64] If we accept the point that they are confession, then that is the end of what in itself is justified from the standpoint of historical science: the distinguishing of the sources according to historical norms. Understood as confession, the narratives as a whole have the validity of a statement of faith: any possible gradation of the sources as of primary or secondary importance finds its criterion not in historical considerations, but in measuring the appropriateness of the content of the confession.[65] Giving

[64] M. Kähler, *Der historische Jesus und der geschichtliche Christus*, p. 45 ('Their witness is already dogmatics'), 4, 108. Similarly also C. Stange, *Zeitschr. für syst. Theol.* 1923-4, part 4, p. 721: 'The situation presented in the Gospels cannot be made comprehensible by purely literary means. In the resurrection of Jesus we have to do with a religious experience'—where to be sure the concept 'religious experience' appears misleading and inappropriate.

[65] H. G. Voigt, *Die ältesten Berichte über die Auferstehung Jesu Christi*, 1906; F. Traub, *Glaube und Geschichte*, 1926; H. E. Weber, *Historisch-kritische Schriftforschung*, 1914, pp. 159 ff. Cf. especially the apt remarks of K. Bornhäuser in *Wirken des Christus*, 1924, p. 251: 'The acceptance or rejection of the resurrection, however, is neither based on scientific deductions nor hindered by them. Neither arises as the result of a "purely scientific process". Nor is it the case that the acceptance of the resurrection of Jesus would *a priori* be an obstacle to

due consideration to the confessional character includes also the possibility of criticism. We have then to ask whether the statement in question adequately expresses the proper sense of the confession and thus of the knowledge of faith, or whether it obscures it.

This recognition that the tradition is determined by considerations of confession and faith also liberates us at the same time from the interminable theological dispute on the significance of the *differences in the resurrection narratives*. Their varied character and manifold form cannot be overlooked. It is found in the statements about the women's purpose in coming to the tomb, about their number and their names, about the time of day, about what happened at the tomb, or in the attitude the disciples are made to adopt to the first news of the resurrection, in the way the picture is painted, and above all in the difference in the place of the appearances—on the one hand in Galilee (Matthew, Luke and John) and on the other in Jerusalem (Luke and John).[66] The fact of a considerable discrepancy in detail is indisputable and can hardly be removed by attempts at harmonizing. The possibility of subjective interference at individual points must be admitted.[67] Now, so long as believing knowledge, which is the over-riding factor determining

---

the right reading of the narratives of the sources. Perhaps . . . the rejection of it is more dangerous still.'

[66] Mention should be made all the same of K. Bornhäuser's hypothesis concerning the name and place 'Galilee'. According to this, 'Galilee' as a place of appearances would be synonymous with the well known gathering place and 'inn' of Galilean pilgrims in the neighbourhood of the Mount of Olives (*Das Wirken des Christus*, p. 257). This attempt at a solution, called an 'apologetic feat' by Althaus, hardly carries conviction. Cf. P. Althaus, *Die Wahrheit des kirchl. Osterglaubens*, note 27.

[67] The attempt to show that the resurrection stories are legendary is possible only on a complete failure to understand the essential character of these narratives, and indeed of the New Testament scriptures altogether. A thorough literary examination of the relevant facts comes precisely to the opposite conclusion: 'They did not tell how Jesus awoke to new life and left his abode in the tomb. Again it is made plain at an important point that here the imagination must not have free rein.' The Easter narrative is not fiction such as was attempted by 'unbridled reciters of the gospel story like the one who wrote under the name of Peter'; rather, 'in the pure reverence with which it veils the miracle, and in its concentration of the will on the service committed to the disciples, it is the complete opposite of all visionary outpourings' (A. Schlatter, *Die Geschichte des Christus*, pp. 528, 524).

The following comment, too, deserves full consideration: 'It is altogether erroneous to suspect legendary motives and assume an infringement of historic dependability wherever the later narrative brings new details. The addition of new features can also have precisely the opposite significance: it can also serve as a defence against legendary transformation.' The later construction of legends in the Catholic Church is the one thing from which the gospel tradition differs very clearly, 'for in the scriptures of the New Testament the tendency towards legendary transformation is opposed and the incomparable worth of the historic facts emphasized' (C. Stange, *op. cit.*, p. 718).

the value of all the Gospel traditions, is left out of account and the historical approach prevails in assessing these differences, this state of affairs will lead to a never-failing source of confusion, muddle and doubt —as is proved by the verdicts of historical science on the resurrection of Jesus. The shifting of the emphasis to an approach which finds its criterion in believing knowledge alters fundamentally the whole attitude to the differences in the narratives. As soon as the traditions are to be evaluated as confessions, differences between them, even to the extent of possible contradictions, require no apology. The variety in the ways of presentation has its ground not merely in the individuality and relativity of men, but also in the abundance and variety of the disciples' resurrection experiences. The difference is not merely a literary one, but has at the same time a substantial ground. *The decisive thing, however, is the complete unanimity in the universal believing knowledge of the resurrection of Jesus itself.* But this fundamental unity in faith usually has its significance curtailed from the historical point of view. The resurrection of Jesus as known in faith is the presupposition of all the New Testament's confessional statements, which are then of course given a varied stamp amid the multitude of man's means of expression and all his limitations.

The establishing of faith as the ground on which knowledge of the resurrection is made possible determines the nature of the theological task and the method appropriate to it. Only the recognition of the basis in faith sets up the link which no abstract method can give with the 'substance' of what is to be examined. Assent to the primitive Christian witness to the resurrection therefore does not by any means rest upon historical probability, but on its believing and confessional determination. Agreement with it thus means not that the dogmatician is left to his own discretion, but that he is bound to the prescribed business of theology, which is open only to the 'thinking of faith'.[68] The recognizing of the faith character does not imply the uncritical acceptance of every

[68] This way of propounding the task of dogmatics has been emphasized by K. Barth, in principle rightly. Dogmatics is concerned 'to see to the rightness . . . the appropriateness of its content', *Dogmatik* I, p. 1, cf. pp. 4, 146, 239-40. Also E. Brunner, *Der Mittler*, pp. 3, 6, 128, 131, 134 (ET, pp. 21, 24, 153, 156, 158 f.); E. Hirsch, *Jesus Christus der Herr*, pp. 9-10, 41 f., 53, 80, especially plainly p. 36: 'The knowledge inherent in this faith is the only theological knowledge there is.' Also Michaelis, *Täufer, Jesus, Urgemeinde*, p. 140. Especially also P. Althaus, *Dogmatik* I, pp. 5 f. The fundamental tendency shown by H. W. Schmidt towards a believing knowledge which includes history is to be accepted, even though his statement in *Zeit und Ewigkeit*, 1927, p. 369 is untenable in its present form: 'If faith says that Jesus Christ is risen from the dead, then it is not for historical science to maintain that the tomb was not empty.'

statement, but it does mean endeavouring to understand the witness in the light of its own most real intention.

With this insight into the necessity for specifically theological thinking in terms of the believing situation, a new relation to historical study is acquired. Now that every heterogeneous, untheological method which attempts to get rid of the aspect of faith must be wrecked by the confessional structure of the resurrection witness and destroys its content, there can therefore no longer be any question of getting behind the resurrection confession in order to find a historic core, but the aim is to understand the 'substance' which is contained in the believing statement but which, apart from it, is not present at all. To qualify the knowledge of the resurrection as believing knowledge does not by any means imply the renunciation of historical research, but it does mean being compelled to alter the presuppositions of the historian's approach. The usual presuppositions so far have been of a philosophical and speculative kind, which seek to rule out the attitude of faith as being a source of error, and thereby force historical research into adopting a false basic position. These underlying presuppositions, whether conscious or unconscious, have to be altered by recognizing the believing character of the resurrection message, and in that way the appropriate transformation of the whole approach of historical science has to be made. Accepting that faith is the presupposition of all knowledge of the resurrection first makes possible the proper pursuit of historical study. A logical proof of the validity of the accounts, and the guaranteeing of them by arguments of an immanent kind, are then admittedly both impossible, but also unnecessary. Rather, the believing confession of the resurrection of Jesus demands as a precondition of knowledge that our methodological principle should be trust.[69]

[69] Cf. W. Künneth, 'Zum Problem der Geschichtsgebundenheit des christlichen Glaubens', *Zeitschr. für syst. Theol.* 1930-1, part 4, a critical examination of the way historical judgments are bound to presuppositions. What W. Elert in *Die Lehre des Luthertums*, 1926, pp. 31 f. says in principle of historical criticism, in further development of Kähler's line of thought, has abiding significance in the context of the resurrection question: 'The attempt on the part of theological study of history to discredit the New Testament writers and discover a historic Jesus *behind* the Synoptic Gospels must be regarded as having failed, because by this means all experiences and utterances of Jesus became dubious, so that it was possible for the absurd idea to arise that Jesus never lived at all. . . . We can . . . see Jesus only through the eyes of these men or not at all. Our assurance concerning this person thus depends entirely on whether we are able to see him in the same perspective as they did. . . .' The assurance of the resurrection of Jesus and the understanding of it are accordingly only to be had from the same standpoint as the New Testament writers, i.e. on the basis of the believing knowledge of the Christian Church. Cf. further W. Elert, *Der christliche Glaube*, 1940, pp. 192 ff., and H. Thielicke, *Vernunft und Offenbarung*, 1936.

Part Two

THE DOGMATIC SIGNIFICANCE OF THE RESURRECTION

THE word of the resurrection of Jesus proclaims a reality. Understood from a systematic point of view, it is *the new and at the same time eschatological reality of life established by God in Christ.* This statement postulates a specifically dogmatic outlook, such as on the one hand is made possible by the resurrection of Jesus, and on the other hand also universally determined by it. The understanding of the reality of the resurrection of Jesus implies a corresponding dogmatic knowledge. The ascertaining of the reality of the resurrection cannot be separated in content from the dogmatic interpretation thereby given, but it can certainly be distinguished in building up a systematic presentation. Our task is now to expound in dogmatic reflection the theological content of the resurrection of Jesus, which was already presupposed in the first part of our study and already at work in the background. The result of this is, that from the most varied angles there emerge *the basic features of a Christian dogmatic, as these are determined by the reality of the resurrection.*

III

GOD'S ACTION UPON CHRIST IN THE RESURRECTION

I. THE FUNDAMENTAL CHRISTOLOGICAL PROBLEM

THE *fundamental question of all Christian theology is the Christological question.* This is not to say that the other discussions of dogmatics on seemingly 'extra-Christological' topics must be set aside as non-essential, but there is no doubt that the question of Christ rightly claims to be the central question of theology. Here is where the decision is made on the meaning of Christian doctrine and thereby on the foundation of the Church in distinction from false doctrine foreign to it. At the same time, however, any deeper study of the problems involved in Christology reveals that a Christian dogmatic can have no room for absolutely 'extra-Christological' elements, since these, too, are in one way or another illumined by Christology. *To begin our theology with the Christological question is therefore always at the same time to venture a statement on the whole of dogmatic knowledge.* The validity of a theology is thus determined in essence by the answer which it gives as a solution to the basic problem of Christology.

What is meant by Christology? Christology is that teaching about Christ which is gained by thinking through in a dogmatic way the believing knowledge which speaks of the encounter with God in Jesus Christ. Its task is the proper grounding and shaping of faith's statements about Christ in a unified system. If Christian faith is the answer to God's word spoken to men in Christ, then it knows of the decision for or against God that is made in Christ. The Christological problem arises when the encounter with Christ appears to be qualified as an encounter with God and the question of God is recognized at the same time to be the question of Christ. Every genuine Christology knows of the claim of the Christ who demands faith and awakens faith in the same way as God.[1] But it knows this only as 'the Christology of faith'.[2]

---

[1] Cf. E. Hirsch, *Jesus Christus der Herr*, pp. 49, 80, on the subject of 'God's presence in Christ'. Jesus is 'essentially God's heart-stirring word to us'.
[2] Cf. P. Althaus, *Theologische Aufsätze*, 1929, pp. 207 ff.

This formal characterization safeguards Christological thinking against the misunderstanding that its conclusions rest upon the disinterested description of given immanent facts, upon the intellectual clarification of psychological and religious experiences or of historical reflections. The Christological question does not arise in the sphere of history pure and simple, but on its frontier, inasmuch as in the fact of Christ there emerges something absolutely unconditional, which is accessible only to faith. We have likewise erected a barrier against confusion with reflection of a philosophical kind which endeavours to expound some metaphysical truth given as such. The content of Christology is on the contrary not subject to the possibility of general recognition and cannot be grasped by philosophical standards of value. Christological knowledge is characterized by the standpoint of faith, appears as a function of faith and is meaningful only in the situation of faith.

What is included immediately and without reflection in the Christian believer's view—namely, faith in the 'divinity' of Jesus Christ—is also the theme of Christology. Whoever thinks he can exclude this central question, utterly misses the real concern and aim of Christological study. It is not the task of Christology to prove the 'divinity' of Jesus, for this judgment of faith is the presupposition that makes Christology's efforts possible at all. But its task is to clarify the relation of Jesus to God and the connection of God with Jesus, to show the quality of this relationship and the theological interpretation of its meaning. The basic problem of Christology is accordingly summed up in the question of what is the proper theological way of dealing with faith's statement of the 'divinity' of Jesus. This basic question may be sub-divided into *the three decisive questions of all Christology. First, what ground is there for the 'divinity' of Jesus?* With what theological right and in what theological sense may this concept be applied to Jesus Christ? *Secondly, how is the unity in our thought of God maintained when we understand the significance of Jesus for faith?* How does Christology safeguard itself against a weakening of the concept of God or against its receding into the background? *Thirdly, how is the specifically Christological concern, which lays the decisive emphasis precisely on Jesus' divine claim, maintained in the face of the concept of God on the one hand and the rationalistic tendencies towards levelling down on the other?*

In the mastering of this basic problem Christological study shows considerable differences. Amid all the multiplicity of individual presentations and their variations in the history of dogma and of theology, three typical forms of Christology can be established.

First, the *Logos Christology* of the Greek Councils and of early Protestant dogmatics, whose insights have continued to work even down to Karl Barth's renewal of the doctrine of anhypostasis and enhypostasis.[3] The ineradicably right element in this essentially metaphysical Christology is its stringent concentration on the divine character of the Logos-Jesus. The divine claim of Jesus is taken absolutely seriously and the demand made by faith in Christ is met. It is further significant that the attempt is made to show the ground of the 'divinity' of Jesus. The philosophical concept of the Logos is selected as an adequate expression of divinity and the divine transcendence of Christ is thereby secured. Moreover, the fact that the Logos-Christ is a secret of faith is given a formal theological safeguard by the paradoxical statements that the human and divine natures exist side by side yet at the same time are also one in the unity of the person. Despite these profound insights, the Logos Christology does not offer a complete solution to the basic Christological problem. It radically breaks down because of its failure to grasp adequately the concept of 'divinity'. The 'divinity' is conceived as an unchanging metaphysical essence of the Logos, and implies the immobile character of an abstractly existing state. The immutability of the divine nature of the Logos inevitably gives rise to speculation about the relation of the two natures with the incarnation of the Logos and because of that incarnation, and about the nature of the *unio, communio* and *communicatio* of their attributes. This metaphysical starting point, burdened as it is by the contemporary philosophy's concepts 'nature', 'person', and 'Logos' which are subject to violent changes of meaning and therefore hinder a proper understanding, forces Christology into unhistoric abstraction, without being able to make clear any living relation between the humanity and divinity of the Christ. But above all, the Logos idea does not make it possible to bring out the reality of God in its relation to Christ. Thus there develops a latent tension between the concept of God and the divinity of the Logos which cannot do justice to the Christological postulate.[4]

In contrast to this kind of Christological metaphysics, *Spirit Christology* strives to pay due regard precisely to the psychological and historical facts and to point out the divine in the life of Jesus himself.

---

[3] K. Barth, *Dogmatik* I, Prolegomena, 1927, pp. 264, 268 ff.; *Kirchliche Dogmatik* I/1, 1932, pp. 435 ff. (ET, §11.2).

[4] Cf. for the criticism of the two-nature doctrine P. Althaus, *op. cit.*, pp. 213 f.; E. Hirsch, *op. cit.*, pp. 48 f. In modern dress the Logos doctrine is found among others in R. Frank, *Wahrheitsgewissheit* II, p. 217, and R. Seeberg, *Dogmatik* II, p. 174.

The thing is to recognize the personal union of Jesus, as the obedient Son, with the Father. 'Perfect obedience is the perfect presence of God' in the true man Jesus. Thus the whole fulness of the Godhead dwells at the same time in the humanity of Jesus, which finds itself in perfect unity of will with God.[5] The value of this Spirit Christology lies in the fact that the thought of God is clearly maintained throughout, without being obscured by metaphysical speculation. The concept of God rightly appears as the dominant factor in this Christology. Christ does not stand as the Logos alongside God, but the Spirit of God dwells directly in Christ. This starting point also makes it possible to ground the divine character of Jesus in his identity of will with God, and thereby to prove his authority. It is reasonable enough that this attitude is combined with a strong emphasis on the historic, personal life of Jesus in its inner relation to his divine claim, so that the concrete movement of Jesus' life in history, which no Christology can dispense with, is brought out in contrast to metaphysical immobility. All the same, the Spirit Christology is no less encumbered than the first. Its decisive weakness is, that it cannot satisfy Christology's central interest in the essential divinity of Christ. The very distinction between nature and will is only possible on a one-sided, ethically voluntarist view of the historicality of Jesus. The maintaining of the theocentricity is bought only at the price of surrendering the specific divinity of Christ. Here the Logos Christology has profounder theological insight, and plainly avoids the danger zone of dynamistic monarchianism and of developing that doctrine in Ritschlian theses which see in Christ the organ of the divine will.[6] Only in the wake of a rationalistic approach is it possible to arrive at the divine authority of the historical Jesus by analysing the determination of his spirit and the attitude of his will. The presence of God in Christ can therefore be distinguished only in degree from 'the presence of God in the perfect Christian'. 'The divinity of Christ', however, as Althaus rightly maintains against Hirsch, lies 'beyond all comparison with any such empirical possibilities'.[7] Moreover, the identification in Jesus' case of divine sonship, which, however imperfectly, belongs to every believer, and divinity does not bring out clearly enough the difference between the 'subject' and 'object' of worship, so that this historico-psychological Christology takes the necessary edge off the offence of the revelation of Christ.

[5] E. Hirsch, *op. cit.*, pp. 74 ff.
[6] Cf. K. Heim, *Dogmatik* II, pp. 67-68.
[7] P. Althaus, *op. cit.*, p. 218.

Taking up again the real concern of the ancient Christian Symbols, recognizing the rightness of Spirit Christology's approach, and fortified by the paradoxical dialectic of Kierkegaard, the *paradox Christology* which embraces the thinking of P. Althaus and K. Heim, and partially also of K. Barth, attempts another solution to the problem. Neither one-sided construction of Christology from the idea of the Logos or 'the exalted one', nor limitation to the divine encounter 'in the historic Jesus', but the paradoxical unity of the essential divinity which demands worship (that is the justification for the 'nature' concept in the Church's doctrine) and the historic, worshipping humanity of Jesus (that is the significance of the approach of historical Christology) is the appropriate expression of Christological knowledge. The 'mystery of the God-man' is expressed in the paradoxical sentence: 'I must believe in this historic man Jesus as my Lord and God.'[8] The 'height of the tension' between the divinity and humanity of Jesus must not be 'reduced' by any psychological or historical explaining. 'Dogmatic Christology' can only 'declare the paradox: The man Jesus gains from us our religious submission and our religious trust that he is dealing with us by the power of God.'[9]

The paradox theology unquestionably represents a ripe form of Christological reflection. It avoids on the one hand all non-historic Logos-speculation on the possible relation between the divine and the human in Christ, while on the other hand it avoids the intellectualizing tendency of Spirit Christology and preserves what is the decisive interest of Christian faith. The acceptance of the paradox permits us to hold without qualification to the divine and human character of Christ, and yet allows room at the same time to develop the concept of God, which is not affected by this Christological antinomy. And yet even this Christological type is also unable to do complete justice to the basic problem of Christology. The paradox Christology by its very nature dispenses with a proper theological understanding of the 'divinity' of Jesus, does without showing what determines the divine authority of Christ and what ground we have for discussing this 'divinity'. This Christology merely repeats the immediate judgments of faith, without giving them any further theological grounding. The pointing out of the paradox does not take us beyond the balanced static relationship between the historic man Jesus and the reigning Christ, i.e. beyond the basic

[8] P. Althaus, *op. cit.*, p. 221; K. Heim, *Dogmatik* II, pp. 9 ff., 58 ff.; K. Barth, *Dogmatik* I, pp. 254 ff.
[9] P. Althaus, *op. cit.*, p. 109; cf. *Dogmatik* II, 1932, pp. 82 ff., 104 f., 108 f.

starting point of the two-nature doctrine. Thus even the concept of God is ultimately unable to become fruitful for the forming of the content of Christology. It is not possible to discuss, within the framework of the paradox, how far and in virtue of what event God acts in and through Christ. The material presupposition for offering divine worship to Jesus, the relation of the history of Jesus to his exaltation or indeed the fact of its being bound up with the idea of pre-existence, cannot be made clear from this standpoint. The paradoxical telescoping of the historic and the divine reality of Jesus on the same plane without any anchor in a definite starting point rules out the possibility of specifically Christological exposition.

To sum up: these three Christological types wrestle seriously with the basic problem, but they always pass one of the questions it contains or do not get the length of a proper answer. Either the action of God recedes into the background as in Logos Christology, or the 'divinity' of Christ is altered as in Spirit Christology, or the grounding of it is dispensed with as in paradox Christology. But this fact that all three attempts are unable to do justice to one part of the Christological task is due to the absence of a concrete starting point for the Christological examination. All three Christological types set out, not from a definite event in the primitive Christian situation, but either from a general statement which was only reached on the basis of this message by abstraction, i.e. from the Logos idea or the spiritual personality of Jesus, or else their basis is the fact of Christ as a whole, in the light of the total witness of the New Testament.[10] The general idea, whether it be that of the Logos or of the Son who is one in will with God, leads to speculative remoteness from the substance of Christology and the obscuring of it by a historical and psychological treatment. The faith of the Church admittedly appears to be in principle an appropriate starting point for the general orientation of Christology, yet it leaves us without a concrete delimitation of the decisive content of faith. To choose the general concept of the New Testament's believing witness, or in general terms the 'fact of Christ', as the key to dogmatic discussion is a highly dubious procedure. For one thing, this renouncing of a concrete event as our

[10] This latter attitude is found in P. Althaus, but especially in K. Heim, *Dogmatik* II, pp. 7-8: 'The doctrine of the Christian faith rests on the fact . . . that God speaks to us through a very definite series of events in history, and that these events have thus eternal significance for us. . . . The presentation of the Christian faith must therefore set out from this point at the heart of human history from which the meaning of the whole becomes plain, from Christ as the faith of the New Testament Church sees him. It is from him that we must acquire the key to the solution of all questions of faith.'

starting point is contrary to the primitive Christian message itself, which did *not* make general religious statements about Jesus, but concentrated upon definite happenings, and brought out one singular event as the essential content of faith and as the ground of faith. Secondly, if we are determined to pay due regard to the very varied believing declarations which we have from the primitive Church, it would not accord with the interest of faith itself to ascribe equal value to all these statements. Undoubtedly, their manifold content is of varied theological quality. Further, in taking a general starting point we are threatened precisely by the danger of shifting the accent on to some secondary peripheral statement, which of course also belongs within the framework of the total witness of the New Testament. With that we have no safeguard against heresy, which exalts a partial truth into the thing that matters most.

The choice of starting point is in fact decisive for the treatment of the Christological problem. The faith of the Church must be grasped concretely in its orientation towards the decisive event. For that reason we cannot avoid the question as to the core of the primitive Christian witness. Thus we have to ask Heim what, then, are the events which 'have eternal significance for us', what, then, in the New Testament faith in Christ is to be regarded as the 'heart' of human history. Our answer to this question takes its cue from the basic insight of the primitive Christian message and declares: *the resurrection of Jesus. Christology has to take its basic starting point in the raising of Christ.* With that, *the theme of Christology is summed up as 'God's action on Christ in the resurrection'*, in which is given the decisive point of reference and direction. From this position a different exposition of the Christological problem is conceivable which goes beyond the three Christological attempts indicated, without our thereby having to leave out of account the justification and the fruits of Christological study so far. Christology is thus essentially to be defined as a *resurrection Christology.* The succeeding discussion has to show how far the resurrection Christology thus demanded is in a position to solve the complex questions presented by the basic Christological problem.

2. THE CHRISTOLOGICAL MOTIVATION OF THE RESURRECTION OF JESUS

The development of a resurrection Christology in terms of divine action upon Christ in the resurrection requires a thorough grounding. The Christological motives of God's resurrecting act are given in two factors:

first in the '*sonship*' *of Jesus*, and secondly in the *preparation in the* '*history of salvation*' for this act of God.

(a) *The Grounding of the Resurrection in the 'Sonship' of Jesus*

The question as to the precondition of the resurrection act of God upon Jesus points back to the question of the person of Jesus. It remains unanswerable so long as Jesus is thought of as a relative phenomenon in the history of religion; thus the solution to it already presupposes the believing knowledge which is aware that the level of religious history has been broken through in Jesus' absolute claim. The theological expression for this transcendental character of Jesus, which does not derive from the relative sphere and cannot be explained in terms of it, is provided by the concept of 'sonship'.

The designation of Jesus as '*Son of God*' is in itself an ambiguous concept and one that still needs Christological clarification. Two interpretations which are untenable in view of the resurrection have to be rejected: on the one hand the identification of the 'divine sonship' of Jesus with divine authority—a view such as underlies the Logos Christology—and on the other hand the emphasizing of the 'parallelism' between the sonship of Jesus and the divine sonship of all believers.[11] According to the latter view, Christians as 'sons of God' would stand in principle in the same relation to God as Jesus, only with the difference that the sonship of Jesus is marked out by the unbrokenness of his communion with God, by the absolute purity of his life which is unrestrainedly filled by the Spirit of God and does not even need justification. Both views have an element of truth in them. The former recognizes the special character of the sonship of Jesus, though of course unduly exaggerated into the fulness of divine power, the latter perceives the difference between sonship and divine majesty, though indeed to such an extent that the unique quality of the concept of sonship is lost. Developing these lines of thought and at the same time rejecting their excesses, we have to notice two elements in the closer definition of the concept 'Son'. 'Son of God' implies, firstly, the closest connection of Jesus with God, unsurpassed by any other relation; it means the personal, spiritual and essential homogeneity with the Father which is expressed in the Son's being his 'image'.[12] This essential divine sonship of Jesus lies beyond all possibility of human comparison and means

---

[11] E. Hirsch, *Jesus Christus der Herr*, p. 76. Cf. on the problems of Christology also Robert Jelke, *Die Grunddogmen des Christentums*, 1929, pp. 91 ff., 102 ff.

[12] Col. 1.15: 'The image of the invisible God, the firstborn of every creature'. Col. 1.17: 'Before all things'. John 12.45; 14.9.

absolute transcendence. Secondly, however, 'sonship' posits at the same time also the difference between Son and Father, the dependence of the Son and the fact of his being conditioned by God. The very concept of 'sonship' stipulates a relationship of necessary disparity and rules out the acceptance of an identity of power, rank and dignity with the Father.[13] Accordingly the essential homogeneity of the Son with God and at the same time his distance from God, since he does not command his divine dignity, finds its theological expression in the concept of 'sonship'. The Christological interest insists on laying down the unique character of the sonship of Jesus, both in relation to God and in relation to man, as the precondition of the resurrection act of God. *The affirmation, 'Jesus, Son of God' describes in theological content an intermediate status of Jesus between God and man.* The concept 'intermediate status' is to be introduced as a provisional term which is to be theologically understood and is used *to safeguard the uniqueness of Jesus' filial status as transcendence and yet not as an expression of divine sovereignty. The 'intermediate status' means the same as the filial status of the pre-existent one.*[14] This concept is accordingly further expounded and deepened by the idea of 'pre-existence', which Christological thinking cannot disregard.

The concept of 'pre-existence' is encumbered by misunderstandings. Two attitudes towards the problem of pre-existence must here be countered.

On the one hand, the idea of the pre-existence of the Son, and therewith every statement altogether about his transcendent being in his relation to God, is rejected as having too little ground and as being not at all necessary for salvation. Thus E. Hirsch thinks any such idea is 'far too disputable' to be included 'among the unsurrenderable pieces of Christian knowledge', for it goes 'beyond the range of experience', threatens the true humanity of Jesus and is not vouched for 'by any sure testimony from the mouth of Jesus' himself. For that reason the 'origin of the life of Jesus' must remain for us an impenetrable secret.[15] The weakness and limitation of Hirsch's Christological position becomes

---

[13] A distinction is thus to be made between the sovereign majesty of God, which the Son does not possess, and the essential homogeneity of the divine image which on the one hand connects the Son peculiarly with God and on the other hand distinguishes him from man.

[14] The expression 'intermediate status' is not to be identified with antiquity's idea of a 'demigod' or a half-human and half-divine being. Both divine majesty and time-bound humanity are things in which the transcendent Son has no part. The concept merely describes the fact of the Son's belonging together with God and at the same time being in subordination to God.

[15] *Op. cit.*, pp. 85 f. Cf. Ernst Barnikol, *Messias und Mensch, Der nichtpaulinische Ursprung der Präexistenz-Christologie*, Kiel 1932.

obvious at this point. His argument against pre-existence is mainly rationalistic and of a critical historical kind, but is not theologically conclusive. It is certainly true that the pre-existence of the Son lies beyond all empirical knowledge; but its thus being beyond all possibility of psychological and rational explanation is entirely as it should be, so that the question of being 'within the range of experience' has to be dismissed from the start. Nor can it in principle ever be possible to attach decisive significance to any attestation by some word or other of Jesus, or to the absence of such attestation.[16] It is certain, however, that both the Pauline and the Johannine witness speak at vital points of pre-existence, without thereby imperilling the true humanity of Jesus. There is no doubt that the statement of pre-existence has a strangeness about it, and in a strict sense is not necessary for salvation; yet it is not the task of theology to trim the primitive Christian witness according to a norm that suits ourselves, but to study the problem and to understand its aim. The attempt to follow up the Pauline insight by discussing the question of pre-existence does not abolish the mystery of the sonship of Jesus, but always remains for secular thought, as does every theological judgment, a disputable paradox.[17]

In antithesis to the giving up of the question of pre-existence, stands the attempt to build a Christology on the basis of pre-existence. The Greek Logos doctrine attempts to make this the starting point for its construction of the drama of redemption. The pre-existence of the Logos then means an abstractly existing pre-temporality, a metaphysical state lying beyond the spatio-temporal mode of being. The pre-existent Logos is thereby understood as already perfect in his divine 'nature', and pre-existence is equated with divine authority. Such metaphysical speculation does not only involve the logically impossible transference to the transcendent of the concept of time with its 'before' and 'after'—and that, too, not merely figuratively but in a real sense—and lead to the

[16] Precisely from the standpoint of historical criticism it would be doubtful whether any 'sure testimony' by Jesus himself exists at all. In that case the same argument could be used to question not merely his pre-existence, but also his reconciling death and his resurrection, since an unexceptionable attestation 'from the mouth of Jesus' is at least disputed. Besides, we have to consider whether the post-Easter situation may not have led Paul to a profounder and more universal Christological knowledge than was possible to Jesus before his resurrection. Cf. John 1.1; 8.58; 17.5, 24; Phil. 2.5 f.

[17] We can therefore say with Freidrich Gogarten: 'Where the pre-existence of Jesus Christ is not held fast, there everything is surrendered, there nothing at all remains of Jesus but a somehow outstanding man whom God has given to the world.' On the other hand we can *not* assent to his identification of the pre-existence of the Son with the divine sovereignty. 'Menschheit und Gottheit Jesu Christi', *Zwischen den Zeiten* 1932, part I, pp. 16 f.

insoluble problems of the relation between the divinity and humanity of Jesus, which in its historic actuality is constantly liable to be impaired. But above all, the understanding of the pre-existence as divine majesty hampers the exposition of the Christological significance of the resurrection, inasmuch as the decisive accents in the constructing of Christology are so shifted by this speculation as to interfere with its meaning.

In contrast to these theories, *the idea of pre-existence is to be taken seriously* precisely *as a peculiar expression not of the majesty of God, but of the sonship of Jesus.* In so doing, 'pre-existence' is not to be conceived in temporal philosophical categories, but is the pregnant description of a Christological fact. I have every reason to be grateful to Althaus for the consideration he has given to the problems I have raised in regard to the apparent necessity of a 'resurrection Christology', and for his critical questions which have made a vital contribution towards clarifying the situation. The relation of the 'pre-existent one' to God and to the Risen Lord must indeed be described as unequivocally as possible. We must alter the terms used in our earlier formulations and say: 'According to Phil. 2.6, the "pre-existent Son" possesses divine being and essence, i.e. (here I agree with Althaus) "identity of being with God" and in that sense "divinity". But he does not yet possess (and here I differ from Althaus) the function of divine authority, the divine sovereignty of Matt. 28.18, which is first bestowed upon the Son through the resurrection. That this teaching is in agremeent with Paul can surely scarcely be questioned.'[18] Two ideas have to be used in further expounding the concept of pre-existence.

Firstly, the pre-existence of the Son means the essential superiority of Jesus in comparison with all other earthly and creaturely existence. The pre-existent one, 'the first-born' Son, 'before all creatures', has as such a special standing in relation to God different from the rest of creation. The divine image in him is not only untroubled by the Fall and by sin, but is also not the same as in man before the Fall, for the pre-existent Son is not the earth-born man, but the spiritual man.[19] Accordingly, as Son his standing in relation to the world is also unique. For that reason he is not a prophet, but *the* Son absolutely, coming from a wholly other dimension. Secondly, the concept of pre-existence includes the statement of the sovereign claim of the Son. To be sure, the Son is not yet in possession of his divine lordship, but the fact that the pre-existent one is the 'first-born' has the result that he is entitled in

---

[18] Cf. Paul Althaus, *Die christliche Wahrheit* II, p. 240.
[19] I Cor. 15.45, 47: 'The second man is from heaven.'

principle to coming sovereignty. His pre-existence is thus the pre-condition of his one day receiving the dignity of Kyrios.

God's act in raising up Christ from the dead finds, firstly, a transcendent ground in the divine sonship of Jesus, which is given a specific interpretation by being understood in relation to pre-existence. *God raises Jesus from the dead because he is his 'pre-existent' Son.*

The significance of the sonship of Jesus for his resurrection has also, further, to be expounded in particular as authentication of this sonship in history. With this we come up against the much debated problem of *kenosis*. According to the particular form of the idea of 'pre-existence', the concept of kenosis will either no longer be maintained at all, or else in the sense of the old dogmatics it will be related to the divine majesty of Jesus. Neither conclusion accords with the Christological task.

The Pauline concept of 'kenosis'[20] does not mean emptying himself of the divine sovereignty—which in fact the Son does not yet possess. Kenosis is therefore not to be identified with a reduction of that original fulness of power which properly belongs only to divine majesty, but not to the Son. The true character of the emptying and humiliation of Jesus lies rather in the change in the status of the Son in relation to God, as also to the world. The status of the pre-existent Son, transcending the world and destined for sovereign divine majesty, undergoes a decisive change when this Son is sent into the sphere of history, i.e. into the situation of the fallen creation.[21]

Christology's interest in the bearing which kenosis has on the understanding of the resurrection of Jesus must be discussed along three lines. First, humiliation means the surrender of the pre-existent Son's rank as the 'first-born'. Taking a place within the immanent system of things puts an end to the status of the Son 'before' and 'above' the world reality as a whole; participating in creatureliness means for the pre-existent exaltedness of divine sonship the entry into a situation which in itself is incongruous, which does not adequately express the filial rank and does not recognize it. This identifying of the Son with the creature, which in itself is 'under' him, takes the Son out of the original immediacy of his relation with God and places him by contrast in a mediated relationship to God which takes place in decisions and is proper only to men. The Son's becoming man is therefore the beginning of his humiliation in the 'servant form' of historicality.

Secondly, kenosis is to be understood as an abiding threat to the Son's

[20] Phil. 2.6 f.; II Cor. 8.9.
[21] Phil. 2.7: 'made in the likeness of men, and being found in fashion as a man'.

unbroken communion with God because of his being placed within the context of the destiny and guilt of fallen humanity. The humiliation of the Son leads on the one hand to a clash with the world of sinners. The Son's union with God in a bond that knows no separation from God must rouse the opposition of the humanity that has cast off God and incur the attack of the demonic and satanic powers that persist in radical divorce from God. The mere presence of God's Son in the fallen creation must kindle the enmity of this world against the one bound to God, i.e. the sinless one. But on the other hand, the Son in this human situation sees his own self under the judgment of divine wrath that hangs over the world. Having become flesh, he shares with a brother's solidarity in the curse of sin and its effects in destruction and punishment, suffers in his 'servant form' with his fellows under the distress of humanity, and knows himself like all creatures subject to the laws of transience and the necessity of dying.

The deepest sense of his humiliation and therefore the significant ground of the relation between Jesus' sonship and his resurrection is found, finally, in the Son's standing the test of obedience.[22] The necessity of the Son's being a servant becomes the decisive confirmation of the authenticity of the sonship of Jesus himself. Accordingly, the central concept for the characterizing of the human situation is that of obedience. Everything depends on how the divine Son bears the changed situation brought about by his self-emptying and lives it through. His exposure to the creaturely and sin-riddled character of human existence raises for the Son the question what is the real will of God and gives birth to the inner struggle for insight into God's plan. Thus the kenosis means having to bow to the darkness and obscurity of God's dealings with him, the pre-existent Son. No rebellion against the servant form that is God's will for him, no demand to be restored to his original filial dignity, no claim to the right of lordship that is grounded in his being the first-born—nothing, amid the constant menace of trials and temptations, interrupted the evincing of filial obedience in the giving, suffering and dying of Jesus.[23] Rather, the obedience of the Son is on the contrary his acceptance of the consequences deriving from the situation of a world that has cast off God, and his unconditional recognition of the fact that God alone is Lord and that this Lord has also the sovereignty

[22] Rom. 5.19; Phil. 2.8; Heb. 5.8.
[23] It is noteworthy that the temptation story in the Gospels takes seriously the Son's right to sovereignty and makes it the starting point for the possibility of tempting Jesus. The voluntary renunciation by Jesus of his claim to sovereignty is the antithesis to the enticement of the devil, Matt. 4.1 f.; Luke 4.5 f.

to act even in contradiction of all filial rights and filial claims. *This obedience of Jesus is* thus *identical with the sacrifice of the filial right to rule.* But the climax and final test of this obedience comes in the agony of the death on the cross as the final surrender of all standing of his own and all power of his own. The humiliation of the Son of God reaches its decisive depth on the cross, in keeping with the utter reprobation of mankind and the loneliness of separation from God in the judgment of death as the fruit of humanity's sin. Only his unconditional obedience binds the Son in his humiliation to the Father. Hence in the obedience of death the sonship of Jesus comes to its perfection, inasmuch as it establishes and proves its genuineness to the very end of his life in history.

We come to this conclusion: *It is because God has brought the pre-existent Son into the world of creatureliness, of sin and of death, that he deals with him also in raising him to glory.* Thus the resurrection finds its ground in the obedience of the life and death of Jesus, the servant of God who is at the same time the pre-existent Son.[24]

(b) The Preparation in the History of Salvation for the Resurrection of Jesus

To see the resurrection from a Christological point of view is not to isolate the resurrection event from history, but rather renders it necessary to show the context in the 'history of salvation' in which the resurrection of Jesus stands, and in which lie the preconditions for the understanding of it. Any separating of the resurrection from the bedrock of history would, moreover, involve the danger of speaking of the Risen One in abstract speculations. The content of the resurrection, even when it stretches far beyond the historic life of Jesus, is always conditioned by the concreteness of the human history of Jesus. Every substantial statement about the resurrection therefore finds itself referred back to the historic presuppositions.[25] The reality of the resurrection throws its light upon *preceding history, so that the latter* in turn *is seen to be directed, as 'history of salvation', towards the Easter event.* The events of the history of salvation have the resurrection as their goal and thus present a comprehensive happening which is qualified by the action of God and provides the essential reason for his subsequent action in the

---

[24] Cf. in agreement with this the observations of P. Althaus, 'Das Kreuz Christi' in *Mysterium Christi*, 1931, pp. 249, 250, 253, 255, 257, 260 f.

[25] The memory of the earthly life of Christ was for the disciples after the resurrection not merely an indispensable means of forming a living picture of the Lord, but at the same time also a 'protection against the imaginative excesses of the cultic imagination', A. Deissmann, *Paulus*, 1911, p. 100.

resurrection. The resurrection life of Christ has its seeds in the work of God's special revelation. Accordingly the preparation in the history of salvation for the resurrection is to be discerned in the line of the Old Testament prophets as well as in Jesus' message of the kingdom of God.

The awareness of a revealing activity of God in history lays the foundation for the recognition that death is not to be the final possibility. The activity of God is always a work of the living God upon the dead. The theme of the history of salvation can therefore be none other than the breaking in of life and its struggle with the powers in the world which are hostile to life. Wherever and however God acts, whether in judgment or in grace, the question of life arises and the pointer to the resurrection is given. With that, *the word of the resurrection* is seen to be *the secret, but effectual, motive of all that happens in the history of salvation*. God acts as the *deus revelatus* in calling to his service men who have not the control of their lives and are subject to death. With this call of God to specific men, a life-process begins among men which does not rest upon themselves and their qualities but has its feasibility and execution only in God. In thus choosing men, God calls them out from the sphere of death and subjects them to his own claim. His claim on all earthly things is judgment and grace at the same time. It is judgment inasmuch as God's electing call destroys the illusion of the human life that clings to itself, and brings to its conclusion the possibility open to man, which can only be a possibility of death. Thus the judging act of God in the destruction of all pseudo-life indirectly makes room for a new possibility of life from God. Divine grace, however, lies already in the claim which demands a relation with God and which as such contains a promise of life. God's dealing with the elect means the beginning of faith, as an admission of the impossibility of their own life, as an act of turning their back on the death-process of humanity not by escaping into illusions, but in hope in God, the living One. Thus the act of God is promise of life, and faith as the presupposition of an understanding of the divine act is expectation of life. God's act in the resurrection has accordingly its antecedents in the call to life and in the promise of life. The story of the patriarchs and the election of God's people ultimately comes under this resurrection perspective, and only in this perspective is it valid as special revelation. In the same way the prophets become bearers of the message of life. Those who are commissioned to speak in God's name bear witness by their word of judgment and salvation to the promised life from God. Beyond all human reckoning and understanding, and even beyond their own subjective views, they are heralds of the all-exclusive divine possibility of the overcoming of death by life. Hence the existence of God's elect, of his people, of his prophets is oriented towards the coming life from God. The reality of life from God is present in the call, the claim and the promise of God. This word of God is the first breaking through of true life, but it points beyond this beginning to a fulfilment. The acts of God under the 'old covenant' have their goal in a fulfilment of life, which the concepts 'Messiah' and 'kingdom of God' characterize as a kingdom of life and peace. *The work of God in the history of salvation becomes a prelude to his work in the resurrection of Jesus.*[26]

This outlook towards the resurrection world of God is expressed to a peculiar degree in Jesus' *message of the kingdom of God*. The concept of the kingdom of God in the primitive Christian sense has of course nothing to do with the idea of a community of moral and religious personalities, but is essentially to be understood as preparation, and partly as proleptic breaking in, of the reality of the resurrection. This resurrection character becomes clear in three directions.

Jesus proclaims the coming of the kingdom of God as fellowship with God and lordship of God. Where God rules, life is established and death dethroned; and where men are admitted to this fellowship with God, they participate in its superiority over death. The kingdom of God is eternal life, and therefore the message of the kingdom of God tells of nothing else but the God who makes the dead alive. The word of the kingdom of God prepares the way for the word of the raising of the dead. Two things are contained in this proclamation: the demand for repentance and the forgiveness of sins. Repentance is the call to acknowledge the situation of death which is ours outside the kingdom of God. It is the radical renouncing of a life ruled by oneself, and turning towards the totally different quality of the life which is from God. If sin, as separation of man from God, is death, then a necessary preliminary to life is the overcoming of sin in forgiveness. The kingdom of God can set in only where there is forgiveness of sin. Hence the forgiveness of sin is the beginning of the divine sovereignty and therewith of the new life. As removal of the root cause of death, the forgiveness of sins becomes the certainty of complete divine sovereignty to come and the guarantee of the resurrection life.[27]

Secondly, Jesus proclaims the message of the kingdom as the 'Son'

[26] Cf. Dan. 7.13; Isa. 52.13 ff.; Joachim Jeremias, *Jesus als Weltvollender*, 1930, pp. 54 ff.
[27] Cf. the detailed and important study by H. D. Wendland, *Die Eschatologie des Reiches Gottes bei Jesus*, 1931, pp. 17, 33, 63, 66, 74 f., 80, 173, 224.

and thereby at the same time as himself the bearer of the divine kingdom. Because the will of Jesus is identical with the divine will, the
divine sovereignty prevails in Jesus, he is *the Messiah* of the kingdom.
God acts now already upon the historic Jesus as a precondition of his
resurrection, by making the Son in his servant form the man through
whom the kingdom of God breaks into the world. Although he is God's
servant and because he is God's servant, God makes the Son the
Messiah, i.e. the bearer of the proclamation about the kingdom and of
his kingly will. If, however, the kingdom of God is eternal life, then the
bearer of this kingdom must also know about this life. Assent to the
rule of God is assent to the life that is from God, and therefore *the
Messiah is he who is on the way to the resurrection.* The Messiah is the
kingdom of God become present, breaking in and under a veil, but he
is also the same who is destined to be the future Lord of the kingdom.
As Messiah, too, the Son stands under the rule of God: as proclaimer
of the kingdom and executor of the divine will, he is the servant of the
divine kingdom, but not yet its Lord. As Messiah the Son knows himself at the same time to be Kyrios designate who even in his messiahship
does not take life into his own hands, but waits for God to act upon him.
The messiahship of the Son is the antecedent of the reality of his
resurrection, not only because the kingdom of God is in history a hidden
kingdom but because the Messiah is not yet Lord. Hence his messiahship is oriented towards the coming lordship of the Son. It is only from
his being destined for lordship that there comes the unparalleled authority of the historic Jesus to forgive sins. This authority, in which the
breaking in of the divine sovereignty is realized, is explained neither by
the spotlessness of his humanity nor by the unmediated union of the
Son with God, but by his messiahship, which as a God-given office can
execute forgiveness only in the name and by the commission of God
but not on its own authority, and especially by his designation to lordship, which looks forward to the act of God in the resurrection. Thus
the forgiving of sins by Jesus, the Son-Messiah, becomes an anticipation
of the post-Easter situation which is grounded in the fact of his being
elected to the authority of universal lordship. The problem of the self-
consciousness of Jesus thus finds its solution only in relation to the
resurrection. The Messiah as Kyrios designate possesses the certainty
of victory over death. He can proclaim his own resurrection 'on the
third day' and in anticipation of his coming divine exaltation can say
of himself, 'I am the resurrection and the life.'[28]

[28] The discussion among New Testament scholars centres on the question

The *miracles of Jesus*, too, have to come under the perspective of acts that point to the resurrection. They are to be understood as manifestations of the divine sovereignty which has become effectively present through Jesus and, as such, 'eschatological foretokens' of the coming act of God in the resurrection. The establishing of the kingdom of God is opposed by the powers of this world, demonic and satanic forces, sin, disease and death, which all stand in an inner association with each other.[29] Miracle then means the partial overcoming of these powers through the might of God which fills the Messiah, but the miracles are at the same time also pointers to the coming exercise of divine sovereignty by the Kyrios designate. If in miracle the sovereignty of God really breaks through, then there is in principle no limit to Jesus' working of miracles. The kingdom of God lays claim to the whole world and therefore miracle overcomes in principle all opposition from the autonomy of a world separated from God, in the soul as well as in the body, even in nature and its law of death. The rule of God which prevails in miracle is a revelation of life. In a special way, therefore, Jesus' acts of raising the dead bear the stamp of signs of the commencing resurrection

---

whether Jesus is to be regarded only as the Messiah designate, who has still to receive his real messiahship (W. Michaelis), or as now already fully the Messiah, who awaits only the revelation of his veiled messiahship (H. D. Wendland). In contrast to both these theories it seems from the standpoint of the resurrection perspective more appropriate, certainly to speak with Wendland of the real, present messiahship of Jesus, but to distinguish from it, as the element of truth in Michaelis' view, the 'lordship' which is still to be imparted to the Messiah-Son. The concepts 'Son', 'Messiah', 'Lord' are not by any means identical, but have each their peculiar theological quality.

[29] Cf. H. D. Wendland, *op. cit.*, pp. 224, 223, 237 ff.: 'The lordship of God has three enemies: Satan, sin, sickness. Sin and sickness are the results of Satan's lordship over men.'

What R. Bultmann thinks can be said of the miracles of Jesus must occasion sharpest opposition. Because 'miracles' according to him are to be considered as the breaking in of mythological ideas, as the making visible of the divine in history, his all too over-simplified and premature thesis is: 'That is the end of the New Testament miracles as miracles.' No less destructive is the verdict which again affects the foundations of the New Testament: 'The belief in angels and the idea of demons in the New Testament' are 'sheer superstition'. 'The Church should quickly do its best to root it out, because it can only endanger the true effect of the kerygma.' Highly significant, and illustrative of the painful situation in which he finds himself, is his verdict: 'The Blumhardt stories are an abomination to me.' *Kerygma und Mythos*, p. 136 (ET, p. 120).

There is no question that in these statements Bultmann has left far behind him the real truth both of the New Testament and also of our knowledge of the world and existence today. 'Miracles', 'angels', 'demons' are, precisely on the contrary, a startling disclosure of the 'authentic' character and underlying background of the whole world system. Cf. O. Bruder, 'Die Heilungen Blumhardts', *Ev. Theol.* 1950, pp. 478 f., and further, E. Michaelis, *Geisterreich und Geistermacht: Der Heilungs- und Dämonenkampf J. Chr. Blumhardts*, Bern 1950; W. Künneth, 'Wunderheilung und Glaube', in H. Siegel, *Der Mensch von heute*, 1950, p. 78.

world. They are a beginning of God's resurrection act—a beginning in which God, through that same son who will become Lord of the kingdom, awakes new life. God acts through Jesus in the miracles, because he will act upon Jesus in the resurrection.

3. THE EXALTATION

The act of God in the resurrection of Jesus is the act of God on Christ in exaltation. The concept of '*exaltation*' means a theological interpretation of the resurrection of Jesus, but not a special act alongside resurrection and ascension. The resurrection of Jesus is identical with his exaltation, whereas the general resurrection of the dead could not by any means be described as exaltation in this specific sense. The risen Christ is at the same time the Exalted One, and the Exalted One is always also the Risen One. For the statement of the exaltation it is decisive to recognize that *God is exclusively the subject of the action in the resurrection of Jesus*. The exaltation of Jesus and—in content inseparably bound up with it—the resurrection of Jesus are therefore to be understood in a strictly theocentric sense.

Irreconcilable with this concept of exaltation are two theses which do not accord with the theological aim of the resurrection message. On the one hand, the act of God in the resurrection must not be described with exaggerated theocentricity as having no presuppositions. The resurrection of Jesus is not an act of sovereign caprice on the part of the divine power of the Creator but has, as we have seen, its inner substantial preconditions. The question why it is precisely in Jesus that the exaltation takes place cannot be left unanswered in favour of an abstract predestinationism divorced from history. Even when theocentrically considered the sonship and historic life of Jesus must not be regarded as having no essential relation to his exaltation.

But on the other hand the exaltation is just as little to be understood as an act of power executed by Jesus himself. In this case the resurrection is seen, not as an action of God upon Jesus, but as an independent act of the Christ Spirit at work in Jesus.[30] Accordingly the 'Redeemer Spirit' which animates Jesus must not die, in order that it can become the operative cause of the resurrection. While this theory does take seriously the significance of the history of Jesus, it both weakens the reality of the death of Jesus and also on the other hand impairs the uniqueness of the resurrection as an act of God. The understanding of the resurrection as the self-awakening of Jesus by the power of his own

[30] Cf. R. Seeberg, *Christl. Dogmatik* I, p. 370; II, pp. 146, 198 f.

TTR E

redeeming Spirit has its root in the Greek Logos doctrine, but not in Pauline theology, whose centre is essentially shifted thereby.

Contrary to this, however, the exaltation means the resurrecting action of God upon Jesus as Son and Messiah, and thus not an action of the Son, but an act of God. Jesus Christ in the resurrection is not the subject but the object of the work of God. It is an act of God, to be sure, which has its meaning and its ground in the sonship of Jesus and his messiahship. The exaltation of Christ by God, however, is in content his exaltation to be Kyrios.

(a)   The Installation as Kyrios

The resurrection Christology is essentially a *Kyrios Christology*. The primitive Christian message declares: *In the resurrection God has made Jesus to be Kyrios.* With the resurrection of Jesus we are therefore given the *concept Kyrios* and in it the key to the *broaching of the problems of Christology*. Kyrios Christology is the Christology whose central basis is the action of God upon Christ in the resurrection.[31]

To discover the dogmatic content of the raising of Christ we must begin with an analysis of the primitive Christian understanding of Kyrios. It is certain that the primitive Christian confession of Jesus as 'the Lord' is of completely unique and decisive importance. The Church summed up its faith in the statement, 'Jesus is Kyrios', and thereby gave expression to the fact that this title adequately meets the interests of faith and that 'if the need for a title of honour was felt, only Kyrios would do'.[32]

Accordingly, the question of what is meant in principle by the 'lordship' attained through the exaltation must be asked in the sense of what the primitive Christians saw in it.[33] Two assertions must first be made

[31] The primitive Christian tradition of the significance of the exaltation to be Kyrios can be described as unanimous and unequivocal. It is the raising of Jesus that first provides the ground of his lordship: Rom. 1.1 ff.; 14.9; Acts 10.42; Rom. 4.24; the possibility of being saved is given only to 'faith in the Kyrios Jesus', Acts 16.31; 15.11; 4.11; Phil. 3.8 f.; 2.11; I Cor. 12.3; Rom. 10.9; II Tim. 2.8; the meaning of the exaltation is clearly seen in Acts 2.34 f.; Heb. 1.13; I Cor. 15.25; and Ps. 110 which is applied to Jesus.

[32] W. Foerster, *Herr ist Jesus: Herkunft und Bedeutung des urchristlichen Kyriosbekenntnisses*, 1924, pp. 11 f., 24, 208. Cf. also E. Lohmeyer, *Kyrios Jesus*, 1928, p. 89: 'This Kyrios hymn (Phil. 2.5-11) is the *locus classicus* of primitive Christian Christology.'

[33] The question of what religious parallels and possible derivations the Kyrios title appears to have, whether it is a general description of the divine nature as such or a special title of the Covenant God of the Old Testament, whether originally a specific deity of Syria, Asia Minor or Egypt was worshipped under this title, whether it is to be related to Roman emperor worship or to be understood from the profane realm as the antithesis of slavery, appears from a funda-

by way of general description. First, the concept 'Kyrios' is to be understood as an expression of the unconditional claim of God in the face of the whole universe. It is an inalienable predicate of the divine majesty. This claim is to be more closely defined along three lines. Kyrios means cosmic lordship, the absolute power of the Creator, potentially and actually. Again, the concept means lordship over the conscience of men, the unlimited moral demand of God on every individual regardless of human recognition of that lordship. But this kyrios-ship of God has, finally, also the special meaning of his lordship over the community of believers. Here the title 'Lord' becomes a special confession of man's faith in, and his dependence on, this very lordship of God.

Secondly, the name Kyrios demands by its very nature an unlimited validity. The lordship of God can tolerate no other lords beside it. Every other lordship is either only derived lordship dependent upon the divine power, or presumptuous lordship, i.e. rebellion. He who is Kyrios is absolute Lord. His lordship is valid for every sphere and all ages; nothing can evade its claim. The title Kyrios has unconditional absoluteness. But this unconditionalness belongs only to God, just because he is the Lord.

In the light of this understanding of the concept of divine lordship, we see the decisive significance of the linking of this Kyrios title with Jesus. His installation as Lord through his exaltation can thus have no other meaning than that of the transferring of the lordship of God to Jesus. The exaltation of Christ in the resurrection therefore means the same as the entry of Jesus into lordship. The exalted Lord is the Risen One and the Risen One is always the Lord. The lordship of Jesus is thus bound to his installation by God in his resurrection act.[34] This basic Christological insight leads to the perception of two things.

The exalting of Jesus to be Kyrios is not the unfolding of an already existing state of lordship but a *novum*, an event of an incomparable kind in the context of God's revealing acts. The transcendent Son, like the historic Jesus, is not yet the exalted One who bears the name of Lord. Rather, Jesus before the resurrection is the one who himself recognizes

---

mentally dogmatic standpoint to be of no consequence. Likewise the discussion as to whether in the use of this term in primitive Christianity the word is taken over from sacred or profane usage, naively or by way of contrast, continuing the former meaning or transcending it, is of no essential Christological interest. Cf. W. Foerster, *op. cit.*, pp. 11 f., 33, 45 f., 117, 57 ff., 78 ff., 90 f.; also W. Bousset, *Kyrios Christos*[2], 1921.

[34] Cf. Acts 2.24, 33, 36; 3.26; 5.30; 7.55; 13.30; 26.8; Eph. 1.20; Col. 3.1; Phil. 2.9 f.; II Cor. 4.14; 5.15 f.; Rom. 4.24; 6.4; 8.11, 34; Gal. 1.1; I Thess. 1.10; I Peter 3.22.

the sole validity of God's lordship and submits himself unconditionally to it. Even the Messiah dies and is not yet the Lord of death. The Christological problem is consequently improperly aggravated when it is considered to assert the lordship of Jesus already in history or in the pre-existence of Jesus. Such a contradiction of the early Christian witness empties God's act in the resurrection of its power. The name of Lord essentially belongs solely to God. God alone commands this name and not by any means the man Jesus, nor the Son of God either. Therefore the installation of Jesus as Lord can only be the act of God and the conferring of the title Kyrios can be understood only in a theocentric sense.[35] It is of supreme importance to recognize that *in the resurrection Jesus receives something from God which he did not until then possess, namely his 'lordship'.*[36] The situation of Jesus before Easter is characterized not simply by the veiling of his messiahship, but primarily and decisively by the fact of his not yet being Kyrios.[37] The lordship conferred on him surpasses qualitatively all predicates of majesty until then ascribed to Jesus, however much these form the precondition of his 'lordly character'. The interpretation of the resurrection as the enthroning of Jesus as Kyrios grasps the inner dynamic of the whole Christ event. Christology has not to speak of a transcendent being of Christ which remains identical in itself. Rather, it knows of a progress in God's dealings with Christ, of a real Christ-event which reaches its climax in the resurrection of the Kyrios. By the resurrection, Jesus is given by God a status which he could not yet have had without this act of God. He has become something which until then he was not and could not be. Thus the installation as Lord becomes the cardinal point of an inwardly dynamic Christology which liberates alike from Logos speculation and from exaggerated paradoxes.[38]

To this there comes also the perception of a second thing which

[35] Cf. E. Lohmeyer, *op. cit.*, p. 69: 'It is God who sets him on the throne of an eternal lordship'; p. 74: 'Kyrios thus means in the first instance the revealed Lord and Ruler of the world; to this honour God has exalted him from the hidden mystery of the son of man and of death.'

[36] E. Lohmeyer agrees, *op. cit.*, p. 50: Jesus receives 'something which this divine form explicitly did not yet possess'. In the exaltation we have to do with 'a peculiar "extra" over and above the concept of form. This "extra" is clearly the honour and status of Kyrios' (p. 51).

[37] H. D. Wendland's view, which in reference to the resurrection of Jesus speaks only of a 'full revealing of the Messiah', of the 'new form of his presence' and of the 'abolition of the paradoxical and ambiguous character which his presence as Messiah possesses', seems unable to do justice to the concept of exaltation to be Kyrios. *Die Eschatologie des Reiches bei Jesus*, pp. 219 f., 222, 241.

[38] E. Hirsch rightly reminds us that 'no immutable, eternally identical relation of Jesus to God' exists. 'The name' is 'not originally Jesus' own, but he only received it': *Jesus Christus der Herr*, pp. 83, 72.

further describes the kyrios-ship of Jesus. The installation of Jesus as Lord means the same as the *conferring of divine majesty*. This grounding of his divine majesty in the resurrection rules out on the one hand any speculative, non-historic metaphysic of the intrinsic divine nature of Jesus, and provides on the other hand a safeguard against becoming exposed to a rationalistic levelling-down tendency by founding his divinity upon the picture of the historic Jesus. What constitutes Jesus' plenitude of divine power is the lordship he received in the resurrection. That, however, contains the unlimited power of God. The dogmatic meaning of the divine lordship of Jesus as given in the concept Kyrios has to be developed in the following directions.[39]

The assertion of the divinity of Jesus poses *the problem of Christian monotheism*. The history of dogmatics is rich in attempts at a solution, ranging from the various forms of modalism and docetism to the flight into modern paradox teaching. There must always come an alteration in the monotheistic concept of God, however, when lordship is conceived as such to be already an inherent property of Jesus. This thesis both contradicts the early Christian witness and is also incapable of doing justice to the idea of God. The result is the doctrine of 'kenosis' and 'krypsis', which speak of Jesus renouncing respectively the possession or the use of the divine omnipotence, yet without thereby being able to remove the dualistic tension between God and the divinity of Christ. The problem is altered, however, as soon as the investing of Jesus with divine power is identified with his installation as Lord. Then the entry into divine lordship is the act of God himself and an expression of his divine will.[40] In conferring upon Jesus the 'name' which is due to God alone, God himself attests himself as the absolute Lord who alone is able to transfer his lordship to another. Precisely because God is Lord, he can make Jesus Lord. The divine lordship of Jesus is for him neither an eternal possession nor a thing snatched or to be snatched. To be sure, Jesus as the Son is destined for this coming assumption of lordship, he has the right to divine power, yet he does not take the asserting of this claim into his own hands, but waits for its fulfilment by God. The divine lordship of Jesus is the gift of God to Jesus. God confers it on the utter

---

[39] Cf. Eph. 1.10 f., 21 f.; Col. 2.10, 15; Phil. 3.21; Rom. 14.7 ff.; I Cor. 15.24 f; I Peter 3.22.

[40] R. Frank, *Die Wahrheitsgewissheit* II, pp. 200 ff. F. Gogarten also agrees: It is God himself 'who in this event, in the death of Jesus Christ, conquers death and robs death of its power, and first and foremost robs it of its power over him who has given himself unconditionally into its (death's) power, even Jesus Christ. And that means nothing else but this: that God raises Jesus Christ from death to life, that he makes him rise again' (*Der dreieinige Gott*, p. 165).

obedience of the Son. The subject of the resurrection is God, who exalts the object of his action to be in turn the subject of the fulness of divine lordship and of the exercise of that lordship. Hence the divine majesty of Jesus is not a power alongside God, but means the same divine lordship bestowed by God himself. Monotheism is not challenged by the recognition of the divinity of Jesus, but rather fulfilled. The early Protestant status-doctrine, too, inadequate though it certainly is in form, has its real interest preserved on the basis of the Kyrios concept. Thus on the one hand the view of Jesus' divinity in virtue of his resurrection is determined by the theocentric outlook, while on the other hand the Christian idea of God takes its bearings essentially from the raising of Christ.[41]

The divine lordship of Christ which is given through the resurrection is divinity in the full sense of the word, not simply a supratemporal *divine essence or divine 'nature', such as can be predicated also of the 'Son' of God.* The divinity of the Risen One is also *not the moral and religious perfection of man* due to his unclouded union with God. The word Kyrios embraces the *whole* Godhead in the extensive sense. It is the ground of unlimited, divine lordship in its full compass, over Church, mankind and the universe. Christ the Lord is absolute Ruler of all creation. At this point, too, it becomes clear that this lordship cannot hold of the historic Jesus, but only of the Exalted One. With the concept of history there goes indissolubly the restriction of power, so that the divinity which, as is the fashion today, is in sharp paradox predicated of the man Jesus in history could always only be an imperfect and restrained divinity. A half-divinity is not divinity at all, and therefore in the strict use of terms this concept is not applicable to the status of Jesus before the resurrection. *It is first through his being installed as Lord in the resurrection that Christ takes the place of God.* The name Kyrios thus becomes the epitome of the plenitude of universal divine power.

The same is expressed by the dogmatic concept of the 'descent into

----

[41] In criticism of the status doctrine it has to be objected that the *status exaltationis* means nothing more than a return of Jesus to the state before the *exinanitio*. This robs the exaltation to be Kyrios of its extraordinary character and weakens the significance of God's action upon Christ.

We must agree with the opinion of Gogarten: 'The divinity of Jesus Christ cannot therefore be understood as if he had attained it through his earthly life. For divinity is not something that could somehow be attained by man' ('Menschheit und Gottheit Jesu Christi', *Zwischen den Zeiten* 1932, part I, p. 13). The conclusion, however, which Gogarten thinks must be drawn, that therefore divine honour must be ascribed already to the pre-existent Son, does not do justice to the New Testament witness to the Kyrios on the ground of the resurrection. The lordship of the Risen One is certainly not an achievement of the Son, but a gift of God.

hell', a statement which can positively *only* apply meaningfully to the Exalted One. The idea of this descent embraces within it the universality, unrestricted by space and time, of the Kyrios to whose kingdom belongs also the world of the dead. Not even this realm can escape his claim to rule. At the same time this concept indicates two things. It points to the judicial office which gives the final decision on life and death and which lies in the hands of the Exalted Lord. This right of lordship is expressed in the 'descent', inasmuch as for the world of the dead, too, i.e. for all generations of men in all ages, no matter whether they have died before or after the resurrection of Jesus, Christ shows himself to be the supratemporal Lord on whom rests the ultimate responsibility for every human fate. But secondly there lies in this concept also the idea of a promise for the whole world of the dead. He who is Lord over the dead is in fact he who was raised by God from the dead. Therefore the lordship of Jesus which is revealed in the 'descent into hell' is at the same time also the promise of a new life that is grounded in the resurrection.[42]

The full divinity of the Risen One implies, further, also the *real* divinity of the Kyrios in the intensive sense. The concept 'seated at the right hand of God' expresses the fact that the lordship of the Exalted One signifies real sovereignty and not a pseudo-government or an auxiliary government. It has the quality of real, essential divine sway.[43] No intensification or perfection of divinity beyond the lordship of Christ is conceivable. Here we see how right was the insight of the Early Church's trinitarian dogma. Any differentiation of degree, however defined, between God and Christ the Kyrios is impossible. In order to characterize the standing of the Exalted Lord, the confession 'Very God' is alone appropriate. The essential point is, however, that the ground on which this confession becomes possible is first laid by God's action in the resurrection. What is ultimately meant by the doctrine of the *coniunctio* of the two 'natures' and the doctrine of *anhypostasis* finds on the basis of the resurrection a fulfilment which liberates it from the inadequacies of the concept of divine nature and from the necessity of defining the divinity of Jesus over against his humanity in such a way that the humanity is curtailed in favour of the divinity. This solution of the Christological problem on the basis of the resurrection certainly does not mean a rational abrogation of the logical paradox of the union

---

[42] See further 'The Intermediate State', p. 270 below.
[43] Cf. also E. Lohmeyer's interpretation, *op. cit.*, p. 52: ' "Kyrios" describes the totality of the divine reality, its form as well as its being.'

of God and man. For the installation as divine Kyrios refers of course precisely to the man Jesus. The Exalted Lord is none other than the obedient Son. But the theologically decisive point is, that we acquire an understanding of the ground of the divinity of the man Jesus, and of the fact that the union of divinity and humanity is not to be taken as a timeless metaphysical principle, but is given only in the concept of Kyrios.[44] Whoever encounters Jesus as 'Lord' encounters God in this lordship of the Risen One; whoever rejects the Kyrios finds himself fleeing from God and in rebellion against God's will. The confession 'Jesus is Lord' therefore means nothing else but the binding of the conscience to Christ as very God, so that we have to say: *where the risen Christ is, there is God, and God is where the Kyrios holds sway.*

With this statement, to be sure, the boundaries between God and Christ do not become fluid, but we have to recognize that since the resurrection of Jesus God can no longer be found apart from Christ but only in the kyrios-ship of Jesus. The characteristic predicate of God is summed up in the statement: *God is the God who has raised Christ: he is the God of the resurrection. Thus because of the Easter event, there can be no other knowledge of God than in and through the knowledge of Christ as the Lord.* Every attempt to worship God without worshipping Christ as Kyrios disregards the action of God on Christ in the resurrection and is therefore in the last resort far from God. Worship of the Kyrios on the other hand does not obscure monotheism, but makes it plainer than ever. It is recognition of God's working upon Jesus and as such always at the same time true worship of God. The cult of Christ, in the sense of worship of the exalted Christ, is necessarily born with the resurrection. Prayer to God, however, since the installation of Jesus as Lord, is now possible and meaningful only 'in the name of Jesus', only '*en kyriō*'. Not Jesus worship, but service of the Kyrios, is therefore the adequate cultic expression of Christian monotheism.[45]

[44] In F. Gogarten's valuable study on 'Menschheit und Gottheit Jesu Christi' we miss any consideration of the Kyrios idea and the resurrection event. Consequently Gogarten never gets in principle beyond the schema of the Early Church dogma. It is only on the presupposition of the resurrection, however, that he is right in saying: 'Where Christology is not concerned with this *coniunctio* as an unfathomable mystery, i.e. with the union of two things that cannot be united, there we can well say that such a Christology is no longer concerned with Christ, with the Redeemer' (p. 13).

[45] The distinguishing mark between Christians and non-Christians was accordingly their calling on the name of the Lord; cf. I Cor. 1.2; 1.10; 6.11; 8.6; Rom. 7.25; 10.13; 15.20; Eph. 4.5; Acts 9.14; Col. 3.17, 'do all in the name of the Lord Jesus'. In this perspective the opinion of P. Althaus becomes dubious: 'The worship of Jesus arose and arises in view of his historic picture, even if certainly only in the light of Easter' (*Theol. Aufsätze*, p. 219). Rather, it has to

(b) The Significance of the Kyrios-ship for the Christological Problem

The recognition of the resurrection of Jesus as exaltation to lordship provides the decisive standpoint for a resurrection Christology. It makes clear that *the construction of a Christology is possible and meaningful only on the basis of this Easter situation*. In this situation is given the focal point for the real understanding of the whole fact of Christ and proclamation of Christ. In relation to the kyrios-ship of the exalted Lord the incarnation and historic life of Jesus are a prelude which in themselves have the character of the fragmentary. Apart from Easter the questions raised by the history of Jesus remain without a proper answer and subject to the caprice of subjective interpretation. The confession to the Kyrios is the only unequivocal answer which is beyond the reach of subjective relativization and on the basis of which sense can be given to the Christological approach. A reconstruction of the history of Jesus which disregards the event of the resurrection not only denies the presupposition on which the tradition arose, but also renounces an essentially Christological answer altogether. *The primitive Christian community looks at the whole of the past through 'Easter' eyes, i.e. with the depth of insight given to it by the resurrection of Jesus*. Its memory of the earthly life of Jesus becomes characterized by the new possibility of interpretation in the perspective of the resurrection. Thus in regard both to content and to method the kyrios-ship acquires a decisive importance for the questions of Christology.[46]

(i) The Significance in Regard to Content

The kyrios-ship of Jesus is not unrelated to the Christological dogma of the Son's becoming man. It is precisely the *incarnation* that often appears in theology to be the central Christian dogma, which even apart from the resurrection expresses the essence of Christianity. In the incarnation there takes place the paradoxical uniting of God and man, eternity and time, word and flesh, so that here we find the whole mystery

---

be put the opposite way round: the worship arises in view of the resurrection of Jesus even if only in connection with his historic picture. Cf. the confession of Thomas, John 20.28: 'My Lord and my God'.

[46] Cf. E. Brunner, agreeing with this: 'The message of Easter first completes the "sentence", the "word", and makes it meaningful. ... Without Easter everything remains in the dark' (*Der Mittler*, pp. 509-10, 522: ET, pp. 563, 574). It is the great merit of W. Michaelis to have pointed out the significance of Easter and Pentecost as the 'medium' through which the history of Jesus first attains contemporary validity. In so doing he has brought out points which are decisive for New Testament theology. *Täufer, Jesus, Urgemeinde*, pp. 133 ff., 138. To be sure, the Easter aspect has to be given the primacy over the Pentecostal one, since the latter is also determined by the former.

of the Christian faith.[47] The attraction of such concentration on the incarnation lies in the possibility of philosophical interpretation and in the openness to the dialectical play of ideas. Exclusive regard to the incarnation dogma, however, presupposes an abstraction which is out of place. It both contradicts the concern of primitive Christian preaching, and is also incapable of showing the ground of the very divinity of the Son with which the dogma deals. The demonstrating of a reciprocal relation between the incarnation and resurrection of Jesus does better justice to the interest of Christology than does the predominating of the incarnation. The miracle of the incarnation is conditioned by the miracle of the resurrection, but equally, we can speak of the resurrection only because we know of the birth of God's Son.[48] Important as it is to recognize this mutual relationship according to which the one statement does not exist without the other and according to which the incarnation cannot be isolated and discussed in abstraction from the resurrection,[49]

---

[47] Cf. E. Seeberg, *Ideen zur Theologie der Geschichte des Christentums*, 1929: 'This basic idea of the Christian religion is undoubtedly the incarnation. . . . This basic idea . . . expresses first of all that the Infinite, necessarily and without reduction of power, must become finite and corporeal, that the Spirit must become word and that the eternal God, who is all and not an existence, must find concrete form and reality in time' (pp. 23-4, 18 f.).

From this standpoint the questions raised by Althaus (*Die christliche Wahrheit* II, p. 240) also find their answer. Certainly 'the historic Jesus claims divine authority', certainly 'he demands faith in himself, he the man Jesus', certainly the Christological problem is 'not first propounded by Easter', but this very divine authority, this claim to faith, are an anticipation of the kyrios-ship for which the historic man Jesus is destined. In the authoritative words and acts of Jesus of Nazareth there break through the first rays of the resurrection, because he is in fact Kyrios designate. It is through Easter that the Christological problem first receives its meaningful interpretation and answer. What scripture passages can be used to show that I have not rightly interpreted the 'Christological content of Easter'? What conclusive theological considerations tell against this 'Christology of the resurrection'? The 'method of Christological thinking' which I employ is dictated by taking the resurrection message seriously. The postulate of a 'dynamic Christology' which derives from the raising of Jesus and looks towards it is one which for the sake of the New Testament witness, as it seems to me, cannot be surrendered. It is obvious on the other hand that 'paradox Christology' can find a place for the significance of the resurrection only in the margin and only as a conclusion, but not in the centre, as alone accords with the primitive Christian witness.

[48] Thus K. Barth, *Dogmatik* I, p. 275: 'The ground of Christ's rising from the dead, and the reason why it must inevitably be taught, is that he is the one who was wondrously conceived and born. That he is the one who was wondrously conceived and born discloses itself, shows itself, makes itself known in his resurrection. Only miracle is the ground of miracle, and only through miracle does miracle make itself known.'

[49] Cf. also F. Gogarten, *op. cit.*, p. 15: 'Only when taken up into, and taken together with, the two facts of the death and resurrection of Jesus Christ . . . is the eternal begetting of the Son by the Father not merely a weird speculation . . . but becomes comprehensible to us as the inconceivable, ineffable love with which the holy God accepts the sinful world.'

yet this relation is not really suited to show the significance of the resurrection for the dogma in question. Incarnation and resurrection are not in fact to be understood as equal foci of an ellipse. The co-ordinating of them is an improper shift of emphasis unknown to the primitive Christian message. To be sure, there can be no surrendering the value of the fact that the incarnation forms a bridge between the unapproachable divine majesty of the Risen Lord and the real humanity of Jesus, and that because of the incarnation the concrete historic life of Jesus is also taken up into God's action in the resurrection, in contrast to the mythologies of the gods in the history of religion—in other words, that the Kyrios is always at the same time the man Jesus. Yet the decisive meaning is not given in the incarnation itself, nor in its reciprocal relationship to the resurrection, but exclusively in the kyrios-ship of Christ. *The incarnation of the Son is neither climax nor conclusion of the whole Christ event, but the beginning of the action of God which makes for the resurrection as its goal.* True, the whole is already contained by implication in the beginning, yet it is only the fulfilment of this beginning in the resurrection that first makes possible a proper exposition of it. It is only on the basis of the resurrection that the birth of Jesus is first understood as a unique revealing act of God and as a divine necessity if the lordship of the Son is to be possible. Because God's work upon Christ begins with the incarnation, the Christmas message is already the promise of the Kyrios. But it is possible to interpret this secret only through the resurrection, in the light of which the predicates of majesty which belong to the 'Lord' are transferred retrospectively to the child in the manger. This transferring of divine honour to the incarnate one, which is understandable from the standpoint of faith, is theologically justified if the process is seen to be retrospective and the ground of it is seen to be in the resurrection. Everything accordingly depends on the fact that the truly human Jesus is the one exalted by God. For the confession of the birth of Jesus as the miracle of divine love, as incarnation, i.e. as the coming of God through Jesus to men, as the breaking in of eternity into time and as the 'becoming flesh' of the 'word'—all this has its validity not in some extraordinary historic event, but in the fact that he who is born in Bethlehem is the Risen Kyrios. The certainty that it is really the 'eternal word' that became flesh, that it is really God who acted in the event of Christ's birth, has its ground only in the certainty of the resurrection.

This comprehensive grounding of Christology which sets out from the resurrection also determines our attitude to the theological interpretation of the 'virgin birth'. In this context fundamental doubts arise regarding the unfortunate attempt of K. Barth to make the question of the 'virgin birth' a central theme of Christology.[50] Although we cannot agree with K. Heim's criticism of the theological evaluation of the virgin birth when he says its 'factuality' has 'to be determined not by dogmatics but by historical research',[51] yet his basic objections are valid also against Barth.[52] From the point of view of the resurrection, however, Barth's acute reflections on the virgin birth appear to cause a shifting of Christology's centre of gravity on to a peripheral point and thus to evade the real Christological task. It is certainly legitimate to develop a 'theology of the virgin birth'. Yet the confession of the 'virgin birth' is in no sense an object of primary Christological interest, but is to be maintained as the classical expression, and one not to be surpassed by any modern formula, of the mystery of the incarnation of the Son, which in contrast to every other earthly birth is a miracle not because his physical parentage was apparently qualified by some divine factor, but because *the* man was born who is the 'Son' and as such the coming 'Lord'.[53]

The material significance of the divinity of Jesus is no less when it comes to understanding the character borne by his *historicality*. The resurrection of Jesus is God's assent to the history of his 'Son'. Thus the resurrection and the history of Jesus stand not merely in an ineradicable mutual relationship, but also in the relation of beginning and consummation. The being and work of Jesus in history form no contradiction to the Risen One, for the latter is not the negation of that history but its fulfilment.

In the resurrection of Christ God himself provides the decisive confirmation of the genuineness of the claim of Jesus. God proves by his action in the resurrection that the man Jesus is the pre-existent man from the transcendent dimension, inasmuch as he perfects his sonship by the conferring of kyrios-ship. God's confession to the sending of the Son and to his obedience in the life of history comes only in the resurrection, and thereby fulfils the Son's right to lordship. In the light of

---

[50] *Dogmatik* I, pp. 272 ff.
[51] The critical and vacillating observations of P. Althaus on the 'virgin birth' cannot satisfy us nor do justice to the concern of the Bible and of dogmatics. *Christl. Wahrheit* II, pp. 215 f.
[52] K. Heim, *Dogmatik* II, p. 70.
[53] In view of the evolution of Roman Catholic Mariology there is certainly a demand for theology to develop on the basis of the New Testament tradition a Christologically appropriate doctrine of the 'virgin birth'. Cf. also W. Künneth, *Christus oder Maria*, Berlin-Spandau 1950.

the resurrection the titles of honour given to the historic Jesus become understandable. He is the Son who in contrast to mankind shares in the eternity of God, and the Messiah who truly bears the authority of the kingdom of God—all statements which under the veil of history bear the stamp of ambiguity, and attain to clarity only through the recognition of the resurrection. It is the lordship of Jesus which first throws light on the true nature of sonship and messiahship.[54]

What Jesus preached and did likewise stands in the light of the resurrection. It is the resurrection of Jesus that first brings a new and deeper understanding of its meaning and a subsequent proof of its rightness. The question whether *the words of the historic Jesus* are to be rated only as wise sayings and prophetic insights of the Rabbi of Nazareth or as words of an incomparable kind is answered for the first time by the resurrection. Unless related to the resurrection, all the words of Jesus lie on the religious-historical plane. They are set free from that relative context only when the prophet who spoke them is something very different, when he is the Exalted 'Lord'. When this is recognized, all the logia of Jesus, the parables, the Sermon on the Mount, the words of judgment, however much they may originally have sprung from a quite concrete situation, are taken out of their place in contemporary history and attain absolute universality. The resurrection makes clear that divine authority is behind them. Thus the words of Jesus retrospectively become 'words of the Lord', which have the quality of the 'Word of God'.[55] Further, Jesus' miracle working also comes into a relation of dependence on the resurrection. Without the coming lordship, the peculiarity of the miracles of Jesus as distinct from other biblical and extra-biblical miracles would only be obscure. The supratemporal meaning of these events is given only when he who works miracles in history is the same as he whom God invests with lordship.

[54] Cf. A. Schlatter, *Geschichte des Christus*, p. 536: 'If in view of the earthly Christ it remained a profound enigma how he could assert eternity of himself, in view of the risen one the idea of eternity was confirmed.'

The argument maintained by K. Heim in his critique of the old status doctrine, that the separating of divinity and servant form robs Jesus of his 'significance as saviour' since it removes 'his divine significance beyond his earthly human reality' (*Dogmatik* II, p. 67), does not affect the Christology presented here. The divinity of the Kyrios has not merely its precondition in the servant form, but the latter derives from the resurrection its meaning. The significance of Jesus as saviour is ensured precisely by his lordship.

[55] Cf. Gogarten, *Ich glaube an den dreieinigen Gott*, p. 166: 'The proclamation both of the Old and of the New Testament finds in the resurrection its divine confirmation and the disclosure of its full meaning.' Further, p. 171: '. . . The resurrection is the fulfilment of the divine promise . . . is God's confessing to his own history, i.e. to the history whose Lord he is.'

Finally, *the action of God in the resurrection of Jesus makes clear the reality of the* 'deus revelatus' *in the historic Jesus.* If the power and the will of God are revealed in a special way in the exaltation of Christ, then the man Jesus is himself already revelation of God in history—a revelation which is perfected and confirmed in the resurrection. At the same time, however, this kyrios-ship implies the exclusiveness of the divine revelation in Christ, so that in conclusion the concept of Christian revelation is also to be defined on the basis of the resurrection.[56]

(ii) *The Significance in Regard to Method*

As soon as the significance of the kyrios-ship for Christology is recognized, theology finds itself confronted by a new situation when it comes to shedding light on the thought-world of the New Testament. The importance which attaches to the resurrection in primitive Christian thinking demands a respect which has a far-reaching effect on method. *New Testament problems*, which on other presuppositions are solved in a way that does not do justice to the New Testament facts, *have to be broached from the key position of the resurrection.* The result is a new attitude to three problems which are important for the understanding of primitive Christianity: the problem of Paul, the problem of Paul and Jesus, and the question of a 'Life of Jesus'.

R. Bultmann rightly avers that 'The understanding of Paul decides the understanding of primitive Christianity.'[57] But what is the basic starting point for the proper understanding of Paul? A glance at the history of *Pauline research* shows not only the intensive effort to master the problems, but also the chaos of opinions and hypotheses. Some seek to start from a central concept of Pauline theology, from the concept of spirit, from the antithesis of *sarx* and *pneuma*, from the idea of reconciliation, from the concept of God, from his anthropology and his understanding of 'being', from his discussion of the law and his attitude to it, or from his eschatological expectation. Others move the emphasis from theological problems to the personality of Paul, to the psychological analysis of his inner life; they speak of his piety, his experience on the

[56] Cf. K. Heim, *Glaube und Leben*, 1926, pp. 433, 302: The primitive Christian message of the resurrection is necessarily absolute and intolerant in the conviction of bearing absolutely *the* truth, *the* revelation. The peculiar vitality of the apostles is indeed expressed in the fact that they know that 'in face of this message there can be only either-or. The message is either true, and then it has absolute significance for all men . . . is for the whole inhabited world the event on which the fate of every individual man is decided. Or the message is false . . . and then we Christians who have built our life upon it are "of all men the most miserable".'

[57] 'Zur Geschichte der Paulus-Forschung', *Theol. Rundschau*, 1929, part 1, p. 29.

road to Damascus, the mystical contemplations of his 'Christ mysticism', of Paul's specific 'sense of life' or even of ecstasy as his basic emotional determination. A third group seek to come nearer to a solution of the riddle of Paul by assuming extra-Christian motifs and religious-historical influences. Thus either the Old Testament tradition of rabbinical Judaism is regarded as the dominant source of Pauline teaching, especially its ritual and sacramental piety, conditioned by hellenistic and gnostic ideas and the mystery religions. Or others champion a synthesis of different sets of ideas, the judicial doctrine of reconciliation, the mystical and ethical doctrine of redemption, Jewish apocalyptic—even the influence of the ancient oriental myth of the primeval man on the world of Pauline faith is seriously considered.

Now it is not to be denied that the abundance of penetrating studies has brought to light much of lasting importance, but on the whole a unified understanding of Paul must be wrecked if the principle governing the world of Paul's theological thinking is missed. Setting out from an arbitrarily chosen and subjectively emphasized idea, which is then usually given a modern reinterpretation into the bargain—from the religious personality of Paul, or from something he has borrowed from the history of religion—inevitably leads to an understanding of Paul which is rationalist, psychological, idealist, speculative and considered in terms of contemporary history regarded purely historically, to an abbreviation and distortion of his theological thought, to an essential misunderstanding of his theological and at the same time existential concern. The result must be that Pauline theology appears self-contradictory and the riddle insoluble, that because the cardinal point is missed then, as A. Schweitzer says, 'the skein tangles itself from the start', and Pauline research is condemned 'to pass off an unintelligible chaos of ideas as Pauline teaching'.[58]

One can agree with Schweitzer also when he says that 'Paul must be understood from a unified basic standpoint if everything he says is not to remain enigmatic'. A comprehensive view of Paul's statements, if it would really understand what Paul is after, must rest on the conviction that Paul's theology interprets itself, contains within itself the norm for its evaluation and is not to be grasped by applying criteria from elsewhere. *Paul's thinking in all his utterances rotates around one unifying centre and that centre is the raising of Christ from the dead.* One of the things which this work seeks to make clear is, that the fact of the resurrection is the decisive point of orientation, as indeed the unbiased judge

[58] *Die Mystik des Apostels Paulus*, 1930, p. 41 (ET, p. 40).

is also compelled to see. In the light of the resurrection the seemingly tangled lines of Paul's thought will unite to form a meaningful systematic whole, a grandiose unified 'world-view', in which the truths that research has discovered about eschatology and anthropology, about spirit, ethics and law, find their place, in the light of the resurrection now no longer inexplicable but illumined anew. To be sure, it remains a striking thing that this very Pauline axis seems to be overlooked, and is considered either to be of no consequence for Paul's basic view or to be an alien intrusion from mythology. The Pauline problem, however, is in essence identical with the question of the resurrection and its meaning for Paul.

The '*problem of Paul and Jesus*' must also assume a new shape in the light of the resurrection situation. If the new world situation since the resurrection is disregarded, then the following picture usually emerges. The person and teaching of Jesus appear to be determined by an unreflected, 'purely spiritual, simple and sober piety',[59] free of theological considerations and untrammeled by faith in certain saving events; his Sermon on the Mount forms the climax of ethical insights and demands whose universal validity remains in dispute; his eschatological preaching is a continuation of the apocalyptic of late Judaism and as such a limited product of its day. Paul on the other hand seems to be of a wholly different stamp, to stand in open contradiction to the 'religion of Jesus' with its simple idea of the fatherhood of God, and indeed seems to complicate it and transform it into universal theological speculations, into a system of facts of salvation. Thus is posed the problem of Jesus and Paul. A solution is attempted either by acknowledging Paul in spite of everything to be the first and 'most congenial interpreter' of Jesus, who developed the inner logic of Jesus' religious ideas and gave them significance for world history through his theology, however many foreign and non-essential elements it may also contain; or else by so completely separating and contrasting Paul and Jesus that Paul's theology is described as a degeneration of the original ideas of Jesus and the attempt is made to get behind Paul and let only Jesus count. In the former case, Paul is understood as admittedly a deviation from Jesus, yet a tolerable one, since the views of Jesus are also still found in him, and in part seem to be made even more profound; in the latter case Paul is rejected as standing in contrast to Jesus.

It is obvious that this way of stating the problem clearly recognizes that Paul brings something new and that therefore something must lie

[59] R. Bultmann, *Die Erforschung der synoptischen Evangelien*, 1930, p. 40.

between Jesus and Paul which can explain his new thought-world. If the cause of this change from Jesus to Paul is not discovered, then the problem presents insoluble difficulties and the result must in every case be far-reaching misjudgments of Paul. The question could therefore be stated thus: What happened after the death of Jesus that inevitably caused Paul to make statements which go further than Jesus and are not in any way grounded in the life of Jesus, yet at the same time without being rebutted by the first disciples as foreign to Jesus and defection from him? The answer can only be: The event after the death of Jesus which stands between Jesus and Paul and fundamentally alters the world situation is the raising of Christ. When this fact is understood, there can be no more talk of a 'Paul and Jesus' problem. This explains the difference between the teaching and acts of Jesus and the thought-world of Paul as a sheer, obvious necessity. Jesus stands in the pre-Easter situation, his works still stand under the promises of the old aeon, his significance has the limitations of the particular, the decisive acts of salvation are still to come. Paul on the other hand knows of the change in the world situation since Easter, he must therefore speak of this event not merely in passing but repeatedly and centrally, faith in the Kyrios expands his theology to become world-embracing, and much that seemed important in the pre-Easter period inevitably passed into the background once men were impressed by the lordship of Jesus. In the light of Easter the inner necessity of the unity and the difference between Jesus and Paul becomes unequivocally clear. For that reason Paul can never be understood as the mere continuer or gifted interpreter of the Gospel of Jesus, but is, precisely in contrast to Jesus and the pre-Easter relation of the disciples to Jesus, first and foremost the apostle of the Risen Kyrios, who has this message to proclaim.

Likewise, finally, *the problem of the 'Life of Jesus'* is also judged in an essentially new way in the light of the resurrection. The interest in a life of Jesus, and the question of what are essentially its basic features, are right and meaningful from the standpoint of the Gospel message, in so far as the life of Jesus is seen in its relation to the resurrection, of which it is plainly the precondition. The extensive efforts in the history of life-of-Jesus research show, however, that in such attempts it is always a case of reconstruction of the situation before the resurrection and without regard to it. With the help of the fresh religious-historical approach of Bousset and Heitmüller who assert 'a vast difference between the primitive Christianity of Palestine and of the hellenistic world', by distinguishing two layers in Palestinian Christianity itself whereby the Baptist sect has a role to play, and not least on the basis of the new form-critical outlook which assumes that the literary shaping of the primitive literature moved in relatively fixed forms according to its own laws of style, the attempt is made to discover the authentic core of the Gospel accounts, i.e. the parts which really make up the life of Jesus. The result is, 'that the entire framework of the history of Jesus is seen to be editorial material, and that thus a whole series of typical scenes which are familiar to us from church use, as also from poetry and painting, are clearly inventions of the evangelists. But the result is a positive one, inasmuch as we now see which parts of the Gospels are ancient tradition.'[60] This kind of research's critical work of dissection clearly leads to the gravest doubts about the life of Jesus. 'We can no longer know the character of Jesus, nor form a clear picture of his personality and his life[61];' 'of the origin and development of his messianic consciousness we can no longer say anything certain at all',[62] and it remains doubtful, too, whether the final catastrophe is really to be traced to the Jewish authorities and not rather to the Roman procurator. To be sure, important remnants of the preaching of Jesus are still discernible. The examination of them leads us, it is true, 'into a great deal of uncertainty, but it does not end in complete scepticism'.[63] That to perceive this must amount for the Christian Church to a destruction of the faith is a point on which this kind of theological study ought at least to be clear.

From this standpoint it also becomes possible to address ourselves to the now much discussed question of the relation of the theological work of Bultmann to the principles of theological liberalism. Bultmann himself and his friends emphatically oppose any identification with liberal theology, and no one denies that Bultmann's concern for an 'existentialist interpretation' of the whole New Testament kerygma has nothing to do with the reductions of liberalism, for which the truth of the New Testament finally shrinks to a few remnants. It will also have to be conceded that Bultmann's intention is to overcome in principle by this means the outlook and theological results of liberalism.

Although we, too, fully acknowledge this, it must nevertheless not obscure from us that the fact still remains that in Bultmann's conception, despite all his new points of view, we have on the one hand a new

[60] *Op. cit.*, p. 14.
[61] *Op. cit.*, pp. 32-3.
[62] *Op. cit.*, p. 38. Cf. also Martin Kähler, *Der sog. historische Jesus und der geschichtlich biblische Christus²*, 1896. Further, E. Meyer, *Ursprung und Anfänge des Christentums* I and II, 1921.
[63] *Op. cit.*, p. 32.

blossom and fruit of the 'old liberalism'. Since this assertion usually encounters sharpest repudiation, it requires to be substantiated in detail.

We maintain our thesis on a threefold basis: 1. As in liberalism, Bultmann adopts an anthropocentric standpoint in his view of events on the plane of history. We do find a deeper understanding of history in Bultmann as compared with liberalism, but the *ratio*, as the critical yardstick which man, the critical observer, applies to the biblical sources is decisive also for Bultmann. 2. In Bultmann, too, as in liberalism, the epistemological principle is methodically to doubt every report which breaks the bounds of the relative and the historical and asserts things that are suprahistoric, inexplicable and transcendent. Even if Bultmann, in contrast to liberalism, is not satisfied with the liberal method of 'selecting' and 'deleting', yet it must not be overlooked that he energetically pursues his own process of critical selection. The method of elimination is one he applies ruthlessly and without restraint. 3. Like liberalism, Bultmann too recognizes the negative results of the 'history of life-of-Jesus research', even though he dissociates himself from their consequences for Christian proclamation by resorting to an emphatic indifference to the 'historic facts' and the 'historical Jesus'. For the understanding of Bultmann's theology the verdict in his book on *Jesus* is therefore still as decisive as ever. Bultmann declares: 'To be sure, I am of the opinion that we can now know next to nothing of the life and personality of Jesus, since the Christian sources were not interested in that, and are moreover very fragmentary and overgrown by legend, and since other sources do not exist. . . . I am personally of the opinion that Jesus did not consider himself to be the Messiah . . . the sources give us the proclamation of the Church . . . critical study shows that the whole tradition of Jesus . . . breaks up into a series of layers. . . . That the Fourth Gospel is a source . . . is out of the question altogether. . . . Within what remains . . . secondary material must again be rejected. . . . By means of critical analysis we can reach an oldest layer, even though we can define it only with relative certainty. Naturally there is even less certainty that the words in this oldest layer were really spoken by Jesus . . . for this oldest layer is also the result of a complicated historical process. . . . To be sure, there is no ground for doubting whether Jesus really existed . . . but such doubts are of no essential significance. . . . Anyone who wishes to set this "Jesus" in quotation marks . . . and regard it as a valid designation of the historic phenomenon . . . is welcome to do so.'[64] Jesus said nothing about his death and resurrection. 'It is true

---

[64] *Jesus*, pp. 12 ff. (ET, pp. 8 ff.), cf. also *The History of the Synoptic Tradition*.

that a few words of such content were put into his mouth, but they do not come from the faith of the Church . . . from hellenistic Christianity.'[65]

This glance into Bultmann's theological workshop shows indisputably not only that Bultmann's theology is dependent upon liberalism's critical-historical principles of research, but also where a 'theology' leads when it loses sight of the fundamental basis of all theological knowledge, namely the resurrection of Jesus. Thus in conclusion it becomes clear again that *a posteriori* every attempt to say something after all of the resurrection of Jesus must utterly fail. The primitive Christian kerygma of the Risen One knows only of the concrete, personal, individual resurrection of the man Jesus of Nazareth, about whom both liberalism and also Bultmann have precisely nothing to say.

On the other hand there is reason to ask: must this starting point of the New Testament's approach not perhaps be described as fundamentally mistaken? Then, since the presupposition is untenable, the end result would also necessarily appear thoroughly dubious. The basis of all such inquiries, however, as we have already pointed out elsewhere, is abstraction from the resurrection—the idea that we can reconstruct from the Gospels the situation before the resurrection. But this assumption is to be repudiated all along the line as irrelevant. *It is an illusion to think that in the Gospels we can get behind Easter and reconstruct a life of Jesus as such, untouched by the knowledge of Easter.* The basic outlook of the Synoptists is conditioned by the resurrection faith, just as all primitive Christianity, Palestinian no less than hellenistic, stands in the perspective of the resurrection. Precisely when Bultmann, too, acknowledges that 'the Church is conscious of owing its existence . . . to the work of Jesus' and 'the picture of the historic figure of Jesus' appears 'through the medium of the Church',[66] when, further, it is quite clear 'that it was not the historical interest that determined the narrative, but the needs of Christian faith and life', and that 'the main emphasis' lay 'on the end, on the story of the Passion and of Easter',[67] then this very insight is not secondary but decisive, and we have therefore to ask what was the ultimate 'cultic' motive which essentially shaped the reports of the life of Jesus. This formative principle is unmistakably given in the resurrection faith. It is only on that basis that a valid understanding of the life of Jesus can be attained and it is possible again for positive,

[65] *Jesus*, p. 196 (ET, pp. 213 f.).
[66] *Die Erforschung der synoptischen Evangelien*, p. 32.
[67] *Op. cit.*, pp. 34-5.

constructive study to take the place of the work of destruction. The evangelists know of the life of Jesus only because they know of his resurrection. The projections of post-Easter knowledge back into the historic life of Jesus are therefore not to be dismissed as 'legendary construction' or 'products of pious fantasy', but answer completely to the 'substance' of the Gospel, inasmuch as the Gospel of the resurrection is in fact a reality. All that can be determined by 'neutral' religious-historical and form-critical methods is for the substance of the life of Jesus wholly immaterial and of no consequence for faith. The observations and insights which come from such researches have value only when they are not regarded in isolation from the total view as governed by the worship of the Kyrios, but can be fitted meaningfully into the whole picture of primitive Christian faith. We know the life of Jesus only in subjection to the resurrection, which at the same time sets us free from bondage to those elements in the life of Jesus which belong to contemporary history, to the sphere of the relative and to the situation before Easter.[68]

[68] That this new basic orientation in method has already been adopted by New Testament scholars is shown not only by the work of Schlatter and others, but above all by the publications of Wilhelm Michaelis, Gerhard Kittel and H. D. Wendland. Thus G. Kittel says: ' . . . Everything up to now was altogether abstraction. The New Testament has of course in reality no wish at all to tell the story of the "merely" historical Jesus. The apostles bear witness of the historical facts to the Church, not in order that the Church may be edified or moved by them, but in order that it may believe and be saved. . . . It is entirely correct when it is stated that the presentation of Jesus in the Gospels stands from beginning to end in the light of the Easter experience. None of the ancient Christians would write a single line about Jesus except out of the certainty of the risen, exalted and ever-present Lord. . . . Only now does the historical picture acquire life and content—more than that: only now does it become real and true. . . . Only one thing solves the riddle: faith . . . only faith is able to interpret the work of the historical method at this point and carry it to a conclusion. There is no value, no meaning in the historical Jesus except when in faith he is experienced and confessed as the living Christ' ('Der "historische" Jesus', in *Mysterium Christi*, 1931, pp. 64 f.); cf. also *Die Probleme des palästinensischen Spätjudentums und Urchristentums*, 1926. Similarly also H. D. Wendland, who makes his task the overcoming of the 'dualism between critical historical study and believing interpretation' and maintains 'the unity of the New Testament revelation' (*Die Eschatologie des Reiches Gottes*, pp. 2 ff.). Cf. also F. W. Schmidt, 'Das Verhältnis der Christologie zur historischen Leben-Jesu-Forschung', *ZTK* 1920, pp. 270 f. Cf. also W. Mundle, *Der Glaube an Christus und der historische Zweifel*, Brunnquell Verlag, 1950. On the lines of M. Kähler, Mundle comes to conclusions which are in essential agreement with the postulates of a 'theology of the resurrection'.

IV

GOD'S DEALINGS WITH THE WORLD
THROUGH THE RESURRECTION OF JESUS

I N the first section of our dogmatic exposition we have discussed the
specific theme of Christology from the theocentric standpoint of an
action of God upon Christ in the resurrection. From the inner logic of
this statement comes the task of inquiring into the significance of this
event for the world as a whole. The action of God in the raising of
Christ is at the same time an action of God upon the world—and that,
too, on the one hand for the grounding of salvation and on the other
hand for the fulfilling of the creation.

I. THE RESURRECTION AS THE GROUND FOR SALVATION

(a) The Grounding of the 'theologia crucis'

It is a decisive insight of recent theological thinking that 'salvation'
can be validly spoken of only when *the significance of the death of Jesus*
for the world is placed in the centre of the picture. The mystery of the
life and suffering of Christ is concentrated on the fact of the cross. Thus
linking up with Paul, and not least looking back to Luther, the *theologia
crucis* is perceived to be the heart of an evangelical doctrine of salvation.
The Logos to which all theology must be related is a *logos tou staurou*,
a word of the cross.[1]

In view of this insight the question arises whether the resurrection of
Jesus has a soteriological determination and if so of what kind, and what
relation the cross of Jesus and the resurrection of Jesus bear to each
other. Does deciding on a 'theology of the cross' mean dispensing with

[1] W. von Loewenich, *Luthers Theologia crucis*, Munich 1929, p. 2. Here he
goes on: 'Can we really expect to reach the heart of the New Testament message
if we circumvent this *logos tou staurou?* . . . The "word of the cross" was thus
the characteristic mark which definitely distinguished primitive Christianity
from the syncretism of the religious world about it.' (Cf. also K. Holl, *The
Distinctive Elements in Christianity.*) Von Loewenich maintains the thesis: 'The
theologia crucis is a basic principle of the whole of Luther's theology', it is the
'theological principle of Luther's thinking', pp. 7-8. See also P. Althaus, 'Die
Bedeutung des Kreuzes im Denken Luthers', *Vierteljahresschrift der Luther-
gesellschaft*, 1926, part 4.

the inclusion of the resurrection in the specific doctrine of salvation, or does the latter require supplementing by the word of the resurrection, or is the connection between the saving character of the cross and the resurrection to be developed in a different direction?

It has first of all to be stated that the saving event of the cross and that of the resurrection are bound together in indissoluble unity, that we are neither given the word of the cross without the resurrection message nor the resurrection message without the fact of the cross, that accordingly it is theologically impossible to disregard either the one or the other. The Risen One is the Lord because he is the Crucified, and the Crucified is the *sōtēr* only because he is the Exalted Lord.[2] We have already shown the connection between the historic life of Jesus and his resurrection, and that makes it necessary to connect also the end of his life with the resurrection and to understand it in that light. Without the Easter event, the cross of Jesus bears the stamp of a purely immanent happening subject to the most varied intra-worldly possibilities of interpretation. Though the death of the prophet of Nazareth who made messianic claims may raise any number of religious questions, yet it still lies on the plane of the relative facts of religious history. It is only because of the attestation of the Risen One that the death of Jesus becomes an essentially theological problem. The possibility of a theological inquiry into the saving character of the cross does not exist at all apart from the resurrection, but is given only in the light of the living Christ. *Thus cross and resurrection stand in the relation of riddle and interpretation* —and indeed in such a way that the very raising of the theological question is conditioned by the answer of the resurrection.[3]

If the inner harmony between the death of Jesus on the cross and his resurrection is perceived, and it has become clear that the preaching of the cross is dependent on the resurrection message, without which the

---

[2] In the primitive Christian proclamation the death and resurrection of Jesus are at first assigned an equal place among the major parts of the confession. Cf. I Cor. 15.1 ff. The resurrection is repeatedly set parallel to the death of Jesus, and it is to both events that salvation is traced. Cf. I Thess. 4.14; Rom. 4.25; 8.34; even the proclamation of 'Christ crucified' in I Cor. 1.23 f. and I Cor. 1.18 obviously does not mean the cross of Jesus in abstraction from the resurrection, but really means the Kyrios whose saving significance finds its characteristic expression precisely in the death on the cross. The *logos tou staurou* at all events does not allow of any antithesis between it and the resurrection of Jesus. Cf. here the most notable study by B. Steffen, *Kreuz und Gewissheit*, 1929, pp. 56 ff.

[3] This has been pointed out by P. Althaus, 'Das Kreuz Christi' in *Theol. Aufsätze*, 1929, p. 2: 'From the standpoint of Jesus' testimony to himself in his lifetime, his end becomes a problem; from the standpoint of the fact of Easter, the cross is in need of interpretation, but at the same time also has light shed on it from that standpoint.'

death of Jesus remains shrouded in total darkness and cannot have any soteriological content, then not only is the giving up of a theology of the resurrection in favour of a theology of the cross unthinkable, but even to speak of a co-ordination of cross and resurrection is hardly proper.[4] The very assertions of primitive Christian thinking, which repeatedly ground salvation not in the cross of Jesus but on the contrary in the resurrection, point in a different direction.[5] Cross and resurrection are bound together in innermost unity, yet in such a way that *the resurrection first makes the cross into that of which faith and accordingly also theology speaks*. The cross is, to be sure, the presupposition for the resurrection of Jesus, but it is the latter that gives the cross its meaning. It is only the Easter interpretation of the cross that lifts the end of Jesus beyond the chances and dubieties of history and makes it a saving event. Theological reflection on the cross of Jesus is essentially rooted in the resurrection.[6] The 'word of the cross' is at the bottom no other than 'word of the resurrection'.[7] For this reason resurrection cannot mean a supplementing of the *theologia crucis* on the basis of a juxtaposition, cannot be a completion of what for the most part was already accomplished in the death of the cross, but *all the statements of the theology of the cross bear the key-signature of the resurrection. Without this key-signature, however, they lose their validity and meaning*. To speak theologically of the cross of Jesus is therewith at the same time to speak of the resurrection, for the latter alone is the root and driving force of the message of the cross.[8] The sense of the theology of the cross accordingly does not lie in itself, but is grounded in the resurrection.

[4] The verdict of P. Althaus, that 'The origin of all theology of the cross lies in the juxtaposition of the cross and the resurrection' (*op. cit.*, p. 2), is misleading to say the least. The concept of 'juxtaposition' does not do justice to the relation that obtains.

[5] Acts 3.15, 26; it is the exaltation to the right hand of God that creates the possibility of *metanoia* and *aphesis hamartiōn*, Acts 5.31; the concept of the *dikaiosynē theou* in Romans, and the idea of the Gospel as the 'power of God' in Rom. 1.16 f., also stand in the light of the resurrection. Above all Rom. 4.25, 'raised again for our justification'; also Rom. 8.10, 34; 5.8; I Peter 1.18 f.; 2.24; 3.18.

[6] It is only on the presupposition of the resurrection that the word of the cross can be a word of glad tidings, of the *dynamis* of God, of the 'wisdom of God'. It is 'offence' and 'foolishness' only because the Crucified is the Lord.

[7] However correct W. von Loewenich's statement, that 'the whole thinking of Paul is dominated by the idea of the cross, is *theologia crucis*' (*op. cit.*, p. 3), yet it is only when the *theologia crucis* is traced back to its real origin in the resurrection of Jesus that the true facts about Pauline theology are unequivocally clear.

[8] Cf. II Cor. 5.15 f.; Rom. 5.10; 6.1 ff.; Col. 2.12 f.; Phil. 3.10 f. Hans Michael Müller has coined the formula, 'The cross with an eye to the resurrection', which does more justice to the aims of a theology of the resurrection: *Macht und Glaube*, Munich 1933, p. 125, cf. also pp. 122, 135 f., 146.

This grounding of the *theologia crucis* in the resurrection determines decisively the theological outlook, in that the *accent falls on the resurrection, which has a pre-eminence over the death*. Because the interpretation of the meaning of the death of Jesus is dependent on the resurrection and because life is 'stronger' than death, the resurrection of Jesus stands in principle above the cross. The resurrection life of Christ means for Paul a higher degree of assurance of salvation than the death of Jesus. Hence every true *theologia crucis* is not only at the same time also a *theologia resurrectionis*, but the latter is the determining ground of the former.[9] When we speak of a theology of the cross, then, in a strictly theological sense, this can always only be one specifically qualified by the resurrection. This supreme importance of the resurrection for the grounding of salvation must now be shown in detail.

The key to the meaning of the cross is summed up in the following general statement: *The raising of the Kyrios is God's confession to the death of Jesus. Thereby God in the resurrection acts on the world in such a way as to ground its salvation.* The exposition of this statement shows substantially how the *theologia crucis* is rooted in the resurrection. *Three things are contained in this verdict given by God in the resurrection.*

The resurrection is the solution of the riddle of the cross. The death of the 'Just One' has the burden of unanswered questions taken from it. The interpretation of this death as the collapse of Jesus' messiahship, as

---

[9] That a *kerygma* of the cross is unthinkable without the resurrection is proved by I Cor. 15.14 ff. Without the resurrection of Christ even a message of the cross would be *kenon*, no reconciliation would be accomplished, the power of sin would be unbroken, faith vain and pointless, the apostles' testimony false, the Christian hope a fantasy, and death an irretrievable disaster. Any dubiety about the resurrection would according to Paul be the same as to reject the Gospel altogether. The pre-eminent interest in the Crucified's being alive is shown by II Cor. 13.4: 'yet he lives by the power of God'.

In three decisive passages it is brought out that the resurrection of Jesus guarantees the salvation of men *'more'* than does his death. In Rom. 5.10 men, although they were still enemies, are reconciled with God through the death of his son, and 'much more, being reconciled, we shall be saved by his life'. Then in Rom. 5.17, in contrast to the fateful interconnection of sin, reprobation and death, the receiving of the 'abundance of grace and of the gift of righteousness' is grounded in his 'life'. The reference is not to the death of Jesus, but to the richness of the life conferred by the resurrection of Jesus. Finally, we have the fundamental confession in Rom. 8.34: 'Christ Jesus who died, yea rather, who is risen again, who is at the right hand of God'. The whole assurance of faith and confidence of victory on the part of those who have been reconciled, chosen and justified is based upon the cross, but 'much more' on the resurrection of the Crucified. This is a fact which systematic study cannot carelessly leave aside. Our talk of the *theologia crucis* thus requires essential reservations, or as the case may be, supplementations. Cf. the declaration by P. Bachmann: 'All our statements so far about the saving work of Christ are therefore also important only in so far as they apply to the Lord who through suffering and death is on his way to the resurrection', *Grundlinien der systematischen Theologie*, p. 98.

the victory of Satan and the demonic triumph of his enemies, is no longer adequate. Because God rescues the Crucified from death, the event is given by God an interpretation which man could not devise and which does not lie in the cross itself. Through the resurrection God shows the death of Jesus to be beyond all earthly possibilities, a divine necessity which reveals his dealings with mankind. The death on the cross becomes in virtue of the resurrection a sign of the divine will which, independently of what men may do, erects unasked this sign in the midst of the world. Thus the death of Jesus is hallowed by God and at the same time chosen by him as the place of the revealing of his salvation. The cross of Jesus is perceived as a result of the resurrection to be the will of God. The will of God is for faith not a riddle, though certainly a mystery. This is the will of God which discloses itself in the resurrection: that as the cross shows, his revelation in the world takes place under a veil, that God deals with men through 'weakness', 'folly' and death. The resurrection marks the cross as the way of God with men—a way which, contrary to the 'wisdom of this world', grounds life by being destroyed. The fact that God in the resurrection confesses to Jesus' death upon the cross as a necessary step in revelation, makes plain the essential nature of his dealings with man. Such dealings with man in this world can only take place in a hidden form, can only be *sub cruce tectum*. The resurrection therefore gives no foundation for a *theologia gloriae* but only for a *theologia crucis*. The cross is not set aside by the resurrection, so that the road to glory would now stand open; rather is the cross conceived as the primal expression of God's saving work upon the world. Jesus' death on the cross is therefore not, as the world must judge it to be, a mark of God-forsakenness, but it is the point at which God in the darkness is dealing with the world.

The resurrection is, further, God's acknowledgment of the death of Jesus as the will of the Son. The resurrection confirms that the will of Jesus to suffer and his obedience unto death were justified. They were not human self-delusion, they were not religious error, not martyr consciousness, but are to be understood in the light of the resurrection as in agreement with God's will and with his plan for man. God's decisive 'Yea' to Jesus' obedience and to his readiness to die, a 'Yea' which the dying man on the cross does not yet hear, is vouchsafed to the Son in his resurrection. God in the resurrection confesses to his suffering, crucified and dead Son. For that reason the death of Jesus must be void of all analogy to the death of other men. It is the resurrection that first makes apparent the unique quality of this death of the Son of God, for quite apart from any possibilities which the world may have had of judging the death of Jesus, it is the resurrection that first establishes its true validity in the judgment of God. In the light of the resurrection the suffering and death of the Son is recognizable as the end of the only man whose end corresponds completely to the will of God, because it was perfect faith and perfect obedience. That the end of Jesus was really a perfected humanity is again only apparent if we recognize the 'divine seal' in the resurrection.[10]

The confession made by God in the resurrection includes also the cross's special significance for salvation. The meaning given by the resurrection changes the 'nevertheless' of his death into a 'because'. Because Christ was crucified, therefore the world is saved by God. *The resurrection is the principle whereby the significance of the cross is made known.* In its light all the imagery which the New Testament employs to describe God's action in the crucifixion becomes possible and meaningful. The death of the Son of God appears as the execution of God's judgment of wrath, as punishment which takes effect in the 'curse of the cross'. Because Jesus submits to this judgment as the Son, his death becomes a sacrifice, and a specifically vicarious sacrifice at that.[11] Thus the resurrection acquires the character of the 'acceptance of the sacrifice of Jesus',[12] which in turn endows Jesus' passion and death with the quality of a work of reconciliation.[13] Further, knowledge of the resurrection lets us see the death of Jesus as a victorious battle with the satanic realm, as the precondition of life and the breaking in of life. The message of reconciling and justifying grace also presupposes the acceptance by God of Jesus' death.[14] These and similar conceptions and ideas are all attempts at interpretation which seek to make clear to us the nature of God's dealings with man in the resurrection of Jesus, in which his death is also involved. The cross of Jesus therefore derives its saving significance from this act of God and from its connection therewith. The death of Jesus procures redemption and reconciliation, it is punishment, sacrifice, a vicarious act, the Crucified is the 'Lamb of God'—all this because in the resurrection God testifies that the fact of the cross is his work, through which he brings about the salvation of the world.

[10] Cf. E. Lohmeyer, *Grundlagen paulinischer Theologie*, 1929, p. 95.

[11] Cf. P. Althaus' observations on exclusive and inclusive substitution, 'Das Kreuz Christi', in *Mysterium Christi*, p. 262.

[12] Cf. R. Frank, *Wahrheitsgewissheit* II, p. 210, where this acceptance is described as 'the chief element in Christian faith'.

[13] Cf. K. Bornhäuser, *Das Wirken des Christus*, pp. 254, 270 ff.; A. Köberle, *Rechtfertigung und Heiligung*, p. 115; B. Steffen, *Kreuz und Gewissheit*, pp. 56 ff.

[14] Cf. C. Stange, *Die Wahrheit des Christusglaubens*, pp. 40, 53.

(b) The Realizing of Salvation in the Resurrection

It is a remarkable feature of dogmatic study of the doctrine of salvation that in formulating it the resurrection of Christ is either completely disregarded or treated only incidentally as a point that might have marginal relevance and be mentioned in conclusion. Justification and reconciliation are spoken of quite apart from the background of the resurrection, with the result that God's justifying judgment appears to be an unchanging state of the mind of God towards the world. God's grace thus takes on the character of a timeless attitude of God towards man, something whose essential and universal truth merely broke through in a special manner in the revelation of the Old Testament and in the preaching of Jesus. If such a conception does not do justice even to the fact of the cross, it does still less to the resurrection message.[15] Such failure to show that the resurrection is an ultimate ground of salvation inevitably leads to a foreshortening of fundamental statements in the New Testament. Thus not only must all that is said of forgiveness and reconciliation lose its decisive seriousness and its depth once it is divorced from the cross and the resurrection, but also the idea of a realizing of salvation in Christ must be relegated to the background. The unity of God's saving work upon man thereby splits as it were into two acts, in that justification and reconciliation on the one hand, and renewal on the other, are torn asunder.[16] Once the resurrection is perceived to be, as we have shown, the foundation of the theology of the cross, and accordingly God's act in the resurrection is understood as his saving action upon the world, then no doctrine of salvation can be validly spoken of save in indissoluble connection with the resurrection. Easter therefore sheds new light on the problems of reconciliation, of justification and of mediatorship.

Just as the resurrection qualifies the death of Jesus as a saving event, so in the same way *the resurrection itself* means *the realizing of salvation as such*. When the resurrection causes us to characterize the cross as 'reconciliation', that is only as it were a description of the other side of the same resurrection reality which is at the same time to be characterized as realization of this reconciliation. Since it makes a reality of

[15] Holl's idea of justification also moves in this direction, *Urchristentum und Religionsgeschichte*, p. 17 (ET, pp. 16 f.).

[16] P. Althaus rightly points out the theological mistakenness of this course: 'Schleiermacher and Orthodoxy alike are both evidence of the fact ... that Luther's idea of justification—which is also that of the New Testament—i.e. the unity of forgiveness and renewal, of the exclusive and the inclusive in the work of Christ, has been lost. It is the task of theology today to recover this insight' ('Kreuz Christi', *Mysterium Christi*, p. 267).

reconciliation, the resurrection fundamentally transcends the promises of future salvation to Israel, and the declarations and acts of salvation that preceded Easter. The resurrection of the Kyrios is the *perfectum* and not the *futurum* of salvation, it is fulfilment, even though that fulfilment is also a guarantee of something yet to come. The resurrection can be the realizing of salvation because it not only enables us to see the death of Jesus as punishment imposed by God, but in awakening Jesus from death remits this punishment, and so liberates from guilt. Jesus' entry into death marks his position before God as that of a *peccator*, or, if we already put the paschal interpretation on it, of one who bears the sin of the world; in the resurrection of this man, however, there is revealed for the first time the possibility of a new relationship between God and the man whom he has judged in death—which means the revelation of a new situation in which God and the sinner are reconciled. God's last word is not the destruction of sinful man in death but the foundation of a new life through the resurrection. *In the raising of the Crucified, it is revealed that the* 'peccator' *can at the same time also be* 'justus'. He can be so only because through the resurrection God deals with the world and because in spite of death the new life, and in spite of sin the new righteousness, is realized in the Risen One. The resurrection of Christ is the proof that God has acquitted the world, but in such a way that in Christ freedom from guilt is accomplished, the enmity is abolished, and thus *a new situation is created which makes possible God's acquitting judgment of the sinner*. In the Risen One the new curse-free relationship between God and man is given. In him the new reality of being objectively reconciled with God has taken concrete form. The essential concern of the theology of the cross is not merely with the proclamation of the grace of God which is bound up with this Christ event: it is at the same time also with the fact that in the risen Christ this salvation by reconciling grace is realized.[17]

If we look at the matter from this angle, we gain an essentially new insight into the fundamental nature of *justification* itself. The ordinary theological discussion on the concept of analytical and synthetic judgments of justification appears from the standpoint of the resurrection to be outmoded or at least only conditionally valid. If we hold on to a

---

[17] Cf. E. Lohmeyer, *op. cit.*, pp. 94 ff. The resurrection provides the 'guarantee for the expiation and blotting out of the curse', 'the affirmation of the fulfilment' (p. 101).

Cf. H. J. Iwand, *Rechtfertigungslehre und Christusglaube*, Leipzig 1930. Cf. also P. Althaus' comprehensive and profound study, *Paulus und Luther über den Menschen*², Gütersloh 1951.

purely synthetic and forensic judgment, we are not taking seriously enough the fact of the realization of salvation in the new situation created by the resurrection. This is no fortuitous circumstance. For this synthetic understanding of justification corresponds to a theology of the cross which forgets its ground in the resurrection and is therefore no longer able in its statements to take account of the new life of Christ. Moreover, such a view of the matter is too closely concerned with the sinfulness of man rather than with God's action in Christ, and too little determined by faith's assurance of God's victory realized in the living Christ. The analytical approach on the other hand is too ill secured against the misunderstandings which see the new life as objectively present in the being of man, as also against ethical rationalizing, which is not wholly corrected even when, as in the case of Holl, this analytical judgment is given an eschatological interpretation. On the one hand it has too little regard to the basic separation of man from the actual reality of salvation this side of death, and on the other hand it fails to discern the decisive implications of *propter Christum* and *Christus pro nobis*, which express the exclusively vicarious character of what Christ has done.

Once, however, we recognize that our salvation was made real in the resurrection, we immediately begin to interpret justification in the following general sense: *God justifies the sinner because of the new situation of being reconciled and justified which is created by the raising of the Crucified. In this situation sinful man, in so far as he participates in it through Christ, is qualified as just before God.* Justification is the pregnant expression used to convey the essential content of God's action on the world in the resurrection. This preserves what is right in the synthetic judgment. Justification does not derive from any quality in the sinner either present or to come, but solely from the act of God. At the same time, however, there remains also the element of truth in the analytic approach, in so far as the Risen One embodies the new reality of justification, which is the foundation of all statements on justification. Justification must be set in strict relation to God's action in the resurrection. This action means declaring just and making just at the same time. The Risen One is always at the same time both forgiver and renewer, both *Christus pro nobis* and *Christus in nobis*. Because of the new situation created by the resurrection, God can show himself gracious to the sinner, can 'declare him just'—this, however, because in Christ the perfected justness of the new life is already realized. If the sinner is existentially connected with the Risen One, then in the Kyrios he is already made just by God, not merely declared just. The two concepts of 'declaring just' and 'making just' are accordingly, when used in separation or in antithesis, inadequate to express unequivocally the fact of the realization of salvation. Everything depends on founding the doctrine of justification in a theology of the resurrection. The realization of salvation, grounded in God's act in the resurrection, changes the situation of man, not indeed empirically but fundamentally and existentially. The Risen Christ in his vicarious action, both in an exclusive and an inclusive sense, has brought about a change in the situation of man, and this change has become objectively real in himself.[18]

With the realizing of reconciliation and grounding of justification in the resurrection of Jesus there goes, finally, the idea of the *'mediatorship'* of Jesus and the concept of *intercessio*.[19] In this the translating of salvation into reality is seen from a different point of view. In the historic life of Jesus before the resurrection there can as yet be no talk of a mediatory function. His task as the Son consists in his perfect obedience. Up to the point of his crucifixion and death he is still wholly subject to the laws of his humanity. The qualification for mediatory office, however, depends not only on being bound up with the common destiny of mankind, but just as much on breaking through the bounds and limitations of that destiny. Only the Kyrios unites these two things within himself: He is the Crucified and as such the Living One; he is one accursed like a sinner and as such also the foundation of salvation; he is the *doulos* and as such also the *Kyrios*. In Christ, man's old life which is in bondage to death and guilt is united with the new resurrection world which is free from sin and superior to death, and it is this that makes possible his mediatory function. Thus the risen Christ brings into being a wholly new relationship to God, which apart from the resurrection does not exist. Through the resurrection God creates a new situation in which man is offered an approach to God despite sin and death. This new approach to God is only made possible through the mediation of the Risen One, for it is in him alone that a new relationship between God and man is to be found. Christ can be the 'advocate', 'high

---

[18] Cf. the notable study by K. Mittring, *Heilswirklichkeit bei Paulus*, 1929, p. 121: 'This righteousness is neither empirical righteousness of life nor a mere ideal pronouncing righteous . . . , but it is an existential constituting of the human situation'. Further pp. 17, 31, 120, 122. Above all also P. Althaus, 'Zum Verständnis der Rechtfertigung', *Zeitschr. für syst. Theol.* 1930, part 4; A. Köberle, *Rechtfertigung und Heiligung*, 1929.

[19] I Tim. 2.5; Rom. 8.34; I John 2.1. Cf. also P. Bachmann, *Grundlinien der syst. Theologie*, p. 89: 'For Paul the heavenly status of Jesus as saviour is the chief foundation of all human salvation and has its basis in the resurrection.'

priest' and 'mediator', who intercedes on behalf of man while man still tarries on this side of death, only because as man he is our 'brother' and as the Risen One is also the Lord who has authority to forgive sins and possesses the life eternal that comes from God. *God makes the Risen One the mediator of salvation, which means that he makes him the only place where that salvation is not merely promised, as in the prophets, but is realized. That is why Jesus is not a prophet, but the mediator.* Jesus' intercession for his 'brethren' constitutes the new relationship to God as one in which man is a child of God. There is no possibility of such a relationship save in the Risen One. For in him sinful man, having lapsed from his original state where such relationship came naturally to him, is again recognized by God as reconciled and justified. It is an error of religious rationalism to regard this father-child relation as a given condition of our human nature. Man's becoming a child of God means the realizing of salvation through the resurrection, because in Christ the union between man and God is restored and made perfect.[20]

---

[20] Cf. also A. Schlatter, *Geschichte des Christus*, p. 531: ' . . . The risen one passes over all their sins and enters into fellowship with them (the disciples). . . . The separation of the disciples from God is overcome; for the glorified Lord joins them as their friend and eats with them his Supper.'

In this context we must point to the remarkable study by E. Schäder, *Die Bedeutung des lebendigen Christus für die Rechtfertigung*, Gütersloh 1893, in which substantially the same principle is examined with regard to the theology of Paul. That is all the more significant since many an error in modern theology comes of failing to recognize the fact that in the resurrection of Jesus Paul 'saw the ground of God's justifying judgment on the sinner' (p. v). For it ought not to be denied 'that according to the apostle's conviction the significance of the death of Christ for our justification stands or falls with the fact of the resurrection of Christ. For Paul the dying of the Lord has its saving value only in conjunction with the resurrection.' Even if we perceive the resurrection to be the absolute act of God alone and therefore reject the statement that 'in his character as Risen Lord the event constitutes the act of Christ in which he . . . breaks the fatal consequences of the exercise of wrath', yet it does express the conclusive and indispensable importance of this event, and we shall agree all the more with the affirmation that 'God brings his reaction against sinners to a stop; that is to say, he raises Christ. . . . If Christ remains in death, then the conclusion from that is . . . that God lets there be no end to the exercise of his wrath upon him. . . . Without the raising of the Lord there is no pardon' (pp. 178-179). 'He who is the representative of sinners in enduring the wrath of God experiences in his own self that expression of the life of God in which God gives up his opposition to sinners and consequently brings the exercise of his wrath to a stop' (p. 185). Here there also comes to its own the idea that the new state of our life is manifested in the Risen One: 'The Risen One as such represents the abolition of guilt.' Reconciliation, redemption, justification are not merely events in history, but 'are valid in the present, because Christ is risen and lives. He who died for sinners and who rose again continues to hold the saving effect of his death and resurrection, our pardon, constantly in his own hands' (pp. 181-182). It is precisely the life of the Risen One that represents the abiding saving effect 'of his bearing the judgment . . . for sinners'.

2. THE RESURRECTION AS FULFILMENT OF THE CREATION

(a) The Problem of a Cosmic Christology

The universal character of the resurrection message is made manifest once *resurrection and creation are related together*. God's action in the resurrection is not concerned with mankind alone, but with the world as a whole. This raises the question whether an understanding of creation can subsist at all wholly on its own, and can be developed in isolation from the event of the resurrection. The recent theological rethinking of the problem of creation has caused men to ask urgently the decisive question where the starting point of a valid doctrine of creation is to be found. At the same time, however, the attempt to bring Christology and the concept of creation into relation with one another is raising questions which seem likely to burst asunder the whole accepted framework of Christological thought. We are faced with the problem of a *cosmic Christology* which must in no sense be a relapse into Greek speculation but rather provides a necessary reminder of primal Pauline ideas. Here the statements of dogmatics concerning Christ will not exhaust themselves in soteriological and hamartiological definitions, as dogmatic theology so far widely seems to think that they do. By introducing thoughts on the creation we endow Christology with a new fulness of content, and at the same time shed new light on the concept of creation from the Christological angle. This also produces a loosening of the rigid conceptions of creation which result from leaving Christ out of account in the doctrine of creation. Fundamentally, however, this whole problem is concerned with nothing less than the absoluteness of Christ. But absoluteness can never be spoken of without relation to the cosmos. Do we possess in Christ the starting point for an understanding and interpretation of the world on the vastest scale? When we ask this question, we are taking seriously the essential meaning of all Christology. Two views, however, militate against the posing of it.

If in the shaping of our Christology we reject all thoughts pertaining to cosmology, then at once we disastrously restrict and curtail our Christological pronouncements. Scepticism in regard to the concept of pre-existence leads to confining the event of Christ to what is historic and no more. Christ is then seen either as a religious and ethical personality or as the Redeemer bringing salvation to the sinner. His death on the cross then comprehends within itself the whole fulness of salvation in respect of human guilt. However untenable the first of these conceptions is, and however necessary the second, yet both are inadequate

TTR F

restrictions of an individualistic, soteriological kind. Christ is related only to the individual, his sins and his salvation, sometimes also to mankind as a whole. Always, however, this kind of Christology remains indifferent to nature and is thus palpably alien to the thought of Paul. It can make nothing of the pronouncements on nature and creation, on original state and cosmic eschatology. Their importance either recedes into the background altogether, or else these ideas are set *alongside* those of Christology in no inner connection with them, still less any dependence on them. The first article of the Creed is thus subordinated or excluded, at all events certainly isolated from the teaching on redemption and on the Spirit. In that case it would be possible to give a completely valid and meaningful account of creation without regard to Christ, and conversely to deal with Christ and the Holy Spirit without taking any account of our belief in creation and the material interrelation between the two. The result of this can only be a lack of understanding for the facts of nature and the story of the cosmos, and that means a shirking of the questions which the world of creation poses precisely for Christian faith. Any purely individualistic, soteriological answer must here lead to complete failure. If we will not venture to set the cosmos in a Christocentric perspective, then the result must be not merely a profound inhibiting of the whole Christological exposition, but also that natural events are abandoned to a scientific rationalist interpretation. *The practice of emptying nature of God since the Enlightenment has its correlate in an individualistically limited Christology*. The renouncing of a cosmic Christology makes us defenceless against a purely immanent view of the world which knows nothing of creation, as also against incursions from the ideal world of gnostic speculation which appropriates the idea of creation and distorts it in an extra-Christian metaphysic.[21]

The new approach made by recent theological thought has led to a recognition of the dangers inherent in a shallow and individualistic Christology. Attempts are being made to put a universal interpretation on the Christ event, and the question of creation is being viewed only in the context of Christian teaching on sin and redemption. Now, though it is unquestionably right to treat the three articles of the Creed as a single and indivisible theological whole, the tendency is nevertheless to conceive of their interrelationship in such a manner that, in reaction to the previous optimistic view of creation, the accent is now wholly on

---

[21] Cf. the ideas of R. Steiner and, in dependence on him, F. Rittelmeyer, who makes use of the theological deficiencies of liberalism in order to introduce teachings foreign to the Gospel.

the veiling of creation's original perfection. The second article, instead of throwing its light on the first, merely casts upon it the shadow of sin and of the need for redemption. The whole texture of the world of present experience is said to bear the stamp of 'fallen creation'. It possesses an 'impure form of existence' which contradicts creation's original perfection.[22] Thus the idea of creation is strictly and centrally defined in terms of sin, i.e. it is oriented not towards Christ but towards the 'Fall'.[23] The cornerstone of this kind of theological thinking is the 'Fall' which includes also the whole cosmos, and to this there corresponds a conception of sin which has undergone a certain metaphysical transformation.[24] Not only mankind but the whole of creation must be seen from the standpoint of the 'Fall'. Nothing is left but a ruined creation that finds expression in this immanent spatio-temporal mode of existence and the transience it involves. Against this sombre background the figure of Christ does of course gain cosmic significance. His work of redemption is by no means directed towards man alone, but has a fundamental openness towards nature and the created world. According to this view Christ is also the restorer of a broken and ruined creation, the renewer of the world's original perfection before the Fall. The resurrection of Jesus in particular may here claim to have taken on the character of a 'reparation' of the original state of the Creator's work.

It is undeniable that such reflections reveal a profound insight into the situation and represent genuine progress in the direction of Pauline ideas, without thereby shifting the accent on to the pre-existent Logos in the sense of hellenistic philosophy. Here Christology is freed from the limitations of individualistic thinking. Yet we may well ask whether a cosmic Christology that is dominated by the Fall is really in a position to understand and make intelligible what is meant by belief in the creation. Despite this new and valuable theological approach, it still remains difficult to see creation clearly in the light of Christ because the concept of creation has become completely dependent on the concept of sin. Once the idea of the Fall dominates the concept of creation to such a degree that creation can be expounded only as an antithesis to sin, then no amount of reflection on the realtion between Christology and creation will really make any essentially new contribution to the under-

---

[22] K. Heim, *Dogmatik* I, pp. 28 f.; II pp. 22 ff.; *Glaube und Denken*, pp. 370 ff.; K. Barth, *Römerbrief*, 1922, pp. 234 f. (ET, pp. 251 f.).

[23] For what follows, cf. the impressive observations by H. W. Schmidt in *Die Christusfrage*, 1929, and 'Die ersten und die letzten Dinge' in the *Jahrbuch der Theol. Schule in Bethel*, 1930.

[24] W. Künneth, *Die Lehre von der Sünde*, Gütersloh 1927, pp. 39 f., 177 ff.

standing of creation. The nature, meaning and purpose of creation derive from the antithesis that has been constructed between it and the fallen, sinful creation, but not from the content of the fact of Christ. Rather, the latter, too, becomes dependent on the Fall, for it is characterized only formally as the restoration of what was lost, which means that in the final analysis the resurrection is set in a causal relationship to the Fall. But such a view does not correspond to the central content of Christology, which, on the contrary, has primarily to be the basis of decisive statements concerning creation.

As against the above theses, we have now to examine the all-embracing importance of Kyrios Christology in regard to the question of creation. *The recognition of the Risen One as Kyrios means something fundamentally new in comparison with the whole created world and is therefore the prerequisite of a thorough understanding of creation.* The raising of Christ implies the necessity of a cosmic Christology, of an *exposition of the concept of creation* not in the light of the Fall but *in the light of Christ.*

(b) Creation in its Relation to the Resurrection

When resurrection and creation are related together we are very forcibly struck by the uniqueness of the fact of the resurrection, and of the Christology which is built upon it. The resurrection is the very heart of cosmic Christology. For this reason, in so far as the concept of creation cannot be properly developed save on Christological lines, the created world must be oriented towards the raising of Christ. *This orientation of all creation towards the resurrection as its fulfilment determines the real fundamental character of creation and provides a Christian doctrine of creation with its deepest meaning.* There can thus be no understanding of creation which is not shaped by the theology of the resurrection. In creation's orientation towards the resurrection there emerges anew the theocentric character of the resurrection event with its bearing on the whole cosmos. At the same time all that has already been said about pre-existence, incarnation, and the reciprocal relationship between the historic life of Jesus and the resurrection is hereby confirmed, summed up and clarified.

Three distinct lines of thought will serve to prove the orientation of creation towards the resurrection. We must deal first with the *incompleteness of the first creation*; then we must clarify the *concept of the 'fallen' world.* Finally we must show that the *resurrection world is the fulfilment of creation.*[25]

[25] H. W. Schmidt's mind is moving in the same direction: 'The problem of

The nature of God's creative will can only be understood if we start from Christ. He is, according to the Epistle to the Colossians, the 'prototype' of every creature. The pre-existent Christ possesses the sonship, the perfect image of God, which God's love seeks to confer on all subsequent creation. What the first-born Son already possesses all creation is to receive after his likeness. Creation is therefore dependent on the 'Son' and on God's dealings with this Christ. This enables Paul to say that 'all things', i.e. the whole reality of the universe, were created by the Son and at the same time also 'unto him'.[26] The 'Son' is thus recognized as the ground and purpose of the created world. His sonship is the presupposition for the creative working of God, the precondition for God's calling creation into being out of nothing. *This created world has its existence not in itself but in the Creator's Christ-bound activity and in its own orientation towards this Christ.* Thus from the first instant of its coming into being, creation stands in expectation of the sonship of God promised to it in the first-born. Creation therefore does not mean existing in the rigid, motionless state of what has been made, been created and merely exists, but rather being on the move towards an end which brings out the meaning of creation by fulfilling it. Creation in accordance with its Christ-centred design is directed towards an action of God which is to come, it moves towards a consummation of its original purpose. The fulfilment of creation, however, is conditioned by the plan according to which God has designed it, a plan which must be understood in essentially Christological terms. But this means nothing less than that the fate of creation is dependent on the fate of the 'Son'. This sonship, however, in no sense represents a perfection that is already static and complete. The first-born is not yet finished, not yet at the end of the road appointed him by the Father. The 'Son', too, as we have seen, bears a promise: as first-born he is the heir to lordship. The 'Son' is destined to receive the Kyrios title from God; the 'Son' awaits an existence which gives him something still higher than his sonship. The sonship of Christ awaits its fulfilment in the resurrection. If the resurrection is the goal of the 'Son's' life, then for the perfection of the created world, bound as it is to Christ, there can be no other goal than the resurrection. Thus *the resurrection of Jesus becomes* the driving force behind creation, *the inner dynamic of creation's development.* The 'not yet' in which the pre-existent Son awaits his kyrios-ship determines the

creation must be posed in such a way that it makes itself felt again with a new urgency precisely in the realm of Christology. . . . Christ is the theme of the creation story' (pp. 20, 59 ff.).

[26] Col. 1.16 f.

'not yet' in which creation awaits its eschatological consummation. 'Resurrection' here becomes a fundamental concept for the consummation of God's creation.

In the light of this Christological interpretation of the idea of creation it is necessary to revise the traditional conceptions of the 'original state' of the created world. The original state can now no longer be regarded as a condition that is perfect in itself, quite apart from Christ, as a life of perfect sonship which beholds God face to face. For even the original state is oriented towards Christ and needs the message of a fulfilment in the resurrection of the Son exalted to lordship; even the first Adam, the natural man, does not command a perfect life that cannot be lost, but is dependent on the 'Son', the second Adam, the spiritual man.[27] The first Adam as a creature of God was created to live in freedom of choice, destined to become the image of God, made for true sonship after the image of the first-born. Hence the first man already in his original state lives in faith, trusting in God's creative plan, and hoping for that plan's Christocentric execution.[28]

This *conception of the original state* has to be distinguished from two theories which have attained importance in theology. One of these identifies the original state with the perfection of paradise; the other takes an idealist view of the matter and in a supralapsarian spirit sees struggle, death and sin as posited by divine necessity already in the original state. Sin and death must not be regarded as the necessary precondition of creation's development towards perfect freedom, if the purity of our concept of God and the gravity of the Fall are not to be endangered. The original state, defined as that which is originally proper to creation, means the state of being created by God as opposed to that of being sinful and fallen. Although the theologian is forbidden to make hypothetical and speculative statements on this original state, to say for instance whether even in that state the laws of the struggle for existence and the inevitability of death were already posited, he nevertheless finds himself compelled to make certain limiting definitions of a fundamental kind. The 'very good' of the first creation does not imply a perfection that excludes all further progress, but rather its relatedness to the resurrection as a predisposition towards the fulfilment of its meaning in Christ, the coming Lord. The content of the 'very good' creative will of God can ultimately only be understood in the light of Christ. Once we

---

[27] I Cor. 15.45 ff.
[28] Here we are in all essential points at one with the view of H. W. Schmidt, *op. cit.*

have grasped this, we are immediately prevented from engaging in any arbitrary attempts to reconstruct an original paradise.[29] Christ cannot be eliminated from theological thought concerning the original state, rather must he be regarded as basically determining the direction in which it must move.[30]

The second question we must pose concerns the relation which the propensities of creation as thus understood bear to *sin and the Fall*, and thus in particular the relation which the incarnation of the 'Son' bears to humanity in its guilt. The first Adam 'falls', turns aside from the divinely appointed path of creation, repudiates his predisposition towards the sonship of God which is given in Christ, severs himself by his own free choice from God's plan and purpose, and so lapses into a condition void of faith and of hope. Man becomes guilty in that he withholds from the Creator his due obedience, trust and hope. Through the Fall, man loses the original expectation of the fulfilment of his creatureliness, the right to resurrection perfection. But the finitude and transitoriness of the creation must be the last word, once faith in the Creator and hope in the completing of his work are lost. Sin becomes its own judgment and itself destroys man by the very guilt he has incurred —in other words, by breaking away from the path laid down by the Creator, man sinks into the meaninglessness of a creation that is severed from God and dependent on itself.

This falling away from the original predisposition of creation must not, however, be individualistically curtailed by relating it merely to man. We have to speak of a 'fallen creation' in the cosmic sense.[31] To recognize this basic fact of a fallen world is to assert the indivisible unity of finitude and struggle, of sin, guilt and death. From this standpoint

[29] Of special significance is the excellent essay by P. Althaus, 'Die Gestalt dieser Welt und die Sünde', *Zeitschr. für syst. Theol.* 1931, part 2, pp. 319 ff. Misgivings are aroused, it is true, by the statements that history, struggle and death are God's 'original will' even if not his 'final' will, and that 'history did not arise incidentally, but it, too, is God's "very good" creation' (p. 335). Althaus is here apparently attempting to establish what belongs to the original, pure creation. Any detailed statement about that, however, means stepping beyond our bounds. We can hardly say, either, that 'the way of faith . . . accords with God's . . . created order' (p. 329), for faith in the original state cannot be equated with faith as we know it in history, indissolubly bound up with sin. The same concept is here describing what is not in fact the same situation. The application of the concept of faith to the original state can only mean that it was not yet the consummated state of 'seeing'.

[30] From this point of view we cannot agree, either, with Dietrich Bonhoeffer's teaching on the original state, according to which the original state is understood in the traditional way as the 'backward projection of hope', *Sanctorum Communio*, 1930, pp. 22 ff. (ET, 1963, pp. 38 ff.).

[31] At this point we plainly depart from the lines of H. W. Schmidt which we have followed together thus far.

it is senseless to distinguish between what is proper to creation and what is result of the Fall. *Two judgments have to be passed simultaneously*: This world as it is actually constituted is both in structure and in content a world of sin and death; yet at the same time, this world with all its interconnected modes of being is *still God's creation*. In the situation following the Fall there can be only an infralapsarian theology, which even in thought *is debarred from all access to the knowledge of the creation in its purity*. It can only take note of the world as it is now and *must see to it that creation and sin are spoken of in the same breath and with equal emphasis*. There is no striving that does not bear the mark of sin even where it seems to be 'ideal', but neither is there any struggle for existence, however terrible, that does not always also draw for its life on the forces that are part of creation. Just as little can we sever the connection between sin and death, and every attempt to find a place for death in God's original creative will is an attempt to escape the ban of the fallen creation. All dying in this world is part of the curse of sin, and yet hidden in all the inevitability of death is also the orderly operation of the Creator's will.

In this fallen world, therefore, we can simply no longer speak of 'created orders'. The concept of a created order would imply a claim to show which orders in our fallen creation are expressions of the original creation. It would then be possible by reverting as it were to these created orders to escape the consequences of the Fall and seek security in these remnants of our original state. Theology, however, must resist the temptation to separate the original created orders from the world of the Fall and to draw a distinction within the world between them and sin. After the Fall there certainly do still remain divine orders; for the world is not a world of sin alone, but is always also still creation. These are the *preserving orders to secure the world against falling into the abyss*. God preserves the world by judgment and mercy. The divine orders within this fallen creation are in part orders of wrath, as a sign that even the world of sin has not fallen out of the hand of God. The order of wrath is God's punishment, is the judgment of all finite creation and the fruit of severance from God, which continues to operate in a ceaseless process of self-destruction. God's order, however, is also a preserving order in the special sense, as an expression of the fact that despite sin and the Fall God will not suffer his creation in his wrath to perish utterly. This concept takes up what is meant by the concept of 'created order', but avoids the misunderstandings it involves, and must therefore duly replace it. In this preserving order we do not comprehend God's original creation, but we do learn from it God's will to preserve his creatures, even in the midst of sin. Thus the order of wrath as a reaction against sin and the preserving order as a protection against sin have always a reference to sin. The concrete order in which the divine preservation is made manifest is thus constantly permeated by sin. Just as the breaking of the preserving order may cause it to turn into an order of wrath, so also the regularity of the order of wrath can serve towards the preserving of creation. Because it remains creation and is on the way to a created end, God preserves the fallen world, by grace and wrath, by law in the special and in the general sense, and by promise. The concept of the fallen world gives expression to the fact that God's original work of creation is under continual threat from sin.[32]

This raises the question of the means by which God overcomes the obscuring and destroying of the original propensities of creation by sin

---

[32] P. Althaus makes plain in the study already mentioned (*op. cit.*, pp. 336 ff.) that this world of ours 'stands in a variegated light'. We have to speak of the 'punishment', the 'grace', the 'love' of God all at the same time. 'History is the expression of the wrath of God at the very point at which it is at the same time also the expression of his love and grace.' 'All one-track thinking and speaking is here a deviation from the truth. Each of the statements seeks to be made of one and the same world, of one and the same death. . . . The conjunction of various different relationships thus makes a metaphysical derivation and explanation of our world on the basis of any one of the three principles impossible.' Precisely because we fully agree with these statements by Althaus, we find his criticism of K. Heim's view of the world as an 'impure form of existence' untenable. Certainly we have to join Althaus against Heim in rejecting every explanation of existence which is derived from the Fall, yet we have on the contrary to join Heim in speaking of the basic character of the world as something that ought not to be. For indeed not only is it theologically impossible, and also empirically dubious, to make any separation between the form of the world's existence as creation and the impure content of the world as sin, *but also, precisely from the standpoint of Althaus' own position, the structure of the world has to be recognized to be determined at the same time also by sin and the Fall.* The objection to Heim would not be that he speaks of the world as 'something that ought not to be'—this statement has to be maintained with Heim as against Althaus—but that he does not speak with equal clarity of the fact that the world is at the same time also still something that God wills, and is therefore preserved by God. *It is precisely the duality and conjunction of the two statements that is the decisive thing.* In this case Althaus' statement, when Heim's insight is included along with it, remains correct: 'In the structure of this world we grasp the love of the Creator' (p. 335).

A similar objection applies to the observation on p. 337: 'It will not do . . . to argue that the world without sin would be free of death and suffering.' Theology, however, standing as it does in the fallen world, can and must just as little maintain that the involvement of the world in death and suffering belongs to the original creation quite apart from sin. This necessary reversal of the proposition appears to us to be lacking in Althaus, and would be a safeguard against the misconception which Althaus himself rejects, that at certain points we can abstract from sin and demonstrate the pure creation. Cf. also the profound study by E. Hirsch, *Schöpfung und Sünde in der natürlich-geschichtlichen Wirklichkeit des einzelnen Menschen,* Tübingen 1931. Here, too, the 'contemplation of the unity of creation and sin as a primal datum' is emphasized, p. 33.

and the Fall and brings to fulfilment what creation was originally meant
to be. The answer to this question is furnished by the *concept of the
resurrection order by means of which God brings the work of his creation to
its consummation.* The resurrection order is therefore always related both
to the original propensities of creation and also to God's preserving
order. Since these orders and their inter-relationships can indeed be
logically distinguished from one another, but cannot be separated in
substance, it is true also of the resurrection order that it involves both
the recognition, restitution and fulfilment of God's creation and at one
and the same time also the recognition, abolition and completion of
God's preserving order. Althaus' suggestion[33] that my position is 'not
completely balanced' appears to me unintelligible, since the simultaneous determining of the world by both creation and sin has been stressed
with all possible clarity.[34] The expression '*co*-determined', which was
used in previous editions in a footnote, will now be avoided in order to
avoid the misunderstanding that we are here concerned with a 'parti-
cularist pronouncement'. This no doubt will adequately meet Althaus'
point. I must, however, take exception to the remark that we must not
distinguish between an 'original' and a 'fallen' creation, if we claim to
be serious in applying the dialectical method to a description of the
world. Necessary as it is for theology to pass a twofold verdict in
interpreting the present character of the world, it is just as inescapably
necessary to contrast in principle an 'original' created world, which is
now in no wise at our disposal, with the present fallen world. If we
refuse to make such a fundamental distinction we run the risk of failing
on the one hand to appreciate the totality of sin and the Fall, and also
on the other hand of searching in the 'fallen' world for actual vestiges
of creation—for the created orders.

The resurrection order has its beginning in the incarnation of the
Son, who in contrast to the Fall of the first Adam points us once more
to the life of free decision as originally created. In the incarnation the
original propensity of creation breaks through. The orientation towards
the Creator is restored in the created man Jesus. Jesus, however, is at
the same time also the 'Son', and as such more than the natural man,
namely, himself the original pattern of all created things, and therefore
the coming Kyrios who brings the created world to its fulfilment.
Christ, the second Adam, is no 'superman', but is the true man who in
the hour of decision remains without sin, who can therefore be the
bearer of the final creation, the bearer of the promise of resurrection.

[33] *Die christliche Wahrheit* II, p. 192.   [34] See p. 175.

The created humanity of Jesus, despite sin and Fall, can become again for all creatures the prophecy of a fulfilment of creation, the pointer towards the new possibility of a rescue from hopelessness to the hope of a new created existence. In the incarnation of Jesus God attests his eternal will to continue in his 'Son'—unhindered by man's fall, undeterred by his sin and guilt and his ever new incurring of guilt—the plan of his creation as it has existed 'from all eternity', and to bring it to its goal in the resurrection glory of the perfect sonship of God.[35] In the Son the continuity of sin in the fallen world is shattered and the God-given purpose of creation is restored.

At the same time, however, the resurrection order which begins already with the Christ of history contains the affirmation of the order of wrath which lies on the world of the Fall. The wrath of God appears as the reverse side of his creative activity, and even in the destroying of the works of man and the bringing of human designs to nothing it testifies to the inviolable nature of the divine will that fashioned the created world. It is as though the order of wrath were clearing a space in which a new order can be set up, and even in its negative aspect it is directed towards the coming resurrection order. The judgment brought upon the finite world by the wrath of God is always indirectly the proclamation of a new world. Hence the resurrection order is the putting aside of the order of wrath—and this in both senses of the term. It puts it aside in the sense of doing away with the situation of the fallen creation and the working of the divine wrath caused by it. At the same time, however, putting aside means also keeping in store. In the resurrection order the order of wrath which is related to sin no longer prevails; yet even in the new order given in Christ the wrath of God remains, as it were, kept in store as the only possible form of the divine will apart from Christ. That the wrath of God should be stored up until the judgment which the order of resurrection brings along with it, is demanded by the seriousness and exclusiveness of God's dealings with the world through Christ. In the same way the resurrection order must be understood as a confirmation of the preserving order. Viewed from the angle of the coming fulfilment of creation, the preserving order is on the one hand a proof of the 'no longer' of the original world of creation, but on the other hand also an indication of the 'not yet' of a final order of things. In the preserving order there is a divine necessity, in so far as its purpose is to make it possible for the world thus preserved by God to be created anew. The preservation of the world implies its suscepti-

[35] Rom. 8.19 f.

bility to—and its dependence on—the action of the Creator in the resurrection. *God preserves creation, not in order to renew its original state again one day, but so that he may fulfil his creative purpose.* We must retain this concept of the 'preserving order' since it gives appropriate expression to the emergency character of the present order of the world and avoids the misunderstandings to which talk of 'created orders' is liable to give rise. The arguments adduced by Althaus in favour of the 'created order' are unconvincing.[36]

This fulfilment of God's creation is summed up in an anticipatory fashion in the exaltation of his 'Son' to be Kyrios. It is only the resurrection that puts the finishing touch to the idea of pre-existence, by bringing the divine image of the Son to perfection in the dignity of the Kyrios. It seems idle to inquire whether the resurrection would have taken place even without the Fall and would have had meaning for man even if he had never fallen.[37] There can be no emancipation from the net of sin and the range of its effects, and yet because of the importance of the idea of creation it is inherently necessary for theology to say: The raising of Christ, as the final consummation of the divine image in the Son who represents the ground, purpose and goal of the creative working of God, must have decisive importance for creation before the Fall as well as for man after the Fall. *Resurrection is therefore to be identified not with the restoration of the original state, but with the bringing of the original predisposition to its final consummation in Christ. It is, so to speak, a second miracle of creation, for which the whole creation waits both before and after the Fall, and which is now made real for the first time in the Risen One.* If the pre-existent Son was the primal pattern of the emergence of creation, the Risen Kyrios is the beginning and prototype of its consummation. In the resurrection the original predisposition and basic propensity of all creation primarily attains its goal, so that the beginning of the Son's lordship provides the ground for the created world's one day ceasing to be the provisional thing it was before. *The resurrection is the dawning of the new creation and points to the coming fulfilment of the hope of a final consummation.* Since, however, the resurrection event really reveals a new creative activity on the part of God, the creation cannot be spoken of with ultimate validity and meaning without including precisely the resurrection. The Christian belief in

---

[36] Cf. *Die christliche Wahrheit* II, p. 192.

[37] The problem of a supralapsarian view of the incarnation was dealt with by G. Thomasius *Christi Person und Werk* I, p. 171. Cf. P. Althaus, *Prinzipien der deutschen froermierten Dogmatik*, 1914, p. 175; H. W. Schmidt, *Die Christusfrage* and, 'Die ersten und die letzten Dinge'.

creation is based not merely on the biblical 'creation story', but far more on the message of the resurrection. The revelation of God the Creator is not an event anterior to, and separate from, the revelation of redemption in Christ, rather is the second the completion of the first, while the first always already inherently contains the second. *Faith in the Creator is not by any means merely confirmed afresh in the resurrection: it is given a new ground and depth.* The recognition of God's action upon the world through the Kyrios necessarily implies also a new conception of creation. The exposition of creation in its relation to the resurrection issues ultimately into the realm of the problems of eschatology.

(c) The Grounding of a Theology of Nature

A grasp of the connections between creation and resurrection makes possible a comprehensive interpretation of the whole universe from this standpoint given in the resurrection. The consequences involved in the theology of the resurrection necessarily lead to a new view of nature determined by the resurrection. What must remain hidden from the autonomous thought of a philosophy of nature that knows nothing of the resurrection, is revealed to that deeper insight which the message of the resurrection provides. The interpretation of nature which is thus made possible is not to be confused with philosophical reflections on nature which elevate intra-worldly ideas of some kind into the principle of interpreting nature. *The foundation of the Christian interpretation of nature is the action of God in the resurrection, which includes also the cosmos.* This is a principle which man cannot lay hold of at will in a spirit of indifference. Accordingly we must plainly speak not of a Christian philosophy of nature, but of a theology of nature. A *theology of nature* is theological reflection directed towards nature as a whole and determined by the reality of the resurrection. Because of its ground it has something to say about the interpretation of nature. In doing so it fills a gap in theology, in which, despite Paul and Luther or for that matter Oetinger, Baader, Dorner, Hofmann, Martensen and Hamann, this sphere of inquiry has received remarkably little attention. When efforts were made to formulate a new view of nature opposed to the rational mechanistic interpretation which natural science has made fashionable, it was these theological omissions which left the door open to ideas alien to the Gospel. In our own day we are once more witnessing an encounter between the new, mighty upsurge of a philosophy of nature and the beginnings of the construction of a theology of nature. This encounter is the more important since the evaluation of nature at any given moment has certain practical consequences and determines the uses to which nature is put.

A detailed theology of nature cannot be attempted within the framework of the present inquiry. An attempt must nevertheless be made to define the basic standpoints for a study of the theology of nature, in order to confirm the principle of the resurrection also in regard to the interpretation of nature.[38]

The essential features of all extra-Christian *philosophies of nature* are of two distinctive types. The one is to be understood as a mystical, pantheistic glorification of nature. Nature is either directly identified with the deity, so that all that pertains to nature already bears the mark of divinity. The life-rhythm of nature is the life of the deity. Whoever wishes to come close to that deity must put himself in harmony with nature and so learn the secret of life, the secret of 'divine Nature'. It therefore becomes the task of religion to do away with the gap between man and nature, now that all distinction between God and nature has also been obliterated. Thus we get the characteristic equation between nature, man and God in which nature acts as the connecting link. From this interpretation of nature there derive the different varieties of nature mysticism, which is not concerned for any personal communion with God but only to be merged into, and unified with, the divine through the medium of nature. A nature religion can also arise, however, when although the identification between God and nature is certainly denied, there is nevertheless an idealization of the natural. In contrast to the technified world of an existence shaped by culture and civilization, nature appears to possess a primal quality, to be still untouched by human hands and therefore a sphere of the revelation of God. All that pertains to nature undergoes a religious glorification, for though nature ranks lower than God, it is nevertheless an expression of the original purity of God's creation. Nature is good, and since this is so, only the holy and unspoiled powers of nature are capable of redeeming man, who

---

[38] A. Schlatter's ideas about the resurrection have the advantage of being ahead of the rest of the theological discussion in affirming the natural aspects of the resurrection of Jesus. Schlatter brings out clearly that the renewal of Jesus' body intrudes 'into the natural sphere'. That testifies to 'the positive relation of God to nature'. *Dogma*, p. 310. Schlatter also sees the significance of the natural in the following further point: against all endeavours which try to open heaven by despising the earth, and think to strengthen the spirit by trampling the natural life, and seek to honour God by dishonouring man, the idea of the resurrection was a sturdy barrier, *op. cit.*, pp. 528, 519, 521. Also *Die Geschichte des Christus*.

A summary review of the ideas of the philosophy of nature is provided by Hugo Dingler, *Geschichte der Naturphilosophie*, Berlin 1932.

has become alienated from nature and debased by civilization. The logical practical conclusion of the glorification of nature is the cult of vitality and of Eros. The mystical, pantheist and idealist assumption of an unbroken divine immanence in nature results in deification of nature on the one hand and redemption by nature on the other.

The other type of philosophy of nature bears a gnostic and Manichaean stamp. It starts from the radical antithesis between God and nature, and asserts an exclusive polarity between the natural and the divine. In the final analysis the determining factor here is the metaphysical antithesis between matter and spirit, between body and soul. Since the divine sphere is conceived in terms of spirit and soul, while nature is seen as the mass expression of matter and body, a connection between the two spheres is unthinkable. Man as a being made up of both body and soul has a part in both realms, but, if he is to preserve the divine character of his soul, he must set himself the task of withdrawing it as much as possible from the world of matter. Thus the assessment of nature becomes wholly negative. Nature, the physical, and indeed all that derives its power of attraction from nature, is a severe hindrance to the unfolding of the soul and to spiritual advancement, and constitutes an unbearable burden to the individuality of man as it strives for freedom. Freedom, however, means being cut loose from the bonds of nature. The world of nature is the antithesis of the world of God. Nature is the materialization of the Fall of immortal spirits and in no sense a sphere of divine revelation. God can only be found by repudiating nature and by overcoming its natural bonds. In place of the glorification of nature this individualistic spiritualism puts contempt for nature, even to the point of seeking the destruction of nature. This dualistic interpretation of the world goes to the opposite extreme of identifying nature with evil and regarding it as the enemy of the divine. The practical attitude towards nature can therefore only be the asceticism which regards the body as an enemy, endeavours to flee from nature, and seeks redemption solely in the realm of the soul.

Both types of philosophy of nature, which in concrete instances are expressed in manifold forms, fail to do justice to the realities of nature. Both interpretations, it is true, contain elements of truth: the one recognizes the importance of our connection with nature and of our nearness to it, the other perceives the otherness and transcendence of the world of God. Yet at the same time both fail to understand certain essential features of nature: thus the former school, in an excessive optimism where nature is concerned, denies the shadow side of nature's life, while the other in an unrealistic pessimism overlooks all that is of genuine value in nature. Both philosophies thus find the way barred in equal measure to an understanding of the resurrection message. The interpretative principle of the philosophy of nature is in both cases immanently given: it is either nature itself, regarded as having an ultimate value of its own, or it is the nature-free soul as an equally ultimate metaphysical datum. Thus the point of view from which nature is interpreted is chosen on the level of nature itself, whether in unity with nature or in separation from it, for even the value of the soul, as an antithesis to the body, takes its bearings from nature. In both cases there is no possibility of a comprehensive view of nature as a whole, for this could only be obtained from a viewpoint of a non-objectifiable kind, i.e. from a standpoint which does not itself belong to the immanent world. Because the philosopher of nature makes his interpretation from within the immanent world, it is neither necessary nor possible for him to derive a principle of evaluation from an act of God in the resurrection. In neither type of the nature philosophies can the phenomenon of death in nature be related to a resurrection, for either death means, in mystical terms, an immediate absorption and submergence in divine Nature, or it is evaluated in terms of a dualistic interpretation of the world as the liberation of the soul. This antithesis to the message of the resurrection on the part of all extra-Christian philosophies of nature is at the same time also the decisive cause of their breakdown when it comes to an understanding and evaluation of nature that accords with reality.

Beyond and above these one-sided and distorted pictures presented by the philosophies of nature, the word of the resurrection provides the key to a specifically Christian interpretation of nature. This theology of nature proceeds neither by the way of a mere surface examination on the basis of the *ratio* nor by that of intuitive contemplation from within but its judgments are the judgments of faith and its knowledge is the knowledge of faith.

It is an intrinsic part of resurrection theology to reflect on the theology of nature. In so doing, the principle of the resurrection gives rise to the following three statements. First, the fact of the resurrection has a relation to nature. If the resurrection of Jesus is understood as a creative act of God, as the fulfilment of the predisposition of all created things, then in the light of the resurrection the question of the existence and purpose of nature enters upon a fundamentally new phase. *Nature can now no longer be regarded as an entity that exists on its own, making its own laws and standing autonomously on its own feet, but it is given a place*

within the creative activity of God that culminates in the resurrection of Jesus
and it can only be properly understood from that angle. Nature is not
something complete in itself, not a factor that bears its own value and
meaning within itself, but it has its true character only in relationship
to the action of God, only in its orientation towards the resurrection.
This brings about a *radical change in the concept of nature,* in that nature,
if its essence is to be grasped in our interpretation, must be interpreted
in general as creation. The concrete ground for bringing resurrection
and nature into relation with one another is to be found, however, also
in the statements about the new body of the Risen One, in which the
new world proleptically comes to light. This clearly indicates that the
resurrection in no way destroys or supersedes the natural and physical,
but rather that it raises it to its rightful position as a thing willed by
God. We can accordingly never regard nature as something opposed
to God. Thus in the Risen One there is no separation between nature
and redemption or nature and grace, but they enter into a relation with
one another of such a kind that the understanding of nature is no longer
simply accessible to all, but is bound to a concrete revelation. The very
concreteness of the resurrection event is of importance in our assessment
of nature, since the direct road to the understanding of nature is closed
to us and we can attain to it only by way of the personality of Christ.
The element of personality inherent in the resurrection demands a line
of demarcation between nature and man and at the same time implies
the distance between the Kyrios and nature. *The fulfilment of nature in*
the resurrection does establish the relation with nature, and yet it is 'more'
than all nature. The relation between nature and resurrection therefore
implies neither identity nor polarity, but means a new view of nature
which comprises both relationship and distance.

This knowledge of the resurrection leads, secondly, to a critical discussion of the evaluation of nature in the two philosophies of nature.
The double face of nature, on the one hand so rich and primary and on
the other so frightening and full of tensions, remains for the philosophy
of nature a riddle which it can escape only by excluding the one aspect
or the other. But this proves the untenable character of its pre-supposi-
tions. It is just this dual character of nature, however, that the resurrection makes intelligible. Nature as a whole bears the marks both of the
Creator's hand and of the Fall in indissoluble unity, and so manifests
at the same time its orientation towards redemption. The antinomies
of nature therefore form a riddle no longer: they are an inevitable effect
of the world's situation as determined by creation, sin and redemption.

From this point of view the solutions offered by the philosophy of nature must be described as erroneous. The idea of a redemption through nature, by merging in the wholesomeness of nature, is utterly invalidated by the reality of the Fall, to the effects of which nature, too, is subject. We have here the error that denies the separation of creation from God and so persists in the illusion of a sinless purity of nature. The opposite persuasion that despises nature and bids man flee from it fails to see nature's character as the created work of God. At the root of such a view lies the dualistic error which ignores God's power over the world and mistakenly identifies the soul with the divine. Both conceptions, however, are ultimately determined by the idea of self-redemption, in that both regard nature's present state as final, and seek redemption in the one case in harmony with this state of nature and in the other in opposition to it. Thus nature is wholly deprived of its progressive and teleological character and there is no grasp of the fact that its essential meaning lies not in its present state but in the knowledge that it exists in expectation of the resurrection.

We are now in a position to sum up this special account of the meaning of nature from the perspective of a theology of nature. There are three things to be said: *Nature is sanctified through God's action in the resurrection.* Sanctification is not the same as sanctity. Nature does not have an inherent sanctity with which it has been endowed by God, but despite the Fall and sin we may believe it to be sanctified by God's new creative act, i.e. to form part of God's plan for the world. What we can observe empirically in nature cannot yet be recognized as sanctified, and the created cannot be distinguished from the sinful. Nevertheless the truth of our proposition is apparent to faith, which alone knows that resurrection does not mean the destruction of fallen nature but the fulfilment of the purpose which the Creator had given it. If nature may be believed to be sanctified, then in faith in the Risen One the natural relations between men, as expressed e.g. in family and nationality, and in the brotherhood of all mankind, are also sanctified. The sanctification of nature expresses the fact that in the resurrection of the Kyrios God has spoken his 'Yea' also to nature as a whole.

Moreover, nature has a pictorial character. *The resurrection is not a figure of the processes of nature, but the changes in nature are a figure of the resurrection event.* Thus the beauty and abundant power of nature is a pictorial presage of its perfection in the world to come; its frailty and transitoriness on the other hand become a figure of the divinely ordained inevitability of death, which in turn demands the resurrection. Its decay and growth become a symbol reminding us of the death and resurrection of Christ. It is of course only the proclamation of the resurrection that gives legitimacy and meaning to the wealth of symbolism of this kind in nature. A nature symbolism divorced from the word of the resurrection sinks back to the pre-Christian level of nature mysticism and nature religiosity. The resurrection cannot be understood from the standpoint of myth, but myth has light shed on it by the resurrection. Because the resurrection is myth's most profound fulfilment, the nature myth can also possess symbolic features which point towards the resurrection. Thus the symbolic character of the course of nature proclaims the resurrection aspect of the meaning of nature.

Finally, nature bears the marks of promise. *In the resurrection nature shows itself as something penultimate and provisional, but nevertheless as something on which there rests God's promise of ultimacy and finality*. The judgment of the resurrection on nature makes clear that in its imperfect state, distorted as it is by the Fall, it is not yet adequate to the real creative purpose of God, but at the same time shows also that the resurrection of Jesus guarantees its consummation. The groaning of creation points beyond the present state of the life of nature, and is made bearable by the promise of the resurrection. In face of the incomprehensible suffering in the created world, the meaning of nature appears veiled. It shines through the veil when faith knows of the promise that is grounded not in such a thoroughly dubious thing as nature, but in the Risen Christ, in whom the new nature has come to life. The promise does not speak of nature developing towards some higher goal, but of its new creation by God. The meaning of nature is, that a breath of the resurrection is wafted through it and enables us to recognize nature as of intrinsic worth. *The conclusion of a theology of nature can be pregnantly summed up in the confession:* 'natura spirat resurrectionem'.[39]

[39] It is above all A. Köberle who has pointed out the necessity of a Christian philosophy of nature. The course is set by his essay, 'Der erneuerte Anblick der Natur' in *Zeitwende* 1928, part 8, pp. 112 ff.; cf. too *Rechtfertigung und Heiligung*, pp. 41 ff., 160 ff. Also his three lectures, *Christentum und modernes Naturerleben*, Gütersloh 1932, pp. 48 ff., and the section on 'Christus und die Schöpfung' in *Die Seele des Christentums*, Berlin 1932, pp. 72 ff. See also p. 287.

V

THE PRESENCE OF THE RISEN ONE

OUR account of God's action on Christ and on the world needs to be deepened and broadened by considering the *presence of the Risen One*. This way of thinking does not clash with the interpretation of Jesus' resurrection as the work of God, but is the logical continuation of the implications of his kyrios-ship. Just as the reality of God can always be conceived only as a present reality, so it is impossible to speak meaningfully of the lordship of the Risen Christ without taking account of its presence. *What we are concerned to do is to show the risen Lord's effectual working in the world.* This raises the question of the actuality of the resurrection, the question of the concept of the Church and the unique stamp set on that concept by the Kyrios, and the problem of a Christian ontology and anthropology.

I. THE ACTUALITY OF THE RESURRECTION

If we are to understand that the resurrection of Jesus implies not merely a transcendent existence but a present actuality, then it is necessary first to clarify our concept of time and then to sketch the essential features of a doctrine of the Spirit.

(a) The Christocentric Concept of Time

The problem of time is very much in the centre of contemporary philosophical and theological discussion. The phenomenological analysis of M. Heidegger and E. Griesebach, the inquiries of R. Bultmann and the investigations of K. Heim and Heinrich Frick all make it plain that for theological statements the problem of time is of paramount importance. Our concept of the presence of Christ will inevitably be formulated in different terms according to our fundamental understanding of time. The question therefore arises, what concept of time is appropriate to express what the primitive Church has to tell us concerning the presence of the risen Christ.[1]

In view of the problems connected with the conception of time that

[1] Cf. O. Cullmann, *Christus und die Zeit*, 1946 (ET, *Christ and Time*, 1951); E. Stauffer, *Die Theologie des Neuen Testaments*, 1948⁵, p. 59 (ET, *New Testament*

have emerged in the discussion so far, the following definitions of the concept which are still to some extent in use in theology must be rejected as inappropriate. First, there is the formalistic concept which, in dependence on Kant's doctrine of space and time as the mutually complementary forms of perception of the world of phenomena, understands time as the form of the world within which the life of man runs its course. Here time appears as a self-existent empty frame, as the given form which is waiting to be filled with the varied content of the world. Man first enters this time form and by his existence turns the vacuum of time into concrete life. Time and existence are therefore separate entities related to each other as form and content. This 'stable conception of time' corresponds also to the naive understanding of time which usually views time as a line which is laid down *a priori* and on which the ego of man is a point that has to travel through the various stations of past, present and future. Time is thus like an infinitely long line without beginning or end, along which world events run their course. Existence is advancing movement within the stationary form of time.[2]

The retention of this static, formalistic concept of time makes it more difficult for the theologian to expound the actuality of the resurrection breaking into the present. If time is no more than an empty form, then it is useless to speak of the Christ event in temporal categories. All the statements about the present and future of Christ which have obviously an important place in the New Testament must then be regarded merely as symbolic and figurative attempts to express an eternal content which can have absolutely nothing to do with the temporal form of the world. To speak of the past fact of the resurrection as something belonging to the present means taking what transcends the time series and is essentially without meaning from the standpoint of time, and attempting to clarify it by forcing it into the formal time schema. To be sure, this method of representation is understandable and inevitable, yet it misses the very thing that really matters. The temporal concept of a presence of the Risen One is then only a relatively valid means of representation, but not the mark of a reality which determines this our present time. The formal concept of time prevents us from understanding the present Christ as reality. Moreover, in terms of this time schema it becomes impossible to explain how a past event in the time series can become contemporary for the present moment, which ceaselessly marches on.

Theology, 1955, p. 75); G. Delling, *Das Zeitverständnis des Neuen Testamentes*, 1940.
    [2] Cf. K. Heim, *Die neue Welt Gottes*, 1929, p. 33 (ET in *The New Divine Order*, 1930, p. 52).

Existence, moving as it does within the framework of time, is accordingly moving steadily away from the event of the resurrection, so that the message of its presence must come into an irresolvable tension with this conception of time.[3]

A second way of looking at time, based upon a metaphysical concept of time, must also be described as inadequate. Here time is certainly not conceived purely formally, but is determined by its content. Time is thus equated with temporality. But temporality means the transitoriness of the content, the experience of existence under the form of the constant alternation of growth and decay. In content and form time is understood as the antithesis of the eternity of God. Temporality is the reality of this world, it is something inferior and anti-divine. It becomes the classical expression of fallen creation over against which stands the world of God, the beyond, whose quality is timeless and supratemporal. Here, too, time and consequently also eternity are described statically in terms of a state that is motionless in itself. Only release from temporality in the manner of Platonism and the mystery religions can bring men into association with the imperishable and divine.[4]

This positing of an exclusive antithesis between time and eternity makes impossible any union of the eternal God with temporal man. On the presupposition of this concept of time the incarnation does, to be sure, have a meaning as the condition that makes possible a proclamation of God in the midst of the temporal sphere. But what we are told of the installation as divine Kyrios involves on the contrary considerable difficulties for theology with this view of time. In this case the resurrection is interpreted as a return of Christ into the supratemporal sphere. The timelessness of the exalted Lord is a *nunc aeternum*, which in its relation to the changing stream of time in this world can also be described as an eternal present. The fruitfulness of this idea, however, is destroyed by the fact that this present is a 'supratemporal' one, and thus for that very reason excludes the effectual working of the presence of the Risen One as a new factor in the content of this our time. The eternal present is timeless, but not a reality within time, and it is on such a reality that everything depends. The union of man with the Risen One is then thinkable only on the basis of mystical efforts to escape from the sphere

---

[3] Cf. Heinrich Frick, 'Die verborgene Herrlichkeit Christi' in *Mysterium Christi*. Frick follows Luther in pointing to the different significance of the spatial and the temporal statements in the New Testament. The former are to be taken as pictures, but the latter as real and literal. 'Thus we see that the spatial and the temporal elements in eschatological language are treated very differently' (p. 319).

[4] K. Heim, *The New Divine Order*, p. 57.

of time. This concept of time also implies a considerable curtailment of the importance of the lordship of Christ. The lordship of the Risen One is apparently restricted merely to the timeless eternal sphere, but does not by any means universally embrace also the temporal existence of man. The concern which is expressed in the concept of 'presence' cannot achieve its ends in theology under these conditions.

In contrast to these theories of time the way has been prepared in philosophy and theology for a change in the concept of time. Under the guidance of these new insights the change in our understanding of time has to be made by asking—in accordance with the fundamental principle underlying any theology of the resurrection—What is the significance of the resurrection reality for the acquiring of a new concept of time? Thus we must *not*, as is usual, *ask what time schema best embraces the resurrection, but vice versa, what concept of time the resurrection demands.*[5] If the resurrection of Jesus is taken seriously as a new reality established by God, then it must also be made the basis of a new understanding of time, in so far as there is of course a connection between this present world of space and time and that of the resurrection. The thing is not to subordinate the resurrection and what is said of the presence of the Risen One to some concept of time, but rather to test that concept in the light of the resurrection. The demand we must make is not for the abstractions of a purely philosophical analysis of time, as if time were a datum that could be apprehended in a purely 'neutral' way and interpreted quite apart from the reality of God's revelation, but for a theology of time, or to be more concrete, a Christocentric concept of time. Scholarly reflection on time must be recognized to be a theological matter, and the definition of the time-concept must therefore be included in the dogmatic discussion. It is in accord with the universal character of the resurrection that it sets a new stamp also on our understanding of time.[6]

The Christocentric concept of time, which is centred on the resurrection, must be developed along two lines. We must distinguish between the temporality of the present visible world and the consummation of time in the resurrection.

It is a fundamental error to suppose that time (whether regarded as a formal datum or in terms of temporal content as distinct from the time-

---

[5] Cf. H. W. Schmidt and F. Holmström, *Das eschatologische Denken der Gegenwart*, pp. 365 etc.

[6] It is significant that H. Frick sees the connection between the problems of time and the Christological question. He demands 'that theology must break with the ideas of time entertained hitherto and develop in their place an independent Christian view of "time" ', *op. cit.*, p. 317.

lessness of the eternal) has an independent existence and is meaningful
in itself. The reality which is meant by the phenomenon 'time' can be
apprehended only from one significant point, to which time is related
and from which it is possible to penetrate into the structure and nature
of time. So long as this point of orientation for the understanding of
time is obscured, the peculiar nature and meaning of the whole time-
complex can be shown only in fragmentary form. If, however, Christ
is recognized as the cardinal point of a theology of time, then in the
light of the resurrection we arrive at the following twofold proposition
concerning the understanding of the temporality of this world: *time is
creation and time is the world form of the Fall*, which means that time is
in form and content identical with the existence of man.[7] Time is then
not a world form that exists as such, independently of man, but is the
existential mode of the life of man as it is now lived as constituted by
creation and Fall, destiny and guilt. But this temporal existence of man
is a unity, so that we cannot distinguish like Karl Heim between the
pure content which came into being through the creation and the impure
form of time brought into being through the Fall, a form to which the
eternal content is bound and by which it is limited. The temporality of
this existence is determined both by the impure form and by the impure
content, but form and content are also always conditioned by the creation. Accordingly the self is also not to be described merely as the
present 'now-point' to which the self is born in ever new creation out of
nothing, as distinct from the past which at every moment becomes
objective in its fulness of content. On the contrary, the self is indissolubly bound up with the continuum of its past as determined by the
fulness of its contents, even although it always stands at the present
point of decision. Thus both the formal coming into being of the self
at every moment and also the content of the past life of this self which
is also carried with it into the present are stamped alike with the marks
of creation and guilt.[8]

The definition of time as creation makes it fundamentally impossible
to think of time as something opposed to God. The qualifying of time

[7] In agreement with K. Heim, *op. cit.*, p. 72: 'Time is the existence of the
fallen creation, i.e. of the creation which has fallen out of its immediate relation
to God. Even as fallen creation it still remains creation, whose whole life comes
from the breath of God. It has not fallen out of the hand of God.' Also p. 65:
'Time is the "existence-form" of our ego, the essence of the mind'. Cf. especially the observations in *Glaube und Denken*, pp. 376 ff.
[8] Cf. A. Sannwald's critical discussion of the theory of time in K. Heim's
Glaube und Denken (1st ed.)—*Kirchl. Anzeiger für Württemberg*, 1931. The
presence of the self appears in Heim to have 'become a moment entirely
without content, that is, a mere mathematical point'.

as creation makes it clear that, like all creation, it is a divine institution with a predisposition towards fulfilment. Temporality in itself does not yet mean remoteness from God; rather is it a divine possibility which enables the Creator's will to take shape and assert itself. Time is not an ultimate fact, but a penultimate one; it is not yet completed, but looks for a fulfilment. Hence time is not to be statically conceived as a motionless world form or a permanent state, but means a perpetual transition towards a goal. Temporality is movement towards the goal of all creation —towards Christ. The reality of Christ is essentially related to time, in so far as the time-bound world of creation was made for Christ and is determined by him. Temporality, however, also implies transitoriness. This, too, can be seen to be meaningful from the point of view of a Christocentric creation. The perishing of all temporal things appears in the light of the resurrection as an act of divine grace, which through the phase of passing away brings the fragmentary to consummation. Thus transitoriness becomes a means of redemption—a redemption which is not supratemporal but uses time to achieve its purpose. On the other hand, however, time as an expression of duration and of continuance also bears the mark of God's preserving of the world. Time is a preserving order of God in which God's creative power despite the Fall, and God's faithfulness, long-suffering and patience despite man's revolt against God, continue to maintain and preserve mankind.[9]

On the other hand, time is the life of the universe as stamped by the Fall. From the Fall have come the wretchedness and curse of temporality. Time makes it impossible for man to retain things of value or to recover them from the past. Time also forbids him to make good or wash out past guilt—and every guilt becomes past guilt the moment it is incurred. This time-continuum with its now determined content is a thing the self must bear as a burden, without being able to get rid of it. The irreversibility of time becomes one of life's afflictions. Thus temporality now appears as the world form in which the wrath of God is active in consequence of the Fall. Time becomes an order of wrath, which allows guilt to mount and the fruits of sin to ripen. The divine judgment of time reveals the emptiness and vanity of man's sinful strivings, which in the course of time break down because of their own instability. At the same time, the transitoriness of things manifests the judging wrath of God that delivers all created things to destruction. The inevitability

[9] Cf. Frick, *op. cit.*, p. 325: 'Time is . . . essentially the "patience of our Lord".' P. 328: 'Precisely this existence that we now have, this continuing life marked by sin and death, is understood by faith to be God's creative time, which he prolongs for the sake of man, in order to save him.'

of death is the judgment of God, which is executed upon all temporal existence. So long as the temporal order exists, marked as it is by sin and the Fall, it is always possible to be far from God and to deny him. Time is visible existence, which bears no immediate relationship to what is non-objective and invisible. Temporality thus implies the possibility of disregarding the real meaning of time's character as a part of creation and of abstracting from Christ as the centre of time and the point from which it derives its meaning. Finally, the experience of the temporal points to the affliction of unfulfilled-ness. The fact of existing in time makes man always feel his limitations, and reminds him of the fateful necessity that has turned his existence into this thing called time which limits or destroys his freedom. Accordingly, time is not only a creative power but also a destructive force.

The second element in the definition of the Christocentric concept of time has to do with the *consummation of time in the Risen One*. It is of decisive importance that the time concept can be applied also to the reality of the resurrection. The very fact that the idea of creation culminates in the resurrection makes it conclusively plain that the usual antithesis between time and eternity is untenable in the hitherto customary form. If the resurrection of Jesus represents the consummation of time, then this means that the teleological character belonging to time as a part of creation attains its end in the Risen One, that the dynamic concept of time finds its consummation in the resurrection. If the time of the visible world is to be understood as the existence of the self—an existence which is admittedly not susceptible to measurement, but can certainly be existentially experienced—then the new time-reality is concentrated in the Risen Christ. *The reality of Christ's resurrection is the 'new' time, i.e. it is not timeless eternity, and not a supratemporality radically divorced from this world, but it is a consummated time, a time fulfilled.* The Christocentric concept of time therefore embraces both modes of existence—the transitory existence which is the old time, and life eternal which is the new time. Over against the pseudo-life of the visible temporal world there appears the true, full life of eternal time. The eternal life of the Risen One is therefore not a mere timelessness without content, but rather contains the whole fulness of a consummated time.[10]

[10] Cf. the legitimate demand of H. W. Schmidt for the introduction of a new terminology, *Zeit und Ewigkeit*, 1927. He speaks of a 'consummate temporality' (*Vollzeitlichkeit*) as the 'possibility of consummated structures'. P. 297: 'Consummate temporality is the consummation which abides in itself and no longer grows beyond itself, but nevertheless does not stiffen into dead motionlessness.' P. 307: time is 'something pre-formal' which is able to provide for the finite and infinite alike the appropriate forms for the various contents. The form of the

The significance of the consummation of time in the resurrection requires to be further expounded on two counts. *First, we must examine the relation between the new, fulfilled time of Christ and the old, broken time.* The new time represents, firstly, the bringing out of the values inherent in the old time as a part of creation. All that is temporal has a hidden eternal meaning within it, which is now revealed by the abolition of the old time in the resurrection. The resurrection becomes a liberation from the misery which sin and the Fall bring to the temporal order. Through the breaking up of the old time form, the positive content of creation emerges in a new form of existence. The view advanced by K. Heim in these terms,[11] which sees the abolition of the time form as a redemption of the pure content from the impure vessel resulting from the Fall, nevertheless requires a passing comment in revision and amplification, since what we have to do with in the resurrection must be not merely a renewal of the form, but also an abolition of time's impure content. It is only with the overcoming of the whole formally and substantially temporal world, which suffers in its totality from the effects of the Fall, that there emerges the true meaning of God's original instituting of time, which likewise determined both its form and its content. Thus the resurrection reality reveals what God originally willed in and through the creation of time, namely (so to speak) a new experience of life without transitoriness.[12] Secondly, however, the beginning of this new time does not mean a mere bringing to light of something already in existence and therewith a restoration of God's 'original time' now freed from sin, but rather the consummation of this 'original time'. In the light of the resurrection it is therefore wrong to say that 'when the results of the Fall are abolished', the 'impure world form returns' again to the pure form 'from which it had come as a result of the Fall'.[13] The new time of the resurrection does not by any means correspond to the 'original time' before the Fall, but the two stand in the relation of predisposition and fulfilment. This makes it evident once more that in the time of Christ there is at once established also a new content that transcends anything of eternity contained in the life of creation till then. We cannot therefore grasp the nature of the consummation of time in the resurrection by using the concept of a restoration of original time. But

---

transitory is described as 'demi-temporality', pp. 265 ff. Cf. also Heim's criticism of the consequences drawn by Schmidt in his attack on dialectical theology, *Glaube und Denken*, pp. 383 ff.

[11] *The New Divine Order*, pp. 83 f.; *Glaube und Denken*, pp. 379 ff.

[12] Cf. also H. Schreiner, *op. cit.*, p. 295, who recognizes the criticism here advanced against the 'negation of time' to be necessary for a biblical theology.

[13] K. Heim, *Glaube und Denken*, pp. 379 f.

thirdly, this newness of time places the life of the resurrection in a paradoxical relation to the temporal existence of sin. The time of Christ is the non-objective reality which remains invisible to the objectivity of the old time. The temporal order that is broken by sin cannot express without contradictions the time that is fulfilled by God. The indirect relation to God which is the mark of the time that is severed from God is no adequate medium for conveying the direct relation to God which belongs to the time of Christ. The nature of the consummation of time is absolutely inconceivable from any standpoint in the time that is as yet unfulfilled. The statements that have perforce to be made on the fulfilment of time must therefore always move either in negations or in exaggerations[14] where our existing time is concerned. Nevertheless it seems advisable *to refrain from using a negative terminology which obscures the fact that the message of the resurrection does not spell the end of the idea of time, but rather brings it to positive fulfilment and preserves a vanished memory.*

The significance of the consummation of time lies, secondly, in its being the ground of the presence of the Risen One. It is only on the presupposition of this understanding of time that it becomes possible for theology to speak properly of the present Christ. Once we realize that time must also be embraced in the new creation, in the reality of the resurrection of Christ, that leads to important conclusions for our conception of the presence of Christ. On the one hand, this insight resolves the tension between the present and the resurrection event in the past; for then of course the resurrection is actually not an element of the old temporal order, in relation to which such a tension would be conceivable. The relation between the present moment in time and the Risen Christ therefore must not be understood as so to speak longitudinal or horizontal in the sense of a linear conception of time. And on the other hand, the new concept of time does away with the severing of time and eternity, for the resurrection does not imply a timeless eternity with which we could only establish communication by surrendering everything temporal. The relation of the present to the Risen One also must not be conceived as an elevational or, so to speak, vertical one. On the contrary, the temporality of the human self, as being created and sinful temporality, possesses an essential openness towards the new time of Christ as its fulfilment and abolition. Temporal existence does not command the new form of being towards which it is predisposed, but its temporal character is no obstacle to its approach to, and the coming of, the fulfilment of time as a present fact. The presence of the Risen One in the midst of

[14] Rev. 7.16 ff.; 21.4, 11 ff., 23 ff.; 22.2 ff.; I Peter 1.4.

this temporal existence can become a reality when there is an encounter between the Risen One and the human self. The relation of temporal man to the present Christ can therefore be described only as an existential one. *The presence of the Risen One denotes a real actualization within the sphere of time*, not a translation into the supratemporal realm. The new time of Christ comes upon the temporal existence of the self in the present moment of encounter—and indeed it does so in such a way that *the eternal life of the Risen One embraces the life of the self and begins in it*. As consummated time it can begin within our still unfulfilled time as a present non-objective reality. Thus the effectual working of the present Christ in this objective temporal world takes the form of a veiled presence.[15] This presence, however, is neither a pictorial representation nor the timelessness of the *nunc aeternum*, but the real, living actuality of the Risen One within the world of time. The life of the resurrection is not divorced from time, but is the new being—in this time of ours a hidden being—which in the existential encounter discloses itself in a non-objective way as the very centre of time and its decisive form. Confronted by the presence of the Risen One, the man concerned experiences his time as the *kairos* which reveals the ultimate nature of the value time and makes possible the Christocentric time-concept.[16]

(b) The Christ Spirit

The actuality of the Risen One cannot be discussed without reference to the Spirit. Some understanding of the Spirit is therefore essential for the concept of actuality. A theological statement on the Spirit, however, can in turn only be made in the light of Christ, so that every doctrine of the Holy Spirit has *the Christ Spirit* as its content. The concept of the Christ Spirit has to be expounded along two lines—first in the context of our understanding of time, and secondly in regard to its relation to the kyrios-ship of Jesus.

The presence of Christ is the present reality of the Holy Spirit. The new time reality represented by the Risen One can become an actual present reality only because it is in character a spiritual one. A spiritual reality, however, is in terms of the fallen world's time present only as a non-objective and invisible one. The content of the new time reality is the Christ Spirit—though certainly not in such a way that form and content could be separated. The new being which has come with Christ is only

---

[15] Cf. also Col. 3.3 f.; *op. cit.*, pp. 243 ff.
[16] Cf. R. Bultmann, 'Das Wort Gottes im Neuen Testament', in *Vom Worte Gottes*, 1931, p. 18.

present where the Spirit is, and the Spirit is only where 'Christ time' is. The Spirit is identical with the eternal life of the Risen One, which is present without breaking through the bounds of the old time; for mystical ecstasy is not the way in which the Christ Spirit works. Thus the concept of the Christ Spirit is the theological expression for the consummation of time in the resurrection.

If the reality of the Christ Spirit is to be described as a present actuality for the broken world of time, then the nature of this Spirit in its relation to time must reveal itself in three ways, in accordance with the character of the temporal world as a creation that is fallen and imperfect but still awaits redemption. First, the Christ Spirit is the creative power behind the universe, which is sustained through this power of the Spirit and, despite sin and the Fall, is permeated by the living forces of the original creation. That this world, temporal as it is, still bears the marks of its Creator's hand and can still be a place where God reveals himself, is the work of the Spirit. The world in its totality is by no means divorced from the Spirit, otherwise it could not exist for an instant. It belongs to the *regnum potentiae* in which the powers of the Christ Spirit are at work. The fallen world is still creation because the Christ Spirit preserves its existence. But secondly, since the world denies its dependence on the Spirit and thinks itself able to be the ground of its own existence, Christ's relation to it in the Spirit must be one of punishment and judgment on its separatedness. The Christ Spirit shows his actuality in the judgment of all finite things. The unceasing process of the dissolution of all temporal existence is not a thing to be explained in purely naturalistic terms, but is a revelation of the power of the Spirit which abandons all that is opposed to God to self-destruction and decrees its doom. The lordship of death in this temporal world is also an indirect reminder of the judging activity of the Spirit who cannot endure outside himself any form of being that is not 'born of the Spirit'. The Spirit of the Risen Christ makes an unconditional claim which rules out all other possibilities, and which therefore in the time of the Fall must always lead to crisis and division. Thus in the existence of the Ego, too, the ever-present Spirit is at work, as 'Holy' Spirit warning and demanding, punishing and destroying. *This draws a new line of demarcation, not between eternity and time, but between holiness and sin, between Spirit and the pseudo-life that is a prey to death.* The third element in the relation of the Christ Spirit to time has to do with the consummation of the temporal existence of creation. The Spirit is at work in time not only as the 'wholly other' reality of the resurrection, but also as a factor which is related to this world and finds in its created predisposition the starting point from which to work. Because there is no antithesis between Spirit and creation and even the world of the Fall is not 'absolutely' Spirit-less, the ever-present Spirit can begin his work of redemption within the sphere of the old time. The advent of the Spirit becomes the promise of a perfected new creation and of a fulfilment of the eternal life which has begun already in our broken time. In the situation of a world fallen in sin the Spirit of the present Christ is a Spirit who forgives and saves from the consequences of the Fall, but at the same time also a Spirit who redeems creation from the fetters of the Fall and fulfils the creative will of God.

The presence of the Christ Spirit must be grasped in all its fulness. This also provides the safeguard against a number of interpretations of Spirit which are likely to obscure the understanding of the Christ Spirit. The Spirit of the Risen One is not to be interpreted in terms of the dualism of spirit and matter, or of soul and body. In that case the Spirit of Christ will belong to the categories of humanity, to the manifestations of spirit in the religious-historical sphere—and that means, to the dimension of the psyche. The things of the psyche, however, are things that are given and possible in the fallen world, and do not take us beyond the sphere of the old time. The Christ Spirit on the other hand is of course the presence of the new time and must therefore never be equated with the spirituality of men. The Christ Spirit stands as it were on the one side, while the existence of the psyche and of matter and the material, summed up by Paul in the concept 'sarx', stands on the other. Consequently the Spirit also cannot be one of the 'objects' one 'comes across' in this world. It is not as such in man's possession and at his disposal. Even the man who as the result of an encounter with Christ is taken hold of by the Spirit does not have the Spirit as a passive possession. For the Christ Spirit is not a deposit always lying to man's credit and encashable any time, but must be understood in an active and not a static sense. Always it is only as one who comes, who meets man and seizes hold of him, that the Spirit of the Risen One is present. He is not present for those who adopt the part of the neutral onlooker, but always only as an existential and personal event, not in the form of abstract ideas but in the concreteness of consummated time. The existential coming of the Risen One into the temporal world is his presence in the Spirit. However vital it is that the reality of the Spirit should not be confused with any intra-worldly factors, it is nevertheless important that a possible starting point for his work is given in the fact of createdness. This createdness does not in itself mean, as R. Bultmann thinks, an 'anterior understanding' for revelation, but it means that it is possible for man to have a decisive existential encounter with the Spirit.

The question now arises as to the ground of this indissoluble relationship between Christ, particularly the Risen Christ, and the Spirit. *We have to ask whether the 'Holy Spirit' can be thought of also apart from Christ*, i.e. whether it is possible to develop a pneumatology as such, which appears only to be completed and specially qualified through Christ.

The previous discussion has established the fact that all God's activity is activity oriented towards his Son's becoming Kyrios. All God's work can essentially be comprehended only under the concept of the spiritual. Thus the creation of the world is a spiritual event, for God's Spirit brings about the *creatio ex nihilo*. But this creative Spirit of God is not by any means merely the Spirit of God in the abstract, but rather the Spirit whose character on the one hand is determined by the 'image' of the Son, and whose aim on the other hand is directed towards the goal of all creation in the lordship of the Son. The creative Spirit of God is marked by his task, his working, and his aim and purpose as a Christocentric Spirit. Just as creation is inconceivable without the Spirit of God, so also it is meaningless unless that Spirit is determined by Christ, for that is the only basis for the idea and reality of creation. There is accordingly no original working of the Spirit of God that does not always centre at once on the Son who is called to be Kyrios. This fundamental principle is also applicable to the spiritual revelations of God in the 'history of salvation'. The prophets impelled by the Spirit of God know of no other divine commission than to promise judgment and grace in view of the coming lordship of Christ. Through them there speaks the Spirit of God who for the Son's sake seizes hold of men and points them to the coming Christ. The Spirit's revelation in history has the Christ as its presupposition, its content and its goal.[17] The connection between the Spirit and Christ can be further shown from the fact of Christ in history. The Jesus of history stands as God's Son in a spiritual union with God, he receives his Spirit in special measure at his baptism to equip him for his mission, and he knows himself to be the bearer of the Holy Spirit as befits the dawning of the kingdom of God.[18] Yet even this fact of the Son's possession of the Spirit points beyond itself to its consummation in the resurrection.[19]

[17] H. Sasse rightly concludes from this: 'Hence the Old Testament is to be understood only in the light of Christ' (*op. cit.*, p. 145).

[18] Luke 4.17 ff. (21).

[19] Cf. W. Michaelis, *Reich Gottes und Geist Gottes nach dem Neuen Testament*,

The very fact that all statements connected with the Spirit point towards the future coming of a Christ-event shows the fundamental importance of the resurrection for the understanding of the Spirit. For this reason there cannot be the same doctrine of the Spirit before Easter and after Easter, but rather in this case, too, the former is further defined and deepened by the post-Easter knowledge. The fact that the resurrection event marks a new departure is plain from the situation before Easter which, though it does know of promises of the Spirit and of partial communications of the Spirit to particular persons, nevertheless knows nothing of any gift of the Spirit which means the realization of a new life. There was no bestowing of the Spirit by the historic Jesus; on the contrary, the baptism of the Spirit and the commandment to baptize are things that depend on the Risen One. The decisive fact, however, is that the resurrection establishes a wholly new relation between Christ and the Spirit. Because the resurrection of Jesus is the fulfilment of all Christocentric statements about the Spirit made till then, it is possible on the ground of the resurrection to speak of the *identity of the Kyrios with the Spirit.*[20] It is therefore only in the resurrection that pneumatology first acquires its essential foundation. This statement requires further exposition on three counts:

The resurrection itself is to be described as an essentially spiritual event. It is the work of God's Spirit, fulfilling the original purpose of creation by means of the resurrection of Jesus. The same divine Spirit who called the world into being after the image of the Son brings about a new form of being in the resurrection of Jesus. The resurrection of Jesus is therefore a new spiritual creation by God, abolishing the temporal world that was divorced from the Spirit and therefore a prey to death. The creative Spirit of God is the Spirit of the resurrection of Jesus. The identity of Kyrios and Spirit, however, does not mean merely that the resurrection rests upon the Spirit, but marks the new reality of the resurrection as essentially spiritual. 'The Lord is the Spirit' is a proposition that goes beyond the Son's relationship with the Spirit before the resurrection. The advance consists in the fact that the Spirit is not merely a possession or endowment, but means the very existence of the Kyrios. The concept 'Spirit' here describes not only the new form of existence but also the content of that existence. To receive the Spirit may be vouchsafed also to men, but to *be* the Spirit is the unique quality

---

Basle 1931, pp. 9 ff.; F. Büchsel, *Der Geist Gottes nach dem Neuen Testament*, Gütersloh 1926. Noteworthy is also K. Barth, *The Holy Ghost and the Christian Life*, ET 1938.

[20] II Cor. 3.17: 'Now the Lord is the Spirit.'

of the Risen Kyrios. The Lord's identity with the Spirit is the measure of the distance that separates the life of the resurrection from the world and that cannot be bridged by any mystical striving. This distance, however, is the same as that between God and the world. The recognition of this raises, finally, the trinitarian question of the relationship between God, Christ and the Spirit—a question to which the resurrection at once supplies also an answer. The resurrection establishes a revealed Trinity and while on the one hand it takes the ground away from all trinitarian speculations before the resurrection or in abstraction from it, it also expresses on the other hand the fact that the Lord is the Spirit and the Spirit none other than the Spirit of God. It is precisely the resurrection that both makes plain the difference between God, Christ and the Spirit —for God's Spirit shows himself operative in Christ—but, conversely, also makes possible an identification, in the sense that because of the resurrection, but not by any means before it, the divine actuality is the same. This means, however, that where the Risen Lord is at work in the present, there the Spirit is working, and where the Spirit is present, there is the presence of God. This is the meaning of the Trinity, and it is possible and legitimate only on the basis of the resurrection. It is not for theology to speak of God's intra-trinitarian relationships, and to do so is to sever its ties with the primitive Christian witness. A legitimate interest in the Trinity, which takes its bearings from the resurrection, shows itself in the Creed's dogmatic concept of *filioque*. The proceeding of the Holy Spirit in equal measure from God the Father and from the Son as the Lord is a necessary expression of the true lordship of the Kyrios. To dispense with the *filioque* means an eviscerating of the lordship of Christ and a devaluing of the resurrection as a basic spiritual reality.

We come to the *conclusion that the Christ Spirit means the spiritual reality of the resurrection,* There is no valid pneumatology apart from the resurrection, and every genuine Christology always embraces a pneumatology.

2. THE CHURCH OF THE LORD

(a) *The Existentialistic Fellowship with the Risen One*

The presence of the Risen One is properly and comprehensively described only when his spiritual actuality in its working in time is recognized as being at once also the reality of the Church. *The Church is identical with the existentialistic fellowship of believers with the ever-present*

Kyrios. We have accordingly to inquire into the presuppositions of the rise of the Church, into the character of this fellowship, into its significance as the beginning of the new humanity, and into the marks of the Church of the Lord.

1. What has been said so far throws a new light on the much-discussed theological problem of the *ground of the Church.* Even if the empirical preconditions for the forming of the Church lie in the disciples of Jesus and in his actions before the resurrection, yet we can certainly neither speak of an instituting of the Church by Jesus nor identify the Church with these disciples. Not only would Jesus' death then mean the breakdown of this institution and the dissolution of the band of disciples, but the Church would appear to be in essence an empirical and sociological entity. But such an interpretation would destroy the concept of the Church. In contrast to this historicizing view stands the idea of the foundation of the Church in the events of Pentecost. We may certainly say that the Church was only 'realized' in the resurrection whereas its conclusive 'actualization' came at Pentecost, and so maintain that 'The day of the foundation of the actual Church of Christ remains Pentecost'[21]; yet the decisive ground on which the Church became possible is to be seen solely in the resurrection. The impartation of the Spirit specially associated with Pentecost is obviously dependent on the resurrection, so that it does not create a new situation but on the contrary reveals the new situation arising from the resurrection. The foundation of the Church is laid in the Risen Kyrios; though it is the events of Pentecost which first bring the spiritual manifestation of this already present and existing reality of Christ's Church.[22]

The Church by nature and essence is exclusively the *Church of the Lord—ekklēsia kyriakē.* The precondition of its existence is the Kyrios; that is why it cannot have had its beginning in the period before Easter, since at that time there could not yet be a confession of the Risen Kyrios. The Church, however, is neither to be thought of as something added on to the resurrection by way of supplement, nor as simply the fellowship of those who believe in the Kyrios. But the Church is the

[21] Thus Dietrich Bonhoeffer, *Sanctorum Communio*, p. 81 (ET, p. 111). The distinction made for dogmatic purposes between the resurrection of Jesus and his ascension appears to us on the other hand to be untenable, since the Risen One is no other than the exalted, 'ascended' Lord.

[22] I Cor. 3.11, the Risen One is 'the foundation that is laid'; Eph. 2.20; Acts 4.11; I Peter 2.4 ff. K. Holl, too, points to the fact that it was from the knowledge of the resurrection of Jesus that there arose 'the basic views which became cardinal for the concept of the Church'. Cf. also H. D. Wendland, 'Der christliche Begriff der Gemeinschaft', *Theol. Bl.* 1930; H. Rendtorff, *Die Kirche des wirkenden Wortes*, 1930.

reality of the present Kyrios in this temporal world. It is the Easter Church, whose spiritual being is identical with the Risen One. Thus we can neither speak of Christ without at the same time treating of the Church, nor can we talk of the Church and at the same time disregard the Risen One; for *the reality of Christ is the reality of the Church in the midst of the fallen world*. The resurrection establishes an objective concept of the Church. The Church must not be confused with a religious fellowship sharing subjective experiences, and it is also misleading to base it on the community's faith in Christ. Rather, the Church of the Lord is a spiritual reality which stands before and above the individual, which reaches beyond the subjective differences and embraces all the individuals in one.

The objective reality of the Church of the Lord is the reality of the Spirit. The presence of the Spirit of the Kyrios, however, is not one that hovers about us free and unbound, otherwise this Spirit could be confused with spiritual things within the world. The resurrection Spirit is word-bound, inasmuch as this word brings us the message of the resurrection of Jesus. The precondition and medium of the Church's becoming present is therefore the *proclamation of the word. The word of the resurrection contains the potentiality of the presence of the Kyrios as a spiritual reality*. Whether and when the Spirit, and thus the 'reality' of the Church, is actualized when the message is proclaimed, stands at the free discretion of the exalted Kyrios. It is not the proclamation that builds the Church, but the Lord himself is the Creator of his Church through the word. He himself turns the Spirit-potential of the word of Christ into the reality of his Spirit, by making his own claim and so bringing about the decision of faith. The faith of the individual and the faith of the community are alike the work of his Spirit. The Kyrios who becomes present in the word sends his Spirit to men, with the result that they are able to believe and their faith is no longer a subjective opinion but a spiritual attitude. Luther's classical remark is thus confirmed: Christ is not merely the ground and object of faith, but *Christus . . . non objectum, sed ut ita dicam in ipsa fide Christus adest*.[23] The Church of the Lord is thus characterized as a Church of the Spirit, of the word and of faith, but in such a fashion that none of these concepts is valid without the others. It is only by uniting the three that we get a true picture of the Church as the Christ-reality which as a spiritual reality is bound to the word and is realized as a living presence only *in actu fidei*.

2. The character of the *Church of the Lord as an existentialistic fellow-*

[23] *WA* 40, 1228.31 f.

ship requires a detailed exposition. This concept implies a new unique relation of man to the reality of the resurrection. This relationship is not to be compared with intra-worldly relationships, since these as possibilities within the immanent world are always already given, whereas this new relationship is established only in action. Nor is this relationship analogous to communal relations of the organic kind. The idea of an organism is one that is static and belongs to the realm of nature, and thus it cannot adequately convey a spiritual reality. Rather, the concept of existentialistic fellowship expresses the fact that it is the Risen One who by being present and addressing man first makes him a personality and thus capable of fellowship, i.e. that he makes a spiritual claim on his whole existence. *It is only through the claim made on it by the reality of Christ that man's existence first becomes true personal being, that it becomes a new existence before God.* Man's becoming a person through the Christ Spirit means that he is a *kainē ktisis*, a new, spiritually determined being, which no longer persists in isolation like the old life, but which as such is always existentially bound to a life of fellowship. *The present reality of Christ calls man into a double I-thou relationship— into the relationship between Christ and the individual and into the mutual relationship of individuals with one another.* It is only in this relationship that true fellowship is realized—spiritual fellowship, which as such can always only be existentially lived in but is not objectively and visibly demonstrable. The existentialistic fellowship with the Risen One means a spiritual relationship of the Kyrios to the individual, but one which is always at the same time also a relationship to the community. The individual believer and the believing community are thus not independent entities which could be separated from the Risen Christ, but they have their existence only in this union with Christ—which means, however, only in the Church of the Lord. It is only the present reality of the Church that makes contemporaneity with the Risen One possible. *Contemporaneity comes about whenever the spiritual I-thou relationship brings man into that brotherhood with the Kyrios which is the basis of the personal fellowship that expresses itself in dialogue.* Brotherhood and dialogue with the Risen One are not possibilities open to the psyche within the immanent world, but spiritual and existential relationships only to be found in the Church of Christ.

Participation in this existentialistic fellowship does not depend on any natural or organic process, nor yet on an act of choice—both of these things can only apply in the case of a sociological entity—but on the action of God in election, whereby man is transposed *en pneumati* into the new reality of Christ.[24] The electing intervention of God is independent of temporal man's 'basic condition' as regards the flesh. It places man into the new spiritual complex of existence which 'fatefully' surrounds man as the new being. The realizing of this election is a hidden process and so cannot be seen by the 'natural' man.[25] The fact that we are caught up into this existentialistic fellowship is not definable as an element of the old complex of being, nor is it an object for analysis by the psychology of religion, but it is declared only as a result of faith and for faith.

What we here mean by the concept of existentialistic fellowship is formulated by Paul as 'being in Christ'.[26] This phrase asserts a contrast between what in themselves are the infinitely many possibilities of the being which man partly finds himself in, partly chooses and partly tries to create anew, and an entirely different possibility of existence which dawns in the midst of the old temporal order—the new life in Christ. *Being in Christ is an expression for the changed situation which is made possible by the resurrection of Jesus and actualized through the presence of the Risen One.* The situation has fundamentally changed in that the man who belongs to the fallen creation is 'in Christ' drawn into the context of the death and resurrection of Jesus as completed events, and therefore 'in Christ' has a part in the actual present reality of the new existence. The words 'buried with him, crucified with him, raised with him, quickened with him'[27] describe the new existentialistic fellowship as a reality that is not merely to come, but is already there.[28] *The concept of 'being in Christ' means neither a mere idea nor an immanent state but is ultimately identical with the revealed reality of the resurrection.*[29]

These assertions are enough to decide whether the concept of 'being in Christ' is to be understood in a mystical sense or not. The idea of a

---

[24] Eph. 1.4; Rom. 8.28 f.; 9.16; 11.32; I Cor. 2.9, 14; II Cor. 5.18; I Peter 5.10, etc. [25] Col. 3.3: hidden 'with Christ in God'.

[26] W. Bousset, *Kyrios Christos*, p. 921; A. Deissmann, *Die neutestamentliche Formel 'In Christo Jesu'*, 1892; *Paulus*, 1925 (ET, *Paul*, 1926). According to Deissmann (*Paul*, p. 140) this formula is found 164 times in Paul. O. Schmitz, *Die Christusgemeinschaft des Paulus im Lichte seines Genitivgebrauches*, 1924; H. E. Weber, 'Die Formel "In Christo Jesu" und die paulinische Christus-mystik', *NKZ* 31.5, pp. 213 ff.; E. Lohmeyer, 'Σὺν Χριστῷ' in the festival volume for Deissmann, Tübingen 1927, pp. 218 ff. Cf. also W. Wrede, *Paul*, ET 1908.

[27] Rom. 6.4 ff.; Gal. 6.14; 2.19; Col. 2.12 f.; II Cor. 4.11.

[28] Specially characteristic is Eph. 2.5 f.: 'made us sit together in heavenly places in Christ Jesus'.

[29] We can therefore speak with K. Mittring of the presence of the 'historic situation of salvation' in Christ, of the 'place at which the salvation of God is present', *Heilswirklichkeit bei Paulus*, 1929, pp. 128 f., 93, 95, 109, 118. Cf. also Col. 1.13; Phil. 3.20; II Cor. 5.1 f. Special mention is due to Friedrich Delekat, *Der gegenwärtige Christus*, 1946, Kreuz-Verlag Stuttgart.

Christ mysticism is essentially at variance with the character of the existentialistic fellowship. The latter is neither to be identified with some kind of religious experience nor with a condition existing in the inner life of the soul, nor is it to be interpreted in substantial and magical terms.[30] The statement of our existential being in Christ is on the contrary an eminently sober and objective expression of the new understanding of the situation. The present-cum-perfect reality of the resurrection does not do away with the boundary between the 'I' of Christ and the 'thou' of man by means of some mystical intermerging, nor does it offer the possibility of exalting oneself in mystical ecstasy above the limitations of the old world time. The essential thing is precisely our participation in the life of the resurrection 'in Christ', not through an abolition of the temporal order, but through the fulfilment already dawning in it. In the midst of a world that is passing away, there is a new eternal existence present in spiritual ways. But sharing in it does not mean mystical identity: it means being rooted in the Church's all-embracing spiritual unity with all its marks of our distinctness from the Kyrios.

3. Further, in the existentialistic fellowship of the Church of the Lord there is established the *beginning of the new humanity*. The old humanity of the fallen world is determined by being 'in the flesh' or by 'being in Adam'. Man stands in the natural Adamite line, in the fateful complex of humanity in sinful and broken world time. 'Being in Adam' is the existence unto self of mankind separated from God, an existence which is subject to death. This inescapable state of man's being in his flesh-and-soul fellowship with Adam is broken through by the reality of Christ in the Church. In the presence of the Risen One there is realized the wholly new possibility, *viz.*—apart from the life 'in the flesh' also the possibility of being 'in Christ'. With this, man's transitory pseudo-life is confronted in Christ with the resurrection life, which is not only a life to come but is actually present, veiled but real, in this existentialistic fellowship. Christ becomes the 'second man' who in his

[30] There can be absolutely no talk of an 'experience of the Spirit-Christ' or of a 'mystic temperature'. Thus A. Deissmann, *Paulus*, 1925, p. 111 (*Paul*, p. 140). The distinction between 'active' and 'reactive' mysticism does not do justice to the facts either, and is liable to make a clear understanding more difficult. Cf. also J. Weiss, *History of Primitive Christianity*, pp. 468 f.; H. E. Weber, *NKZ* 31.5, p. 223; *Eschatologie und Mystik im Neuen Testament*, 1930. For the sake of theological clarity it is to be regretted that A. Schweitzer, too, speaks of a 'mysticism of the apostle Paul' although in actual substance he makes clear the fundamental difference between the mysticism of religious history and the Pauline relation with Christ. Cf. also E. von Dobschütz, 'Wir und Ich bei Paulus', *Zeitschr. für syst. Theol.* 1932, part 2, pp. 262 ff.

collective person sums up the new humanity, i.e. the humanity which
has part in the Christ life. The spiritual reality of the Risen Christ
begets a new creation, which appears in the spiritual community. This
is the new creation, which begins already in this world of time, in so far
as the Spirit is present, as surety, 'seal', 'earnest', 'firstfruits'.[31] Because
the Spirit of the Risen Christ dwells in the community, the Church of
the Kyrios becomes the dawning of the new reconciled humanity that
lives from eternity. As a spiritual entity, the Church has the character
of the 'body of Christ', which embraces the new creation and the new humanity. Christ as head of the body is at the same time also head of the
Church and head of the new humanity. The new, 'reborn' man is the man
who lives from his existentialistic fellowship with the Risen Christ. The
sinful separation is overcome through the existential 'I-thou' relationship.
Thus the spiritual reality of the Church of the Lord is at once the heart
of the new humanity and the profoundest fulfilment of its purpose.[32]

4. This way of viewing the Church as an existentialistic fellowship
with the present Kyrios must determine also the characteristic marks of
this Church of the Lord. Even if this is not the place to expound a proper
doctrine of the sacraments, we must nevertheless indicate how their
essential characteristics and their meaning must be understood in the
light of the presence of the Lord in his Church. If *to speak of the Church
is to speak of none other than the Lord who lives in his Church,* then the
notae ecclesiae, the sacraments, can in turn also ultimately be understood
only in the light of the resurrection event which determines the Church's
faith in the Kyrios and is constitutive of the reality of the Church of the
Lord.[33] *The sacraments of the Church are resurrection sacraments.*

From the standpoint of the history of religion, it is not at all difficult
to find practices and formulae especially in the sacramental celebrations
of the mystery cults that are analogous to the sacramental marks of the
Church,[34] The specifically Christian character of the view of the sacra-

[31] Eph. 4.30; II Cor. 1.22; 5.5; Eph. 1.14; Rom. 8.17 f., 23 f.
[32] Reference should be made to two studies by Dietrich Bonhoeffer, who
has vital things to say in this context: *Sanctorum Communio,* 1930, pp. 15, 34,
64 ff., 70 f., 85 f. (ET, pp. 28, 84 f., 99ff., 106f., 114), and especially *Akt und Sein,*
Gütersloh 1931, pp. 103, 128 f., 132 ff., 145 (ET, *Act and Being,* 1962, pp. 123,
148, 157, 172 f.). He sees 'Christ existing as Church', 'the Church as a unity of
act and being', p. 99 (120). Also noteworthy is his presentation of the doctrine
of man 'in Adam' and 'in Christ', pp. 131 ff. (155 ff.).
[33] Cf. on the question of the sacraments, A. Schweitzer, *Geschichte der
paulinischen Forschung,* p. 169 (ET, pp. 216 f.); *Die Mystik des Apostels Paulus,*
1930, pp. 222 f. (ET, pp. 227 f.); O. Fricke, *Die Sakramente in der Protestant-
ischen Kirche,* Tübingen 1929, makes important observations on the fundamental question.
[34] C. Clemen, *Religionsgeschichtliche Erklärung des Neuen Testaments,* Giessen

ments in the primitive Church, however, only emerges in the light of the resurrection as the fundamental principle of the Church of the Lord.

As to the *nature of the sacrament* as the primitive Church conceived it, we have first of all to make the following fundamental points. Sacraments are the visible signs, 'the visible proclamation', the concrete expression, of the fact that something new has happened and is now present, that an old form of being which hitherto existed has passed away and a new kind of existence has dawned. The understanding of the sacraments therefore turns on the resurrection and depends on the reality and present actuality of this event. Thus sacrament means the objective and earthly = objectual happening of a spiritual = 'heavenly' = non-objectual event.* One might describe the peculiarity of a sacrament by the paradoxical concept of 'non-objectual reality'. Both elements belong indissolubly together: the objectivity of the substantial event, as a sign that the substantial ground of the new being is given independently of man in the perfect-cum-present of the Risen Kyrios, and the non-objectuality of the same event, since the life of the resurrection is a spiritual reality and the presence of the Kyrios can be apprehended only in faith. If the Lord of the Church, in keeping with his omnipotence and omnipresence, is himself the Spirit who works irrespective of the subjective decisions of men, then the church sacrament which bears witness to him must give expression to both things: the objective reality of a new existentiality and also the spiritual character of this sacramental relationship.

This view of the sacraments contrasts both with the objective and magical conception and with the subjective and symbolical idea of a sacrament. According to the former, the sacrament becomes an *opus operatum*—which does indeed preserve its objective character, but overlooks the fact that the Lord is the Spirit over whom man even in a sacramental act has no power and who can be known only in the faith awakened by the Spirit himself. The other view does indeed recognize that even in the sacrament we have to do with a spiritual reality that calls for faith, but overlooks the fact that the essential character of the sacrament is misunderstood if the subjective element is decisive and the

---

1924; W. Heitmüller, *Taufe und Abendmahl im Urchristentum*, Tübingen, 1911; R. Reitzenstein, *Die hellenistischen Mysterienreligionen*, Leipzig and Berlin 1927.
  * 'Objectual' is an attempt to render in English the meaning of *gegenständlich* as opposed to *objektiv*, though both terms are normally rendered by 'objective'. 'Objectual' (*gegenständlich*) means having the character of an object or thing in space, whereas 'objective' (*objektiv*) means the character of having existence (whether material or spiritual) independently of the observing subject.— *Translator.*

reality which transcends the self is lost. A valid concept of the sacraments must thus be adequate to the paradox of the revelation of Christ.

When it is the resurrection which determines the way we understand
the sacraments, then they are *two in number*. The *perfectum* of the resurrection and the presence of the Risen Christ demand a twofold sacramental reference. Thus Baptism as an act performed only once is the
sacramental, i.e. objective and non-objectual expression of the completed saving event, while the Lord's Supper in its repeatability is the
earthly and spiritual representation of the presence of the new life.

The meaning of *Baptism* then derives from its being parallel to the
raising of the Crucified.[35] Two basic ideas are decisive here: first, that
of destruction or dying, second, that of renewal or life. We can recognize
the necessity of Baptism when we realize the state of the old, sin-marked
and death-ridden being to which natural man is irretrievably condemned. This old being must accordingly perish. But for the first time
it is overcome in Jesus' death and resurrection. That is why Baptism
can only mean being baptized 'into Christ Jesus', and more specifically
'into his death'. Man must not remain as he is; what has been till now
in its corruptedness, must be killed, laid aside. Thus Baptism means in
the first instance the ending of the old aeon as a finished event of decisive
significance which is objectively and fundamentally valid for all who are
baptized. Secondly, however, with our Baptism there begins in princple
a new state, our ingrafting into the body of the Lord, our implanting
into the spiritual presence of the new aeon and, finally, the promise of a
consummation of the resurrection life that has thus begun.[36] Baptism
is the substantial expression of the new creation that has begun with the
resurrection; it is the sacramental event, transcending all subjective
baptismal experiences, which is the guarantee of participation in the
resurrection Church of the new aeon. It is a real ingrafting, but a
spiritual one and therefore one that is recognizable only for faith and
exists only for faith. If the resurrection is the eschatological event, then
Baptism, too, partakes of this character, for it is only on the ground of
the resurrection that an act of Baptism has any meaning. The spiritual
relationship which is given through Baptism cannot be abrogated, since
the Lord's claim on the membership which begins in Baptism cannot
be abrogated even though on man's side that membership may well be
impaired or even destroyed.

[35] Rom. 6.3 ff., cf. also Gal. 3.27; Col. 2.12; Titus 3.5.
[36] Cf. Luther (*Catechism* IV): 'Just as Christ was raised from the dead, so
we also are to walk in a new life.'

Our understanding of the *Lord's Supper*, too, is grounded in the resurrection. The Lord's Supper is the typical festival of the Church, living as it does in the situation between the old world and the new. The Lord's Supper is of course not merely a feast commemorating the death of Jesus, but is primarily a cultic act in which, firstly, surety is received for the mediating of salvation by Christ on the ground of his reconciling sacrificial death, but in which, secondly, existentialistic fellowship is experienced with the exalted and spiritually present Kyrios. This at once makes of the Lord's Supper an eschatological feast that looks towards the consummation of the new world, a communion of those who are prepared to leave the old aeon behind in the expectation of the parousia of the Kyrios. In this cultic act our fellowship in the destiny of the Risen One reaches its climax, in that the life-giving spiritual power of the ever-present Lord communicates itself to the congregation at the Table as an earnest of the fulfilling of fellowship in the new cosmos. For the Church the Lord's Supper is the power-house of the new being in the midst of the world of transience, the place where the conflict between existence in the flesh and in the Spirit reaches its tensest, but at the same time is resolved by the Spirit and by faith. The presence of the resurrection reality is experienced in the Supper, and by celebrating it the existential fellowship with the Kyrios is strengthened. Hence bread and wine are not merely the substantial expression of the objective coming of the new world to man, but also a pointer to the full life of the resurrection that is conferred in Christ and embraces also the life of the body. The celebration of the Lord's Supper in the primitive Church as the heart of its fellowship and the seal of its spiritual existence 'in Christ' would be inconceivable apart from the resurrection. It is only this event that first gives rise to the repetition of the last fellowship meal with Jesus —to be sure, with a fulfilled, spiritual meaning given by the event of Easter. The host at this meal is the invisibly present Kyrios, who through this eating and drinking institutes fellowship with himself and among the celebrants, and out of his own new existence confers in spiritual ways upon the fallen, the sinners and the guilty the new resurrection life. In the Lord's Supper the existentialistic fellowship with the Risen One takes concrete and visible form. It is the resurrection feast of the Church, which in partaking of this meal recognizes in special measure that it has a part in the life of Christ.[37]

The marks of the Lord's Church communicate no new content, but,

[37]Hence word and sacrament according to Article VII of the Augsburg Confession are definitely to be understood in the light of the resurrection of Christ.

reveal in concrete form that the life of the Church is the life of the Risen One.[38]

(b) The Ethical Dynamic of the Church

If the word of the Church of the Lord is to mean a real presence of the Risen One, then an ethical power and vitality must find expression within it. The spiritual presence of the Kyrios is incompatible with ethical ineffectiveness and impotence within the Church. The answers to the questions of Christian ethics, and more especially the questions of ethical renewal, of sanctification, and of the possibility and meaning of Christian action, are already decided by our theological attitude to the resurrection. If we neglect the significance of the resurrection and deal mainly with reconciliation in the sense of a one-sided theology of the cross, then we shall tend to be equally one-sided in putting justification in the centre to the exclusion of the idea of a *nova vita*, and pointing out the dubiousness of all ethical possibilities open to the justified man. However much may be said for dialectical theology's use of such methods as safeguards against pietistic distortions of evangelical ethics, yet the first thing is to make the new reality of the resurrection life our starting point, and to take seriously the fact that resurrection opens the way for the Spirit and communicates the Spirit—which, however, means that it contains within it an effectual formative power and an ethical dynamic. It is only from this standpoint that we can then go on to inquire how theology has to expound this *dynamis* of the resurrection Spirit in the midst of the fallen world.

Two basic statements have to be made about the *ethical dynamic of the Church:* 1. *The ethical dynamic is a present reality only as the spiritual power of the Risen One.* 2. *All ethical effectiveness on the part of the Church must be seen as a work of the Kyrios.*

The ethical power of the Lord's Church results from its existential union with the Risen One. His Spirit alone is the life-creating Spirit of the Church.[39] Only the gift of the Spirit connects fleshly, physical man

---

[38] Cf. I Cor. 10.16 ff.; 11.23 ff. Further, E. Lohmeyer, *Kyrios Jesus*, 1928, p. 66: 'The celebration of the Lord's Supper was for the primitive Christian believer a surety for two things: the certainty of the presence of the Lord, and the certainty of his eschatological coming.' Cf. also E. Sommerlath, *Der Sinn des Abendmahls*, Leipzig 1930. W. Elert, *Die Lehre des Luthertums*, p. 58: 'The congregation as such derives its certainty of having him in its midst . . . from the common celebration of the . . . Lord's Supper. The Church would have no interest in this celebration, if it were not certain that the exalted Christ, whose presence it here perceives, is identical with him who unites in himself the life of man and of God.' Likewise W. Elert, *Der christliche Glaube*, pp. 433 ff.

[39] Cf. O. Schmitz, 'Der Begriff δύναμις bei Paulus', festival volume for Deissmann, Tübingen 1927.

with the living Lord. Thus everything depends on the contact established between the Church and the Risen One, for the dynamic of the Church is grounded solely in its dependence on the Spirit of the Risen Lord.[40] That brings out the fact that the dynamic of the Church is not a dynamic of its own. The Church does not by its own resources have spiritual life-forces and ethical powers at its disposal as a possession of its own. Nor is it distinguished from other communities by special ethical qualities in such a manner that the moral excellence of its conduct would justify the Church itself to the rest of the world. The life within it is a spiritual life and its dynamic is a Christ-dynamic. This means, however, that the Church is alive only in so far as it is filled with the power of the resurrection and is thus really an existentialistic fellowship, but that as soon as its union with the Kyrios is severed, it is the same as any other human religious fellowship. The ethical principle animating the Lord's Church is therefore decisively determined by its existential contact with the resurrection reality and is therefore as far removed from idealist autonomy as from Judaistic heteronomy. The error of the autonomist view and of all idealist philosophy is, that the spirit of man is equated with the Holy Spirit: it possesses creative power of its own and has no need to be bound to God. On the other hand, the error of heteronomist and Catholic philosophy is the belief that fulfilment of the law and submission to an alien authority brings eternal life. But the binding of the Church to Christ is not heteronomous, since the Church only exists at all in and because of its being thus bound, and the ethical authority of the Risen One is thus not something that stands outside the Church but is identical with the authority of the Church. The Church therefore has no authority in itself—that would be a human and relative authority—but only in Christ. Autonomous and heteronomous thinking are still under the ban of fallen creation, still on the hither side of the fact of Easter, and can know nothing of the Spirit. Both views are deceiving themselves in their illusions concerning the power and possibilities of our being. As against all this, the ethical dynamic of the Church must be understood as Christonomy, since it depends exclusively on being spiritually bound to Christ.[41]

We thus see that the ethical activity of the Church does not have its norm and centre in itself, but that its centre of power is transferred from man to the Kyrios. The ability to act is not a neutral possession, but

---

[40] Cf. Eph. 3.16; 4.4; Gal. 4.6; 3.2; 5.22; 6.8; II Cor. 3.6; Acts 3.6, 16; 4.10, 30.
[41] Cf. ἔννομος Χριστοῦ, Rom. 6.12 f.; 7.4; 8.12; 12.1 f.; 13.14; Gal. 5.16, 25; Phil. 4.13; Col. 2.16, 20; II Cor. 7.1 f.; 12.12.

only arises at every moment from the link with the actual presence of the Lord. Thus the Church becomes a spiritual function of the Risen One, in which everything depends upon its spiritual direction by Christ not being interrupted. This spiritual guidance of the Church by the Kyrios is made manifest in the moment of concrete decision when some quite specific commission of the Lord motivates and directs the action of the Church and the individual amid the abundance of possibilities. The certainty of being directed by the present, risen Lord is the basic assumption behind the ethical attitude of the Church.[42] Since, however, this guidance is spiritual, it cannot be objectively established or observed, nor can it by any means be unequivocally recognized by its effects. Likewise, form and content of this spiritual commission vary according to the individual and concrete diversities of life, so that the recognition of it must be utterly impossible to any unbelieving scrutiny. Spiritual leadership by the Kyrios is a certitude of faith, and not a matter of empirical demonstration. This certitude of faith need not express itself in specific moods or in clear insights, for it is knowledge of the presence of the Lord, but not *a priori* knowledge of the concrete content of his will. The will of the Kyrios is in principle unconditioned, and hence not bound to the conditions and orders of the fallen creation, so that his commands cannot simply be read at sight from the concrete situation. Were this possible, it would always be the Church's own will that was making the decisions. The Church, however, knows its whole existence to be dependent on the Kyrios, and the only will it possesses is bound to him. Its will is not driven by any independent dynamic of its own. The Church has therefore to listen to, and wait for, the concrete word of its Lord and then to act in accordance with the commission it receives. Even its execution of such a commission is not always accompanied by subjective certainty as to the rightness of this action; the possibility of doubt and error is always present in this world, but the carrying out of an action must be believed (though it admittedly cannot be known) to be ordained by the Kyrios when such action takes place in existential decision before the Lord. The spiritual directing of the Church by the Risen One is always an existential one.[43]

---

[42] Acts 8.26; 13.2; 16.6, 7, 9; 18.9; 19.21; 20.22; 27.23 ff.

[43] Cf. the observations of K. Heim, who was the first to bring out and develop in ethics this fundamental idea of the New Testament, *Glaube und Denken*, pp. 415 ff. Heim expounds the theological understanding of the fact that an 'invisible accent' is laid by the Holy Spirit on relative phenomena and words, so that they become the 'authoritative rule' for me through the principle of 'dimensional cleavage'. His criticism of K. Barth here manifestly touches the weakest point in Barth's theology. P. 433: 'The living Christ guides his Church

This insight leads to the second proposition: that we can speak of ethical effectiveness on the Church's part only as the work of the Kyrios. The work of the Christ Spirit is a universal one and embraces the entire man at every point in his life's acts and his relationships with the world, all of which are thus directed towards one ethical centre, towards a central orientation point. The *dynamis* of the resurrection extends to the depths of ethics, to the individual ethical questions of everyday life. The Christian ethic is therefore a Christ-centred, revealed ethic, a spiritual ethic of the resurrection.

Firstly, through the fact of the resurrection and its spiritual presence the whole ethical situation is fundamentally changed. *Ethical activity* is then no longer action of man in view of some goal of his own choosing —whether to fashion his own life after some idealistic pattern and raise himself to a higher existence, or to create a humane and harmonious world which will bring the greatest possible happiness and wellbeing, or to ensure his own religious significance as a means of attaining salvation. Ethical activity is a reaction springing from the new living reality of the Risen One. It is this that is the basis of the Christian ethic, and all moral conduct is only a proof of Christ's spiritual presence in the concrete situation. This implies a complete reversal of the whole ethical approach. It is not the moral code itself which is the motive force, but the working of the Spirit.[44] The Church's spiritual aliveness, which does not come from itself, has therefore nothing to do with assiduous activity on man's part, with supremely intense vitality of body and soul, or with exceptional morality. This excludes every form of an ethic of achievement, an ethic of duty and of justification by works. In the raising of Christ as a perfected act the whole process of salvation is complete, and does not require any addition or continuation.[45] To regard the ethical imperatives as a condition of salvation is in fact a mark of the pre-Easter situation in the old aeon of the law. Any relapse into a theory of merit means a lapsing from the spiritual fellowship of Christ. Likewise, there is in this new spiritual sphere of the Church's life no place for mystical quietism or for libertine enthusiasm. Any

according to his promise by his Spirit . . . thus he gives us for the situation in which we stand, for the καιρός, the word for the hour.' For further development cf. E. Brunner, *The Divine Imperative*, ET 1937, pp. 68 ff., 111 ff.

[44] II Cor. 4.7: the power 'not of us'; cf. E. Sommerlath, *Der Ursprung des neuen Lebens nach Paulus*, Leipzig 1927.

[45] Cf. R. Bultmann, 'Das Problem der Ethik bei Paulus', *ZNW* 23, 1924, pp. 123 f.; W. Mundle, 'Religion und Sittlichkeit bei Paulus in ihrem inneren Zusammenhang', *Zeitschr. f. syst. Theol.* 1926-7, part 4, pp. 456 ff.; H. D. Wendland, 'Ethik und Eschatologie in der Theologie des Paulus', *NKZ* 1930, pp. 757 ff.

relinquishment of action and of purposeful activity—whether on the part of some esoteric sect that has turned its back upon the world, or by people who feel they have full possession of the Spirit and thus think themselves exalted above the concrete demands of life—makes obvious the absence of the Spirit. The Spirit of God in man is always supremely practical, even if not at man's disposal as a possession of his own. This Spirit shows his power, not somewhere beyond, or in abstraction from, the old, sin-distorted world, but precisely in it. Even as the Church represents the work of the Spirit, so also the work of the Church which has become the organ of the Spirit is at the same time the work of the Spirit.[46] Action is for the Church both possible and necessary since its life is spiritually bound up with the Kyrios and so lies open for the working of his Spirit.

This also answers the question whether we can speak in the Church of 'sanctification'. Sanctification must be understood as a proof of the new Christ-life,[47] as a reflection of the resurrection within the Church.[48] Sanctification is not a meritorious moralistic act on the part of man, but is the working of the Spirit as a confirmation of the present power of the Kyrios in battling with sin and temptation despite defeat and guilt in the sphere of the old aeon. The Church has been renewed 'in Christ', its life in God's world is already a real fact, even if a hidden one, and because of this it can be summoned to sanctification, to that conduct of life which accords with its spiritual existence. It is not for the attaining of this new, Spirit-conditioned situation, but as expressions of it, that the imperatives and admonitions have their force. Sanctification means that by reason of the new existential being in Christ we are actively ready for the workings of the Spirit and willing to live by them. Even as the Spirit is never an infused *habitus* and possession of man, so also sanctification can never be the work of justified man. Rather, sanctification is persistent and daily openness towards the formative power of the Spirit, and readiness to be moulded by it. One could put it paradoxically: sanctification is passivity towards the Spirit and at the same time the working out of this *laisser-faire* in activity determined by the Spirit.

The spiritual work of the Church must be concretely described as a

[46] The Church is the 'workmanship' of God, 'created in Christ Jesus unto good works', Eph. 2.10.   [47] Eph. 4.12 f.
[48] A. Köberle in his study on the problem of sanctification has also clearly called attention to this decisive connection between sanctification and the new aeon: 'If for faith there is no such actual receiving of the Spirit, then neither is Christ risen. Then the old aeon with the full weight of the obligations of the law still lies upon the earth.' *Rechtfertigung und Heiligung*, pp. 117, vii, 155 ff., 136, 150.

revelation of *agape*. The Church of the Lord is its true self always only by being at the same time the Church of *love*. The resurrection has changed the relationship of man to those around him. The self-seeking of the 'I'-relationship has been broken through by the 'I-thou' relationship established in Christ, which first sets man free for the claims of his fellows. Man in the existentialistic fellowship with Christ becomes a brother, and the man still outside this fellowship becomes a neighbour who is consciously or unconsciously waiting for his new humanity, because the reality of the resurrection is valid also for him. The acknowledgment of these relations of brother and neighbour, and the assent to the claims thereby made, reveals the love of God which is spiritually present in the Risen One taking concrete shape within the Church. Thus *agape* becomes the fundamental principle of the new spiritual mode of existence, which in the fulness of its concrete possibilities is free from any kind of casuistry.[49]

Out of the changed ethical situation that results from the resurrection there arises a *new conception of life on the part of the Lord's Church*. In keeping with the existentialistic fellowship, this new conception of life must be determined by the basic attitude of *discipleship*. Discipleship can now no longer be misunderstood as *imitatio Christi*, for that would be an empiric process void of spiritual quality. The concept of discipleship is again only to be understood in the light of the spiritual intervention of the Kyrios in the existence of the Church in calling it forth, while the Church accepts and follows this call of the Lord and in so doing changes the direction of its life and orients it towards Christ. Thus on the one hand discipleship is defined as obedience and surrender to the Lord, even to the point of martyrdom, which is not a self-chosen work but a spiritual event in which the new situation of the resurrection Church in the midst of the world of death finds concentrated realization as at a focal point. On the other hand, however, the conception of life as discipleship is a spiritual joy,[50] is marked by the knowledge of the change in the world situation and has therefore an incomparable assurance of victory, which produces 'a wholly new art of dying'.[51] The spiritual conception of life on the part of the Lord's Church is deter-

---

[49] Cf. the important study by W. Koepp, 'Merimna und Agape'in the festival volume for R. Seeberg, 1927, supplemented in W. Koepp, *Panagape* I, 1927, II, 1928. Noteworthy is also Eduard Ellwein, *Vom neuen Leben: eine systematische und theologiegeschichtliche Untersuchung zur Lehre vom neuen Leben*, Munich 1932.   [50] Hence: 'Rejoice in the Lord!', Phil. 4.4.
[51] C. Stange, *Zeitschr. f. syst. Theol.* 1923-4, p. 710. A. Schlatter, *Geschichte des Christus*, p. 531, speaks of the 'triumphant assurance: Death, where is thy sting?'

minative for the whole of the community's existence and so necessarily affects also its whole life, soul and body.[52]

The Christian ethic has no illusions, since all the Church's action takes place on the stage of the fallen world. But the Church's moral standard is at the same time also full of power in this world, because it is the work of the Spirit. That is why the ethical dynamic of the Lord's Church is itself the visible symbol and proclamation of the new coming world of Christ and reflects the fact of the presence of the Risen Christ.

3. THE POSSIBILITY OF A CHRISTIAN ONTOLOGY

The turning of the latest philosophy towards ontology, and the theological existentialism which is connected with this, have led to a new and deeper understanding of reality and have laid bare the real problems of being, to whose difficulty modern man, too, is alive.[53] While the philosophical approach seeks, in strict abstraction from any metaphysical interpretation, to provide an analysis of the structure of being, it is obviously the interest of the theologian to raise the problem of the presuppositions underlying all ontology, of the value and interpretation of ontological statements, and so to assert the concern of religion. Here the question at issue is, whether a philosophical ontology can provide the foundation for a Christian dogmatic, or whether Christian faith already implies from the start a quite specific understanding of existence and must reject a so-to-speak 'atheistic' ontology as inappropriate. We must also ask whether every ontology does not in some way or other provide a starting point for the Christian proclamation, so that every understanding of being contains within it an 'anterior understanding' of the idea of revelation.

Once we accept the postulate of a theology of the resurrection, the problem of ontology is clearly defined. Unquestionably this department of thought gains a special importance in relation to the resurrection message. Nobody can be blind to the essential connection between a philosophy of 'Dasein'* and the new knowledge of existence which is

---

[52] Cf. the Church's hymns of resurrection and of victory; also the unique sense of life, governed by the resurrection, among the so-called 'Gospel Christians' at the time of the Bolshevist persecutions in Russia.

For the immediate relation to the *sōma*, cf. I Cor. 6.15 where Paul rejects unchastity in view of our membership in the Body of Christ. Cf. also O. Schmitz, *Lebensgefühl des Paulus*, 1922.

[53] Cf. M. Heidegger, *Sein und Zeit*, 1927 (ET, *Being and Time*, 1962, with German pagination in margin); the volume on ontology of the *ZTK* 1930, part 5, with studies by R. Bultmann, K. Löwith and K. Heim; K. Heim, *Glaube und Denken*, pp. 23 ff., 107 ff., 139 ff., 270 ff.

* The word '*Dasein*' is left untranslated in this section, since it is already

grounded in the resurrection. From the standpoint of a theology of the resurrection, it is true, every abstract philosophical ontology that takes no account of the Christian revelation is seen to be a way of thinking that does not grasp the ultimate depths of reality. If a man knows nothing of the world of the resurrection, he is also incapable of a proper view of the datum 'Dasein' in its totality and a proper grasp of its meaning. Conversely, however, from the viewpoint of a theology of the resurrection it is possible to construct a Christian ontology. Christian ontology claims, firstly, to possess its own independent understanding of 'Dasein' which takes up into itself the insights of philosophical ontology, and secondly, to be able also to solve the problems raised thereby. After all that has been said so far, we may venture the proposition: *Christology is ontology, i.e. there is no understanding of 'Dasein' that is in touch with reality and that disregards the Christ reality.* It is the latter that makes possible ontological knowledge. That is why the New Testament knows of no ontology save the *resurrection ontology.* The latter becomes the answer to the ontological problem. H. Schreiner raises the legitimate question whether the concept of an 'ontology', which connotes something 'static', would not be better abandoned. In face of this it must be pointed out that through the resurrection this concept is given a new 'dynamic' content. Schreiner's object is presumably also achieved by his more recent observations on 'eschatological perspective' and 'dynamic'.[54]

(a) Existence and the Fact of its being called in Question

(i) The Problematicalness of Dasein

Man does not find himself primarily as a sinner burdened in his conscience, but as a man, as one who is. First of all, linking up with Heidegger, we find the following basic features of the understanding of Dasein. That his life is, is the absolutely unshakable reality and at the same time also the great riddle that confronts him. Man experiences his existence as an overpowering destiny under which he has been placed without being asked, and into which he has been inextricably woven. Destiny, however, implies a being that comes upon us irrespective of any personal decision of our own and makes this destined being into our own peculiar Dasein. Human existence is the expression of a

---

reasonably familiar in English discussions of Heidegger. In most German philosophy it means simply 'being' or 'existence'. But in common parlance, and in Heidegger, its use is restricted to *personal* being.—*Translator.*

[54] Cf. *Die Verkündigung des Wortes Gottes*, p. 296.

primordial dispensation, inaccessible to reason, which has thrown man into Dasein[55] as an individual with precisely these particular existential characteristics at a quite definite point of time, and an equally definite point in space. The person of a man is thus identical with the reality of his Dasein. 'Man's "substance" is not spirit as a synthesis of soul and body; it is rather existence.'[56] Existing man is confined within the world of what is, existentially fitted into the cosmos in natural ways and therefore, in consequence of this 'Being-in-the-world', is also succumbed to this world,[57] a part of its cosmic destiny, serviceable to its demands, 'making provision' for its questions. The existence of man thus of itself becomes the decisive question addressed to his life—which means, however, that his Dasein, in so far as he understands himself, calls itself in question. The very reality of his existence alone is enough to make man one who is questioned.

This fact of being existentially called in question is made more profound by the intentional structure of existence, which is always directed towards something. The Dasein of man is never a being in itself and only for itself, is no isolated being of the 'I' severed from the being-complex of persons and things, but is always, as Heidegger says, a 'being-with'. 'A bare subject without a world' is 'never given' and 'just as little is an isolated "I" without Others'. 'The others', too, are 'not proximately present-at-hand as free-floating subjects along with other Things',[58] but show themselves in their interwovenness with the world around them. Existence therefore means having a common destiny of being with others, with the cosmos, finding oneself in perpetual movement with a 'Thou', being turned towards the being of community. Dasein posits at once an 'I-Thou' relationship, it is a perpetual quest for the 'thou' in reference to which the 'I' first finds itself, in reference to which it understands itself and so perceives its own existence, unfolds itself as a real 'I'. The original predisposition of man towards conscious and understanding Dasein only comes to fruition in reference to his neighbour. Being alone, the 'solitary being-for-itself of the "I", is something wholly secondary—namely, the result of an act by which the "I" has shut itself off from the "thou" '.[59] The condition that makes this possible, however, is given precisely in the intentional directedness

[55] M. Heidegger, *Sein und Zeit*, pp. 135, 199.
[56] Heidegger, p. 117, cf. pp. 46 ff., 52 ff., 63, 180, 304.
[57] *Op. cit.*, pp. 175, 222, 254.
[58] *Op. cit.*, pp. 123, 114, 116, 118, 120, 124. Cf. also F. Gogarten, *Politische Ethik*, 1932, pp. 7 ff.
[59] K. Heim in *ZTK* 1930, part 5, pp. 333 f.

towards the other. The 'I', as a quest for the 'thou', is always at the
same time the attempt to supply a response to the other questing 'I'.
There is thus no Dasein without responsibility; for the ontological
problem is more closely defined as an ethical one. Man therefore lives
in the situation of an existence which stands in question and which, as
one concrete set of relationships supersedes another, is constantly
oppressed by questions. Thus life goes on subject to the question which
its Dasein puts to the 'thou', but also subject to the question which
cosmic being puts to all real being connected with it, and in view of
these questions it becomes aware of its 'questionableness'.

The fact of man's being called in question finds its basic expression
in the peculiar quality of his consciousness of life, in the subject's
'state-of-mind',[60] which according to Heidegger is ultimately to be
characterized as 'care' (*Sorge*) and 'anxiety' (*Angst*). While it is true
that care (*Sorge*) is not to be understood as 'tribulation and the cares
of life', but as the 'basic existential-ontological phenomenon'[61] of
'concern' (*Besorgen*) in and for the world, nevertheless this concept
makes clear precisely the fundamental necessity inherent in being—the
necessity of having to question and of being questioned. This condition,
however, determines the basic mood of anxiety. Anxiety itself has the
character of a latent question and of being questioned. It is in fact a
reflection of the enigmatic character of the world, of the uncertainty
and questionableness of existence. The man who feels anxiety in the
world is aware of the uncanniness (*Unheimlichkeit*) of our being, and as
one who is homeless (*ein Heimatloser*) amid this problematical reality he
asks after his home (*Heimat*). 'That in face of which one has anxiety
(*das Wovor der Angst*) is . . . the world as such. . . . In anxiety one feels
"uncanny" . . . but here "uncanniness" (*Unheimlichkeit*) also means
"not being at home" (*das Nicht-zu-hause-sein*).'[62]

The reality of life accordingly manifests itself not as a being that is
motionless and complete, not as a being that is grounded in and at peace
with itself, but as an original, and in essence ontically and structurally
problematical existence. Dasein is destinedly intentional and as such is
an everlasting question to man.

[60] *Op. cit.*, pp. 134 f., 140. ['State-of-mind' is the accepted translation of
Heidegger's *Befindlichkeit*, though the idea of 'mind' is not present in the
German term, which refers rather to how a man finds himself, how he does. Cf.
'Wie befinden Sie Sich?', the common phrase for 'How do you do?'—*Translator*.]   [61] Pp. 57, 68, 180, 193, 196, 212, 277, 290.
[62] Pp. 187-188, 186, 191, 251, 265 f. [The connection obvious in German
between 'uncanny' (*un-HEIM-lich*) and 'not being at home' (*nicht-ZU-HAUSE-
sein*) cannot be reproduced in English.—*Translator*.]

(ii) *The Boundary of Death*

The problems of reality are by no means exhausted by the structure of Dasein as we have so far described it, but come to a head in a quite peculiar way when we take cognizance of the *death boundary* of all existence. The reality of death's inevitability has been given strikingly little attention in customary philosophic and theological discussion, yet all that 'is' is in its ultimate depths clearly and inseparably determined by it. Death is not an event that represents a factor outside of life, but a fact that is integrally constitutive of the nature of existence. It must be regarded as an 'existential phenomenon',[63] as a happening without which this Dasein would not be what it is, as a life-destiny that is still 'outstanding' and yet at the same time a basic element of life itself. 'Being-in-the-world' is fateful, always 'a being-towards-death'. 'The "end" of Being-in-the-world is death.'[64] 'Dasein, as thrown Being-in-the-world, has in every case already been delivered over to its death. In being towards its death, Dasein is dying factically and indeed constantly.'[65] Man, who by a primordial dispensation has been called into Dasein, is with this existence of his bound to death; as one who is, he is succumbed to temporality,[66] and without his being consulted he is on the way in this temporality towards a boundary of Dasein.

The reality of being is the reality of death. Death bounds all that 'is' in this world. Death is a cosmic phenomenon that causes all natural things to pass away, and subjects to its laws man who after all cannot live in the world a life that is being-in-itself. This world which is the world of this life is essentially a world of death. This life is therefore essentially not a consummate life but a pseudo-life whose content is a certainty of death, and existence-towards-death. The existence conditioned by the death boundary is therefore a veiled life, is certainly a predisposition for life, but not true life. Death obscures our authentic life, posits its ontological bogusness, turns life into a problem. Both the being of the world and the existence of man are therefore always a being that is menaced by the death boundary.

The fact that existence thus stands under the threat of death as an inescapable certainty causes the temporality of Dasein to be felt as an exigency, and has a decisive effect on man's 'basic state of mind', his consciousness of life. Above all, the knowledge of being limited by death reveals even more clearly things which in themselves, to be sure, are already implied in existence. The certainty of death means the

---

[63] *Op. cit.*, p. 240.　　　　[64] P. 234.
[65] P. 259.　　　　[66] Pp. 234, 326 ff., 330, 386, 419.

impossibility of there being any substitute when it comes to having to die. The certainty of death is always entirely personal, and the limitedness of Dasein means being directly addressed by this fact. The other is of course subject to the same necessity of succumbing to the threat of an end to his existence, and cannot 'in death' take away from us this piece of personal Dasein.[67] But secondly, the understanding of being-towards-death makes clear the removal of any possibility of escape from death. To attempt to escape from dying, i.e. from the boundary experience of Dasein, means failing to understand this Dasein's real nature. Every existence is bounded by death, and therefore to have existence is tantamount to being unable to flee from the end.[68] All being moves towards its end, and is on its way towards its boundary. The problem of being is therefore always at the same time the problem of death.[69]

In our acknowledgment of the death-line the problematical character of reality assumes its extremest and sharpest form. The recognition that such is the nature of existence extends the problem beyond what in the first instance are purely ontological findings, and makes it the quest for an answer to the problem posed by reality as a whole.

(iii) *The Question of Meaning*

The problem of being, when it is properly understood, is always the *question of the meaning of this being*. Even propositions intended only to have ontological application imply a question, the question of meaning, whose solution first provides the essential understanding of true existence. Every attempt to understand presupposes the existence of a meaning, and if Dasein asks about its own meaning, then it is only in answering its questions that we have a basis for the decisive knowledge of being.[70]

Our examination of the problems of reality has not so far led us to the concept of God, or of sin, but our discoveries appear to have been entirely confined to the sphere of the purely immanent. And yet any

[67] P. 240.

[68] From this standpoint the further modification of the structural elements of Dasein by death becomes comprehensible. Thus 'care has its most primordial concretion in Being-towards-death. . . . Thrownness into death reveals itself to Dasein in a more primordial and impressive manner in that state-of-mind which we have called "anxiety". . . . Anxiety in the face of death . . . is not an accidental or random mood of "weakness" in some individual; but, as a basic state-of-mind of Dasein, it amounts to the disclosedness of the fact that Dasein exists as thrown Being *towards* its end', *op. cit.*, p. 251.

[69] Developed further in H. Thielicke, *Tod und Leben, Studien zur christlichen Anthropologie²*. Cf. also the legitimate critical queries of P. Althaus on this problem: 'Der Mensch und sein Tod', in *Universitas* 1948, part 4.

[70] Cf. K. Heim, *Glaube und Denken*, pp. 279 f., 295 f., 307 f., 319 f.

serious exploration of reality as such implies a process governed by 'more' than immanent and ontic considerations. Knowledge of the innermost structure of existence creates an awareness of the limit of all immanent existence, an appreciation of Dasein's closed character due to birth and death as the two points of destiny that impart to existence its peculiar character. But both the true knowledge of reality and the experience of Dasein's limited character confront us at the same time also with the question as to the possibility of another reality, a transcendent being. No matter whether this transcendence really exists or is identical with 'not-being', the problem of being as such certainly requires the raising of this question which reaches out beyond the immanent world. This question in turn has the character of a question of meaning; for to ask about the meaning of existence points beyond life's being as it is—namely, threatened by death—to a 'something' which can give Dasein its meaning. The question of meaning is therefore essentially religious in character; the very profanity of Dasein is that of being which seeks for meaning and is directed towards meaning, and as such is never without a religious quality.

The problematical character of Dasein, which has been shown in principle to derive from man's being called in question and his limitation by death, raises a twofold series of questions as to the meaning of reality. First, the primordial givenness of the existence of man and the world confronts us with a decisive Either-or. Either man's existential fate is relative and fortuitous being, his being-in-the-world is a result of irrational chance and accordingly the totality of all that 'is' is empty of meaning—or the primordial establishing of Dasein is subject to a law of higher, unconditional necessity, and contains within it an appointed purpose and the possibility of its fulfilment. A meaning can be given to existence, however, only by starting from an absolute normative point, from a central point at which the purpose of life and of the world is fulfilled, and which redeems being from its relative possibilities. But secondly, the question of meaning, if it is really to lead to an answer valid for the totality of being, must be defined as a quest for life, i.e. for a genuine, everlasting life, for an unlimited Dasein. No element of the immanent world, no mere idea, can liberate us from the death boundary, but only a new fact, a reality in the realm of being, which forms the basis of a new existential possibility. This would provide the foundation for a fulfilling of the purpose of Dasein, while without it the effort to find a meaning would be condemned to failure. We should therefore regard these two possible lines of inquiry as merely two sides of the same question of meaning, for the point of reference from which meaning is derived must have an existence not threatened by the death boundary, and the new reality in the realm of being must have not only a transcendent character but also the ability to provide 'co-ordinates of meaning' for the immanent sphere of being.

Our understanding of reality leads to the fundamental insight that the being of all existence as it is, quite apart from any special religious evaluation, already provides in itself a primordial religious reference, which becomes manifest in the question of the meaning of Dasein.

(b) The Ontology of the Resurrection

Raising the question of being has led to a new way of formulating the problem. We are now concerned with the problem of Dasein, of life as such. Is there any answer to the question of meaning raised by our existence that is threatened by death? This question of being which is asked by man is met by the primitive Christian message of the resurrection. In the form of a *resurrection ontology* it gives a threefold answer.

(i) The Dependence of Existence upon Christ

The Dasein of man, like that of the world, is not harmoniously self-contained, not perfect and complete, not capable of life and creative of life. Rather, it is oriented towards an existence in which, as unbroken life not subject to death, the concept of being is fully realized. Whether this life really exists or is merely a postulate and a product of wishful thinking, is something that cannot be determined at the level of this pseudo-life and within the scope of it. But the moment we receive the word of the resurrection, there dawns on us the basic insight that this orientation of all existence is no arbitrary turning to ask a meaningless question, but that in the final analysis it means dependence on Christ. If Dasein is built for Christ, then it can also only be understood in the light of Christ. This fundamental relatedness of existence to Christ is of far-reaching significance.

The claims of the resurrection message, as they encounter man, do not meet a world which because of its own vitality has no need of this word. On the contrary, they meet with the fundamental ability to hear on man's part. This openness is not a subjective and individual thing, but is grounded in the structure of Dasein as such. The subject may turn aside without interest from the resurrection message, yet the one common destiny of all life is turned towards it in the expectation of a fulfilment of life. Conversely, the reality of the resurrection of Christ is

related to the brokenness of our Dasein, and the latter in its own
questionableness possesses the possibility of understanding the former.
The resurrection message therefore finds its starting point primarily
not in some specifically religious question, not in man's consciousness
of God, or his sense of sin and guilt, but in the very being of the world
as it is. For this reason it is universally directed to all men alike, irrespective of their differences in race and nationality and in culture and
history, since all alike are called in question by being as they are, and
all alike have the ability to receive the decisive answer that gives meaning
to life. This universality of the resurrection message proves its unconditional character and the validity of its claims. The decisive thing is
therefore that man should attain to the ripeness of knowledge of his
life-situation, so that through growing insight into the questionableness
of his Dasein he may come to the readiness to hear. Thus every serious
ontology, even if it achieves only a fragmentary grasp of the reality of
Dasein, can become a *paidagōgos eis Christon*. That creates the presupposition for Dasein to convince a man that the reality of the resurrection concerns him existentially, lays hold of him directly in his own
Dasein. The ontic fact of being dependent on Christ is turned by the
encounter with the resurrection message into being thrown upon the
present Kyrios. The destiny of being thrown into the Dasein of this
world has its counterpart in the destiny of being implanted into the new
world of Christ. The resurrection existence stands in a homogeneous
relationship to the original predisposition of man's Dasein, and that is
why it is the answer to the question posed by that Dasein.

If our Dasein is dependent on Christ, then that provides the starting
point for a new *anthropology*. Man comes to a truthful understanding of
himself neither from himself nor from his relation to the world around
him, but only by being directed towards Christ and directed (judged)
by Christ. The concept of 'being directed' (*Gerichtetsein* = both 'being
directed' and 'being judged') has both a positive and a negative element.
Man's being directed means firstly, that he is made right (*richtig*) for
the first time through Christ, that his life is given the proper direction
(*Richtung*) and is put in order. But secondly, it also means the testing
which eliminates all that is wrong (*unrichtig*), the regular measuring by
rule (*Richtschnur*) which proves his life is not acceptable and rejects it.
Accordingly, in the new being of Christ there is grounded a Christian
anthropology, which arrives at a threefold verdict on man:

Man's Dasein is not to be understood by ontological analysis, but in
the light of God's new creation in Christ it is to be regarded as creature-

liness. The destiny of existence is not an arbitrary dispensation but an expression of the creatureliness which depends on a Lord. Creaturely being, however, does not exist of itself but by the power of its Creator; it is not an eternal but a limited being. But the power that establishes and limits our Dasein is no blind fate, but God the Creator. To be dependent and limited means not being a creative lord but being a creature that cannot have the command of its existence but waits for its Creator to act. Existing as man is thus not being one who is merely there, but being one who stands in relation to God. This relationship to God is cardinal for the concept of man and of existence. Man's being called in question by the problematical character of his Dasein is therefore the creature's being called in question by the Creator. The unceasing questioning to which existence is subject discloses the inescapable dependence of all creatures on God's revelation in Christ. Through this the questionableness of our Dasein loses its meaninglessness. It becomes full of meaning and directed by its meaning when we recognize that God holds his creation in his hand despite all that seems irrational to the creature, and that in the Risen One he speaks his assent to the world he has created.

The second finding is not a supplement to the first, but is essentially given along with it. Existence is not to be understood merely as creation willed by God, but also as a being that ought not to be. The mere tracing of the structural outlines of being does not in itself furnish a proper knowledge of existence, still less does it mean attempting to attain a rational understanding of the appropriateness of its being as it is. The trouble caused by the tensions of our Dasein, and the fact of the world's being-towards-death, both testify not only of creatureliness but also of the state of a creation that is fallen and enmeshed in sin. There is no such thing as man-in-himself who in the abstract, without any relation to God, could be understood in his 'pure' Dasein. Man can always only be conceived at once as a sinner, whose Dasein is never pure but always stained. The fact of being directed towards Christ takes us behind the outward picture of existence to the causes that determine this being as it is, and so robs the phenomena of Dasein of their claim to rightness and original truth. The existence which is broken by sin and the Fall looks out for a correction and in its very distortion knows that it is dependent upon the redeeming being of the present Christ. In the light of the reality of the resurrection there is every reason for the meaninglessness of the creature's existence when it abides by itself and repudiates its direction towards Christ. Dasein as

Christ-less being is empty of meaning, and only when related to the existence of Christ has it any relation to a meaning.

But the fact that our creaturely and sinful existence is directed by Christ also points beyond our present condition towards the coming reality of the resurrection. Our Dasein is a reconciled Dasein that is moving towards a fulfilment. The fact of its being dependent upon Christ brings out the truth, that this questionable existence is not our ultimate being, but a penultimate one. The question about the meaning of life makes it plain that our empirical being is not a real life but a pseudo-life. The fulfilment of the meaning of all life comes about only in the promise of a resurrection world, and is present in the witness of the Spirit, which breaks into the existence that is waiting for it. To dispense with a resurrection ontology therefore means accepting the fragmentary character of our Dasein as an ultimate reality and so dispensing with any knowledge of the meaning of existence.

(ii) *The Changed Meaning of the Fate of Death*

It is possible to speak of a resurrection ontology because in the resurrection event *the conquest of the fate of death* is concretely and fundamentally established. If the connection between death and Dasein is obvious, and indeed is such that all existence can have its reverse side only in death, then Christ's conquest of death must link inseparably the resurrection life and our present Dasein. The consequence of this is a radical change in the meaning of the fate of death. It is therefore precisely at the critical point of the problem of death that the ontological significance of the reality of the resurrection becomes evident. It is in the interpretation of death that the character and value of a world-view becomes especially clear. From the vantage point of the resurrection, we are able to adopt the following attitude as distinct from other attempts to interpret the problem of death.

First, quite apart from knowledge of the resurrection, there is the naturalistic interpretation of death. Death appears to be the necessary end of all life and is one of the series of natural processes. The dying of man is but one variant in nature's universal sequence of life and decay. Even this scientific statement, if it is meant to be more than a mere working hypothesis, contains an interpretation. If it is meant to account for the whole phenomenon of death, this interpretation suffers from the fact that it cannot see the whole of nature from the standpoint of creation and sin and must necessarily misunderstand the nature of death which in fact, even in the case of an animal, is something other than the beginning of a physiological process of disintegration. As soon as the question of meaning arises, this naturalistic view of death forms the basis for a number of possible interpretations, some optimistic, some pessimistic. Death in nature has a general purpose which is easy to demonstrate by naturalistic argument, in so far as death is everywhere the presupposition of life. Death is the 'evolution motif' for man and must be included as part of the ontic system, it belongs to the 'existential structure of Dasein'.[71] However accurate the observation underlying this interpretation is as such, the interpretation itself is nevertheless a superficial one, since it fails to take adequate account of the distress engendered by transience and the grievous sharpening of the problem in the fact that man must die. The optimistic interpretation thus provides no satisfactory solution of the problem of meaning.

Of a different character are the attempted solutions which do indeed also recognize death as a necessity of nature, but at the same time are alive to the intolerableness of this unceasing threat and its uncanniness. Any optimistic disguising of the situation seems impossible. Once the essential structure of existence is taking seriously, three different positions are conceivable. Either the inescapability of our having to die drives us to feel the practical impossibility of Dasein, i.e. to despair. Or we seek by the way of illusionism to flee from the death boundary by losing ourselves in the nearest possibilities offered by everyday life and being absorbed in the public sphere.[72] Whereas the first method abandons any kind of struggle for life as hopeless, the other is under the spell of 'latent anxiety' and bears the stamp of an unauthentic and alien Dasein. The man who thus 'flees from his death' into illusion is repeatedly overtaken by it.[73] As a third possibility there remains the attitude that is partly fatalistic and partly heroic. Here we no longer ask whether the fate of death is meaningful or otherwise, but are filled with deepest scepticism and resignation, having without illusion seen the whole of reality for what it is. At the same time, however, we are heroically resolved to accept the fate of Dasein, given as it is to death.[74] This

---

[71] Thus M. Heidegger.

[72] Cf. Heidegger, *op. cit.*, pp. 184, 189, 192.

[73] Heidegger points to the repeatedly aggravated temptation 'to cover up from oneself one's ownmost Being-towards-death'. 'This evasive concealment in the face of death dominates everydayness stubbornly' in that man strives for 'a constant tranquillization about death' (*op. cit.*, pp. 251, 253). These attempts to flee in the face of death, 'giving new explanations for it, understanding it inauthentically, and concealing it', the constructing of an 'untroubled indifference' of this kind, makes an attitude of real assent to existence impossible and only 'estranges' Dasein from its 'ownmost potentiality-for-Being' (pp. 254 ff.).

[74] M. Heidegger, p. 305: 'As Being-towards-the-end which understands—

resolute attitude, which is not lacking in bitter irony towards the optimistic view of Dasein, makes itself 'free for death', 'as if' such conduct
were meaningful.[75]

Alongside of the naturalistic conception of death there is the ethico-
religious interpretation. According to this last, the secret of death cannot
be revealed through the categories of the natural, but we are here
concerned with a happening which presupposes a relationship to God
and has to be approached from the standpoint of religion. It is recognized that no philosophical reflection, but only a theology of death, can
attain to the understanding of its meaning. Here, too, three interpretations are possible, frequently in combination with one another. If the
interpretation is based on the Greek conception of the soul, then death
is welcomed as a liberating of the soul for immaterial being. The meaning of death is accordingly that it opens the way to the higher world of
souls. This solution of the problem is of no significance for our corporeal
Dasein, since redemption applies only to the soul. Secondly, death is
evaluated as a process of purification, by which God brings about the
necessary cleansing of sinful man. Dying makes possible the elevation
of the soul and its further development in purity and freedom from sin.
In this view, Indian elements are intermingled with those of anthropo-
sophy and of Roman Catholic theology. Finally, death is seen primarily
as the terrible judgment of God, which reveals the wrath of God that
lies upon the world. This is the original Jewish way of looking upon
death. The inevitability of death is the fruit of sin and the result of the
Fall. In death man falls irretrievably into the hand of God, body and
soul, without being allowed to postulate an after-life. Behind death there
stands the infinite majesty of God, and the meaning of it is, that in
death God punishes the sin of man.

Such attempts to interpret the fate of death disregard the resurrection
and know nothing of it. Over against them stands the meaning given
to it by the theology of the resurrection. Here the elements of truth in
the naturalistic interpretation, as well as in the ethico-religious and

---

that is to say, as anticipation of death—resoluteness becomes authentically what
it can be.'
[75] A typical and outstanding example of the heroic attitude is O. Spengler in
Man and Technics, ET 1932. He speaks of 'proud scepticism'; 'Optimism is
cowardice'; 'To hold on to the lost post without hope, without rescue, is our
duty' (p. 104). Cf. also R. Bultmann, 'Die Geschichtlichkeit des Daseins und
der Glaube', in *ZTK* 1930, part 5, pp. 360 ff. Bultmann is therefore right when
he says, 'That resoluteness, where it is ontically realized in the factual Dasein's
being shattered on the reef of its death, letting itself be thrown back on its own
there-ness (*sein Da*) and . . . thus deciding resolutely for itself, is a resoluteness
of despair.'

particularly the Jewish and biblical view, are taken up again and given their proper meaning. The decisive basic insight which must determine all interpretations of the destiny of death is this: *In the resurrection of Jesus the power of death is broken. Death is not the end, but the last word is with the Resurrection. The Risen Christ is the surety that God's ultimate will is not death, but life.* From this standpoint we reach a twofold conclusion about the meaning of death.

The fate of having to die must be taken absolutely seriously, for it is God's radical 'No' to the world of the Fall and of sin. In death God shatters our whole existence. Naturalism is right in this: that death is a real end which comes to our whole life. Death is the curse of sin and reveals God's claim to judgment from which there is no escape.[76] Every glorification and idealization of death is unrealistic and pointless, because in it God executes his annihilating judgment. The heroic acceptance of Dasein and of death is also wrong, because what this attitude accepts is not the will of God as the Lord of death, but the sinful nature of the world as it is. Such heroism becomes the Titanism in which even in the hour of death a man still refuses to recognize God, but only seeks himself as the sinner who bids even death defiance. Because the Risen Christ is he who has passed through the death judgment of God in full assent to his will, it is possible on the ground of the resurrection for faith to say 'Yes' to the 'No' spoken by God in the inevitability of death. The meaning of death lies in the action of God, who shatters the Dasein that resists him.

Secondly, however, death in the light of the resurrection becomes also at the same time the revelation of God's grace, and this in two respects. In death God releases man from sin and from the consequences of the Fall. Death becomes redemption for the sinner, a passage to the resurrection life. The fate of death is a liberating fate only because the Risen Christ is the victor over that fate.[77] But secondly, death becomes the road to the freedom of the resurrection life because it does away with man's creaturely limitations and makes creation free for its consummation by God. So long as man still stands on this side of the death boundary, the redeeming will of God has not yet achieved its purpose with his creature.[78] In view of the Risen Christ death loses not only terror, but also its quality of being a curse, for in this perspective we can well say that the meaning of the ending of all existence is, that God

---

[76] Rom. 6.23. [77] Rom. 8.23.

[78] P. Althaus goes so far as to say: 'It is of God's love that we *may* die. We not only *must* die, but we also *may* die', *Zeitschr. f. syst. Theol.* 1931, part 2, p. 333.

is making room for the new existence of the resurrection. Death as a passage to the eternal life of the resurrection has, however, nothing to do with the idea of a liberating of the soul by death. Just as death affects our whole existence, so our physical being, which is destroyed in death, is also on the way to a new resurrection existence. Our having to die is a sign of God's redeeming love—albeit inseparably bound up with the judgment of his wrath—which in the reality of the resurrection of Christ waits with a new Dasein for his fallen creatures.

The changed meaning which the resurrection enables us to read into death makes plain that it is only on the basis of this insight that it can be meaningful to assent to our Dasein. It must be a broken assent, in so far as it refers to existence as creation or sin. It is therefore also an assent to death as judgment and grace. The verdict of Christian ontology is as far from an optimistic view of our Dasein as it is from a pessimistic one, and as far from illusionism as from scepticism and proud heroism. It expresses that realistic attitude of which every serious ontology stands in need.[79]

(iii) *The Ground of Life in the Resurrection*

The ontology of the resurrection speaks of Christ as the fulfilment of the meaning of human Dasein and of all existence. In the resurrection the new, real being-from-God breaks through. It is the new dimension that becomes a central point of orientation for all Dasein. Because this new reality of the existence of the Risen One liberates from the distress and the curse of transience, human Dasein is not merely a 'being-toward-death', but in orientation towards the resurrection a 'being-towards-life'. In the resurrection life of Christ a new ground of life discloses itself which sets the pseudo-life that is bounded by death free from its questionable character. The resurrection existence is the Dasein which is freed from death, and which is itself no longer called in question but on the contrary calls in question all being that is on this side of the death-line. From the standpoint of the ground of life in the resurrection, all Dasein is asked whether it really possesses life, or is a being that is on its way to an end. Hence the resurrection life cannot be tested from

---

[79] The ways of expressing the connection of Fall, creation and death which were used in my work on *Die Lehre von der Sünde*, 1927, pp. 200 ff. are ones I can no longer retain today, since they do not bring out sufficiently the unity and contemporaneousness of the things here expressed. Cf. also A. Köberle, 'Das Rätsel des Todes und seine Überwindung', in *Die Seele des Christentums*, 1932, pp. 156 ff. Reference should likewise be made to K. Heim's study on 'Ewiges Leben' in *Leben aus dem Glauben*, 1932, p. 77. Cf. also the most notable and sensitive study by P. Althaus, *Vom Sterben und vom Leben*, Gütersloh, 1950.

the standpoint of the pseudo-Dasein of man, but the latter knows of
true life only when it knows of the resurrection. Hence, too, the reality
of eternal life cannot be constructed by any process of thought, but is
present only in the existence of the Risen One. Only this personal
reality in the realm of being is mightier than all opposing ideas, representations and imaginings, and superior to all the other ontic facts.
According to the ontology of the resurrection we have to distinguish
between two modes of existence: the death-ridden, bogus, Christless
Dasein with its laws of transience, and the death-vanquishing, true,
Christ-bound reality in which the *nomos* of the living Spirit reigns.[80]
'Being-in-the-world' stands in contrast to 'Being-in-Christ'.

*Through the resurrection message man is given a new possibility of
existence.*[81] This means, however, not only a promise of life but the
possibility of existential contemporaneousness with the present Christ.
The resurrection reality is present and can become for man's existence
the ground that sustains it. Everything therefore depends on a connection being established between the existence of self and the existence
of Christ. This connection is made existentially 'in the Spirit' and 'in
faith', so that the self which has become questionable in its own eyes no
longer remains oriented upon itself as the centre of Dasein, but knows
itself bound to the existence of Christ. With this decisive change from
'being in the world' to the 'being in Christ' which is a present existential
reality and thus does not require any flight from the world, the new
change in being has already in principle become an actual fact. The
existential event of this change in our Dasein is the beginning of a
present dying already before death, in that our old being is recognized
as sinful and contrary to God and the judgment of God on this Dasein
is accepted. With this there arises the will to a life that comes from God,
which is the beginning of the dying of that self-will which assented to a
life without God. But at the same time this change means surrender to
the present Christ and so the beginning of eternal life in the midst of
our old Dasein. We give up clinging to the old fragile Dasein, in order
to find the fulness of life in Christ. He who has attained to this being in
Christ stands now already upon the ground of life given in the resurrection, although his Dasein as it was till now decays to an end. Because
the resurrection existence is present and contemporaneous, we can say
in spiritual terms that he who is bound to Christ is already passed from
death to life (John 5.24). The life of Christ has spiritually become the

[80] Rom. 8.1 f.
[81] II Cor. 5.16 f.; Gal. 6.15; II Cor. 2.16.

life of the believer, so that we can now speak of the Risen Christ dwelling in the Dasein of the self.[82]

As soon as the reality of the resurrection is recognized as the ground of life, and the grounding of our Dasein in it has existentially taken place, there comes a change in the situation of human existence which has far-reaching consequences. When a man lives on the foundation of the resurrection, his threatened Dasein becomes now already in faith a liberated being, since he knows that in the Christ-being which embraces and carries his own being, the powers of death have already been overcome. Man's 'state-of-mind' thereby becomes different. He no longer sees himself thrown into the uncanniness of Dasein in which there can be no home for him, but 'in Christ' he has found his true Dasein which, to be sure, he was seeking in all his questioning hitherto, but could not recognize. *Out of the uncanniness of his being-in-the-world he has come home to the being-in-Christ which was waiting for him, and therefore now already, though still standing in the old temporal order, he is spiritually 'at home' with Christ.* If the Christ-Dasein is a being that is authentic and true, then man is released in principle from the untruth of his own existence which repeatedly drives him into illusions and lies, then the basic attitudes of his being—anxiety and care—are transformed into the spiritual attitudes of faith and love. The restlessness which is given in his ontic structural disposition is overcome by the peace which comes from the world of the resurrection. This explains why the 'peace of God' that passes all understanding cannot be a work of man or a human mood, but is bestowed as the spiritual gift of the Christ-existence. The new being imparts knowledge of the meaning of real humanity. This knowledge makes it possible for the fellowship relations of 'being-with' and 'being-towards-the-other' to be understood anew for the first time in all their depth and to be shaped anew in love. The other in his Dasein finds himself in the same death-marked situation. His call can be really heard only when there exists an 'I-thou' relationship consummated in Christ, which at once reveals who the other needs. In view of the death situation there can thus be no help for that other from prosperity or philosophic altruism, but only through the proclaiming of the resurrection as the one remedy for the one predicament of existence. This proclamation always realizes itself at once in love, acts on the basis of the new ground of life, as a crystallization of the present existence of

---

[82] The classical formulation of the meaning of Christian ontology is in Paul's words, 'to me to live is Christ', Phil. 1.21; 'I live; yet not I, but Christ liveth in me', Gal. 2.20; Rom. 14.7; cf. also Rom. 8.11, 'the Spirit dwelleth in you'.

Christ. Man's frantic attempts to safeguard his life against catastrophe and threats become meaningless when he stands on the ground of life in the resurrection. There is no secure Dasein without Christ. That is why the man who is bound to Christ abandons his self-chosen safeguards in order to have his life secured in the eternal life of Christ. This attitude, too, brings a 'freedom' and openness for death. Yet it does not come from the resoluteness of a Titanic heroism, but on the ground of the victory of the life of Christ over death. Christian resoluteness does not draw its strength from itself, but from Christ. The Christian's being free to die means therefore that he is free for the true life, for Christ.

In the context of the present inquiry, a Christian ontology cannot be discussed in detail. We have only been concerned to show how far it is possible on the ground of the reality of the resurrection to develop a Christian ontology that exists in its own right. The basic features we have worked out are meant to indicate the direction which in our opinion ontological reflection must take if the basic insights of the Gospel are to bear fruit.

Part Three

THE RESURRECTION AND ITS
CONSUMMATION

THE argument so far developed has repeatedly brought us to the problems of *eschatology*. These became acute in the discussion of Christological questions, of the doctrine of creation, of the Spirit and the Church; they are most closely interwoven with the problem of time, and stood in the background of our reflections on the theology of nature and on ontology. This not only confirms the finding of almost all the most recent theology—that Christian eschatology simply cannot be properly presented on the outskirts of dogmatics as a concluding chapter—it also follows of necessity from the theme of this present work, since we cannot speak other than eschatologically of the resurrection of the Kyrios. Thus even where the concept of 'eschatology' is not explicitly used, the present inquiry is essentially eschatological in character, for both the action of God in the resurrection of Jesus and the effectual working of the Risen One are alike always directed towards an eschaton.

The question of the theological meaning of the resurrection of Jesus comes to its conclusion in the concept of the *consummation of the resurrection reality*. When we say this, we are gathering up together once again the various lines of dogmatic thought so far indicated, and giving expression in a special way to their basic eschatological character. A theology of the resurrection, if it adheres consistently to its governing principle, produces a specific eschatological kind of thinking. In this section we are therefore concerned with *three things*: first, with *the methodological problem of the grounding of a Christian eschatology*, secondly, with *the essential description of the basic features of a resurrection eschatology*, and finally with a *statement about the 'aeon of Christ's lordship'*. Our task here cannot be the detailed exposition of all eschatological questions and their solutions, which would in any case be unnecessary in view of a series of important eschatological treatises, but our aim is, to make a contribution to the eschatological problem from the viewpoint of the theology of the resurrection.

VI

THE GROUNDING OF A CHRISTIAN ESCHATOLOGY

THE question how best to lay the foundations of a Christian doctrine of the 'Last Things' meets in the first instance with three possibilities, which have played a decisive part in the theology of the past and have still not been completely eliminated even today. There is the attempt to build eschatology on the Platonic and Aristotelian idea of immortality, even if in a modified form; secondly, there is the grounding of it on the reflections and perspectives of philosophical and speculative thought[1] and finally, there is the biblicist effort to find the starting point in individual eschatological statements, ideas and images of the Bible. While the first two views contain elements which are alien to Christian thought, the last is to be taken entirely seriously, even if it cannot by any means accord with faith's thinking out the Christian doctrine of salvation. The main arguments in Althaus' criticism of the biblicist position are by no means unjustified, even if it has to be emphasized that the substance of the biblicist pronouncements is not by any means lost to us as a result of this criticism, but can receive new significance by being approached from a different angle.[2] It is certainly a valid argu-

---

[1] Cf. C. Stange, *Das Ende aller Dinge*, 1930, pp. 6 ff., 16 ff., 43 f.; G. Hoffmann, *Das Problem der letzten Dinge in der neueren evangelischen Theologie*, Göttingen 1929, pp. 10 ff. Cf. also Otto Michel, 'Grundzüge urchristlicher Eschatologie', *Zeitschr. f. syst. Theol.* 1931-2, part 4, and 'Unser Ringen um die Eschatologie', *ZTK* 2. Further, Hans Steubing, 'Das Grundproblem der Eschatologie', *Zeitschr. f. syst. Theol.* 1929, part 3, p. 461. On the basis of what has been said so far it is no longer surprising that what R. Bultmann calls 'eschatology' has nothing to do with the eschatology of the New Testament and in fact stands in irreconcilable antithesis to it. Since the history of the world has gone on and the parousia of Christ has not taken place, the mythological character of all these apocalyptic ideas is according to Bultmann proved, and that 'puts paid to the expectation of the coming Son of Man'. The idea of his 'own translation into a heavenly world of light' is also for Bultmann not merely 'rationally inconceivable' but also 'meaningless'. Accordingly the phrase about the 'Last Day' can also only be understood as 'mythological talk'. *Kerygma und Mythos*, pp. 18, 21 (ET, pp. 5, 8).

[2] P. Althaus, *Die letzten Dinge*[3], 1926, pp. 77 f., 88 f. On the other hand we cannot agree with Althaus when in his criticism he casts doubt on the 'sureness of the foundation' of the biblicist theory: 'His theory has become impossible for us today. Between him and us lies the age of historical criticism' (pp. 54 f.,

ment against this kind of biblicism to say that an isolated appraisal of individual promises cannot provide a sound foundation for an eschatology, and furthermore that the pre-Easter character of these eschatological pronouncements is an obvious limitation. This criticism has therefore not to be levelled in principle and in every case against paying attention to individual eschatological pronouncements, but merely against the manner in which the biblicist makes them the ground of his eschatology.

Since these three possibilities accordingly cannot be seriously accepted by the theologian, we are faced again by the question of the proper starting point for eschatological thinking. *What, however, is really meant by 'Christian eschatology'?* As long as we interpret this concept in the traditional way as the doctrine of the 'Last Things' or of the 'End of all Things', as teaching about 'eternity', the 'life after death', the 'future life', etc., we have still not by any means expressed the specifically 'Christian' concern. The fact that it knows about eternity, about an end, about things to come, does not of course distinguish the Christian faith in any way from non-Christian eschatologies. Nor does Christian faith make use of abstract formulations, which are always a gateway to alien ideas, but it speaks of the concrete content of the future for which it waits. The peculiarity of Christian eschatological thought, however, expresses itself in the concept of 'hope'. The Christian Church is eschatologically minded, not because it knows about death and eternity, about the boundary situation of Dasein and the judgment of God, but because a very definite hope is alive within it, which embraces the end of all things and the whole future and puts its characteristic mark upon them. Once we understand *Christian eschatology as the doctrine of the Christian hope*, then this also solves the question of the foundation of eschatology. If eschatology is concerned with the Christian hope, then this excludes a multitude of possible motivations of the most varied kinds, which, while they can show 'that' man waits for a future, and 'why' he does so, and 'what' he hopes for, are yet unable to prove his right to such expectation, and the point of it. Here is the dividing line between the certainty of Christian hope, which knows on what it is founded, and the uncertainty of non-Christian expectation, which vacillates uncertainly between speculative presumption, fantastic wishful thinking, and despair. To those, however, who ask what Christian hope is founded on, what is the ground of its certitude and its meaning, the primitive

88 f.). This concession to critical historical research seems in my opinion to be neither valid in content nor correct in method.

Christian proclamation gives an unequivocal answer. *The ground of the Christian hope* is not in prophetic predictions or in visions of the future, not in individual words and sayings of Jesus, not even in the person of Jesus or the wholeness of the Christian faith whose paradoxical structure demands an eschatological fulfilment, but *solely and decisively in the reality of the resurrection of the Kyrios* in which all these other insights are summed up and confirmed. The resurrection of Jesus is the principle which governs a Christian eschatology. If the resurrection message, constitutive as it was for the faith of the primitive Church, is not to be emptied of meaning and have its eschatological content impaired and devalued, it is the knowledge of the resurrection that must be made the ground of our eschatological statements.

In order to illustrate further the importance of the resurrection for eschatology, let us examine the standard work on Christian eschatology by P. Althaus, and the eschatological teaching of C. Stange in which the debate with Althaus is contained. We must inquire in particular what is assumed to be the foundation of eschatology and whether this is in harmony with the word of the resurrection which determines the Christian hope.

The foundation of Althaus' eschatology seems at first sight to be wholly in accord with the required principle of the resurrection. 'Our hope of consummation has . . . a strictly Christocentric ground. It should be explicitly emphasized that in this respect the fact of Christ is always the fact of the Risen Christ. . . . Eschatology thus rests upon the fact of Easter, as does the whole Christian position. . . . The Risen Christ is the foundation of our eschatology. . . . In the Risen Christ . . . the goal of our hope . . . is already present and perceptible as a beginning and surety.'[3] Now, it all depends decisively on whether this insight is the all-determining foundation, or whether other factors are also given a part, and secondly, whether in developing the eschatological trains of thought the resurrection principle attains to thoroughgoing normative application.

Unquestionably, various grounds are adduced by Althaus which can be regarded as the starting points of Christian eschatology. The ground of his axiological thinking is found in a reference to the certainty of God which must be distinguished in the first instance from the certainty of salvation. Every encounter with God has eternity within it. 'The certainty of God, being a certainty of judgment, is a certainty of eternal death and so of "immortality".'[4] But again, the ground is given in the

---

[3] *Die letzten Dinge*, pp. 56-57, cf. also pp. 60, 74.   [4] *Op. cit.*, pp. 31, 29 f.

love of God which breaks through in the word of forgiveness. 'The certainty of the love of God' leads to confidence in an everlasting fellowship with God.[5] C. Stange rightly asserts against this that here we have fundamental statements which are derived not from the fact of Christ, but from 'the general relationship of man to God'.[6] Again, when it comes to proving that the Christian hope implies a 'teleological eschatology', we have plainly a system of argument that disregards the resurrection principle. Thus at this point the ground is traced to the paradox of revelation and salvation, i.e. to the relationship of tension that is given in Christian faith.[7] The objection might indeed be made that all these statements about an axiological and teleological derivation of eschatology are already 'essentially included' in the fact of the resurrection and only represent a more detailed unfolding of the fact of Christ.[8] But the method by which the eschatology is constructed largely shows that it starts from abstractly defined concepts which are then afterwards given a Christian content, so that at all events the affirmed grounding of eschatology in the fact of Christ, and particularly in the Risen Christ, is not safeguarded against being co-ordinated and combined with ideas from other, partly philosophical, sources—and that means, against being improperly relegated to the background.[9] That these misgivings in face of Althaus' grounding of his eschatology are justified is evident if we examine the consequences which result—or to be more exact, which fail to result—from his approach.

In two cases where Althaus reconstructs eschatology in a positive way and develops the peculiar content of the Christian hope—in the questions of the 'new world' and of the 'new corporeality'—it is easy to show his obvious divergence from the lines of the resurrection of Christ.

On what does Althaus found the Christian hope of a new world? If the fact of Christ is the starting point, one might expect an indication of how far Christ, and in particular the Risen Christ, is of decisive importance also for nature, for history, and for the world as a whole. Althaus, however, avers: 'The grounds for expecting a new world must be discovered through probing the depths of the meaning of *our* world, that

---

[5] *Op. cit.*, pp. 33, 239.   [6] *Das Ende aller Dinge*, p. 208.
[7] Althaus, *op. cit.*, pp. 36 ff., 44 ff.   [8] Cf. pp. 28, 56.
[9] This is rightly perceived by Eduard Thurneysen, 'Christus und seine Zukunft', *Zwischen den Zeiten* 1931, part 3, p. 187: 'From the standpoint of method it has to be noticed that Althaus sets out from a general conceptual definition of the problem. . . . Into this conceptual framework he then sketches the Christian eschatology', though to be sure it is then 'repeatedly burst through and broken open'.

is, from a Christian philosophy of nature and history.'[10] Nature, history and culture are not merely 'means to an end', but there lies in them 'an independent meaning, a special purpose of God'.[11] Nature must also 'be an end in itself according to the will of God, a manifestation of his life, of his inexhaustible fulness and beauty'. The shaping of culture, the mastery of the world and the values of history are not only 'tasks for the builders', but are important 'at the same time precisely also for their shape and structure' in so far as eternity is in fact 'the perfection of beauty, as also of goodness and truth'. For 'the tasks which God allots us here and the work which he has us do are like prophecies which await their fulfilment. . . . All organizing and symbolizing activity points beyond itself to a "new world" which is wholly used by and filled with the Spirit.'[12] Now it is undeniable that these remarks are of value and worthy of our serious consideration, but the question here is whether the above line of argument is not much more a philosophical than a theological one. These ideas which justify the expectation of a new world have not been derived from the fact of Christ, but from reflection on the philosophy of culture and of nature. The consummation of nature, history and culture has been deduced from the meaning already latent within them. All this, however, destroys the force of the fundamental principle of the strictly Christocentric grounding of the whole of eschatology and makes plain the contradiction between the starting point and the heteronomous philosophic points of view which are put forward as independent epistemological grounds of the eschatological hope. The fact of the resurrection declares precisely that the 'meaning of our world' is always at the same time also meaningless, that a purely philosophical insight, even if it is deepened by the idea of God, cannot possibly furnish the ground for expecting a new world. Althaus has endeavoured to come to grips with this criticism,[13] and believes that he must still hold fast to his method of anthropological and cosmological deduction. He says: 'At the least, the indissoluble connection between the corporeality and the worldliness of our Dasein must surely be shown by anthropological and cosmological reflection. . . . And Christological grounding surely does not mean that the Christological insistence on the corporeality of the Risen Christ and the assent to the natural world which is implied by Easter could be a substitute for anthropological and cosmological reflection on the essential corporeality and worldliness of our being.' Here we must make plain that we, too, hold that the Easter faith has by

---

[10] *Op. cit.*, p. 251.
[12] Pp. 252, 254 f.
[11] *Op. cit.*, p. 251.
[13] *Die letzten Dinge*, 1934, pp. 334 f.

no means to take the place of necessary theological reflection, and that for this reason Althaus' arguments are of undeniable importance. The real question is, however, whether such findings even apart from the resurrection of Jesus have an autonomous validity of their own, or whether it is the reality of the resurrection which first establishes their legitimacy. It is this question that differentiates a 'theology of the resurrection' from all theologico-philosophical attempts to endow nature and the world with a meaning which is given and recognizable in itself.

The value of nature, culture and history is really not disclosed by any penetrating insight into their nature, which in itself appears full of contradictions, antinomian, and at one and the same time both full and empty of meaning—not even when it is set in the perspective of the idea of creation, for even that idea remains a question and a postulate if it is without the unconditional action of God in Christ to give it meaning. For it is only in the light of that event that earthly values acquire the character of 'prophecies' of some future consummation. A meaning and value of its own can hardly be said to belong to the world apart from the impartation of meaning which is revealed in the reality of the resurrection.

The foreign foundation which conflicts with the Christocentric starting point becomes still clearer in the question of the new corporeality. Althaus says: 'Precisely here everything depends on a really adequate grounding.' Since for Althaus, too, eschatology is determined by the fact of Easter, the logical development of that would have to be to ground the hope of a new corporeality in the Risen Christ. Althaus, however, evades the dictates of his own Christ principle and asserts: 'In the face of this question—and it is most important to say this explicitly—the recollection of Jesus' resurrection provides no help.' It 'gives us by itself alone no adequate ground for the hope of a new corporeality. . . . The question remains whether it is really legitimate to deduce the mode of the Lord's heavenly existence directly from the way he manifested himself to men's earthly senses.' 'The most elementary epistemological considerations must here enjoin caution; the resurrection of the body of Jesus is here not the solution but itself a part of our problem.'[14] In another passage Althaus asks, 'Who can say whether the body in which Jesus appeared to his own was actually the "heavenly body"?'[15] Since according to Althaus' view it is impossible within the context of the New Testament witness to the resurrection of Jesus to draw any 'conclusions as to the relationship between the new corporeality and the

---

[14] P. 257.   [15] P. 263, note.

earthly body',[16] the argument for the new corporeality in support of the Christian hope finds itself dependent on general philosophical and epistemological considerations. Thus the value of the body is held to be that it represents 'the instrument of experience and of action', the expression of 'fellowship' and of 'personal life', and indeed 'the expression of the life of the soul with God'.[17] And so Althaus reaches the conclusion 'that in the living relationship between body and soul there is expressed an independent part of the divine intention which must necessarily find its fulfilment. This and this alone is the real meaning of our hopeful message of "the resurrection of the body".'[18] Althaus is certainly right when he says, 'It is plain to see that our grounding here is completely parallel to the line of thought in which we acquired the certainty of the "new world" ',[19] but this very grounding is alien to his own fundamental principle.

Here again the observations on the meaning of corporeality must be accorded the fullest recognition, but they receive their validity only *a posteriori* on the ground of the bodily resurrection of Jesus. If the resurrection is disregarded, man's bodily existence has undoubtedly just as much questionableness as meaning in it, so that instead of a new corporeality one could postulate with equal justification also the annihilation of our corporeality. Scrutiny of the essential relationship between body and soul never provides a ground for hope, but leads only to a question which requires an answer in revelation. And in view of the fallen state of the world we cannot speak of recognizing corporeality as an independent part of the divine purpose, unless we know of the redemption of the body in the resurrection of Jesus. In Althaus' eschatology, the ground given for the hope of a new corporeality is a purely philosophical postulate which is not derived from the logic of the fact of Christ.

That in this specific context Althaus never gets down to a real explanation of the importance of the resurrection for the grounding of eschatology, may well be designated as the weak point of his eschatology. It is certain that Pauline eschatology makes the perfecting of our earthly corporeality definitely dependent on the bodily resurrection of Jesus, and it is certain also that 'the hopeful message of the resurrection of the body' is justified only in relation to the Risen Christ. Althaus' argument stands under the shadow of historical criticism which prevents him from taking up an unequivocal attitude towards the event of the resur-

[16] P. 263.   [17] Pp. 259 ff.
[18] Pp. 261-2.   [19] P. 262.

rection. Thus for Althaus the primitive Christian witness to the resurrection is obscured by problems which are out of harmony with the basic trend of his own eschatology. Once the resurrection of Jesus' body becomes a problem and his 'heavenly' mode of being is called in question, then it is quite true that the only way left open for the grounding of the new corporeality is to have recourse to philosophy; then, too, the question whether the resurrection of Jesus is real at all becomes dependent on philosophical norms from outside the substance of the matter itself, while the foundation which is laid in the resurrection independently of all human speculation and philosophizing as the ground of the Christian hope is ultimately destroyed and the comprehensive significance of Christ's bodily resurrection is ignored. Even if the Gospel narratives are left out of account, the 'heavenly' body of the Risen Christ is explicitly mentioned by Paul.[20] But even apart from this testimony, the very nature of the resurrection compels us to the same conclusion. It would have to be asked in what form of being the appearance of the Exalted One is to be conceived, if not a 'heavenly' one. Since the idea of an earthly and natural body cannot be entertained, there would remain only the possibility of some kind of indefinable, intermediate form after the manner of spiritualist and occult phenomena. The Risen Christ appears to his disciples *precisely* as the heavenly Lord from whose lordship it is impossible to separate the *doxa* which is also a determinative mark of his corporeality. Or are we to entertain the untenable thought that in raising Christ God did not yet create his full, new heavenly corporeality? Either we take Jesus' resurrection seriously, and then with the recognition of this reality the appearing of the Risen One in a 'heavenly' body is a matter of course, since no other possibility exists at all—or we play down the significance of Jesus' bodily resurrection, and then it is impossible to see how the resurrection can be prevented from evaporating into an empty idea of immortality. It is true enough that 'the words of Jesus and the utterances of Paul do not allow us to give a description of "the new body" '.[21] But neither do we obtain such a description from philosophical reflection. The fact of the new corporeality is the content of the resurrection message, and stands in no need of any supplementary philosophical grounding, but must in fact reject anything of the kind as a failure to appreciate the nature of the resurrection.[22]

[20] I Cor. 15.40 f.; Phil. 3.21; Rom. 8.17; I Cor. 2.8; II Cor. 3.18; Phil. 4.19; Col. 3.4; II Thess. 2.14.   [21] P. 262.

[22] In complete agreement with this is W. Elert, *Der christliche Glaube*, 1950, who rightly says: 'In particular we have to reject all reflections which seek to

Thus Althaus' attempt to think through the formulation of a Christian eschatology is constantly broken into by philosophical considerations, even though the consequences of this are rejected so far as his theology is concerned. At all events, it is plain that in Althaus there are various starting points and arguments which impair the essential unity of his eschatological thinking and which not only partially exclude the principle of the resurrection but also obscure it.[23]

The grounding of Stange's eschatological teaching, which seeks expressly to deal with the 'Christian hope', its 'ground and its aim', has also the appearance of being fundamentally Christocentric. 'Here, then, is the point from which we have to set out in eschatology: any eschatology that is theologically possible must have its starting point in our faith in Christ'—in this, Stange completely agrees with Althaus.[24] Indeed, the purpose of his critical examination of Althaus[25] is precisely to emphasize the uniquely Christian elements in eschatology.[26] In Althaus 'Christian eschatology has been intermingled with idealist notions',[27] and in face of that it must be pointed out 'that we cannot attain to the concept of eternity with the aid of idealism, but only with the aid of Christianity. The concept of eternity bears a peculiarly Christian stamp.'[28] In the light of Luther and 'in the spirit of scripture' Stange arrives at the following thesis, on which he builds his eschatology. 'The concept of eternity is used in a Christian sense only when we employ it to reflect our view of the peculiarity of the life and person of Jesus.' 'The concept of eternity . . . is a quality concept', which comes to us by reason of the peculiar quality of Jesus' life.[29] Here Stange has found a fruitful starting point for the development of his eschatology. What really matters now is how Stange interprets this eternal quality

---

understand the new corporeality on the basis of our experiences of the necessity of corporeality for human existence' (p. 648).

[23] Althaus even in the revised edition of his eschatology (4th ed. 1933, pp. 116 f.) still holds fast to the 'necessity of an anthropological grounding of our hope of new corporeality'. He grants, however, that the statements in the 3rd edition, p. 257, were 'in actual fact hesitant as they stand' and 'could not be repeated as they stand'. Thus Althaus, too, attains to the thesis that 'the bodily resurrection of Jesus Christ is the ground of our hope for the body'—though indeed without drawing the consequence of this position which is theologically the only tenable one. The result is, that Althaus' teaching on the new corporeality still maintains the vacillating attitude of 'both . . . and'. Precisely the 'mutual grounding of each other' which is provided by anthropology and by the certainty of the bodily resurrection of the Lord hardly does justice to the demand for an unequivocal Christian eschatology.

[24] *Das Ende aller Dinge*, pp. 204-5.

[25] *Op. cit.*, pp. 98 ff., 103 f., 123 ff., 138 f., 205 ff.   [26] P. 73.

[27] *Op. cit.*, pp. 4 f., cf. also p. 107: 'Eschatology becomes the victim of the speculations of the philosophy of history.'

[28] P. 63.   [29] Pp. 76-77.

of the life and person of Jesus. The resurrection message could here attain its due place if the connection were brought out between the resurrection as ground and the hope of eternity as result, and if the concept of eternal life were described concretely as the life of the Risen Christ. But it is all the more astonishing that the importance of Jesus' resurrection for the grounding of eschatology recedes well into the background, even although Stange is one of the theologians who have very vital things to say on the question of the resurrection. The resurrection of Jesus is always mentioned only incidentally and spoken of only in general terms, but not by any means treated as the central point that determines all eschatological thought.[30] The consequence of this is, that in disregarding the Easter event Stange cannot describe the quality of eternal life, or the 'otherness of the life of Jesus', in any other way than by saying that in Jesus' case 'the inner life is the precondition of the outer', that 'life is eternal when the inner creates the outer'.[31] 'And indeed we gain the impression that eternal life is distinguished from everything else that we call life by its inwardness and depth.'[32]

This argument undoes the original starting point of Stange's eschatology. The separation of the concept of eternity from the resurrection of Jesus drives him to an ethico-religious definition of terms which is by no means safeguarded against slipping into that idealism which Stange himself deplores.[33] The very thing that Stange makes a reproach to Althaus breaks through in his own writings, namely, the fact that philosophical ideas repeatedly threaten the 'Christian-ness' of his eschatology. Instead of an emphasis on the reality of the resurrection life we find the idea of life which, to say the least, is misleading; in place of the witness to the consummated corporeality of the Risen Christ, we have abstract talk about the inwardness of the life of Jesus.[34] Thus it is easy to understand, too, that biblical grounds are by no means the only ones used to establish the validity of eschatological statements, but that use is likewise made of empirical, rational and ethical norms.

The examination of the problem of the grounding of a Christian eschatology shows in a striking manner the theological tendency towards numerous varieties of failure to find the basic starting point in the reality of Christ's resurrection, as also the conflict between the resurrection principle and other ideas part theological part philosophi-

---

[30] *Op. cit.*, pp. 79, 80, 81, 85, 125 f.
[31] P. 89.   [32] P. 96.
[33] Thus Thurneysen, *op. cit.*, p. 188: 'It is impossible to see how any real distinction from speculative idealism can still be found here.'
[34] Cf. pp. 80, 202.

cal. The grounding of the Christian hope, however, can reasonably take place only on the basis of the resurrection event. For a Christian eschatology there can, as was self-evident to primitive Christian thought, be no other sustaining ground than God's own word of the resurrection.

VII

THE ESCHATOLOGICAL EVENT OF THE RESURRECTION OF JESUS

THE resurrection of Jesus is not an occurrence which merely forms a link in the chain of eschatological events, nor is it only a fact that is of special importance for eschatology, but it has to be understood as *the* eschatological event pure and simple. The reality of the resurrection is already the eschaton, and does not merely have a relation to it. All the Last Things have their ground in the Risen Christ and are bound up with him. That is why the resurrection is the ground of the Christian hope of eternal life and of our knowledge of the consummation of the world. *To speak of the End means to speak of the significance of the resurrection of Jesus, which casts its light also upon history, but whose significance is a hidden one and awaits its fulfilment in the* Telos.

I. THE ESCHATOLOGICAL CHARACTER OF HISTORY

(a) The Question of the Meaning of History

The concept of history denotes that mode of existence in which men and their various associations, bound to a past heritage and directed towards an end, stand in continual concrete personal decision and in action and reaction upon each other, partly in the form of attraction and partly of repulsion. History is therefore not a mere condition but an active happening. In its essence it cannot be objectively apprehended but can only be understood through the act of decision. The historic is always at the same time also the temporal and that is why true history is always present in the moment of a new occurrence and yet stands in continuity with the past. Historic life always has a goal, it is determined by a purpose, it is teleologically oriented time. Nevertheless, as time it is limited and is threatened by the fact that all historic life comes to an end. Of course, the supra-individual life of history outlasts the individual, but the span of time involved is not identical with eternal life. So history appears as a confused tangle of human purposes and strivings which are repeatedly brought to an end by death, and as the ceaseless rhythm of human growth and decay.[1]

Historicality therefore does not in the first instance imply meaningful order, comprehensive unity and inherent completeness, but manifests a fundamental questionableness. Existence in history confronts us with the question what is the aim of historic life and growth, what is the norm by which history is governed, and how the responsible decisions of historic existence are to be made. To ask about the nature of history is to ask about its meaning. But history is the plenitude of human possibilities, all of which bear only the stamp of relativity and yield no meaning that could be absolute. So long as there is no establishing of a meaning for historic life, however, there can be no *one* history (which would be to presuppose a quite definite order) but only histories, historic possibilities, a variety of points of view but no norm-determined unity. From this question of meaning which historic existence so relentlessly forces upon us there results the struggle on the part of the philosophy of history to find a meaning in history. The philosophy of history therefore strives to bring order into history's chaos, to employ empirical or *a priori* standards of value in order to answer the questionableness of history. It is a kind of thinking which represents man's grandiose attempt at interpreting the whole of history in terms of some given idea, as though the thinker could have the meaning of history at his command. The problem of the meaning of history, however, is decisively summed up in the question whether the end and goal of the historic process is life or death. Since the philosophy of history cannot command the answer to this question, it cannot get beyond the 'as if' attitude.[2]

At bottom there seem to be two typical possibilities for the philosophical interpretation of history. One is the essentially idealist view of history which sees it as an upward movement and a unity of meaning. Hegel's thinking on history represents this view in its classical form. History here is the dialectical upward development and perfection of the absolute spirit. In history the absolute spirit of the world attains self-knowledge in the spirit of man and for this reason historic growth is endowed with redemptive power and has the future in its possession.

[1] Cf. Hans Jürgen Baden, *Der Sinn der Geschichte*, Hamburg 1948, pp. 50, 281, 314. As an example of a theology of history grounded on the resurrection we may cite W. Künneth, *Der grosse Abfall*, Hamburg 1948. Special notice is merited by Reinhold Niebuhr, *Faith and History*, 1949.

[2] Cf. H. D. Wendland, *Geschichtsanschauung und Geschichtsbewusstsein im Neuen Testament*, 1938.

Even though E. Hirsch 'in conscious opposition to Hegel' refuses to confuse 'God's life and power' with the human spirit working in history,[3] yet his interpretation of history still belongs to the same fundamental type of philosophy of history. For all his recognition of the fact that the history of man is 'fragile and imperfect' and interwoven with 'unrest and fear',[4] yet for him, too, the ground of the meaningfulness of historic life is given in the fact of the human spirit and in the specific religious and ethical character of the conscience. In all historic reality 'a supra-historic element is mysteriously entwined', and history is related to 'something eternal' with which 'the individual soul' unites itself 'by the acceptance of a specific duty'.[5] Because it is of 'the deepest nature of the spirit' to be 'certain of its power and truth', it stands in an inward relationship 'to an Ultimate and Absolute'.[6] The 'foundation stone' of Hirsch's conception of history is therefore expressed in the thesis: 'The history of man, both as a whole and in detail, can be understood only by him who discerns its metaphysical core and its religious reference.'[7] The 'heart' and 'meaning' of history is to be sought in 'what belongs equally to every point and moment of historic life— but that is the direct relation of the human spirit in all its motions to something beyond history, to something eternal'.[8]

The characteristic mark of this mature form of idealist and theistic philosophy of history is to be seen in three points: in the optimistic belief that history has a meaning, in the direct 'givenness' of this meaning for the human spirit, and in the grounding of this meaning in a general idea of the supra-historic. The human spirit, thanks to its relation to things eternal, has accordingly the meaning of history at its disposal, and requires no further special disclosure of that meaning, since it has itself at all times open access directly to the ground of the meaning. Fascinating though it is, this attempt to solve the problem nevertheless arouses misgivings. This view of history seems to take too little account of the profound questionableness of the historic life that is moving to its end. The dichotomy of the human spirit is not resolved even by its relation to the supra-historic, and the attempt to apply a norm therefore always remains ambiguous and misleading. Even our knowledge of the truth is always at the same time called in question in history by falsehood and error. Since such truth can never be more than fragmentary, the relation to the eternal must always be precarious. If,

---

[3] *Deutschlands Schicksal*, 1922, p. 23.   [4] *Op. cit.*, p. 23.
[5] Pp. 16-17.   [6] Pp. 18 ff.
[7] P. 14.   [8] P. 48, cf. p. 62.

however, the eternal is something more than a mere concluding idea of God, if it is the actual reality of God, then the meaning of history cannot possibly be grounded in the relation to the eternal. This relation to God can in fact just as easily reveal precisely the complete lack of meaning in all human history, can show historic being to be a lie, and reply to the question of the end of human development with the answer of annihilation and death. This kind of 'ethicism' makes it doubly necessary to recall that by the standards of eternity there exists in history no perfect obedience and no perfect fulfilment of duty. That, however, renders even the 'metaphysical core' of history useless as a possible ground of its meaning. The question of meaning raised by the philosophy of history cannot in this perspective be answered in favour of life.

In contrast to this conception is the other interpretation of history which sees it not as an ascending movement, but as one of descent and decay. This philosophy of history has found impressive form on the one hand in the thought of O. Spengler,[9] and on the other in Erwin Reisner's book with the significant title 'History as the Fall of Man and the Road to Judgment'.[10] Here history is the scene of the relative, of the fateful course of events, of the different 'truths' but not of the truth. Hence it is impossible to speak in history of a comprehensive meaning that imposes a pattern on all the parts. It cannot be the task of the philosophy of history to disclose its meaning, or to impose one on it, but rather to disclose the meaninglessness of all history. According to Spengler, the proper attitude to the life of history can only be scepticism. The belief in progress is therefore nothing more than a 'piece of foolery', a 'sentimentality'. Man himself is in fact a 'beast of prey', a 'rebel'.[11] 'Every higher civilization is a tragedy. The history of man as a whole is tragic.'[12] What Spengler sees as a destiny inherent in nature is given greater depth by Reisner through his practical, ethical approach. The distress of history does not derive from an undeserved fate but consists in guilty decisions. History is the antithesis to redemption; it is the result of a godless act and of man's continuing 'Fall'. It is true that all history is directed towards an end, but this end is not the goal that consummates an evolutionary process, it is the judgment. The answer to the question of meaning is: In history no meaning can arise, for its end is death.

This pessimistic view of history, no matter whether it is based on fate

---

[9] *The Decline of the West*, but also *Man and Technics*.
[10] *Die Geschichte als Sündenfall und Weg zum Gericht: Grundlegung einer christlichen Metaphysik der Geschichte*, Munich and Berlin, 1929.
[11] *Man and Technics*, pp. 19, 42.   [12] *Op. cit.*, p. 90.

or on ethics, is relatively justified as a counterblast to the tendencies towards glorification which imagine they can discover 'God in history'. Unquestionably, this view of history recognizes factors which make it impossible in principle to construct a meaningful picture of history. The forces which shape history are not merely constructive and progressive, but to a far greater extent destructive. Significant in this view is, further, that in the first instance it does not seek to answer the question of meaning at all, but by probing more deeply into the riddle of history renders the question posed by it still more profound. But this interpretation of history, too, is open to serious criticism. It will not do simply to overlook the elements of rightness and truth in the idealist approach. Undoubtedly guilt and meaningless fate are woven into the texture of history; but does it not also reveal meaningful order and creative life? To regard the life of history simply as the result of the Fall does of course have the attractiveness of all one-sided views, but is surely hardly the whole truth. Ultimately, the answers of both the sceptical and the idealist view of history alike represent an inadequate judgment which anticipates a possible interpretation that comes from an entirely different dimension. The pessimistic attempt at interpretation, too, moves on the plane of immanent facts and knows nothing of a 'transcendent' bestowal of meaning.

Both these types of philosophy of history contain an eschatological element. The first speaks of a relationship between the historic and 'a last word'; the other speaks of the way of history leading to a final end in death and 'judgment'. That is an outline of the essential trends followed by the philosophers of history, who practically all seek for a meaning in history and in their attempted solutions point indirectly towards it whether negatively or positively, yet without actually being able to find it.[13]

Yet in face of all these attitudes it must be asserted that there can be an answer to the question of the meaning of history only if there is *a centre of history*, a *point of reference, by which an orientation of all historic happenings can be achieved*. It is to the special credit of P. Tillich that he has pursued the problem of a philosophy of history along these lines and has determinedly raised the question of 'Christology and the interpretation of history', and of 'eschatology and history'. 'To engage in Christology really means to describe the place where an Absolute

---

[13] G. Simmel, *Die Probleme der Geschichtsphilosophie*, 1907; E. Hirsch, 'Grundlegung einer christlichen Geschichtsphilosophie', *Zeitschr. f. syst. Theol.* 1925, part 2. Also Otmar Spann, *Geschichtsphilosophie*, Jena 1932.

Source of meaning enters history and endows it with meaning and transcendence.'[14] Tillich defines the character of the 'focal point of history' by saying that it is the place 'at which the principle that gives meaning to history is perceived'.[15] The establishing of this centre makes a universal claim, because the 'transcendent meaning of events' which is thereby given is 'the eschaton'.[16] As the Ultimate, however, it is unconditional and 'not the fortuitous and dubious result of a process of development'; rather, 'every happening, however small or however great' participates in the eschaton.[17] The concept of a centre or focal point of history is a religious category and should not be thought of as a 'secular possibility'. Hence it is 'only for faith that Christ is posited as the centre of history'.[18] The constitutive principle of history, however, cannot be 'the place of demands', but must be 'a meaningful kind of being'. Christ is 'anticipatory fulfilment', and 'a sacramental reality'.[19]

These extraordinarily important statements of Tillich's can be made fruitful for the solving of the problem of the philosophy of history. Indeed, the question seems in actual fact to be already solved by the above reflections of Tillich's on the theology of history with their basis in the Christian revelation. He recognizes that the 'principle which is the concrete source of meaning' is Christ, 'a personal life that is entirely determined by its relation to the transcendent'.[20] In face of that, it remains only to ask what Tillich understands by the word 'Christ'. Is Christ for him the same reality as is meant by the New Testament when it speaks of the Risen Kyrios? This question, however, is an absolutely decisive one, and we must make the following observations: The historical personality of Jesus is of no interest for Tillich's philosophy, and for this reason he also knows nothing of a resurrection reality. 'Faith includes no facts', not even the event of the resurrection. The question of Christ as the focal point of history has nothing to do with the 'unanswerable question of the historical facts'[21]; this, however, robs the concept 'Christ' of its historic concreteness. 'Christ' becomes for

---

[14] *Religiöse Verwirklichung*, pp. 110-111, 128 ff. (ET in *The Interpretation of History*, 1936, pp. 242 f., 266 ff.).
[15] *The Interpretation of History*, p. 250.
[16] *Op. cit.*, pp. 250, 270.
[17] *Op. cit.*, p. 274.
[18] *Op. cit.*, p. 260.
[19] *Op. cit.*, p. 262.
[20] *Op. cit.*, pp. 248, 259 f.
[21] *Op. cit.*, pp. 264 f. One could agree with this judgment were it not that in Tillich it means a radically sceptical view of history altogether. His criticism of E. Brunner is symptomatic: 'It is his weakness that he does not allow the questionableness of the empirical to stand in all its radicality, even to the point of including the non-existence (of Jesus)', *Religiöse Verwirklung*, p. 290, note 27 (notes omitted from ET).

Tillich an idea wholly free from history, a symbol, an expression of the transcendent element in history which gives it meaning. To engage in Christology therefore does not mean to look back to a historic past, but 'to contemplate the centre of history as it is laid before us and to strive to uphold its claim to be valid as the centre of *our* history'.[22]

In view of these assertions Tillich's philosophy of history means in essence a relapse into that idealist attitude which he himself rejects. That which gives meaning is that which in itself can show up any time; it is the Absolute and Transcendent, which breaks into the individual's present life with 'power' and makes its claim upon him. What this Absolute is in essence, we cannot say. Christ as the centre of history certainly does not by any means represent the first, and at the same time also completed, breaking in of this absolute bestowal of meaning, so that the latter would be bound to the fact of Christ, but he is merely the supra-temporal symbolic expression for the existence of a real meaning which shimmers through history, but which is not by any means grounded in Christ nor bound to him. Christ is not regarded as the ground of the meaning of history but rather as the symbol of that meaning. The Christologically determined focal point of history can therefore only be established in Tillich by means of a metamorphosis of the specifically Christian content. Under the influence of the message of Christ, Tillich borrows from that message his vital knowledge of the focal point of history, while at the same time denying the ground on which that knowledge becomes possible. Thus his efforts in the philosophy of history have a formally Christian stamp, while their content has fallen away to philosophical speculation. Tillich's solution to the problem of the meaning of history therefore necessarily succumbs to an illusion, in so far as we then imagine that on the ground of a universal impression made by an Absolute we have that meaning at our disposal, whereas in fact we cannot have it at all, since there is no guarantee whatever for the validity of the universal relation that gives the meaning. If there is no 'fact of Christ' as an event which provides in all concreteness a ground of meaning, then the content of the whole philosophical edifice collapses. However important the things Tillich has said of the structure of the focal centre of history, it is equally true on the other hand that the content of his Christological pronouncements is inadequate. The question of meaning, which is a question of life or death, ultimately remains open in Tillich; it is a postulate without a valid answer.

[22] *Op. cit.*, p. 265.

The criticism of Tillich has shown that there can be a decision on the question of meaning only when there is a concrete living reality which guarantees the meaning. We cannot come to know of this reality, however, by way of the philosophy of history, but can only speak of it in expounding the Christian's believing knowledge of history, i.e. in terms of a *theology of history*. This of course implies something that is in sharpest contrast to any systematized philosophy of history, and means taking the stumbling block of the message of Christ—and the Risen Christ at that—as the directing principle of a theology of history.

(b) The Risen Christ as the Focal Point of History's Meaning

We can only treat of Christ as the focal point of history, which gives it meaning, if by 'Christ' we understand the reality of the Risen One. That this grounding of its meaning is bound up specifically with the resurrection of Jesus, and not only in a general way with the person or the cross of Jesus, is no accident. A historical fact as such—and here Tillich is right—cannot be treated as a focal centre of meaning since, being itself on the plane of history, it shares to the full in history's questionable character and indeed itself raises a question as to its meaning. The historic person of Jesus as such stands among the relativities and conditionalities and cannot have an unconditional character. The same is true of the fact of the cross. It is itself the most intense form of the question as to the meaning of history. In it there is concentrated the meaninglessness of all that happens in the sphere of history, and the answer which it is able to give points towards death. As against this, it is only in the resurrection of Jesus that history's focal point of meaning is given. On the one hand, being itself an event related to history, it can give an answer to the question which history poses; on the other hand, as a reality that transcends history, it possesses the unconditional and universal quality necessary to what gives meaning. The decisive question as to the last word on historic existence as a word either of life or of death, is given an unequivocal answer by the resurrection of Jesus. The Risen Christ is *the* living reality absolutely, and hence the reality in which the sole guarantee for the meaning of history is given. On this ground we are justified in speaking of Christ as the focal point of history and in agreeing with Tillich's formal conceptual presentation—not with the intention of giving a new content to the framework constructed by a philosophy of history, but because we recognize that this insight on the part of the philosophy of history is itself dependent on that content.

This *concept of history's 'focal centre of meaning'* expresses the fact that the resurrection of Jesus is the eschatological event. Because the resurrection of Jesus is the centre of meaning, it is at the same time also the last word for all historic life. The converse of this is also true: because Jesus' resurrection is the last word, it can also be the centre that gives meaning to history. If the resurrection of Jesus is the eschaton, then at the same time the eschatological character of history is revealed and confirmed in it. From this it follows also that it is only on the ground of the resurrection of Jesus that it can be made clear whether and to what extent we can speak of meaningful history, and what this meaningfulness implies. The basic knowledge which the theology of history provides of the eschatological centre of meaning in the Risen Christ involves two things: 1. The focal centre of meaning implies the possibility of an orderly orientation of all history towards the eschaton, and 2. the possibility of a special interpretation of history from the eschatological angle. Thus the *resurrection of Jesus becomes the starting point for a new Christian view of history.*

Man's chaotic movements in history continue to succumb to a disorder which defies every unifying principle, and to the arbitrary application of relative standards of value, until the establishing of a normative point provides a guarantee of orientation and of overcoming the hopeless fragmentation of historic life. The subjective selection of such a central point is indeed always being attempted, but never leads beyond the relativity of the historic, since only an absolute authority which is independent of all that is subjective can be the basis of meaning. Its absoluteness involves also the impossibility of proving this central point of meaning, whose claims can of course be challenged at any time, but whose justification is shown in the unfolding of its meaning.

Once we recognize the resurrection of Jesus as the eschatological focal point of meaning, then all the happenings of history are oriented towards that centre as though drawn by the power of a magnet. This, however, brings about a unifying process which resolves the clashes and combinations in the maelstrom of history and orders its multiplicity of movements into a whole. It is only through this reference point that the various 'histories' are fitted together to form one single history, i.e. the *history of mankind.* The histories of peoples, races and cultures, without losing their peculiarity are liberated from their relativity to find their place in the over-arching complex of mankind. The concept 'mankind' is a concept of the theology of history which gains its meaning only from the reality which is Christ. The concept of the history of mankind has therefore an eschatological character, in that through Christ all human life in history, divisive and mutually oppressive and destructive though it is in itself, is gathered up into a unity which as such can never be the product of human development or the result of human efforts, but represents an ultimate end towards which history is directed, which we know of in faith, but whose consummation is beyond any earthly grasp. The Risen Christ turns history into the history of mankind. In saying this we are recognizing two things. First, the resurrection makes it plain that all men apart from the reality of Christ are in the same situation. The multiplicity and contradictoriness of their life in history is merely the concrete and individual expression of universal history since Adam. The history of mankind is on the one hand history 'in Adam', though it can be understood as such only from a standpoint which lies beyond that history. Only when we know of Christ do we know that all men, despite their sharpest differences, are uniformly directed 'in Adam' towards a single eschaton. Secondly, in the perspective of the resurrection, history is recognized as an inner unity, because in the light of the Christ event the whole situation of mankind is to be regarded as being subject to the same eschatological determination. The new humanity established in the Risen One is the reality which has the same validity for all men who are 'in Adam', and which thereby gathers them into the new unity 'in Christ'. This reality of the new humanity 'in Christ', however, is not a fact of history, but an eschatological one towards which all history is uniformly moving. That history is the history of mankind is therefore established also in view of the coming Christ-humanity.

Secondly, because of the centre of meaning in the resurrection of Jesus, history is qualified as *saving history*. Saving history (*Heilsgeschichte*) does not mean a 'sacred' (*heilige*) history, which in contrast to secular history would be distinguished by its peculiar metaphysical character. If that were so, salvation (*Heil*) and therewith the meaning of history would be secularized into a factor in history. But neither does saving history mean the transcendent reference of all historic life from which it has its meaning, so that saving history could be so to speak the inner meaning of history, discoverable everywhere, and all history would become so to speak the transparency through which the central meaning shines.[23] The description of history as saving history is intended, on the contrary, in a strictly Christocentric sense. But this

[23] P. Tillich's interpretation necessarily moves in this direction, for he can say: 'In so far as history is given, it is given as saving history' (cf. *The Interpretation of History*, p. 256).

means that saving history is always a history of preparation for the
eschaton of the resurrection of Jesus and then for the eschaton of all
history, which is guaranteed in the resurrection of Jesus. Two things
are included in this: from the standpoint of the focal centre of meaning
in the resurrection, the saving history which is a preparation for the
eschaton is to be understood on the one hand as *prophetic history*, and
on the other as *missionary history*. All historic happenings before the
establishing of the centre of history have their eschatological meaning in
the fact that in the form of presentiment and interpretation history is
oriented towards the reality of the Risen One which fulfils its meaning.
This prophetic history is indirect, unconscious and ambiguous in the
context of the phenomena of religious history, but it is direct, clear and
unequivocal in the history of the 'Old Covenant' and in the prophets
of Israel. The meaning of history is a Coming One, who is expected as
the salvation of God. The whole of saving history, whether in distorted
or in pure form, reveals the expectation of the meaning of all historic
life, which is not confirmed until the resurrection. Thus it becomes the
prophecy of a new life, whose end is not death. After the establishing
of its focal point, however, history becomes missionary history. Now the
life of history is one through the midst of which there runs missionary
endeavour sustained by the ground that gives history its meaning.
History since the resurrection has its meaning in the fact that in it the
consummation of all history in the eschaton is being prepared for
through the publishing of the message of Christ. Its meaning is once
again an eschatological one, in that all mission, while certainly knowing
of the salvation fulfilled in Christ, nevertheless still waits for the consummation of that salvation. The new period of history which begins
with the resurrection differs from the preceding one in having a peculiar
eschatological direction. God's leaving the nations to themselves and
'winking at' sin is succeeded by missionary history[24] as the sending of
the resurrection Church into the world. With this begins a new saving
history, as a history especially of grace and repentance, such that the
historic life of the Church, because it knows of the eschaton and there-

---

[24] It is noteworthy that in Paul, too, these reflections on the philosophy of
history are found in the context of the raising of Jesus. The cardinal point for
his view of the world and his interpretation of its history is the resurrection of
Jesus. In Acts 17.30 f. the beginning of a new period of history is marked by the
end of the 'times of ignorance', and explicit reference is made to the need for
metanoein and *pistis* in view of the coming judgment of the world—but all this
on the foundation of the fact 'that he hath raised him from the dead'. Cf. W.
Lütgert, *Reich Gottes und Weltgeschichte*, 1928, p. 53: 'The cross of Christ and
his resurrection is the eternal law of history.' Cf. also K. Heim on world mission
in *Leben aus dem Glauben*, p. 239.

fore of the meaning of history, is seen to be the essential core of this era of history.

The special theological interpretation of history which takes its bearings on the eschaton of the resurrection of Jesus *can be summarized in the following three ideas: the focal point of history's meaning involves for it crisis, promise, and responsibility.*

As soon as the life of history is seen in the light of the End, all glorification of history and all belief in the meaningfulness of the present nature and further development of history vanishes. History becomes something penultimate and inconclusive, which is irredeemably the prey of death. What the sceptic and pessimistic philosophy of history asserts is confirmed: in view of the fact that the reality of the resurrection lies beyond death, historic life is not something whose meaning is unequivocally disclosed in the progressing rhythm of historic growth, it is not the scene of the victory of truth and righteousness, but the destructive realm of demons hostile to God. If the purposely anti-divine will which lays hold of man as a force of temptation and destruction and shapes his historic existence is described as demonic, then history appears in all its meaninglessness as the place of material and spiritual devastation. History means the dominance of the brutal, lie-infested will to oppression and the assertion of a state of disquietude for the removal of which the theology of history can see no possibility within history. Thus history bears not only the imprint of the fate of death, but also the marks of ethical guilt. History is a continuing Fall; that is why the Son of God was crucified in it. But because he who was rejected and crucified in history is also the Risen One, the whole of historic existence is placed by him in its final crisis. History is threatened by the eschaton of the resurrection, and the servant of that eschaton is death.

At the same time, however, history is placed under an eschatological promise by the resurrection of Jesus. The eschaton of the resurrection of Jesus, to which all history is directed, is not a timeless transcendence out of all relation to history. This is made clear precisely by the Risen One, who to be sure is the exalted, yet also the historic Christ. Thus the historic is not destroyed by the resurrection, but rather taken up into a new reality. The resurrection of Jesus is therefore not an abstract supra-historicality, but a concrete fulfilment of history. Thus a new light falls from the Risen One upon the whole life of history, giving it a new meaning. From this standpoint it becomes possible to speak also of a value in history, of God's continuing creation, which reveals itself in the preserving orders of history and its strictly regular laws. History is then no longer merely the scene of forces separated from God, but is also a work of God which has an eternal meaning. Here the element of truth in the idealist philosophy of history becomes clear. Of course, the knowledge of this meaning is not given in itself, but is imparted and confirmed only when all history is taken up into the promise emanating from the Risen One. The Risen One, as the historical Jesus, guarantees the right to historic being and the meaning of all historic action related to the eschaton, despite all the questionableness of what emerges in history. *The meaning of history has its ground not in history, but in Christ.* It is therefore the basically eschatological direction of the life of history which ultimately gives it its meaning. Standing as it does under the promise of the resurrection, all history waits not only for death, but beyond that for its consummation in life. The consummation of history means being liberated from the historic order of wrath and from the fate of death. The resurrection of Jesus is the final solution to the question of the meaning of history, because it alone can give the answer of life.

This links up with the third idea, that of responsibility in history in view of the *telos*. Life in history is always a life of responsible decision. As long as it does not have its norm in the focal point of meaning, it is lived in ways that are conditional and fortuitous and bound to relative values. The absolute claim which comes from the focal point of meaning in the resurrection guides the life of decision to greater clarity and depth. Responsibility in history comes to maturity when the eschatological viewpoint becomes the standard of conduct. It is not the consequences of our conduct which decide the meaning, but in that relation to the ultimate in which we live in absolute responsibility the meaning proves itself—a meaning which is not given, but is existentially experienced. History's being directed towards the *telos* gives it the highest possible tension, and it is only in the eschatological perspective of the resurrection that this tension can be a meaningful one. To exercise responsibility in history is to know that history, precisely because it is moving towards its consummation, is always on the way to judgment, but at the same time, that our everyday decisions, both small and great, must be made in obedience to the part appointed us by destiny in the life of history. From the eschatological viewpoint there lies an accent of eternity on every responsible decision. Thus the life of decision in history is experienced at one and the same time both as being subject to the last judgment that comes from the resurrection of Jesus and as entering into the grace which has the last word and whose consummation embraces also our historic existence.

2. THE HIDDEN NATURE OF THE RESURRECTION AEON

Once the resurrection of Jesus is understood as the eschatological event, then this brings out, further, that the dawning of the resurrection aeon is given in the Risen Kyrios and that this is the beginning of the last and eternal reality.[25] In the Risen Christ the whole existence of the new aeon is summed up proleptically: the *resurrection of Jesus is an anticipation of the new world of God*. This endows the resurrection of Jesus with the character of a turning point in the ages, in such a way that the old aeon is still present as the new aeon begins. The resurrection appears as a dividing line through time, so to speak as a vertical line coming from God which meets the plane of the old aeon so that from

[25] This gives dogmatic significance to ideas which were put forward for the first time by A. Schweitzer in the context of his eschatological view of Christ. In contrast to Greek and oriental mysticism there is a 'dynamic dualism' in Paul, according to which the world happenings in which the relationship of God and man is expressed take place in historic events which press towards a *consummatio mundi*. The decisive incident in the world's life, however, is to be seen in the raising of Christ. 'The beginning of this concatenation is marked by the resurrection of the Lord, the end by his parousia' (*Paul and his Interpreters*, p. 224). According to A. Schweitzer's interpretation of Paul, the turning point in the world's life which is brought about by the resurrection of Jesus is so radical that as a result there arise two world-epochs, the old aeon and the new aeon that now begins, which however have no relation to each other, at all events not an evolutionary relationship. It is true that the apostle sees 'an intermingling of the still natural and the already supernatural state of the world', yet 'it is as if he assumed that there are no ties linking the present world-epoch to that in which Jesus lived and taught, and as if he were convinced that as a result of the death and resurrection of the Lord there now exist conditions which in their utter newness abrogate all that he taught and compel us to a new foundation for ethics and to far-reaching insights concerning his death and resurrection' (*op. cit.*, pp. 244, 245 f.). Whereas A. Schweitzer reproduces Paul's world-view in these terms, yet regards it as an opinion subject to the limitations of its day and therefore does not ascribe any abiding religious and theological significance to it, the theology of K. Heim is strongly influenced by these ideas. The assertion that the resurrection of Jesus is the breaking in of the new aeon into time is emphatically stressed by K. Heim: 'Into this world of the hoping and the hopeless, of the Jews and the Greeks, comes the *euangelion*, the "joyful news", the peculiar perfect tense, which runs through the whole preaching of the apostles: the world's turning point, renounced by the mystics and watched for in breathless tension by the hopeful, is already come.... The transforming of the world is now only a matter of time. The form of this world is passing away. Everyone who believes in Christ enters now already in unseen ways into the community of the future which awaits its consummation.... The news that the turning point is already come was tremendous. It brought about an utterly new attitude towards the world.... In contrast to all these imperatives, demands and exercises which harrassed and troubled men, the message of the apostles began in a totally different way. It began with a perfect indicative' (*Glaube und Leben*, pp. 431 ff.; *Die Weltanschauung der Bibel*, p. 86). The standpoint of the resurrection requires our full agreement with Heim's observations. Cf. A. Schweitzer, *The Mysticism of Paul the Apostle*, in which he puts the finishing touches to his view of Paul as presented above. With this, the representation we have here given of the basic views of Pauline theology is confirmed in all essential points.

this event onwards the 'new epoch' is already in being together with the old world epoch. Since the resurrection we have to distinguish between two periods of time: our provisional existence and the reality of the resurrection, the aeon *kata sarka* and the aeon *kata pneuma*. In relation to the turning point given in the resurrection, there is in the old aeon a 'before' and an 'after' analogous to the changed situation 'before' and 'after' Easter, in that precisely as a result of this event a new possibility of existence is now a present reality in the midst of the old epoch. If to stand in the old aeon means being subject to the laws of transience and death, of sin and of the Fall, so that the cosmos, too, suffers from the same helplessness and futility as man and therefore in this epoch of death is 'burdened', 'groans' and 'travails', then to stand in the new aeon means partaking of the eternal life of Christ, being saved from the effects of the Fall and knowing of a redemption that embraces the whole world. On the one side there is the validity of the law, on the other the Risen Christ as 'the end of the law'. As long as we think that we are still under the law, and at the same time that we can recognize the new aeon, we have not yet grasped the change in the world since the resurrection of Jesus.[26] Over against the sovereignty of the 'powers of darkness', 'the Prince of Death', the demonic forces in the old world epoch, there stands in the resurrection aeon the 'Prince of Life', the sovereignty of the Kyrios, the victory in principle over all that destroys life.

This dawning of the new world epoch in the resurrection of Jesus does not result in the end of the old world epoch, but in a relation of mutual conflict and interpenetration between the two aeons. There is indeed no immanent continuity between this present existence and the new life, but the new world epoch is here in the midst of the old, whether man recognizes this reality or denies it. The two aeons stand in a relationship of presence and contemporaneity in respect of time, but in regard to substance they are in a relationship of antagonism. The old aeon is the visible and objective mode of existence, while the aeon of the resurrection on the contrary is the invisible and non-objective reality. The world which has dawned in the resurrection is a hidden one for the hitherto existing aeon. This makes it clear that since the turn of the ages a new reality can interpolate itself into the old visible world by reason of the hiddenness of its existence, in such a way that the

[26] From this standpoint we can understand Paul's passionate struggle against all judaizing compromises, since to adopt them is the sign of a relapse into the pre-Easter attitude, which is tantamount to a betrayal of the Gospel.

concepts of 'hiddenness' and 'visibility' become characteristic descriptions of the two presently existing aeons.[27]

The 'hiddenness' of the resurrection aeon marks it as an eschatological factor. The importance of affirming this hiddenness is far-reaching, since it largely depends on that whether we properly understand the resurrection of Jesus at all.

The term 'hiddenness' can have a twofold meaning. It can mean that hiddenness which is the radical opposite of 'openness' and excludes not only all relation to what is hidden, but also all knowledge of its nature and essence. This kind of hiddenness belongs to the reality of God apart from his own revelation. Of the *deus absconditus* nothing can be said, since there is no possibility of any revealing disclosure. Here hiddenness does not by any means imply only what cannot be seen, but still more what cannot be known. The hiddenness of God is then identical with his absolute transcendence that excludes all contact with the world. This concept of hiddenness must not, however, be applied to the resurrection aeon. That would mean that the resurrection of Jesus is merely a limiting statement, and a synonym for timeless eternity or unapproachable transcendence, so that the resurrection is not really a revelation at all and any statement about it appears fundamentally impossible.

By hiddenness, however, we can also understand a revelation reality which has attested itself so that we can know of it even though it remains withdrawn from our actual sight. Here, hiddenness is most definitely not an expression of transcendence, but it implies the veiling of something which because of revelation is already there, but is invisible. Hiddenness, in the sense of veiling, and revelation are not two opposites, but mutually qualify each other, for God's revelation in the world is possible only if it takes place under a veil and the hiddenness of revelation can be meaningfully spoken of only when there is some knowledge of that which conceals itself. In this case hiddenness does indeed imply an inability to see, yet at the same time also an ability to have knowledge of the thing that veils itself. Thus hiddenness in this sense applies to God precisely not as *deus absconditus*, but as *revelatus*.

After what has been said so far, it is only this concept of hiddenness that can express the present reality of the resurrection aeon. The hiddenness of the resurrection can of course only be spoken of in the judgment of faith. The hiddenness exists indeed as such, even apart from faith; but the knowledge that the Risen Christ is there as a hidden presence

[27] Cf. H. Schaedel, *Die neutestamentliche Äonenlehre*, 1930.

is impossible for unbelief, and given only to faith. The meaning of the hiddenness of the resurrection of Jesus must now be more closely examined.

If *the resurrection of Jesus is an event which is veiled*, then we must reject every attempt to conceive that resurrection as a visible happening in which the Crucified reveals himself in divine majesty. Because the resurrection is a hidden reality, the idea of a rehabilitation of Jesus, as rejected by the world and now exalted by God, represents a fundamental misunderstanding. Here there is a decisive parting of the ways between the Evangelical and the Catholic understanding of Christ. The latter fails to recognize the hiddenness of Christ, which has not been abolished since the resurrection of Jesus, but rather established for the first time in its fullest sense. Of course, as with every revelation of God, we must speak of the veiling of the Son and the Messiah even before the resurrection, but in view of the divinity of the Risen One and the fact that the resurrection aeon has now begun, the hiddenness has come to be of fundamental importance. If we believe that the veil has been done away by the resurrection and a *status gloriae* established by it, then it is necessary to make this resurrection glory visible to all the world and thus also credible to all the world. It is this basic attitude which explains the efforts of the Catholic Church to represent the majesty of the Risen Christ objectively in the Church's splendour and power and to make the world of the resurrection visible within the Church's organism. This objectivizing of the lordship of the Kyrios finds its concrete expression in his papal representative, who vicariously embodies the visible manifestation of Christ the King rehabilitated by the resurrection. Whereas the attitude of faith is appropriate to the hiddenness of the Risen One, the realizing of the glory of the resurrection in the Roman Catholic Church calls for seeing, for the impression of power and for the stirring of the emotions.[28]

The result is, that the resurrection of Jesus is wrongly appealed to for the rise of a Church of glory and a *theologia gloriae*. But the denial of the hiddenness of the resurrection in this ecclesiastical and theological view destroys the resurrection message at a vital point. As against this, it is understandable that the Evangelical Church conceives of itself as a Church of poverty whose glory is hidden, and as a Church of the cross

[28] Cf. K. Heim, *Das Wesen des evangelischen Christentums*, 1929, pp. 45 f.; (ET, *Spirit and Truth*, 1935, p. 78); also *Die neue Welt Gottes*, pp. 46, 53, 57 f. (in *The New Divine Order*, pp. 73, 83, 89 f.), 71, 77; *Dogmatik* II, p. 86. Cf. also H. Frick on this point, and also on the understanding of hiddenness, *op. cit.*, pp. 299 f., 308, 311 f., 321 f., 327.

founded on a *theologia crucis*; with equal justification, however, it has
to know itself to be the bearer and guardian of a theology of the resurrection which in contrast to all falsifications is incapable of divesting
Jesus' resurrection of its hiddenness. The *theologia resurrectionis* must
not be equated with a *theologia gloriae*, which is not a possibility open
to man in the fallen world; its relation to such a theology is like that of
the truth to an error which believes it can appeal to the truth.

The hiddenness of the resurrection aeon is an insight which the
theology of the resurrection cannot lose. If in the resurrection the
Kyrios were to cast aside the veil, then the resurrection would be an
event visible to all mankind and accessible also to unbelief. The resurrection of Jesus would in that case partake of the nature of proof and
would no longer need to call forth a decision of faith. Consequently it is
also mistaken to attempt to explain the resurrection of Jesus as a partial
parousia—which only serves to obscure our understanding of both
parousia and resurrection alike. The resurrection is not in fact a fragmentary visible manifestation, but the beginning of the resurrection
world under a veil. As the eschatological event the resurrection aeon
must be hidden from the world of the penultimate. If the eschaton were
visible, then it would be an object in this world and a conditional entity.
It is only because the eschatological reality of Jesus' resurrection is a
veiled one that a continuance of the old aeon is conceivable despite its
presence, and only thus is the lordship of the Risen One no part of the
conditionalities of this world. So long as this world lasts, the Kyrios can
exert his universal lordship only under a veil. But it is precisely by
being King in secret that the Risen One can exercise his absolute claim
upon the world as a whole. Thus the hiddenness of the resurrection
aeon is the ground on which a lordship of the Kyrios is possible without
objectification, and thereby without limitation of his power and without
annihilation of the old aeon. Because of the veil, the majesty of the
Kyrios becomes bearable for the world of the Fall. The hiddenness of
the new aeon is thus seen at the same time to be an expression of grace.
The attempt to make visible the reality of the resurrection means either
profanation, or else fanaticism which fails to grasp that the resurrection
is the beginning of God's eschatological acts and attempts to anticipate
the eschatological consummation.

If the resurrection aeon is a hidden reality, then that means that all
dogmatic statements on the meaning of Jesus' resurrection are set in
this key. Our assertions about God's action on the world through the
resurrection or about the action of the ever-present Risen Christ, or

about the opening up of a new world perspective with the establishing of a new interpretation of the world, are valid only when their content is set so to speak within the bracket of the concept of 'hiddenness'. There is no point in the old aeon at which this invisibility of the resurrection reality can be broken through. The new Christ-epoch, like the Christ Spirit and the Church of the Lord, is not a thing-like phenomenon that can be observed, measured and represented, but an invisible reality which is known not by psychic means, but solely in faith. If the existential relation to the present Kyrios is not conceived as an encounter in the secrecy of faith, then it must be secularized and become Christ mysticism. That indeed is precisely the characteristic feature of Christ mysticism: that it does not take the hiddenness of the Risen One seriously, but seeks to break through the veil to see, to enjoy and to uncover. In contrast to this, the existentialist fellowship with Christ assents to the veiled presence which discloses itself not to ecstasy but to faith. The same is true of the hiddenness of the spiritual dynamic of the Church. Here the boundaries are most precise between fanatical activism and ecstatic sanctification cults and also inactive quietism, and faith in the working of the Holy Spirit. The hiddenness of the Spirit determining conduct does not involve dispensing with the ethical shaping of life in ways that become visible, just as the invisibility of the Lord's Church does not mean the abandonment of all objective realization of its life, but it makes plain that all the effects of the Spirit do not make the Spirit himself visible and that the Church's objective results provide no measure of the living reality itself. In much the same way, we can also speak only of the veiled character of the meaning of nature, of the secret quality of the eschatological orientation of history, and of the hiddenness of the focal point of history. It is only the concept of the hiddenness of the resurrection aeon that safeguards the theological view of nature and of history against the tendency towards a Christian glorification of nature and an idealist glorification of history. So also Christian ontology lives not by seeing the new Dasein but by faith that the new man is 'hidden' with Christ in God.[29]

The hiddenness of the resurrection aeon which is already now invisibly present *contains an eschatological tension*. The eschaton of the resurrection reality, as the event by which creation and redemption are fulfilled, is on the one hand already present under a veil, but on the other hand the visibleness of the old aeon continues to exist. The eschatological tension accordingly lasts so long as the hiddenness of the resurrection

[29] Col. 3.3 f.; I John 3.2.

has not yet reached the unveiling of the consummation. The hiddenness of the resurrection aeon accordingly determines an intermediate stage between the resurrection of Jesus and the final consummation by which the hiddenness is ended. As long as the hidden lordship of the Kyrios endures, faith is not yet made perfect in sight. But the trouble about the eschatological tension is, that in this time of the hiddenness of his kyrios-ship the possibility still remains for the old world to resist the new Lord. The veiling of the resurrection aeon means a time of unbelief, for which the message of the resurrection is a 'stumbling block' and 'foolishness'. It provides room for the struggle of anti-Christian forces against the lordship of Christ and for satanic revolt against the breaking in of the world of life. This is the time of seduction and of apostasy, precisely because the Christ aeon has already dawned.[30] Faith begins to doubt the truth of the revelation given to it, and the gravity of its decisions becomes the greater for the enormity of the responsibility. Thus the continuance of the power of death in the old aeon also becomes a burden to the faith which knows of the eternal life of the new aeon.

In keeping with the situation between the resurrection of Jesus and the consummation in the *telos*, the outlook of the Christian believer has an orientation which is essentially eschatological in character. Faith looks back on the one hand to the finished act of salvation in the Risen Christ. It knows itself spiritually united with the world of the resurrection actually present, and it has a part in its life. But on the other hand faith also looks forward, for the hiddenness of this life presses for a disclosure in the eschatological future. Thus the believing community is harnessed in between the perfect tense of the resurrection of Jesus and the future tense of the *telos*, itself wearing the veil that is over the resurrection aeon—and is for that reason a waiting and hoping Church.

[30] Ideas belonging to demonology and satanology cannot be eliminated from the thought of Paul, nor from the conceptual world of Jesus. The demonstration of Zoroastrian influence would be no argument against the validity of such statements.

VIII

THE AEON OF CHRIST'S LORDSHIP

THE consummation of the resurrection reality is summed up in the statement of the 'aeon of Christ's lordship'. In it there comes the unfolding and realization of that which had its beginning in the eschatological event of the resurrection. But we can speak properly of the lordship of Christ in its consummated form only when on the one hand we conceive it in a specifically eschatological perspective and when on the other hand we expound it as the *telos* in all the fulness of its manifold appearances, activities and phases.

I. THE ESCHATOLOGICAL PERSPECTIVE

At this point we must ask what kind of thinking is appropriate in principle and in method to the biblical revelation. This raises the problem of the Bible's eschatological 'world view' and at the same time requires us to show the grounds of that linear thinking that is so characteristic of the eschatological perspective.

(a) The Biblical View of the World

(i) The Rejection of the Longitudinal Dimension

There is certainly no lack of dispute among modern theologians as to what we must understand by the eschatological outlook in the Christian thinking that derives from the resurrection of Jesus. The biblical thinking which unfolds in a longitudinal dimension encounters resolute theological opposition. *An eschatological view that is essentially linear and longitudinal implies the necessity of a 'succession' of events: it means a horizontal progression in which the whole eschatological process moves lengthwise.* Such a view, however, is always rejected wherever time and eternity are sharply opposed to one another in philosophical ways. Since according to this theory all the lines of time run together into a suprahistoric point of eternity, there can then only be a simultaneousness in the eschatological statements and events, but never a succession of eschatological stages. This means that all longitudinal perspectives are abandoned in favour of a vertical one, so that only perpendicular parallels, but not horizontal extension in length, are recognized as legitimate forms of expression for theology.

The theses of Althaus provide an example of this: 'It is impossible to order the objects of our expectation in a clear succession of historic events in time.' Any attempt to do so must lead to 'hopeless difficulties'. 'The consummation here and beyond cannot be related in terms of succession, despite our temporal impressions of the temporal succession of death and the Last Day.'[1]

Althaus therefore sums up as follows: 'Eschatology does not present a picture of the Last Things as a sequence first of death and then what is beyond death, secondly of the end of history followed by what is beyond history.' We have therefore 'to teach along with the whole Church the essential unity and substantial simultaneousness of death and judgment, of homecoming to Christ and resurrection'.

The objection to every kind of linear thinking is given added force by the following philosophical and theological considerations. The concept of 'preparation', of a 'preliminary stage', and the idea of a later 'completion' logically contradict the concept of 'consummation'. Rational reflection says: either the fulness of salvation begins after death, in which case all that still comes after that is robbed of its force; or else a real decision is to be awaited only at the Last Day, in which case death is not as yet followed by salvation and the hope of going home to Christ is therefore robbed of its force. The logical dilemma between devaluing the judgment of death in favour of the Last Judgment and *vice versa* devaluing the Last Judgment in favour of the judgment of death is according to Althaus irresolvable. But Althaus believes that he can get round this logical difficulty by means of a doctrine of concomitance and intermingling instead of succession. Thus logic achieves a victory over the linear perspective of the Bible's eschatological world picture and over the proliferous fulness of primitive Christian thinking, which expresses itself precisely in terms of this longitudinal dimension.

Particular weight attaches to this problem of perspective in view of the assertion of an 'interregnum' under the special rule of Christ. Undoubtedly this conception has a most unhappy history both in the Church and in theology—so much so that both in the official teaching of the Church and in dogmatics, scripture passages of this kind are usually passed over in silence. There seems to be all the more justification for such theological aloofness, since the great Confessions of the Church and the Reformation reduce the eschatological world picture of

[1] *Die letzten Dinge*[4], pp. 75 f.

the Bible, and restrict the manifold variety of biblical statements to those bearing witness to the return of Jesus to judgment, to the general resurrection of the dead, and to eternal life. On the other hand it was believed one could appeal to Article XVII of the Augsburg Confession, with its rejection of the doctrine of the 'millennium'. It was precisely this doctrine which was in continual danger of misuse by fanatics and gave scope for the discussion of this range of questions by groups and personalities who are outside the Church and do not stand within the orbit of what is recognized by the Church's theology. These assertions about the 'millennium' with their lack of theological safeguards and their fundamental want of adequate grounding have brought discredit on the biblical 'substance' itself and on a concern which theoretically is not to be so lightly rejected.[2]

Against this very kind of 'millennial' thinking Althaus brings his comprehensive criticism to bear.[3] His attack is from four different directions:

The idea of a Messianic interregnum, so his argument here runs, derives from Zoroastrianism and is the legacy of late Jewish apocalyptic of the kind to be seen in the Apocalypses of Enoch, Baruch and II (4) Esdras. To be sure, the pointing out of this, though doubtless historically necessary, does not seem at all conclusive, since it does not as yet imply any judgment on the truth of the actual content. The ideas of angels and of satanology are also found in the same sources without Althaus making theological objections to them. So it would have to be asked why specifically the statements about an 'interregnum' must be rejected as untenable.

Secondly, this critical attack cannot claim to be in accord with scripture either. Althaus is compelled to concede that the message of Paul in I Cor. 15.23 ff. and of John in Rev. 20 unquestionably speaks of an 'interregnum' under the lordship of Christ, but in face of these Bible passages it is necessary according to Althaus 'to take seriously our fundamental principle that obedience to the word of God does not bind us to individual theological ideas of primitive Christianity, but in fact makes us free in regard to them'. This Reformation principle must certainly be accepted, yet here the counter-question has to be asked: In these scripture passages do we not, also and precisely in Paul, have to do with central insights which we cannot ignore without dangerously curtailing the biblical truth? Is it not here a matter of grasping the

---

[2] J. Sickenberger, 'Das tausendjährige Reich in der Apokalypse', *Festschrift für S. Merker*, 1922.   [3] Cf. *op. cit.*, pp. 286 ff.

peculiarity of the Bible's eschatological thinking as such, which resists our modern attempts to level it down? Nor must we disregard the fact that bound up with this are other important statements which cannot be passed over in silence but must be given their proper right. The statement that 'The dead in Christ shall rise first' (I Thess. 4.16), taken in conjunction with the phrase, 'If by any means I might attain unto the resurrection of the dead' (Phil. 3.11), makes it plain that Paul has in mind a progression in the eschatological consummation and doubtless in terms of Rom. 8.17 ff. lays down distinctions. In face of this scriptural fact it is necessary, in contrast to Althaus' critical thesis, to demand on the contrary that our theological thinking should be corrected by this scriptural insight and that the latter should not be obscured.

A third objection is: 'The time for the fulfilment of Old Testament prophecies has come to an end with the coming of Christ.' This thesis could hardly be proved theologically, if it is understood that the resurrection of Jesus is a first eschatological fact which aims at a consummation. The first coming of Jesus is certainly the beginning of the fulfilment, but not as yet the final consummation—which also explains why a great number of prophetic promises have in fact not yet been fulfilled.

Finally, the idea of the 'interregnum' as a 'pre-consummation' is rejected as theologically untenable and contradictory. 'In both respects it comes to grief on the point of the relation between the millennium and the return of Christ.' The consummation of the Church and the consummation of the world must not according to Althaus, be separated from one another. The general resurrection and the consummation of the Church are not isolated from each other. 'Our resurrection is not only our own resurrection, but the complete renewal of the world.' 'Between the two aeons, between history and the consummation . . . there can be no intermediate stage.'

These critical reflections unequivocally establish the antithesis to the longitudinal dimension of the perspective in which biblical thinking sees the world.

(ii) *The Grounding of the Eschatological Dynamic*

The question this raises is, Does this postulate of static simultaneity accord with the eschatological perspective of biblical thought? We have not, however, to ask whether the thesis fits logically into the rational pattern of thought, and whether conversely the eschatological dynamic of the biblical view of the world shatters our powers of thought and for that reason must be rejected as discomfiting. In accordance with the conclusions that arise from the theology of the resurrection, we have to state that *biblical eschatology is essentially determined by the principle of succession and progression.* To be sure, we agree with Althaus that it is impossible to order the eschatological events 'in a clear succession'. That is neither the task of biblical theology nor its real concern, but of course the vital thing is, to make plain the essential features of this linear eschatological thought. There is no doubt, however much this insight may run counter to what has so far been the eschatological thought pattern of accepted theology, that this very idea of successive stages is the characteristic feature of primitive Christian and biblical eschatology. Precisely if we would understand it, it is essential to pay attention to the longitudinal dimension, the eschatological horizontal. The special grounding of this, too, is given in the reality of the resurrection of Jesus.

First of all we have to take seriously the central biblical concept of *aparchē*, 'firstfruits', 'beginning'. The following impressive testimonies must be understood anew in their essential theological content. The Risen One is designated as 'the firstfruits of them that slept'. This assertion, however, introduces a process of development, a succession of stages: 'But every man in his own order: Christ, the firstfruits . . . afterward they that are Christ's . . . then the end' (I Cor. 15.20, 23 f.). The same line of thought is to be found in I Thess. 4.14 ff.: because the resurrection of Jesus is the foundation of all hope for the future, God through Christ will bring the dead with him to glory, whereby 'the dead in Christ shall rise first; then we which are alive'. The statement of hope for the future is here just as important as the differentiation between 'before' and 'after'. This Pauline insight is confirmed to be general to primitive Christianity by the differentiation between a first resurrection and a later general resurrection in Rev. 20.5. Entirely in harmony with this are the statements: Christ is 'the firstborn among many brethren'; the Christians therefore appear as the chosen from out the *massa perditionis*, and so as the beginning of a new humanity (Rom. 8.29). They are 'firstfruits of his creatures' (James 1.18; Rev. 14.4), 'firstborn of every creature' (Col. 1.15 f.). Here again the clear succession of stages is brought out. Christ—Church—mankind—cosmos. The Church is 'firstfruits', provisional part, first beginning, on which lies the promise of perfection (Rom. 11.16). Through these assertions runs the fundamental idea that from the first fruits there comes a ripening and a further development up to the harvest.

Secondly, the eschatological dynamic expresses itself in the tension which is characteristic of biblical eschatology. The resurrection of Jesus marks the situation of the Christian community as one of 'waiting'.[4] Since the Easter act of God, the world is secretly on the move. The Church therefore lives in eager expectation of that consummation of the kingdom of God which has begun with the resurrection of Jesus. The long-suffering of God waits for 'fruits' while the Church of Jesus is summoned to wait 'in patience'. It waits for the 'redemption of the body', and as 'firstfruits of the Spirit' the Christians 'long for' the hour of consummation (Rom. 8.22 ff.), and look forward to a cosmic renewal (II Peter 3.13). Again from the concept of 'waiting' comes the progressive sequence of sowing, increase of growth, and bearing fruit until the harvest day of God (John 4.35; Rev. 14.15 f.; Gal. 6.7 f.). This expectation on the part of the Church, however, is more particularly one of most intense movement, because it is a burning desire to reach the goal, to win the prize of the contest, to triumph in the race, i.e. to be one of those present at the 'pre-consummation' of the first resurrection.[5]

The classical witness to this most tense eschatological expectation is furnished by the seer John with his vision of the course of the 'last' events in their necessary succession. The 'souls of the martyrs', although already secure in the peace of Christ that belongs to the new aeon, cry out in face of the continuance of the great tribulation on earth, 'How long?' Still the consummation of the lordship of Christ in all its fulness has not yet come, still there is tension and waiting not only within the confines of the old aeon, but also a longing on the part of those who 'are fallen asleep in Christ' (Rev. 6.9, 10 f.). The idea that death, the consummation of the Church and the end of the world should be simultaneous is here out of the question. Every attempt to neutralize or exclude what we know of a 'church expectant' must be condemned as contrary to the Bible.

A third argument, to which special weight must be attached, draws attention to the fact that biblical eschatology is conditioned by thinking in terms of aeons. The essential features of this doctrine of aeons again begin to manifest themselves in the light of the turning point in the resurrection of Jesus, that absolute, eschatological turning point of the ages. Hence we have to do with the development of the essential features of the Bible's grandiose eschatological picture of the world, with the biblical doctrine of the aeons which supplant each other and follow

[4] James 1.3 f.; Gal. 5.5; Titus 2.13; Heb. 9.28.
[5] Phil. 3.14; I Cor. 9.24 f.; I Tim. 6.12; II Tim. 4.7; Heb. 12.1; II Tim. 2.5.

each other. Even this insight will not enable us to arrange the Bible's statements about eschatological things in a logical and flawless order, yet neither is it the task of theology to construct a rational system of eschatology by dispensing with vital insights of primitive Christian faith, but the important thing is to present the whole of the primitive Christian eschatological witness in scientific form, even when that means breaking the bounds of our logical way of thinking.

This seeming departure from the usual way hitherto taken by the recognised theology of the Church does not by any means imply that we renounce all claim to legitimacy as measured by the Confessions and take our stand on the Reformation principle of recognizing the Bible alone as *regula et norma*. On the contrary, it would be a disastrous misunderstanding of Luther if we were ready to let the still unexhausted wealth of biblical insights remain buried merely because the Confessions do not speak explicitly of them. Article XVII's criticism in the Augsburg Confession is directed not against the biblical witness of Revelation 20, but against the misuse of it. The fanatical visionary ideal expressed in the *'judaica opinio'* that the *'pii regnum mundi occupaturi sint'*, that an earthly Christian world kingdom is to be asserted parallel with other earthly world kingdoms, has nothing to do with the real concern of eschatology. The judgment of the *Augustana* rightly rejects any confusing of fanatical millenarianism with an eschatological realism.[6]

With regard to the fundamental significance of the biblical doctrine of aeons, we have to consider the following aspects.

The resurrection of Jesus is the decisive proof that God, according to an eternal plan, despite all the circumstances of the present, through all the happenings of history and through the whole course of the ages, is guiding all things to his own predetermined goal. 'It is a question', as E. Stauffer says, 'of the absolute temporal priority of God's plan and will over all the "accidents" of history.'[7] The hidden wisdom of God at work already before the beginning of the successions of aeons, the

---

[6] Contemporary theology should not forget that not only the theology of the Early Church, but also Lutheran theologians like R. Frank, K. von Hofmann, W. Löhe, H. Bezzel, to say nothing of such Württemberg fathers as Bengel and Oetinger, very definitely took the Bible's eschatological view of the world seriously and knew of a doctrine of aeons. R. Frank (*System der christlichen Wahrheit* II, § 47, 6, 463) emphatically brings out the 'successive stages of the consummation', the 'provisional character of the goal', and thus an 'eschatological development'. Significant is his verdict: 'And altogether, the appeal to the Confession of the church (Article XVII of the Augsburg Confession), on the ground that it rejects the millennium, rests upon an unhistorical and literal approach which is such a misjudgment of its confessional character that we must refrain from refuting it on this one point.'

[7] *New Testament Theology*, p. 54.

divine *oikonomia*, designs and executes its world plan, which culminates in the resurrection of Jesus and from that point onwards presses on towards the final consummation.[8] The vital point, however, is the biblical principle of a development by stages of this divine plan of salvation. But that gives the idea of a partial pre-consummation its theological necessity and its fundamental importance. In accordance with this 'economy', God's plan of creation and salvation does not realize itself at once, not with a single stroke which produces the total transformation, but through a succession of world periods, of 'ages', of 'aeons'. In the perspective of Jesus' resurrection, the place of the metaphysical separation of time and eternity is taken by the advancing universal divine plan of worlds and ages—namely, that 'mysterious, hidden wisdom of God which God ordained before the world unto our glory' (I Cor. 2.7), so that only 'in the ages to come' will the riches of God's grace be disclosed in all its fulness (Eph. 2.7). All 'ages' are exactly defined by God and fulfil their part in a strict sequence, one following after the other, *in saecula saeculorum*. There is thus an 'eternal progression of aeons according to God's 'eternal' plan. Biblical eschatology, therefore, thinks essentially in terms of the course of the aeons, their emergence and their consummation. It is a case of aeon periods which, measured by our standards of time, are 'eternal', apparently 'supra-temporal', although they, too, are not by any means unlimited. An 'eternal aeon' accordingly represents a segment within the divine world plan, without it being possible to say of such an aeon that it is 'timeless', that it is without beginning and without end.[9]

To understand the doctrine of aeons, we must recognize that the biblical view of aeons has the character of perspective. Just as from the standpoint of an observer, the trees in an avenue immediately beside him stand far apart, and then behind and before him come ever closer

[8] Cf. Eph. 3.2; 3.9-11; Col. 1.15-17; John 1.3-10; Heb. 1.3, 10.

[9] The concept 'world-epoch' to render *aiōn* is an inappropriate term in so far as our present idea of time and chronology is valid only for a tiny sector within the vast periods of the aeons. The different meaning of the words used in the biblical concepts *'olam* and *aiōn* as distinct from *chronos*, the word for earthly time, therefore must not be overlooked. 'Aeon' can accordingly be understood to mean eras and periods of time whose endless succession is used to describe the concept 'eternity'. Aeon can also mean infinite time, in the sense of the eternity of God—which, however, means that the concept is then identical with something beyond time, since God always was and always will be. Again, aeon can mean a long, yet limited period of time, a world epoch, a world age, in contrast and distinction from the 'eternity' of God. Finally, it must not be overlooked that there is not one single world-epoch, but a countless series of successive world-periods, as is typically expressed in the antithesis of 'this age' and 'the age to come' (cf. H. Sasse in *TWNT* I, 1932, p. 197).

together until they finally appear to merge into a single point, so for the biblical eye the present aeon is widely extended and painted in great detail—all the more so, since within it lies the focal point of the eschatological perspective, the resurrection of Jesus—while the preceding and succeeding aeons are presented in shortened perspective, so that the 'beginning' and 'end' of the sequence of aeons find mention only in a single sentence. The important thing however remains, that we have to do with a succession of aeons.

The theological purpose of this exposition of the Bible's eschatological view of the world, with its perspective of the different aeons and of their progressive dynamic, is to overcome the unbiblical curtailment of the eschatological statements of primitive Christianity which widely prevails in theology and in the Church and to bring out plainly on the contrary their richness and flexibility. It is a question of understanding the tremendously dramatic quality of the biblical view of the world, of leading away from the static philosophy of circular thinking or a metaphysical dialectic and on to the biblical dynamic of Christian eschatology, of advancing from the flats of foreshortened theological statements to a grasp of the eschatological depth-dimension.

(b) The Intermediate State

If the eschatological perspective establishes a succession of stages in the 'end events', then that implies in principle the possibility of an 'intermediate state', that is to say, a form of existence between death and the resurrection of the dead. Theology takes a divided attitude towards this complex of questions, whose problematical character must not be overlooked.

(i) The Criticism of the Concept

The critical attitude on the part of theology towards this problem has found twofold expression. The round rejection of the possibility of any 'intermediate state' at all is found in P. Althaus. In consistent pursuit of his time-eternity metaphysic, he sees the crux of the problem in the question of the balance between the hope for the individual and the hope for the kingdom, of the relationship of the invidividual to the community, to humanity, to the cosmos, of the individual consummation in its relation to the total consummation. Accordingly there must arise an intolerable conflict between the coming to Christ of the Christian through his death, and the appearance of Christ at the last day before the whole world. The more perfect the state after death is conceived to be, the more the importance of the parousia is diminished. This leads

Althaus to speak of a 'disastrous either-or', for there is a complete lack of unity in the results of theological reflection—a double judgment, a double life, and a double consummation. Thus what should form a unity is torn apart: body and soul, the individual and the community, the fate of men and the fate of the world.

Hence Althaus frames the following postulates: 'We can only escape from this if we refrain from ordering the two elements of hope, the world beyond death and the last day, in an objective succession. . . . Is time as we know it not everywhere bordered by, and stranded upon, the last day? Does the last day not as it were lie all around us, so that for all of us our dying makes us contemporaneous with the end of history, with the coming of the kingdom, with the judgment?'[10] The idea of an 'intermediate state' would accordingly make the resurrection of the dead 'empty of meaning and a matter of indifference'. ' "Before" the resurrection we know nothing save death, and that the dead are in God's hand. That is enough.'

In the face of these arguments we must ask what it is that determines such a judgment. Certainly, it does not derive from the ideas and the world view of biblical eschatology. It is obviously derived from the logical principles of philosophy and the fundamental ideas of a metaphysic of timelessness. Is it permissible to reduce what are indisputably biblical insights for the sake of a logical system? It is not with a flawless ordering of events in an 'objective' succession that we have here to do, but with the recognition in principle of a series of stages. But wherever theology is resolved to teach a world development and world perfection according to God's eschatological plan, there the 'intermediate state' also finds a necessary place.

H. Thielicke, too, has taken a critical attitude to the problems of the 'intermediate state' in question here,[11] although he exercises very notable caution in his judgment. If we radically pursue to its conclusion, as Thielicke does, the idea of the total dying of man as a whole person, in which there can be no dividing of man into body and soul, then it seems a simple step, and one demanded by logic, to exclude the possibility of an 'intermediate state'. If we assume the complete extinction of the psycho-somatic Ego in death, then dying can logically be followed only by the resurrection as a *creatio ex nihilo* without an 'intermediate state.'

Thielicke himself, however, has rightly had misgivings as to whether this 'theological roundedness' of the argument does justice to biblical

[10] *Die letzten Dinge*⁴, p. 152.　　　　[11] Cf. *Tod und Leben*, 1946.

thought. 'Might it not be that this roundedness means at the same time a constriction as compared with the richness and the flowing abundance of biblical statements?'[12] In face of all the insistence on logic, a feeling of scepticism begins to arise. The reason of man cannot be the final authority; it is itself involved in the Fall and subject to limitations. The 'illumination on one side spells a darkening on the other ... therefore caution is required'. At all events, Thielicke avers, the dying of the whole person is no criterion to be set against the declarations of scripture and these must not be dismissed as 'heterogeneous' or 'relics of hellenism'.

Thus in regard to the 'intermediate state' Thielicke comes to the following conclusion: There are indeed no central biblical statements on this subject, but all the same it is undeniable that there is a 'relatively frequent recurrence' of those statements about an 'intermediate state'. That before the resurrection of the dead there 'is something in the nature of being at home with Christ, and conversely also being far from him, must be acknowledged'.[13] This 'intermediate state', however, must not be regarded as determined by human characteristics which last beyond death, not by the quality of the 'soul', but by 'the character of my Lord, who cannot leave me'. 'At all events this statement does not in any way provide for a doctrine of immortality nor for the assumption of a division of the Ego. The biblical anthropology is consequently neither confirmed nor called in question by the statements about an intermediate state.'[14] Thus Thielicke's position, unlike that of Althaus, definitely leaves the possibility of an 'intermediate state' theologically open, however reserved his judgment.

(ii) *The Meaning contained in the Concept*

In developing the biblical eschatological perspective we are compelled, contrary to all critical objections, to make a positive theological assertion concerning the 'intermediate state'.[15] *What makes an 'intermediate state' possible is God's eschatological dealing with man which is grounded in the resurrection of Jesus and which by successive stages leads man towards the perfection which God has planned. It is here ultimately*

[12] *Op. cit.*, p. 218.   [13] *Op. cit.*, p. 220.   [14] *Op. cit.*, p. 221.
[15] Under the influence of the statements of the Bible I find myself having to alter my negative views on the 'intermediate state', as advanced in my work *Unsterblichkeit oder Auferstehung*, Berlin 1930. The biblical view is moreover confirmed also by the experiences of Christoph Blumhardt. I would refer also to Wilhelm Horkel, *Botschaft von Drüben*, Munich 1948; and Paul Le Seur, *Nach dem Sterben*, Wuppertal 1950, with whom I fundamentally and gladly agree. Cf. also W. Mundle, 'Das Problem des Zwischenzustandes', *Festschrift für A. Jülicher*, 1927.

a question of 'being transformed' into the image of Christ 'from glory to glory' (II Cor. 3.18). Thus we agree with Thielicke that the foundation of such an 'intermediate state' lies not in man himself, not in the immortal soul, not in a division of the Ego, but solely in the work of God, in that relationship of man to God which is confirmed in the resurrection of Jesus. This communication with God, however, is valid for every man, even for the godless (Ps. 139.8, 11 f.) because this relationship has its ground not merely in the quality of the personal spirit of man, but above all in the will and plan of God.

The meaning of the 'intermediate state' lies in its being a partial pre-consummation, an intermediate and preliminary stage towards the coming total perfection. As a state of 'being in between' it has the character of 'waiting'. Waiting characterizes the whole basic situation of man after the Fall: human existence becomes a waiting for redemption, for consummation. The real meaning of this waiting, however, is grounded in the resurrection of Jesus. Without this, 'waiting' would be without hope, a permanent torture, a mere waiting for judgment. When related to the Risen One, however, there is a hopeful, blessed and joyful waiting. The waiting of the 'intermediate state' is anticipatory joy, and as such certainly true joy, but not yet the joy that is finally fulfilled and perfected for all who fall asleep in faith in Christ. For the unbelieving, however, this waiting becomes painful and distressing, because of the mystery of God's forthcoming action.

Theologically, therefore, the 'intermediate state' can be spoken of only in such a way that at once two lines are drawn which bring out clearly the provisional separation which takes place between men immediately after death. According to the Bible man comes to 'Sheol', to the realm of the dead, each 'to his own place'.[16]

For the non-Christian and the unbeliever, the 'intermediate state' means an existence far from God. Even this mode of existence involves differentiation. The measure of the anguish corresponds to the measure of the guilt, of the apostasy and of the separation from God. Anguish and remorse can here make plain the difference between this and the earthly mode of existence, because once earthly limitations have been overcome, then indeed the true insight is given into the situation as it is before God.[17] Secondly, this state is characterized as one of waiting in dire distress for God's final judgment of rejection. As a marginal possibility and a last offer of rescue, there is then for the 'godless' in this intermediate state the fact that the lordship of the Risen Christ

[16] Luke 16.28; Acts 1.25.   [17] Luke 16.19 f.; Matt. 5.26; 18.34.

embraces also the world of the dead. The Gospel proclamation of the Kyrios who 'descended into hell' attains here the vital fulness of its splendour.[18] But with the assumption of this last message of salvation in the 'intermediate state' for the world of men before and apart from Christianity, a positive relationship to God is once more restored. Thus the resurrection of Jesus sheds a special light on the 'intermediate state', which accordingly does not have the neutral character of a merely imperfect mode of being on the part of the dead, but must be understood as a disclosure of the true situation of man without Christ. This being in 'hell' means an existence of dire tension, of torturing unrest in the knowledge of having failed to attain life's goal—an existence in which our utter and complete dependence on the Risen One is made unsparingly plain. The state of waiting in 'hell' 'between' death and resurrection does not mean purgatory in the sense of an anthropological possibility of self-cleansing or purification in the next world, but implies a clarification of man's in itself hopeless situation in the light of the resurrection of Jesus. To take seriously the credal phrase 'descended into hell' is to discover the rightfulness and the necessity of a theological discussion of the 'intermediate state'.

The second line of thought which seeks to define the 'intermediate state' relates to those who believe in Christ. To their union with Christ there corresponds the peace and blessedness which is now unbroken and no longer restricted and veiled by the limitations and sufferings of earth. Four things according to scripture are characteristic of this 'intermediate state'.

Those who 'are fallen asleep in Christ' rest in the peace of God; they are liberated from the struggle, toil and suffering of their earthly pilgrimage; they 'sleep' under God's eyes and are secure in God's hand.[19]

Yet at the same time this 'resting' is not equivalent to some euphemistic phrase about 'being in death', but denotes the conscious joy of 'being at home with the Lord'.[20] 'The dying of Christians means their departure to the heavenly Kyrios.'[21] Hence this 'intermediate state' is in contrast to 'hell' a 'life in paradise',[22] the joyous arrival at the goal, a blessed foretaste of the glory that is in process of fulfilment.

But thirdly, this life in the light and power of the Risen Christ during

---

[18] I Peter 3.19; Eph. 4.9 f.; Phil. 2.10; Col. 2.15; I Tim. 2.10; Rom. 10.7; Acts 1.18; 2.24.
[19] I Thess. 4.13 ff.; II Peter 3.4; Luke 23.46; Heb. 4.9 ff.; I Peter 4.19; Matt. 27.52; I Cor. 15.20; Mark 5.39; John 5.24 f.; 8.51; 11.26; I John 3.2, 14.
[20] II Cor. 5.8; Phil. 1.23.
[21] E. Stauffer, New Testament Theology, pp. 210 ff.
[22] Luke 23.43; Rom. 14.8.

the 'intermediate state' must not be misunderstood as a monotonous existence in the form of a 'sleep of the soul'. Despite all the 'resting from their labours', it denotes activity and conscious personal being on the part of the disciples who have fallen asleep in Christ. It is a question here of their new membership of the 'church above' which in intimate union with Christ exercises a priestly service while in the intermediate state. This service takes shape by beginning the 'heavenly liturgy' of adoration and praise on the one hand and of intercession and blessing on the other. An effectual working of the 'church of the firstborn which are written in heaven' and of 'the spirits of just men made perfect'[23] may be legitimately spoken of in this sense.[24]

Finally, however, it is plain that even in this state of 'having come home' there is an element of 'not yet'. This 'intermediate state' does indeed mean having reached the goal, but not yet the final goal, not yet the whole fulness of the riches of heaven. It is a partial anticipation of the consummation in the form of communion with Christ—it is a pre-consummation—but not yet the resurrection of the body, not yet the glorification which is bound up with the appearing of Jesus. This idea of a blessed waiting for a final consummation cannot be eliminated from primitive Christian thought. There remains the longing for a 'house which is from heaven', which is 'eternal'.[25] The pre-consummated Church of those who 'have come home' knows of the dire struggles of the Church militant, and waits for its ultimate victory until 'their

[23] Heb. 12.23.
[24] At this point the Roman Catholic doctrine of the ministry of the 'saints' has established itself, though certainly by perverting the biblical facts. Quite apart from any higher ethical quality being ascribed to the 'church of the saints', that 'church above' is never the object of an appeal for intercessory support. The extension of these ideas by the richly imaginative speculations of Mariology is well suited to bring the whole primitive Christian view of a 'church above' into discredit. It thus seems all the more misguided when H. Asmussen takes up the ideas of Roman theology, but certainly not of the New Testament, and speaks emphatically of the peculiar 'place' which Mary occupies in the realm of the redeemed. It is certainly true that every believing Christian 'is redeemed for admission to a definite place' (*Maria, die Mutter Gottes*, 1951), but we are told nothing of how such stations are organized and must not go beyond the limits set us. The ascription to Mary of an extraordinary priestly ministry in heaven, however, oversteps these boundaries, is the product of theological speculation, and prejudices the Christological substance of the Christian proclamation. True as it is that the Confession of the Evangelical Lutheran Church recognizes the priestly ministry of intercession by the 'saints in heaven' (II Macc. 15.14), nevertheless their 'invocation' is passionately rejected. But as far as the invocation of Mary is concerned, it is said unequivocally in clear rejection of this 'false doctrine': 'For what need would there be of Christ, if Mary could do it?', *Conf. Aug.* XXI, 10, 14 f., 27 f. Cf. *Apologie* XXI, also W. Künneth, 'Mariologie—lutherische Tradition oder Irrtum?', *Deutsch. Pfarrersbl.* Nov. 1951, No. 21.
[25] II Cor. 5.1 ff.

fellow-servants also and their brethren should be fulfilled'.[26] This state of waiting in the pre-consummation is therefore not eternal but lasts until the eschatological reveille which comes with the parousia and the consummation of the Church, and on the other hand until the judgment of the world and the resurrection of the dead. For the disciples who have fallen asleep this waiting period of the 'intermediate state' strains towards the coming of Christ's kingdom and the consummation of the whole cosmic world.

Thus biblical eschatology speaks of an 'intermediate state', despite all theological assertions of a philosophical or rational kind. This truth E. Stauffer, too, has rightly rescued again from oblivion: 'The theology of the New Testament is *theologia in conspectu mortis*. For that reason alone the question, "What becomes of our dead?" has been a cardinal one for it from the start.' Primitive Christianity is 'unanimous in its fundamental conviction that death does not yet bring the final solution. The state after death is only an intermediate solution which points beyond itself to the final state which is to come. It is on this last, therefore, that the interest of the early Christian thinkers is concentrated.'[27]

2. THE ACCOMPLISHING OF THE ESCHATOLOGICAL REVELATION

The consummation of the resurrection reality is summed up in the revelation of the lordship of Christ. Its accomplishing is marked by a series of events and takes its course in realities of the 'new' aeon, which admittedly cannot be ordered in a logical succession but rather partially overlap and intermingle with each other, but which we are nevertheless compelled to distinguish in thought. The accomplishing of the eschatological consummation therefore cannot be represented in the form of a number of points in a straight line, but has to be described by a series of statements standing side by side and by an exposition of various complexes of ideas, and only when we have taken all these into account and coordinated them with each other can we reflect the fulness of the Bible's eschatological insight.

(a) The Parousia of the Risen One

The understanding of the parousia stands in closest connection with the knowledge of the resurrection of Jesus. The parousia has its pre-

---

[26] Rev. 6.11.
[27] *Op. cit.*, pp. 210-13; cf. also Christian Stoll, 'Das Schicksal unserer Toten', *Jahrbuch des Martin-Luther Bundes*, 1946, pp. 62 f.

supposition in the reality of the resurrection, and brings the unveiling of it. The resurrection reality in the *telos* accordingly means from the viewpoint of the parousia the *emerging of the Risen Kyrios from his hiddenness*. Here, too, there again arises the question so important for eschatology: What is the character of this event of the parousia of the Risen One? In view of the new understanding of time and the world, it cannot be understood as the supra-temporal presence of Christ which is always in the process of coming. For in that case the parousia would in fact be no unveiling at all for this *world*, and therefore no consummation of the reality of the resurrection. But if the event of the parousia is not to be thought of in terms of the supra-temporal, just as little is it to be regarded as something that happens at the end of history.[28] A factual reality occurring at the end of history would indeed be seen in this world, but conversely would be no unveiling of the Risen One, for it is in the very nature of this world that it involves veiling, limitation, and renders impossible what the parousia is really meant to be. The event of the parousia can accordingly in substance be theologically understood only as the visible dawn of the new aeon of Christ's rule. With that we have defined also the form of the parousia, *viz.*—as the event of the consummation of history. The 'appearing' of the 'return' of Jesus is neither a timeless point in eternity nor a final point in the sphere of history, but the dawn of consummated historicality. This definition preserves to the full the purpose behind the idea of the parousia. On the one hand it brings out that in the parousia it is not a question of a mere idea or symbol but of the concrete reality of the historic Jesus, the Jesus crucified in history, who reveals himself as the Kyrios to this world which he has reconciled and to these men who have rejected him. To that extent it is correct to say that it is precisely history which must experience the unveiling of the Risen One. But on the other hand it is made clear that the parousia leads to a consummated history, that the overcoming of hiddenness brings about the renewal of historic man and the abolition of the laws of history that belong to the old aeon. History consummated in the parousia is history freed from the limitations of the old world. Thus the parousia surpasses all our powers of conception, not indeed destroying history, but taking its fruits and meaning up into itself and fulfilling them.

The parousia accordingly presents itself as the beginning of a world transformation, even if not yet of a final world consummation. The

---

[28] In criticism of the end of history, apocalyptic and millenarianism, P. Althaus has illuminatingly said all that is necessary, *op. cit.*, pp. 77-136, 142.

total world renewal introduced by the parousia has not yet attained its final fulfilment, for even the reign of Christ that begins with the return of Jesus bears the marks of the pre-consummation of the world, and is the prelude to the coming new creation. That the aeon of Christ's reign is not yet the *telos*, is one of the decisive insights of primitive Christianity[29] and as such must not be overlooked.

Two things are expressed in the parousia: first, the manifesting of the Risen One as a King in his glory, and also, secondly, the manifesting of the victory over the power of Satan.

In the parousia the lordship of the Kyrios is consummated in so far as it reveals itself to be an unbroken one. So long as the veil of the old aeon keeps hidden the majesty of the Kyrios, his lordship can be disputed and his death on the cross can be misunderstood, whether as a judicial murder, or the sacrificial death of an idealist or the punishment of a blasphemer. Correspondingly, the Church of the Lord, because of the hidden nature of the lordship of Christ, bears the 'form of a servant' until the parousia. The parousia of the Risen One is the decisive event in which all the dissonances arising from the hiddenness are removed and the glory of the Kyrios which was inherent already in the resurrection is made fully manifest. The Risen One discloses himself as the King in his glory, whose triumph the entire new world must serve. The parousia of the Risen One is the only possible proof of Christ, the only possible proof of God. For it is only when the hidden Lord becomes the manifest King in his glory that all resistance to his claim to rule collapses, that indeed every possibility of rebellion has the ground removed from under it. The 'return' of the Kyrios not only sets the crown to the recognition given by faith, for which what was hitherto invisible now appears in visible form, so that in the parousia faith itself is transformed into sight, but now it comes also to the recognition of the Kyrios by unbelief, which sees itself convicted of rebellion against Christ and at the same time, in the light of the unveiling, as broken rebellion. Whether belief or unbelief is in the right, is shown unequivocally only by the parousia. Thus the resurrection faith waits eagerly for its confirmation and consummation in the parousia in which it is made manifest for all the world to see, including also the opposition, that Christ is the Kyrios, and in which the confession of his lordship is consummated in a universal confession.[30] Before the parousia there can be no world confession, for the rise of such a confession is an eschatological event.

---

[29] I Cor. 15.23, 24 makes a clear separation between the two events.
[30] Phil. 2.10 f.; 3.20; Rev. 22.17, 20.

At the same time, the parousia shows itself as the unveiled triumph of the resurrection victory over the power of Satan. It thus becomes God's decisive assault upon the dominion of Satan in all aeons. When, in accordance with God's plan for the world, in God's eternal wisdom[31] Satan's time has run its course and the satanic world empire has grown to fullest maturity, God intervenes. He intervenes through the 'Son' who since the resurrection has been the hidden victor and the Kyrios. Christ's victory in the parousia takes place through the uncontested overthrow and destruction of the anti-Christian empire and its anti-Christian 'church'. This is the theological meaning of Revelation 19 with its witness to the 'binding of Satan for a thousand years'. This is not an indication of time in the sense of earthly chronology, but the description of a definite period of aeons. In contrast to the ideas of Zoroastrian dualism, it is clear here that the 'binding' of Satan does not take place in the 'struggle' between two equally matched parties, but is a sovereign act of the superior power of the Kyrios. Thus for the first time since the original creation the seductive power of Satan's influence is nullified. The rule of Christ reveals itself as the 'new' aeon liberated from all domination by Satan.

The course of the old world epoch and of history do not manifest the superiority of Christ; on the contrary, they are proof of an empire that is in opposition to God. When, however, in the parousia the hidden rightful King emerges from his concealment to be unrestricted Lord, then at once the whole demonic fruits of world history are thereby judged and the fall of Satan from his presumptuous world empire determined. The parousia is the revelation of the final victory of the Risen One over all demons of the old aeon, and the final subjugation and disarming of Satan.[32] So long as theology does not venture to utter such statements, it is still under the spell of rationalism, which prevents it from a really

---

[31] Rom. 11.33.

[32] The 'theology of the resurrection' embraces the fundamental assertion that satanology is not a marginal comment in the Bible which can be overlooked or eliminated, but on the contrary represents a central truth of eschatology. Eschatology without satanology is a thoroughly questionable, unbiblical caricature, for primitive Christian thought can be understood at all only against a transcendent world-background which is satanic. We must therefore speak of a satanic primal rebellion in which this prince of angels who had been created by God misused his freedom and declared against God in order to set up 'being as God'. Grounded upon falsehood and disobedience, this break in the harmony of the heavenly aeon of the angelic realms is the prototype of the seduction of man and the ground on which it was possible. The battle-front of the resurrection of the Kyrios is therefore directed essentially against this power of Satan. Cf. John 8.44; Jude 6, 9; Job 1.6; I John 3.8, 10; Eph. 2.2; II Cor. 4.4; 11.14; 12.7; II Peter 2.4; Luke 8.30; Rev. 20.10.

profound understanding of the triumph of the resurrection message precisely where the conquest of these forces is concerned.

(b) The Exaltation of the Church of Christ

Inseparably bound up with the parousia of the Risen One is the exaltation of the community of Christian believers to be with their Lord. For in keeping with the parallel with the resurrection of Jesus, we have the resurrection of the community as the revealing *consummation of the Church of the Lord*. The fate of the 'head' of the 'body which is the church' is the fate of the community; that is why the resurrection embraces not only the individual but also the collective entity of the Church. An individualistic pursuit of independent eternity, which sees the resurrection only in relation to its own Ego, has no place in Christian eschatology. Rather, the individual is fitted into the whole and has his value only as a 'member' of the body. If the Church has a part in the resurrection aeon which has already dawned and in the eschatological tension, while all the time it is engaged as a whole in battle, is despised and endures persecution, then it has also a part in the unveiling of its life in Christ. In analogy to the obedience of Jesus in his life in history, the Church as the community of the 'brethren' of Christ is required to practise believing obedience even to the point of martyrdom. To the exaltation of him who was obedient 'unto death' there corresponds the resurrection of the now suffering Church. Thus the martyrdom of the Church has the closest relation to eschatology.[33] During the old aeon the Church cannot be justified before the world; that is why all ecclesiastical attempts to make the Church appear as an earthly power must amount to betrayals of the truth of eschatology. Only through the consummation of the resurrection does there come the rehabilitation, not by the Church of itself, but God rehabilitates the Church before the world.

In particular, this statement about the consummation of the Church of Christ involves three affirmations:

The parousia of Jesus leads first of all to the special encounter of the Risen Lord with his chosen Church which awaits him. In this insight lies the element of truth in the idea of a 'catching up' of Christ's Church to its Lord. This event of the exaltation of the Church, however, is identical with the concept of the 'first resurrection'.[34]

Of the 'first resurrection' there has oddly enough usually been little

---

[33] Cf. the expositions in Rev. 7.9-27; 20.4 ff.; 6.9-11; 2.10; 3.5, 12; 14.10, etc.
[34] Rev. 20.5; I Thess. 4.16; I Cor. 15.23.

mention in the eschatological researches of theology so far, although scripture contains clear references to it. To leave it to the sects to distort these statements is an error on the part of standard church theology, which has disastrous consequences. These biblical statements are anything but marginal comment, for there can be no doubt that the apostles strive passionately to ensure that the faithful shall have a part in this first resurrection. All eschatological interest is centred on this 'being there' when the Lord comes, this 'having a part' in his appearance. This first resurrection refers to the Church of Christ, both to the members who have already 'fallen asleep' and who now in the 'intermediate state' are already 'at home with the Lord' but still await their consummation in the resurrection, and also to the 'living members'. The exaltation of the Church in the first resurrection, however, means 'being changed'.[35] There is thus no question of the continuation of our present physical mode of being, for to have a part in the kingdom of Christ is impossible for the natural man, for 'flesh and blood'.[36] Thus the first resurrection brings about the awakening of the Christian believers for their participation in the aeon of Christ's lordship.

Secondly, the exaltation of Christ's Church means the receiving of the glory of the resurrection. In biblical language a variety of images and comparisons are used in order to express this fulfilment of the expectation and longing of the Church. The hour of union between the 'bridal Church' and the 'bridegroom', of 'the marriage of the lamb', of the 'great supper' has come. The struggling, suffering Church which dies with Christ is crowned, receives the crown of victory, the palm of victory, the prize. The 'race', the battle, the struggle of faith reaches its goal.[37] The images also at the same time describe the appointing of the members of the Church by Christ as 'kings and priests', i.e. their being called to an incomparable task of lordship in communion with Christ.[38] With this exaltation there comes, further, the 'manifestation of the sons of God' awaited by the whole cosmos.[39] Unquestionably we have here to do with an exceptional distinction and pre-consummation conferred on the Church of Christ in contrast to the rest of mankind, 'before' the universal second resurrection of the dead.

It is thus made plain, thirdly, that the aeon of the lordship of Christ is also a lordship of the Christian Church together with Christ. This lordship, contrary to Israel's nationalistic and messianic idea of lord-

[35] I Cor. 15.51. [36] V. 50.
[37] II Tim. 4.7, 8; I Peter 5.4; I Cor. 9.25; I Tim. 6.12; James 1.12; Rev. 2.10.
[38] Rev. 1.6; 20.6; I Cor. 6.2; Matt. 19.28; Luke 22.30.
[39] Rom. 8.17-19; II Cor. 14.17; Col. 3.4.

ship, is not an earthly or worldly one, not a *regnum mundi*, but a spiritual one which becomes effective in a new 'world epoch'. This insight gives meaning to what is said of the 'millennium'. Once again it would be a mistake if theology failed to do justice to the universal significance of the kingly and priestly lordship of the Church. Certainly it appears necessary to discuss this with caution and restraint, and in all soberness to refrain, as the biblical references themselves do, from all closer definition and embellishment.

The basic idea of these biblical allusions, which cannot be fitted chronologically into our view of time and the world, moves in principle on the following lines. The 'new' aeon is no longer subject to Satan's power, and therefore his powers of destruction can no longer take effect.[40] Hence the lordship of Christ includes the last comprehensive possibility of a conversion of the 'nations' to Christ. While in the sphere of the present 'old' aeon a Church of Christ is gathered 'out from' all peoples as a 'little flock', the aeon of Christ's lordship provides at once the great and essential missionary period for the pagan world. From the 'firstfruits of the resurrection', the Church exalted and triumphant, there flow without hindrance priestly powers of renewal for the conversion of mankind. The 'mystery' of Rom. 11.25, 26 might also find its answer at this point, namely, in the 'saving of the fulness of the Gentiles' and the redemption of 'all Israel'.

The inconceivability and otherness of the aeon of Christ's lordship forbids us to develop these thoughts any further or to enquire into the 'how' of these possibilities. The only thing that remains of theological importance is the stress laid upon the role which the Church of Christ plays in the dramatic course of the eschatological events. *The Church of Christ itself belongs to the 'eschatological' events and to the 'last things' and is on the way towards a special consummation.*

(c) The Judgment of the World

At the judgment of the world, the great day of the world harvest, the parousia of the Risen One is consummated as the Judge of the world. He can be the Judge because he is the Lord to whose function the divine office of Judge belongs. But he can be Judge in particular of the 'living and the dead' because he is the living Lord who has passed through the realm of the dead, the life-giving Spirit who has the power of eternal life.[41] *His function as world Judge corresponds to the world-wide power of his lordship.* Thus the parousia is also the manifesting of the Risen One

---

[40] Rev. 20.3.   [41] Rom. 14.9; I Cor. 15.12 ff.; Acts 17.31.

as the Judge whose claims were certainly announced to men in the hiddenness of the new aeon, but just as certainly also not heard. It is only at the parousia that the judging word of the Kyrios becomes one the world cannot fail to hear. The coming of the Risen One as the Lord of world judgment contains two specific ideas.

The judgment of the Kyrios always begins at once upon the encounter with Christ. Where belief in Christ arises, there also man is judged in his conscience. He who believes is already judged and has the judgment behind him, for indeed he already has part in the life of the resurrection aeon. The believer has already experienced Christ as his Judge. Nevertheless he still has the judgment continually before him, because he stands in the old aeon and until death participates in its sin, and also because the new Christ-life is a hidden one. The believer is thus always at the same time on his way towards the 'judgment'. Accordingly, the 'last judgment' in the parousia means two things for the believer: firstly, the unveiling of the life which man already possesses in faith, which means the manifesting of the sinner's acquittal by Christ, about which the believer already knows; and secondly, the renewed awarding and confirmation of the life of the resurrection, because of the sin which clings continually to the believer in the old aeon and which therefore means even for faith a persistent threat to his acquittal, so that before the parousia the believer, being a sinner, is still always faced by the dual possibility of life or death. The parousia judgment is therefore for faith both an unveiling of present grace and a renewed justifying of the sinner. In this context it must not be forgotten that the exalted Church of Christ, the 'children and sons of God' who now bear the image of the Son of God, also have an active part in the world judgment. Once the decisive crisis lies behind them, in which by faith in Christ they have passed through death to life, the disciples as Jesus' faithful followers unto death have been proved and preserved through suffering and the cross and for this very reason are competent to judge others and to exercise with Christ the office of judge. With that the whole picture has radically changed: those who were accused and condemned before the world become the judges of the world.[42] The norm for this judgment is provided by the Gospel, i.e. by the attitude of man towards Jesus Christ, by the reconciling work of the 'Son', and so by the outcome and fruit of each individual's life.[43]

[42] I Cor. 6.2, 3.
[43] Judgment according to works, Matt. 12.31 f.; 16.27; Mark 4.24; 3.28 f.; II Cor. 5.10; 11.15; II Thess. 1.6 f.; II Tim. 4.14; I Peter 1.17; Rom. 2.6; Rev. 2.23; 20.12; 22.12.

From this there follows, secondly, the character of the world judgment for the unbelievers. It proves to be not only the unmasking of their life in its remoteness from God, but also the inevitable carrying out of their rejection. In negative analogy to the relation of faith to the judgment this means: unbelief, too, is in fact already judged through its rejection of the Christ-life. It really judges itself, by choosing death in preference to Christ. Its reprobation has therefore already begun before the parousia and in the old aeon. Thus it appears entirely logical to go on with Stange to say that because the godless have no part in Christ, they also have 'no part in eternal life'. They pass away with the earthly world. There is 'nothing in them which outlasts death'. There is really no annihilation of the godless either, 'since there is nothing there which can be annihilated'.[44] And yet we must not follow the argument on these lines to its end. For then the idea of judgment in general, and of the judgeship of the Risen One in the parousia in particular, would be robbed of its gravity. Rather we must say: The public unmasking of unbelief in the last judgment cannot mean that the absence of the godless proves they have 'fallen to destruction', but at the judgment on the 'last day' it will be revealed that the existence of the unbelievers was all along a lost one belonging to death, and at the same time Christ, whom they sought to escape, is really their Judge. Then, however, this unmasking leads to the carrying out of their rejection which only now ensues as so to speak a second act of judgment. This conception of the judgment admittedly involves the logical difficulty of showing in what form of existence the godless appear at the last judgment, since they can have no part in the world of the resurrection and the old aeon has passed away. Intellectually, the problem cannot be resolved. Rational objections, however, where an eschatological thought-complex is concerned are never convincing arguments when they are not in agreement with the substance of eschatology; on the contrary, they only prejudice the theological content. Nor is it the task of theology to force the irrationalities of Christian eschatology into a logical system, but on the contrary to expound their meaning. The world judgment necessitates the resurrection of all the dead to judgment.[45] This resurrection is the 'second resurrection', as distinct from the exaltation of the Church of Christ. The dualistic outcome of the world judgment has in all its harshness and sharpness a biblical foundation. The result of the

---

[44] C. Stange, *Das Ende aller Dinge*, pp. 158 f.
[45] Matt. 25.46; 11.24; 13.30 ff.; 3.7 ff.; Mark 4.29; Luke 2.34; 7.35; John 5.29; II Thess. 1.5 f.; Phil. 1.28; I Peter 1.17; II Peter 2.5 f.; Rev. 20.11.

last judgment consists in the final division which takes the place of the temporary division in the 'intermediate state'. This means, on the one hand, the resurrection of the 'blessed', the 'pardoned', the 'saved' to the 'eternal life' of unbroken communion with God; and on the other hand, the revelation of the 'accursed' who arise 'to everlasting damnation'. This damnation is 'the second death',[46] which represents not annihilation but being bound in a state of conscious remoteness from God, and being shut out from the life of God.

(d) The New Creation

The resolution of the eschatological tension comes with the revelation of Christ's lordship. This brings the emergence of the resurrection world from its hiddenness, and the unveiling of the hitherto hidden *resurrection aeon*. Thus the consummation in the aeon of Christ's lordship does not consist in the world's development reaching its conclusion, but in the unveiling of what is already present in principle in the reality of the resurrection. The affirming of a consummation therefore does not take us in principle beyond the resurrection existence, but asserts a complete unfolding of the eternal life which has begun in the Risen One.

(i) The Consummation of Time

The consummation of the world by a new creation can be properly spoken of only when clarity prevails concerning the concept of time which is inextricably interwoven with the concept of the world. The consummation of the world cannot in general be otherwise described than as the *consummation of time*, since every existing reality is always a temporal reality. In accordance with our presupposed view of time, the consummation of time is to be conceived as follows:

The lordship of Christ does not denote the end of time in some supra-temporal point of eternity. This would not be the consummation of time, but the annihilation of time in timelessness. If the end of time is a timeless eternity, then there is no sense in speaking of a consummation of time, and then the concept of a new 'world' must also be rejected as inappropriate. So long as all theological statements on eschatology lead to a colourless and formless concept of eternity, which might then just as well be interpreted as Nirvana, the naive millenarian

[46] Rev. 20.14; 14.10 f.; 20.6; 21.8; 22.15; Matt. 7.23; 25.41; 13.39 ff.; John 3.36; II Thess. 1.9; Heb. 6.2; Mark 9.48; Luke 13.28; Rom. 9.3. Cf. G. Heinzelmann, *Das ewige Leben*, 1917.

eschatology still has its value as a counterweight. On the other hand, however, the conception of the termination of time does not do justice to the concept of consummation either. Consummation as the termination of time, as the terminal point of the course of time, is of course no new time and therefore not consummated time either. This conception does indeed seek in a realistic way to hold fast to the reality of time and to prevent its being resolved into mere non-being, but it does not lead us beyond the sphere of the old aeon. As distinct from all this, the consummation of time means neither the terminal point in our time nor a supra-temporal point in eternity, but the unveiling of the new time-form and the new time-content of the now present resurrection aeon. The old time is, indeed, swallowed up in the new time, but in such a way that time as such, i.e. whatever in and of time is capable of fulfilment, is not destroyed but attains to consummation. Consummated time is indeed no more conceivable than timelessness, but it is not a matter of no consequence whether the new world may be spoken of deliberately in temporal categories or not. These categories must always be inadequate means of expression, because they are taken from the old aeon, yet the fundamental right to employ them comes of the knowledge that the new world represents *not* timelessness but 'time-fulness'. Accordingly, the 'new world' does not imply the monotony and sameness of eternity, but the manifoldness and movement of a fulness of life. Thus in the light of this insight, too, it is entirely meaningful to speak of different acts within the reign of Christ, of 'periods of time' which of course must not be understood in terms of the chronology of the old aeon and must not be equated with it, and of events which take their course in the new world.[47]

(ii) The Resurrection of the Body

If the consummation of the world is in the first instance to be understood in a general way as the consummation of time, then in particular it is equivalent to the *fulfilment of that hope of resurrection from the dead which is grounded in the resurrection of Jesus.* And indeed, world consummation implies a twofold resurrection or resurrecting, namely, that of the individual and of mankind, and that of the cosmos.

The concept of *resurrecting* is the appropriate expression for the eschatological action of God. It has the characteristics, on the one hand of taking death absolutely seriously, and on the other hand of being

[47] Cf. I Cor. 15.24. Paul knows of different acts within the new aeon, and for all their soberness his statements are yet most highly dramatic. Cf. also K. Heim, *Die neue Welt Gottes,* pp. 44-45 (in *The New Divine Order,* pp. 71 f.).

unreservedly theocentric. To speak of resurrecting is to know that the conquest of death is no human possibility, and that death, precisely by coming upon man in his totality of body and soul, casts man in his totality upon God. To speak of resurrecting is therefore to know also at the same time that resurrection, in analogy to the resurrection of Jesus, is a consummating act of new creation by God, which embraces equally the whole of man, and which is a possibility given only by God and known only in faith. If death is the breaking of man in both body and soul, the problem arises as to the continuity between this man and the man of the resurrection. In terms of the analogy with the Risen One, the continuity is given in the preserving of his individual spiritual person. From the theological standpoint, however, this very fact indicates man's utter dependence upon God, since all earthly supports and securities have been destroyed. This theocentric assessment of all anthropological possibilities applies in principle also to all statements about the 'intermediate state'. There is therefore only one sole possible and meaningful way of preserving man's personal spiritual being between what he now is and what he once was—not in some sort of immortality that belongs to the old aeon and does not extend beyond it, but in God alone. The Spirit, as the guarantor of the coming resurrection, establishes this connection as assured in the God who is revealed in Christ. Hence the certainty of resurrection, being grounded in God and independent of all human and earthly conditionalities, is an unshakable and unconditional certainty.

The more detailed statements about the resurrection of the individual man can be worked out in a Christian eschatology only in the light of the resurrection of Jesus. The Risen One is first among the brethren who follow, and therefore his new corporeality is the pattern for the work of God which brings about the coming resurrection of their bodies. The hope of a *new corporeality* is grounded in the bodily resurrection of Jesus. Corporeality, however, is precisely the concrete expression of a definite individuality, of man's unique, concrete spiritual person. Thus through the midst of death the identity between the mortal individual life and the eternal life of the resurrection is preserved by God. If Christian hope is directed towards a bodily resurrection, then there is also sense in expecting in the resurrection a consummation and renewal of the concrete peculiarity and value of personal life, as manifested in the characteristics of nation and race. But inasmuch as the corporeality of the resurrection is something 'new', there is no means of gauging what undergoes a new creation in the resurrection. Only the 'fact' of bodily resurrection is certain in the Christian faith.[48] The spiritual corporeality of the resurrection no doubt implies the identity of the individual and personal, yet not an identical or reconstructed form of the fleshly body, but the newness of a spiritual body.

(iii) *The New Cosmos*

The resurrection of Jesus has been recognized to be an event of cosmic breadth and depth. If it is of world-embracing significance, as is shown by its relation to creation, nature and history, then the consummation of the resurrection reality necessarily implies the resurrection of the *whole cosmos*. The new world embraces at one and the same time the new corporeality of the individual and the renewal of the cosmos. A new corporeality can exist only in the context of new time, new space and renewed nature. The resurrection of the cosmos is the consummation of the original creation of God, to become a new reality of creation which no longer requires the preserving orders.[49] Thus there comes the fulfilment of what Christian ontology and the Christian theology of nature hope for in faith. It is precisely the statement of the renewing of the cosmos that is the clear antithesis to all rationalistic emasculation of eschatology. Everything depends on this concrete existence, this corporeality, this life in nature and in history, being taken up into the resurrection life of Christ and its consummation. It is a question of regaining the primitive Christian realism which has nothing to do with a naive materialism but gives expression to the specific peculiarity of the Christian view of the world. Thus the very concept of the 'resurrection of the body' may also be a valuable safeguard against all spiritualistic dilutions of the faith. The Risen Christ is the whole Christ, and therefore the consummation also embraces the whole of 'the world'.[50] To the 'realism' of the resurrection of Jesus there corresponds the realism of the world to come. In particular, that means

---

[48] Cf. Rom. 8.11; I Thess. 4.14 f.; 5.10; II Cor. 4.10 ff.; 5.15; I Peter 1.3; 1.21; Col. 1.18; 3.1 f., etc.; cf. also W. Elert, *Die Lehre des Luthertums*, p. 74, and *Der christliche Glaube*, pp. 644 f. Cf. also A. Schlatter, *Dogma*, p. 308: 'That the Head of the Church has the glory of eternal life is the decisive thing in the work of Easter, and the result of it is then also for us liberation from our temporal and earthly aims and the assurance of eternal life.' Striking, too, is Stange's verdict: 'The difference between Christian faith in the resurrection of the dead and belief in the immortality of the soul is not that it springs from a cruder psychology, a more material view of the life of the soul . . . but that it is affirmed by a religious consciousness which is anchored not in the wishes of man but in his conscience' (*Zeitschr. f. syst. Theol.* 1923, p. 732). Further, C. Stange, 'Die christliche Lehre vom ewigen Leben', *Zeitschr. f. syst. Theol.* 1932, part 2, p. 277. Cf. also Martin Peisker, *Christliche Dogmatik*, 1932, pp. 68 ff.

[49] Isa. 65.17 ff.; II Peter 3.13; Rev. 21.1 ff.; 22.1 ff.

[50] Excellently expressed by E. Thurneysen: 'The world into which we come

that the lordship of Christ attains its universal operation in the world of the new creation. In contrast to all non-cosmic spiritualization, this new cosmos is to be interpreted as the fulfilment of the visible, the consummation of the physical, the perfecting of the corporeal. Cosmic life always means infinite multiplicity. Accordingly the lordship of the Kyrios over redeemed humanity and the rest of the liberated creation is one organized according to various tasks, hierarchies and orders of rank.[51] Hence 'eternal life', as it takes shape under the lordship of Christ and as a result of it, can be understood only paradoxically as profoundest rest and peace on the one hand and intensest activity on the other. Its characteristic mark is not monotony but a manifold abundance of richness, power, beauty and blessedness.[52]

With this new creation of the cosmos, God's plan of creation has reached its goal. In it a saved humanity attains to the image of the Son which marks the 'children of God' and into which they are ever increasingly transformed 'from glory to glory'.[53] The Church of Christ as the 'firstfruits' is followed by the harvest of the saving of all nations. The redemption of mankind, however, is followed by the transformation and renewal of the cosmos, in which the laws of the struggle for existence, of suffering and of transience, no longer prevail, but 'all things are made new'.

(e) The Telos

These conclusions do not yet, as might appear, bring us to the end of eschatology. The aeon of the lordship of Christ is not yet the final goal of the ways of God. God's plan of creation, which has been unfolding itself for aeons and in aeons, aims at a perfect communion with freely and willingly obedient creatures. This raises the question whether the existence of men and angelic powers who are damned must not contradict the divine goal of perfection. We have to enquire whether God's unqualified will to love and the 'universal reconciliation' through Christ can let damnation have the last, eternal word. This raises the problems of 'apokatastasis' in an urgent form.[54]

---

in the future of Jesus Christ is thus not another world, it is this world, this heaven, this earth, but both of them having passed away and been made new. It will be these woods, these fields, these cities, these streets, these men, who will be the scene of redemption. Now they are battlefields . . . one day they will be fields of victory' ('Christus und seine Zukunft', Zwischen den Zeiten 1931, part 3, p. 209).

[51] Cf. the Pauline concepts 'principalities', 'powers', 'authorities', 'dominion'.
[52] Rev. 21 and 22.
[53] II Cor. 3.18.
[54] Acts 3.21.

(i) *The Problems of* Apokatastasis

The following reflections on the final outcome and final goal of the world merit consideration. They are concerned with three hypotheses which cannot be said to be theologically tenable.

First, there is the attempt to ground the 'restoration of all things' on a 'natural theology' of man, in the feeling that any severity in the idea of judgment should be avoided. Here we have the effort to overcome every dissonance for the sake of a harmonious picture of the world— that is to say, on the ground of philosophical argument. The result, however, is a disastrous emasculation of the decision-character of this life, such as meets the needs of modern 'enlightened thinking and secularism'. Such theses are unequivocally contradicted by the statements of the Bible. Rational, human methods of proof cannot endow the *apokatastasis* with any validity.

Likewise, secondly, the idea of a kind of evolutionary process, which similarly fails to take seriously the decision-character of life, misses the point of genuine *apokatastasis*. Here a gradual development and rising purification leads progressively up the ladder of countless individual decisions to the stage of that harmony in which all contradictions are resolved. This possibility of development, specially effective precisely after death, has found rationally convincing supporters from Lessing via Schleiermacher and E. Troeltsch to R. Seeberg. 'The consummation can only be conceived in terms of a progressive purification and raising of the finite spirit until it becomes wholly one with God.'[55] In this idea it must not be overlooked that the concept of 'progressiveness' is here applied as a human possibility, in complete contrast to the exclusively theocentric determination of the doctrine of aeons in biblical eschatology.

The third hypothesis teaches the annihilation of the godless, and by means of this radical solution attains the result of complete harmony and absence of tension in the *telos*.[56] While holding fast to the gravity of the decision on life and death in this life, this theory avoids the dualism of a damned and a redeemed humanity, and attains the monism of the all-dominating kingdom of God in the *telos*. But to this rationalism, too, the theologian must take exception. If 'eternal death' is interpreted as the extinction of existence, then not only do we lose the concept of man's personal freedom and responsibility, but his being judged by God is changed from an 'eternal world judgment' into the

[55] Cf. E. Troeltsch, *Glaubenslehre*, 1925.
[56] Cf. the influence of R. Rothe and A. Ritschl upon T. Häring, Kirn and F. Traub, and especially C. Stange, *Das Ende aller Dinge*, pp. 147, 158, 198.

innocuous form of a finite, limited, this-worldly act of judgment—indeed, it is even turned into its opposite by the fact that the annihilation of existence is a kind of 'release'. There is no denying the obvious contradiction of scripture, for the 'consuming fire' of God[57] means precisely *not* the destruction of man, but his being compelled to exist before the holy majesty of God.[58]

In face of these mistaken hypotheses the following points must be noted. The unqualified decision-character of life must be maintained, and the personal responsibility which precisely in death does not come to an end, but rather to its fullest maturity, must not be given up. The result of this is by logical necessity a dual outcome for man, with the dangerous possibility of failing to reach the goal, eternal life.

With this clear, uncompromising statement, however, the theological reflection which bases itself on the theology of primitive Christianity has not yet concluded its task. We have still to ask whether the doctrine of the dual outcome for man is revelation's last word on eschatology—i.e. really its only word—or whether alongside of it we have to demand the recognition of yet another, second necessary truth without thereby doing away with the dualistic picture of the future outcome. The two-track character of theology must here be asserted again.

The mystery of the divine *oikonomia* contains the statement about the *apokatastasis*. This idea, however, is no ground for resting or for false security, and no 'exhaustive description of the end',[59] but represents an ultimate consequence of the doctrine of the aeons, and as such a theological necessity. Accordingly, it is solely a question of the biblical grounding of the *apokatastasis*. Three ideas will serve the further exposition.

The omnipotence of God's love and grace does not rest until its ultimate goal is achieved. The election by God, which begins partially and progressively with the individual, moves on through the Church, yet does not end even with the election of the Gentile and pagan world, but rather has for its *goal* also *the election and bringing back of his whole godless, lost mankind*. This miracle of election does not abrogate the decision-character of faith.

Secondly, redemption and the lordship of the 'Son' reach their goal only when 'all his enemies' confess Christ as their Lord. This confession of Christ is only universal and valid when all men, too, in their hope-

---

[57] Heb. 12.29.
[58] Cf. Matt. 25.46; Mark 9.44 ff.; Luke 14.24.
[59] Cf. P. Althaus, p. 187.

less, lost, damned state, as well as the powers that are hostile to Christ
have of their own free will found the way back from their self-incurred
torment. The essential thing is the final realization of the freedom to
return, of the new obedience, and of the possibility of new knowledge
which will grow into a fully valid confession of Christ. The blood of
the Saviour of the world and the victory of his resurrection are valid
also for the godless, for the cosmos, for *ta panta*, all things.

Finally, the following vital statements of scripture confirm these
eschatological borderline possibilities. The decisive chapter on the
resurrection in Corinthians speaks impressively of the 'putting down'
of 'all rule and all authority and power', of a completeness of Christ's
lordship which is realized without limit or hindrance, and indeed even
of the 'destroying' of the 'last enemy', of 'death', which must here no
doubt be identified with the power of Satan.[60] God pursues his final
purpose of 'having mercy upon all',[61] on the ground of the once-for-all
reconciling and saving of all.[62] The fulfilment of the world's purpose is
attained only when the whole of creation, the universe, is gathered
together in Christ as its Head and all creatures of the visible and invisible world bring adoration, praise and honour to the 'Lamb of God'.[63]
Without an insight into the all-embracing importance of this final
eschatological idea, it would not be possible to grasp properly the concept of the *telos*.

(ii) *The Lordship of God*

Standing as we do on the limits of eschatological knowledge, it is
necessary in conclusion to introduce one more Pauline idea in this
dogmatic context. It is the *idea of the handing over of the lordship to God
by the Kyrios*.[64] This idea is derived from the concept of the kyrios-ship
of Jesus. The lordship of the Risen One means the taking over of a
commission from God. In the parousia, this commission is visibly
carried out. In the execution and fulfilment of the kyrios-lordship comes
the consummation of the reality of the resurrection. Christ's lordship
has fulfilled its final task and attained its ultimate perfection when 'all
things' have been 'subdued unto the Son'. This unlimited subjection
to the lordship of the Son is the ultimate logical conclusion of the
theology of the resurrection. The commission to rule which was given

[60] I Cor. 15.23-27.   [61] Rom. 11.32.
[62] Col. 1.20; I Tim. 2.4; I John 2.2; Rom. 5.18.
[63] Eph. 1.10; Col. 2.15; 4.10; Phil. 2.10, 11; Rev. 5.13; and also John 1.19;
12.47; Luke 23.34; Ps. 145.19; Num. 14.21; Rom. 3.3 f.; 11.29; 10.19; 15.8;
I Cor. 13.13; John 20.23; Matt. 16.19; 18.18 f.; Luke 15.1 f.
[64] I Cor. 15.24-28.

to the 'Son' in the resurrection has attained its eternal goal. With this, however, the communion with God, which was founded by and in the Son and is now disturbed no more by any creaturely being or any power inimical to God, begins in unbroken purity and perfection.

The eschatological perspective now converges for our thinking on one single point: the handing over of Christ's lordship to God, the Father. Once the commission assigned to the Risen One is completed, the aeon of Christ's lordship comes to an end. Then the Kyrios hands back his lordship to the Father and remains, in relation to God the Father, the Son subject to God the Lord.[65]

The goal of all eschatology, as of all life, is not Christ but God alone; yet God alone through Christ and his resurrection. The consummated *telos* is the kingdom of God, but that means, 'God all in all'.

In this lordship of God, the aeon of God's eternity, the world plan of creation and redemption reaches its climax and goal in accordance with the *oikonomia* and *sophia* of God. The image of God in redeemed humanity, and the equality of that humanity with the Son, takes the form of the communion with God which is realized in freedom and love. It is at the same time a communion with the triumphing angel worlds, in union with the whole of the rest of creation, now liberated and shining with new, imperishable life. The lordship of God is only to be described as eternal life in millionfold variety and abundance of riches, as a ceaseless growing and ripening and bearing fruit out of the love of God and to the love of God in Christ.[66] This eternal life is at the same time the eternal hymn of the aeons to the honour and glory of God.

This message is the mighty finale of biblical eschatology, which has its ground and centre in the theology of the resurrection. It runs: God alone is Victor. 'To him be glory for ever and ever.'[67]

[65] I Cor. 15.24, 28.   [66] I Cor. 13.2.   [67] II Tim. 4.18.

EPILOGUE

THE present work is an attempt to expound in a strictly systematic way the word of the resurrection of the Kyrios without curtailing what was proclaimed in the primitive Church as the resurrection message. It was therefore necessary to consider theologically the reality of the resurrection of Jesus and its dogmatic meaning. This provides the basic features of a theology of the resurrection. The outline of a resurrection theology cannot say everything: much could only be touched upon and many dogmatic questions have to remain open. The dogmatic sketch here constructed from the standpoint of the resurrection and with an eye to the resurrection would not claim completeness, but believes it can provide an extension to the range of theology. Its vital concern, however, is to turn the eyes of systematic theology towards this central part of the content of the Gospel.

Our study has led us to the following summary conclusion: *The raising of the Christ* is *the* act of God, whose significance is not to be compared with any event before or after. *It is the primal datum of theology, from which there can be no abstracting*, and the normative presupposition for every valid dogmatic judgment and for the meaningful constructing of a Christian theology. Thus *the resurrection of Jesus becomes the Archimedean point for theology* as such, not derivable from empirical reflection, and established beyond any religious *a priori*. All theological statements are oriented in one way or another towards this focal point. There is no Christian knowledge of God which does not acquire its ultimate fulness and depth from the revelation of God in the Risen One. The constructing of a Christology without an understanding of the Kyrios is inconceivable. Pneumatology, too, has no other content than the reality of the Spirit of the Exalted Christ. The concept of the Church, as well as that of Christian ethics, is essentially determined by the resurrection of Jesus. Important insights into creation and nature, into history and existence, cannot be acquired without the resurrection faith. In it alone is there the possibility of a universal interpretation of the world.

Christian faith exists only where the resurrection of Jesus is acknowledged to be a reality. Its heart is the living Christ. It is in the Risen One that the whole life of mankind ultimately comes to a decision. The ultimate decision, however, is that between life and death.

The word of the resurrection of Jesus is the assault of life upon the dying world. It is decisive. Out of this assault there grows the faith that knows: *Extra resurrectionem nulla salus.*

INDEX OF SUBJECTS

INDEX OF NAMES